How to Implement Market Models Using VBA

How to Implement Market Models Using VBA

FRANÇOIS GOOSSENS

WILEY

Library of Congress Cataloging-in-Publication Data is Available

ISBN 978-1-118-96200-8 (hardback) ISBN 978-1-118-96198-8 (ebk)
ISBN 978-1-118-96199-5 (ebk)   ISBN 978-1-119-06583-8

Cover Design: Wiley
Top Image: ©iStock.com/pixel_dreams;
Bottom Image: ©iStock.com/awstok

Set in 10/12pt Times by Laserwords Private Limited, Chennai, India
Printed in Great Britain by TJ International Ltd, Padstow, Cornwall, UK

Contents

Preface

Graduate students and practitioners coming to the area of quantitative finance may be daunted by the abstruseness of stochastic matters, coupled with the austerity of scientific programming languages. Learning these disciplines is a challenge that some are reluctant to tackle. Then, to get some hands-on expertise of complex valuation issues with an easy-to-learn programming language, without delving too deeply into the theory, proves to be an attractive alternative: this is what this book invites you to do. For this purpose, VBA has been chosen for its accessible code and its connection with Excel and its easy-to-use spreadsheet format.

What sort of financial applications may be run in VBA?

Contrary to common belief, you can run a lot of complex pricings with VBA, almost as fast as in C++ even if VBA is not going to compete with C++ as the engine of big risk management systems. This book will not specifically address the computing performance topic: for a comprehensive approach to this see, e.g., Webber (2011). However, one thing to remember is that, not only in terms of accuracy, but also in terms of computational cost, VBA is an efficient tool to get fast and in-depth understanding skills on complex derivatives.

How this book can help you

To complete a pricing project from scratch is a road paved with challenging steps. If you are holding this book it means you are already a VBA developer, or you intend to become one, and you have some taste for quantitative matters: it is already a good start. Guiding you through the technical obstacles and making you familiar with the means to fix them is the ambition of this book. The quicker you complete your first Monte-Carlo algorithm or tree-based pricing program, the more self-confidence you get, if you are a newcomer in applications coding. To strengthen this self-confidence, no aspect of quantitative issues must remain in the shadow: you will probably notice that barrier option valuation theory and yield curve modeling are developed in detail, for they illustrate best the key notions of stochastic calculus.

Knowledge prerequisites

No VBA knowledge is required. The essentials presented in this book should suffice. You must have basic notions of analysis (continuity, derivability, integration) and linear algebra basics (matrix calculus). In the capital markets domain, you must be familiar with vanilla derivatives (forward contracts, European-style options) and, preferably, have some knowledge of the common risk management issues, such as delta or gamma positions. As regards the stochastic calculus theory, this book helps you to apply theory with a practical approach.

Structure of the book

Chapter 1 delivers the essential syntax and vocabulary elements to start coding algorithms in VBA; some emphasis is put on matricial calculus, as it occupies a prominent place in numerical algorithms and Monte-Carlo scenarios.

Chapter 2 introduces common algorithms that fix unavoidable numerical problems in the course of a pricing algorithm. In fact, every valuation program will encounter at least one interpolation or optimization hurdle at some stage of the algorithm.

Chapter 3 gives the reader an opportunity to check his knowledge of the capital market fundamentals. For complete VBA beginners, it also provides some training exercises to put into practice VBA techniques, such as loops. In a second part, one key aspect of the stochastic calculus theory, the change of probability measure is addressed. This technique is implemented via barrier options pricing.

Chapter 4 deals with numerical solutions that are called in aid when no analytical solution is available: to put it bluntly, it fixes 99% of the problems. This is the core material of the book, since every pricing algorithm refers more or less to one of the recipes presented in this chapter.

Chapter 5 deals with classes of assets that are valued using Monte-Carlo simulation methods. It covers multi-asset and path-dependent instruments. Variance reduction techniques are logically investigated in this chapter.

Chapter 6 addresses widely used yield curve models and the critical calibration issues. It introduces first Hull & White and Gaussian short rate models, secondly Heath-Jarrow-Morton and LIBOR market forward rate curve models.

Chapter 7: as a widespread standard stochastic volatility model, Heston's is here presented in detail. Some recipes to tackle exotic pricings using this model are developed. In addition, one paragraph is devoted to SABR.

Chapter 8: in this chapter, our yield curve modelings are put into application to implement numerical algorithms aimed at some "standard" interest rate exotics: CMS Swaps, Cancelable Swaps, and Target Redemption Notes. Solutions resulting from different models or numerical methods will be compared.

Acknowledgements

My thanks go first to the staff of Wiley for their patience and assistance in the unenviable task of correcting the manuscript.

I would also like to thank the practitioners and principal lecturers at the Paris Dauphine and Paris-Sorbonne universities who provided time from their busy schedules to review or comment on this book. Advice and encouragement given by Sofiane Aboura especially have been of great help in completing the work.

Last but not least, I would like to express my gratitude to the authors, some are mentioned in the bibliography, who succeeded in making quantitative finance an appealing matter: I owe them an incurable taste for financial algorithms.

Abbreviations

ATM	At-the-money (options)
BGM	Benhamou/Gobet/Miri approximation method (Heston model)
BS	Black–Scholes
CMS	Constant Maturity Swap
HJM	Heath-Jarrow-Morton model
IRS	Interest Rate Swap
LMM	LIBOR Market Model
OTC	Over-The-Counter
RNG	Random Number Generator
RV	Random Variable
TARN	TArget Redemption Note

About the Author

François Goossens has 12 years' experience in Java and VBA programming of pricing algorithms. As a consultant, he currently trains students and young practitioners in computational finance through VBA coding. Prior to that he ran, over 15 years, interest-rates and equity related trading desks with Credit Lyonnais and Ixis, and was strongly involved in exotic derivatives' management.

François graduated from École Centrale in Paris.

CHAPTER 1

The Basics of VBA Programming

1.1 GETTING STARTED

To access the VBA editor, point to the *Developer* (VBA menu on the ribbon). In case this menu is not visible, proceed like this:

Office 2007   Click the Microsoft Office Button

then click on Excel Options (bottom right). Point to *Popular* and mark *Show Developer tab* in the Ribbon check box, then OK: the Developer tab is now displayed on the ribbon

Office 2010 and beyond   Point the *File* menu and select *Options*
Click on *Customize Ribbon*, and mark Developer

> ☑ Insert
> ☑ Page Layout
> ☑ Formulas
> ☑ Data
> ☑ Review
> ☑ View
> ☐ Developer
> ☑ Add-Ins
> ☑ Background Removal

When you click on Developer, Excel displays a minimum of three *groups*:

- **Code**: this is the group from which you open the VBA editor
- **Controls**: user interface components, to create Windows-like applications
- **XML**: converts XML files into Excel files and vice versa.

From the Code group, click on "Visual basic" icon (far left). If you work on a newly created file, the VBA editor looks like this:

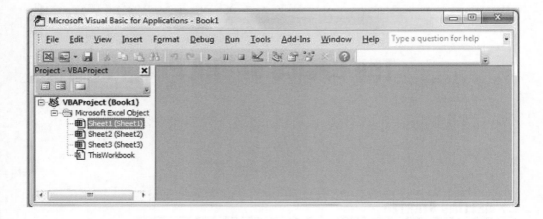

The bar on the top provides three especially useful menus:

- **View**: a menu that lists windows editing information regarding the code execution. Also hides or shows the project explorer (on the left). At creation, the project reduces to three open sheets and an empty *module* named **ThisWorkbook**. As new contents are added in your project, they appear in one of the following items:
  - **Module**
  - **Class Module**
  - **UserForm**
- **Insert**: from this menu, you can add modules to edit your procedures, or class modules if you need to create customized objects. You can also build UserForms from this menu.
- **Debug**: from this menu, you can toggle breakpoints where the execution of the code is interrupted. To track algorithmic mistakes, you can also activate the execution step by step (shortcut F8) and watch the changes in some variables, displayed in the **Immediate window** or **Local variables window** (see View menu).

You cannot write any code on the central gray colored zone: all the procedures must be coded within a module.

The specific ThisWorkbook component contains macros that are executed automatically at the opening of the workbook or when special events, such as the updating of one sheet, come up.

1.2 VBA OBJECTS AND SYNTAX

VBA objects are essentially visible pieces of Excel applications. This definition includes sheets, ranges of cells, icons on the ribbon, and custom interfaces.

To handle objects, one must specify their **types**. For instance, a range of cells is given the type **Range**. To locate a Range in the Excel application, we use its physical coordinates on the sheet. For instance the cell "D5" is identified by

```
Range("D5") or [D5]
```

A range of cells (e.g., D5:F8) is identified as

```
Range("D5:F8") or [D5:F8]
```

Objects of the same type can also be pulled together into a **Collection**, a set of indexed elements. We list below some common collections of objects in VBA:

- **Worksheets**: collection of worksheet-type in a file
- **Sheets**: collection of worksheets + charts + dialog sheets
- **Cells**: collection of cells within a range
- **Workbooks**: collection of Excel application files open at the same time.

How do you access an element of a collection?

- either through the <u>name</u> of the element (e.g., Worksheets("VAT"))
- or its <u>index</u> (e.g., Worksheets(2): 2nd Excel sheet tab)

We highly recommend designating the cells of a sheet through their coordinates (i,j). For example

```
Cells(i,j)
```

denotes the cell at the intersection of the i-th *row* and the j-th *column* of the sheet.

You must be aware that charts are members of the sheets collection, just like worksheets: if your project includes charts, you must be aware that the order has changed in the collection.

1.2.1 The object-oriented basic syntax

Between objects, there exists some kind of hierarchy, or ties of belonging. By nature, an Excel sheet belongs to the Worksheets collection, and itself contains a collection of cells. The collection of worksheets itself belongs to a Workbook instance.

Therefore, the comprehensive identification of an object should mention its "pedigree". In other words,

```
Range("D5")
```

denotes an object that is not completely defined since its location remains vague.

Which worksheet does this cell belong to?

In which workbook (more than one Excel file can be open at the same time)?

To link one object and its parent, we use the **dot** character "." For instance

```
Workbooks("Bonds").Worksheets(3).Range("D5")
```

provides a more exhaustive identification of the cell.

Also, cells are somewhat complex objects that have numerous properties: color, borders, values, etc. To access one property of an object, we similarly use the dot character. For instance

```
Range("D5").Column
```

denotes the number of column D, i.e., 4.

1.2.2 Using objects

When populating an Excel sheet with data and formulas, you are probably used to performing actions such as activating a worksheet, or copying and pasting a range of cells. In VBA, the piece of code needed to copy values displayed in [A3:D8] is, for instance,

```
Range("A3:D8").Copy
```

This statement does the work, and no return value is expected. However, things are generally different when manipulating objects: when you change anything in an object, you generate a new instance of this object. The modifications operated can involve two kinds of attributes: **members** and **methods**.

Members   Members are used to describe an object. For instance, borders, background, or font type are members of a Range object. These members are themselves objects, but, in contrast to their **parent**, they are **not visible**, and are thus somehow abstract. Therefore, to access these members, we again use the dot symbol.

For instance, the **Interior** and **Font** members aim to describe the background aspect and the font properties of a Range.

To color in red the font of the characters displayed in "A1"

```
Range("A1").Font.Color=vbRed
```

To turn the background color of "C1" blue

```
Range("C1").Interior.Color=vbBlue
```

VBA provides a kind of *code assistant*: A list of relevant properties and actions pops up as you start coding the ID of an object followed by a dot. For instance, if you start writing

```
Range("A1").
```

the following list will pop up:

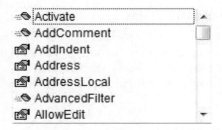

Members are identified by the icon   .

When you nominate a cell and want to perform some arithmetic operation on its value, you may omit the member **Value**, for the sake of conciseness, probably about developers' demand. The statement

```
Range("A2")=Range("A3")+1
```

is therefore valid, and is equivalent to

```
Range("A2").Value=Range("A3").Value+1
```

Methods   Methods are actions carried out on objects (iconized by   in the code assistant relevant list):

- Some do not return any value, such as

```
Range("B3:D8").ClearContents
```
 (clears all values in the range B3:D8)

```
Range("B3:D8").Select
```
 (puts the focus on B3:D8)

- Others return **instances** of the same object type (objects with specific properties): among them, we can quote **Offset** and **End**:

  - **offset** shifts the location of one cell to another position on the sheet. This method returns a Range-type object.

    ```
    Range("B3").offset(n,m)
    ```

  [B3] indicating Cells(3,2), Range("B3").offset(n,m) points to Cells(3+n,2+m)
  - **End** locates the last cell which is not empty in some direction. The arguments of this method are xlDown, xlUp, xlToRight, xlToLeft.

    ```
    Range("B3").End(xlDown)
    ```
    (finds the last non-empty cell in column B, from B3)

    finds the last non-empty cell in column B, from B3.

1.3 VARIABLES

As an experienced Excel user, you have probably already given names to cells or ranges of cells. You can do the same with any type of object in VBA, including RANGE or WORK-SHEET.

This section will explore how to handle variables in accordance with the category they belong to, i.e., either **basic** or **Object type**. Thereafter, we will address the specific cases of **Variant type** variables and **Constants**.

1.3.1 Variable declaration

Basic variables The VBA developer can ignore matters regarding memory management. All you need to know is that the name of the variable is a reference to the physical location of your variable in the memory, or, in short, its address. One thing that you must be aware of is that the memory allocation depends on the precision required when handling the variables: A decimal value needs more memory than an integer. To mention the variable type at creation is good practice.

To declare a new variable and specify its type, write

```
Dim [VariableName] As [VariableType]
```

Below is a list of some commonly used types:

```
Byte
Integer
Long (Integer > 2*10^9)
Single (decimal)
Double (decimal double precision)
String (chain of characters)
String*n (bounded to n characters)
Date
Boolean
```

For instance:

```
Dim yield As Single
Dim clientName As String
```

To make the code more concise, use shortcut notations:

```
$ for String
! for Single
% for Integer
```

and group declarations in one single line:

```
Dim vol!,rate!,spot!
Dim client$
```

It is recomended that you initialize the variable(or **instantiate**) when it is created. For instance:

```
Dim vol!:vol=0.3
Dim client$:client=Sheets("clients").Range("B2")
```

It is possible to code several short statements on the same line, separated by ":".

Scope of variables   When declared inside a procedure, a variable is **local**. For instance the variable varName declared as follows:

```
Sub ProcName()
Dim [varName] As [Type]
End Sub
```

is not visible outside ProcName. When the execution of ProcName terminates, varName is ignored. If you declare it at the top of this module, as in the following example

```
Dim [VarName] As [Type]

Sub ProcName1()
[statements]
End Sub
Sub ProcName2()
[statements]
End Sub
```

varName in that case is seen from all the procedures within the same module. Dim, alone, is equivalent to **Private**. If you need this variable to be **Global**, i.e., visible to all code in the project, not only one module, add the directive **Public**.

You may omit to specify the type of variable (shame!) when creating it: the default type given by VBA is **Variant**, a kind of catch-all type. It can store any kind of data, except bounded strings. Variant will be introduced shortly after Arrays, since it is more or less related to matrices.

Object-type variables   Object variables, unlike data, have different properties, not only values. Declare them with Dim, but initialize them with the directive **Set**. For instance:

```
Dim zoneYields As Range:Set zoneYields=Sheets("yields").Range("B2:B11")
```

You can also declare several object variables on one single line:

```
Dim zoneYields,zoneVols,zoneSpots As Range
```

Constants   Unlike variables, constants store values that cannot be changed in the course of the program. The objective is obvious when considering the number PI, for example: an explicit Id, such as **PI**, is surely more concise and explicit than 3.14159265. They are declared such that

```
Const PI=3.14159265
Const VAT=0.205
```

Besides custom constants created by the developer, VBA provides **native constants**: they are passed as arguments of VBA/Excel functions, generally values of type **Long**. VBA assigns explicit names to these values.

In the following examples:

```
[B5].Interior.Color=vbRed
[B5].end(xlDown).Select
```

the hidden values of vbRed and xlDown are
vbRed=255 and xlDown=-4121

The Variant type   By default, the **Variant** type is assigned to any variable not declared explicitly. In practice, you can store any kind of objects in a variable declared as Variant, even an array of values (see §1.3.3 below).

The declaration statement is similar to other basic types, i.e.,

```
                    Dim v As Variant
```

A Variant type variable can even be assigned a Range-type object, which is convenient when you need to use VBA functions (in fact, only Range-type values can be passed as arguments to VBA functions).

For instance, this declaration:

```
                 Dim w As Variant:w = [B3:B8]
```

is correct.

1.3.2 Some usual objects

Some objects are unavoidable: **Worksheet** and **Range**. In this section, we outline the way they are commonly handled.

Worksheet   For instance, to initialize a worksheet named "wk" and assign it the 2nd sheet of the active Excel Workbook, write:

```
Dim wk As Worksheet: Set wk = ActiveWorkbook.Worksheets(2)
```

You can change dynamically (although this is not recommended) the name of the worksheet that appears at the bottom of your Excel workbook:

```
ActiveWorkbook.Worksheets(2).Name ="Bonds"
```

Once a worksheet is activated, you can refer to it using ActiveSheet:

```
ActiveSheet.Columns(1).Interior.Color = vbBlue
```

Worksheet collections   The Worksheet object is a member of the Worksheets collection, that itself contains a collection of child objects:

- Cells
- Comments (all the comments in a sheet)
- ChartObjects (charts in a given sheet).

Some current members and methods

Members:

- Name
- Visible
- Password

Methods:

- Activate (select the whole sheet or the top right cell of a range)
- Copy
- Paste
- Protect

Range Range type may refer to:

- one cell
- a range of cells
- a collection of several ranges of cells.

For instance, if you want to create a range named "SwapRates" containing

- a range of <u>maturities</u> displayed on [A3:A12]
- a list of <u>currencies</u> on [B1:F1]
- some <u>swap rates</u> on [B3:F12]

the relevant code will look like this:

```
Dim SwapRates As Range
Set SwapRates = Range("A3:A12, B1:F1, B3:F12")
SwapRates.Select
```

When selecting SwapRates, pay attention that Selection is to designate [A1] alone, although the whole range is highlighted:

	A	B	C	D	E	F
1		EUR (%)	USD (%)	JPY (%)	GBP (%)	CHF (%)
2						
3	1y	0,86	0,51	0,38	0,77	0,18
4	2y	0,87	0,55	0,39	0,99	0,82
5	3y	0,92	0,62	0,41	1,01	1,17
6	4y	1,05	0,74	0,49	1,15	1,42
7	5y	1,27	0,95	0,6	1,27	1,68
8	6y	1,45	1,15	0,68	1,46	1,9
9	7y	1,61	1,33	0,82	1,64	2,05
10	8y	1,75	1,48	0,98	1,82	2,2
11	9y	1,88	1,63	1,13	1,98	2,3
12	10y	1,98	1,76	1,2	2,13	2,4

Range collections A Range type object is the parent of four collections:

- Cells, of course
- Columns
- Rows
- Areas.

In our example

```
Areas(1) = [A3:A12]
Areas(2) = [B1:F1]
Areas(3) = [F3:F12]
```

Actually, the number of rows and columns in SwapRates are those of the <u>first</u> element in the collection, i.e., Areas(1) (as an illustration, SwapRates.Rows.Count=Areas(1).Rows. Count).

Some current members and methods
Members:

- Interior
- Font
- Borders
- Formula
- Count (provides the number of cells inside a Range).

Methods:

- Copy
- Paste
- Activate
- Resize
- Offset
- End.

1.3.3 Arrays

An array is a set of objects of the same type, ranked with a numerical index. The size of an array can be:

1. <u>fixed once and for all</u> when it is declared, or
2. <u>omitted</u>,

In any case, the objects' type must be declared.

1: When the size of the array has been specified at creation, such as in the example below:

```
Dim tabYields(10) As Single   'or
Dim tabYields!(10)
```

it cannot be resized in the course of the program.

If omitted, the size of an array can be modified dynamically: use **ReDim** to modify it:

```
Dim tabYields!()
Dim n1%:n1=10
ReDim tabYields(n1)
Dim n2%:n2=15
ReDim tabYields(n2)
```

Before populating an array, it is imperative that you redimension it (ReDim directive): if not, the VBA error message emitted is unfortunately insufficiently explicit.

When using the ReDim statement, all the elements of the array are erased. To avoid this, add **Preserve** to the ReDim statement.

```
Dim tabYields!()
ReDim tabYields(n1)
ReDim Preserve tabYields(n2)
' the n1 first elements remain if n2>n1
```

The lower and upper bound of an array are given by:

```
LBound([Name of the array])
UBound([Name of the array])
```

By default, the number 0 is the first element in an array. You can force the lower and upper bound in the array declaration:

```
Dim n1%, n2%
n1 = 10: n2 = 15
ReDim tb!(n1 To n2) ' first element is number 10
```

You can also set the lower bound of every array in a module to 1: type:

```
Option Base 1
```

on top of the module, outside and before any procedure.

NB: Omitting the size of an array at creation is almost automatic since the settings of financial applications need to be dynamically adjusted, as a general rule.

An array can have more than one dimension: a two-dimensional array is called a matrix. For instance, to declare a dynamically resizeable matrix, write:

```
Dim MatrixName!()
 [Statements]
ReDim MatrixName(n,n)
```

Another example: to declare a three-dimensional fixed-size array where the first element of the second coordinate is indexed by 1:

```
Dim MatrixName!(5,1 to 10,10)
```

1.4 ARITHMETIC

Math operations   Numerical operations are standard. The code for

$$M \times (1 + r)^n$$

is

```
M*(1+r)^n
```

Attention must be paid to precedences. Brackets have to be added to avoid miscalculations. For instance,

```
M/(1+r1)/(1+r2) is equivalent to  M/((1+r1)*(1+r2))
```

while

```
M/(1+r1)*(1+r2) equals (M/(1+r1))*(1+r2)
```

Some operators are specific to integer operands:

```
7\3   '  returns the integer result of the division i.e. 2
7 Mod 3  '  returns the integer remainder of the division i.e. 1
```

Comparison operators

```
= , > , < , <= , => , <> (not equal to)
```

These operators compare two data and return a boolean value (True or False). For instance,

```
Dim bool As Boolean: bool=(45<3)   ' bool=False
```

The comparison operators are widely used in conditional statements (see below).

Binary logical operators   Binary logical operators also perform comparisons, but uniquely between boolean values:

```
And , Or , Xor

X And Y   '  returns True if and only if X and Y are true
   4>3 And 8>9 = False

   X Or Y   '  returns True if one at least of the expressions is true
   4>3 Or 8>9 = True

   X Xor Y   '  returns True if one exactly of the  expressions is true
   4>3 Xor 8>9 = True
   4>3 Xor 9>8 = False
```

Unary logical operator   This operator takes one single operand:

```
Not

  Not X '   returns False if X is true,
  In that case, Not(Not X) returns True

Not (Not 3 > 2) '   returns True
```

Conditional statements

if...then   The if...then...(else) statement evaluates a condition. If this condition is met, some code is executed. Alternative actions can be carried out if the condition is not met:

```
If [Condition] Then
    [statements]
End If
```

Additional conditions may be inserted:

```
Dim TaxInc As Boolean
Dim Total!, DutyFree!, VAT!
```

```
If TaxInc Then
    Total = DutyFree
ElseIf VAT = 7.5 / 100 Then
    Total = (1 + VAT) * DutyFree
Else
    Total = (1 + 12.5 / 100) * DutyFree
End If
```

Select Case...   The Select...Case statement can run several blocks of statements, contingent on the value taken by one single variable:

```
Select Case Variable
    Case Value1
        [statements if Variable=Value1]
    Case Value2
        [statements if Variable=Value2]
        .
        .
        .
    Case Else
        [Statements if Value does not fit conditions above]
  End Select
```

Intervals may also be evaluated:

```
Dim AgeClass$, Age%

Select Case Age
    Case 1
        AgeClass = "baby"
    Case 2, 3
        AgeClass = "SmallInfant"
    Case 4 To 7
        AgeClass = "Infant"
    Case 8 To 17
        AgeClass = "Young"
    Case 18 To 64
        AgeClass = "Adult"
    Case Is >= 65
        AgeClass = "Senior"
End Select
```

Loops   A loop is a block of statements aimed at being executed repeatedly. The number of iterations can be predetermined or contingent upon the evaluation of one or more conditions. Three situations may come about:

- the number of iterations N is known:

```
For k=1 to N
[code]
...
Next k
' the code is executed N times
```

- the statements are repeated as many times as the number of elements in a collection. As an example, dealing with a collection of cells:

```
For each Cell in [Name of the collection]
[code]
...
Next Cell
```

- the following block repeats an action <u>as long as</u> a condition (boolean value) is met:

```
While [condition]
[code]
...
Wend
```

or the block repeats an action <u>until</u> a condition is met

```
Do
[code]
...
Loop Until (While)
[condition]
```

Do While...Loop allows you to insert the **Exit Do** statement, in case the sequence of iterations needs to be interrupted: For instance:

```
Dim d As Date,n%
d=CDate("01/01/2020")
Do
n=n+1
if d<Date() then exit do
Loop Until
DateAdd("yyyy",d,-n)-Date()>0
```

Most of the time, different loops can achieve the same task: the more concise the better.

1.5 SUBROUTINES AND FUNCTIONS

Subroutines and functions are both procedures, i.e., blocks of code that complete a specific task. In addition, <u>functions return a result while subroutines don't</u>. The following issues deserve some consideration:

- the **scope** of the procedure. When a subroutine or a function is created, you must decide in which module this procedure is supposed to be run (main procedure), or called from another procedure. For instance, the following statements

```
Sub ProcName([Arg]), etc.
```

or

```
Private ProcName([Arg])
```

create procedures only visible in the module in which they are edited. To be called from other modules of the active workbook, add a **Public** directive:

```
Public ProcName([Arg])
```

- the **passing mechanism** Unless otherwise specified, arguments are normally passed to subroutines **by reference** (syntax **ByRef**):

```
Sub ProcName(Arg)
```

is equivalent to

```
Sub ProcName( ByRef Arg)
```

When an argument is passed by reference, any change made in its value within the called procedure remains effective outside this procedure. Reference here designates equally the address and the data registered at this address.

When an argument is passed by value (**ByVal**), a copy of the variable is made and passed to the procedure, so that any change in the copy will not impact the value of the passed variable.

The example which follows will underline the difference: given the procedures invSingle1 and invSingle2 performing both the inversion of Single type variables,

```
Sub invSingle1(s!)
s = -s
End Sub
Sub invSingle2(ByVal s!)
s = -s
End Sub
```

Running the procedure testPass below

```
Sub testPass()

Dim x!: x = 1
Dim y!: y = 1
Call invSingle1(x)
Debug.Print x
Call invSingle2(y)
Debug.Print y

End Sub
```

we get (in *immediate window*)

```
-1
1
```

VBA does not allow us to pass arrays by value.

1.5.1 Subroutines

To create a subroutine, just type

```
Sub [Name of the procedure]
```

VBA completes the code, adding

```
End Sub
```

For instance, a procedure that scans through a range of cells in sheets(1), and fills the empty ones with the next cell up, could look like this:

```
Sub CheckData()
Sheets(1).Activate
Dim zoneData As Range:Set zoneData=Range([B3],[B3].end(xlDown))
```

```
For Each cell in zoneData
if isEmpty(Cell) Then Cell=Cell.offset(-1,0)
Next Cell
End Sub
```

Subroutines may accept arguments: in that case, these arguments may be regarded as parameters of the procedure. For instance, in the code below

```
Sub RetrieveData(Market As String)
 Worksheets(Market).Activate
End Sub
```

'Market' denotes the name of the sheet where the bulk of data to be retrieved (and dealing with Liffe exchange) is stored. We guess that the same block of statements can apply to other markets (different sheets). To call a subroutine from an external procedure:

- use **Call** if some arguments are to be passed, or
- just write the name of the subroutine should this not be the case.

In the example below, a main program calls successively RetrieveData and another procedure OtherProc taking no argument:

```
Sub MainProc()
Call RetrieveData("Liffe")
OtherProc
End Sub
```

NB: Arguments of a subroutine need not to be enclosed in round brackets.

It is highly recommended to mention not only the type of argument, but also the return type. Obviously, the type of argument must not be omitted.

1.5.2 Functions

To create a function, use the keyword **Function** and specify the type of the returned value:

```
Function [FunctionName](list of arguments) As [Type of returned value]
 [Statements]
 FunctionName= value to be returned
End Sub
```

For the function to return a value, add the statement

```
FunctionName = result to return
```

The value returned can be a single value or an array of values: In the second case, add parentheses to the type declaration.

Here is an example of a daily changes calculation. The argument is an array of market quotes, the value returned is an array of daily variations.

```
Function DailyVar(Quotes!()) As Single()

ReDim t!(UBound(Quotes))
For i = 1 To UBound(t)
    t(i) = (Quotes(i) - Quotes(i - 1)) / Quotes(i - 1)
Next i
DailyVar = t

End Function
```

1.5.3 Operations on one-dimensional arrays

In this section, we display some examples of procedures where arrays are passed as arguments:

- function deleting one element in a list:

```
Public Function DelFromList(t!(), e!) As Single()

ReDim result!(UBound(t) - 1)

i = LBound(t)
While t(i) <> e
    result(i) = t(i)
    i = i + 1
Wend
For j = i To UBound(t) - 1
    result(j) = t(j + 1)
Next j

DelFromList = result

End Function
```

- function merging two sorted arrays of single values:

```
Function Merge2List(a!(), b!()) As Single()

Dim la%, ua%, lb%, ub%
la = LBound(a): ua = UBound(a): lb = LBound(b): ub = UBound(b)

ReDim t!(ua - la + ub - lb + 1)

Dim i%, j%, k%
i = la: j = lb: k = 0

While i < ua And j < ub
    If (a(i) < b(j)) Then
            t(k) = a(i): i = i + 1
        Else
            t(k) = b(j): j = j + 1
    End If
    k = k + 1
Wend

While (i <= ua)
    t(k) = a(i): i = i + 1: k = k + 1
Wend

While (j <= ub)
    t(k) = b(j): j = j + 1: k = k + 1
Wend
Merge2List = t
End Function
```

1.5.4 Operations on two-dimensional arrays (matrices)

First of all, let us point out that Excel can perform some basic matrix operations: multiplication, transpose, inversion, etc. So can VBA proprietary functions.

However, these functions reject two-dimensionnal arrays of numerical values for performing the product of two matrices. As a consequence, working with Excel/VBA proprietary functions binds you to process solely data stored in an Excel sheet. This is definitely not compatible with standard programming rules.

Nevertheless, since you may be concerned to check your self-developed functions (e.g., inverting a matrix, or calculating a pseudo-square inverse), it is useful to become familiar with Excel functionalities.

The proprietary Excel function Let us consider two ranges of cells named A and B to be multiplied:

1. Select with the mouse the area where you want your solution to be located in the Excel sheet and choose the relevant function in the Excel drop-down list, here **MMULT**: first, ensure that

$$\text{Number of columns (A)} = \text{Number of rows (B)}$$

The format of the selected range C must be (given C=A.B)

$$\text{Number of rows (A)} * \text{Number of columns (B)}$$

2. Provide ranges A and B as inputs of the function MMULT in the pop-up dialog box
3. Press **Ctrl + Shift + Enter**: if you click on "ok", the result is the top left element of the matrix alone.

VBA customized functions Some of Excel functions have their equivalent in VBA. More precisely, these functions are **methods** of a wide VBA object called **WorksheetFunction**. Therefore, you must mention the parent object when using one of these functions, as in the example below:

```
Dim A, B, C As Variant
A = Range("B25:C26"): B = Range("E25:E26")
C = WorksheetFunction.MMult(A, B)
```

WorksheetFunction is itself a member of **Application**, the patriarch of all existing VBA objects.

Multiplication The following code shows how to multiply two arrays of numerical values (of type Single in our example). First of all, we have to check the dimensions of the arguments, which is achieved by **Mdim**(m#()). As a matter of fact, VBA functions do not perform dot products, for instance.

```
Public Function Mdim(m#()) As Integer

On Error GoTo Dimension

  For DimNum = 1 To 3
    ErrorCheck = LBound(m, DimNum)
  Next DimNum

Dimension:
Mdim = DimNum - 1

End Function
```

Next, the function **MatMult**(m1#(), m2#()) performs the appropriate multiplication, taking the dimensions of m1 and m2 into account:

```
Public Function MatMult(m1#(), m2#()) As Double()

Dim dim1%, dim2%
dim1 = Mdim(m1): dim2 = Mdim(m2)

Dim res#()

Select Case dim1 * dim2

    Case 2
        If dim1 = 2 Then
            ReDim res(UBound(m1, 1))
            For i = 1 To UBound(m1, 1)
                res(i) = 0
                For K = 1 To UBound(m1, 2)
                    res(i) = res(i) + m1(i, K) * m2(K)
                Next K
            Next i
        Else
            ReDim res(UBound(m2, 2), UBound(m2, 2))
            For i = 1 To UBound(m1, 1)
                For j = 1 To UBound(m2, 2)
                    res(i, j) = m1(i) * m2(1, j)
                Next j
            Next i
        End If

    Case 4
        ReDim res(UBound(m1, 1), UBound(m2, 2))
        For i = 1 To UBound(m1, 1)
            For j = 1 To UBound(m2, 2)
                res(i, j) = 0
                For K = 1 To UBound(m1, 2)
                    res(i, j) = res(i, j) + m1(i, K) * m2(K, j)
                Next K
            Next j
        Next i

End Select

MatMult = res
End Function
```

Transposition of a matrix

```
Public Function matTranspose(t#()) As Double()

ReDim res#(UBound(t, 1), UBound(t, 2))

For i = 1 To UBound(t, 1)
    For j = 1 To UBound(t, 2)
        res(i, j) = t(j, i)
    Next
```

```
Next
matTranspose = res
End Function
```

1.5.5 Operations with dates

Date type variables are created just like basic variables. The reference *Date* points to today's date:

`Dim Today As Date: Today=Date`

Setting payment schedules is a permanent concern in financial activities. Here are some functions specifically devoted to these tasks:

- DateAdd
- DateDiff
- Weekday().

DateAdd adds a number of periods (days, months, quarters...) to a date passed as argument and returns the resulting date. The first argument is a string value figuring the period. For instance, to add 6 months to today's date:

```
Dim TodayAnd6M As Date: TodayAnd6M = DateAdd("m", 6, Date)
```

Value	Period
"yyyy"	year
"q"	quarter
"m"	month
"d"	day
"ww"	week

DateDiff returns the number of time periods between two dates. The periods are those of the DateAdd function:

```
Dim nb_of_months%: nb_of_months = DateDiff("m", Date, TodayAnd6M) ' returns 6
```

Weekday returns an integer representing the day of the week. By default, the first day of the week is Sunday:

```
Dim DayOfWeek%
DayOfWeek = Weekday("01/01/2012")
' returns 1 for Sunday
```

To modify the convention, use the optional argument **FirstDayOfWeek** in the function definition:

```
Weekday(ArgDate, Optional [FirstDayOfWeek])

Weekday("01/01/2012", vbMonday) ' returns 7
```

The function *PayDates* below sets up a cash payments schedule, given

- the expiry date **tenor**
- the periodicity of the cash flows period in number of months ("1m","2m",...)

Prior to the setting of the schedule, you must merge the Target Holiday Calendar and the week-end days in order to determine the first business day following:

A
Target holidays
12/25/2012
12/26/2012
1/1/2013
3/29/2013
4/1/2013
5/1/2013
12/25/2013
12/26/2013
1/1/2014
4/18/2014
4/21/2014
5/1/2014
12/25/2014
12/26/2014
1/1/2015
4/3/2015
4/6/2015
5/1/2015
12/25/2015
12/26/2015
1/1/2016
3/25/2016
3/28/2016
5/1/2016
12/25/2016
12/26/2016
1/1/2017

```vba
Public Function PayDates(tenor As Date, period$) As Date()

Dim d As Date: d = tenor
Dim n As Long: n = 0
Dim i As Long

Dim tempDates() As Date

Dim f%: f = CInt(Left(period, Len(period) - 1))
Dim m%: m = Fix(DateDiff("m", Date, tenor) / f)

ReDim tempDates(m) As Date

While d > Date
    tempDates(m - n) = d
    n = n + 1
    d = DateAdd("m", -f * n, tenor)
Wend
```

```
ReDim targetDays(Range([A3], [A3].End(xlDown)).Count -1) As Date

i = 0
For Each cell In Range([A3], [A3].End(xlDown))
    targetDays(i) = cell
    i = i + 1
Next cell

ReDim WEdays((tenor - Date) / 3) As Date '  size by default 1/3 > 2/7

Dim temp As Date: temp = Date
i = 0
While temp < tenor
    temp = temp + 1
    If Weekday(temp) = 7 Or Week-
day(temp) = 1 Then WEdays(i) = temp: i = i + 1
Wend

ReDim Preserve WEdays(i)

Dim holidays() As Date
holidays = MergeDateList(targetDays, WEdays)

For i = 0 To m
    While testList(tempDates(i), holidays)
        tempDates(i) = tempDates(i) + 1
    Wend
Next i

PayDates = tempDates

End Function
```

1.6 CUSTOM OBJECTS

1.6.1 Types

A *type* is a user-defined type of structure that stores closely associated data together in a single object. For instance, if you intend to price instruments like bonds that have more than one term in common, such as maturity, nominal, coupon, or frequency of interest payments, you should be interested in creating a custom object named, e.g., **bond** and declare it as follows (you may notice the absence of *Dim* statement):

```
Type Bond
    Nominal As Single
    Market As String
    FixedRate As Single
    Period As String
    Maturity As Date
End Type
```

To create a variable named Tbond1 of type Bond, write:

```
Dim Tbond1 As Bond
```

To access an element of a Bond variable, you must relate to the name of the parent variable: in our example, to place 1000000 in Nominal data, write

```
Tbond1.Nominal=1000000
```

You can also declare arrays into your Type definition and even nest other custom types into it. For instance, suppose that:

1. You have created a custom type Nominal, with two elements, the amount and the currency name:

```
Type Nominal
    Amount As Single
    Market As String
End Type
```

2. Then, you can declare an interest payments schedule CoupDates, more detailed than a unique maturity in the body of the type definition: your Bond definition may become:

```
Type Bond
    Capital As Nominal
    FixedRate As Single
    Period As String
    CoupDates() As Date
End Type
```

1.6.2 Classes

Types are custom objects with limited abilities. Since they handle no custom methods and provide no control over what values are alloted to their elements, they are like a static data structure. For instance, you would be interested to verify that a cash payments schedule complies with the target calendar: this has to be done in an outside procedure. In this section, we introduce **class modules** where you can edit the definitions of new objects that are somewhat similar to Java or C++ classes.

Defining a new class   From the *Insert* menu in the VBA editor, add a new class module to your project. Change the default name in the properties window into something more explicit. As an example, let us create a new class, named Bond:

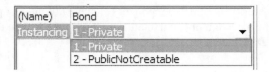

```
Dim Nominal As Single
Dim Market As String
Dim FixedRate As Single
Dim Period As String
Dim Maturity As Date
```

By default, the class is declared **Private**, thus accessible only in the project where it has been defined. To use this class in another project, we will select **PublicNotCreatable** To create a new *instance* of the Bond class, i.e., define a variable called BOAapr2017 for instance, just type

```
Dim BOAapr2017 As New Bond
```

You may want to make the elements available throughout the project and also give some of them default values when an instance is created:

1. Declare the elements as **Public**
2. Hardcode the default values in the **Class_Initialize()** procedure. The definition of your class in the editor looks like this:

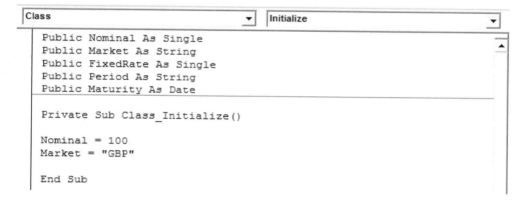

```
Class                              ▼   Initialize                        ▼

    Public Nominal As Single
    Public Market As String
    Public FixedRate As Single
    Public Period As String
    Public Maturity As Date

    Private Sub Class_Initialize()

    Nominal = 100
    Market = "GBP"

    End Sub
```

To handle the values set or retrieved from an object, we use **Property** procedures:

1. Get Property to retrieve an element
2. Let Property to initialize an element
3. Set Property to assign a reference to an object.

Some code can be embedded into those properties, allowing appropriate actions to be taken when assigning values to the object elements, such as raising an error if values are invalid. The piece of code below creates a new Bond object named oblig and uses the Let Property to instantiate oblig.Maturity while checking the date relevance:

```
Public Property Get Expiry() As Date
    Expiry = Maturity
End Property

Public Property Let Expiry(tenor As Date)

ReDim target(Range([A3], [A3].End(xlDown)).Count -1) As Date
    i = 0
```

```
For Each cell In Range([A3], [A3].End(xlDown))
    target(i) = cell
    i = i + 1
Next cell
    If testList(tenor, target) Then
        MsgBox ("invalid maturity: not a business day")
    Else
        Maturity = tenor
    End If
End Property
```

1.7 DEBUGGING

1.7.1 Error handling

In this section, we will focus on runtime errors, and discard banal omissions such as "for without next" or variable declaration omissions. A runtime error occurs when a statement of the program cannot be executed properly. The origins of such interruptions are usually:

- a division by zero
- an overflow error (e.g., when an algorithm diverges)
- a call to an element of an array whose index is beyond the length of that array
- a call to a local variable or procedure out of the module where it has been declared.

When it happens, the program stops and the faulty statement is highlighted. Moving the cursor over the edited code shows you the current value of variables at the time of error. If you wish the execution to continue normally, then type *On Error*.

On Error Resume Next   When an error is encountered, VBA resumes the execution on the next line. An error number is recorded as a value of the **Err** object.

After testing Err.Number, an appropriate action can be taken:

```
On Error Resume Next
...
    x=Sqrt(y)
    ' runtime error when y<0
    If Err.Number <> 11 Then
        y=-y
    End If
```

On Error Goto <line label>:   The execution is transfered to the line following the specified line label, ignoring all the lines in between.

```
Dim price!
On Error GoTo DefaultVol:
    vol = sqrt(Var)     ' can cause an error
    price= ' some code involving vol '

DefaultVol:
    vol = 0.3 ' the default value in case var<0
    Resume Next
```

1.7.2 Tracking the code execution

Activate **Debug** on the Menu bar. VBA displays four groups of items:

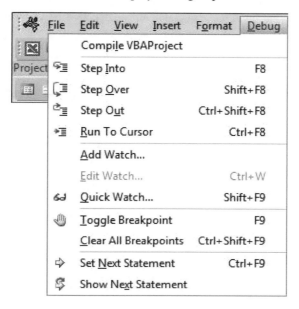

These items can be activated in conjunction with windows that aim to change some lines of code at the very moment of runtime or display information in the course of the program execution:

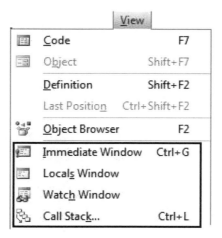

Immediate window   You can use this window to display the value of some key variables at some point in the program execution. Type

```
Debug.Print <Name of variable>
```

You can also use this window to add commands when the execution is in break mode. To place a break point on a line, put the cursor on that line and press F9 or choose "Toggle Breakpoint":

the line appears with a brick background. You cannot place a breakpoint on variable declaration lines (you can if you redimension one array). In the course of runtime, VBA pauses immediately before processing this line, which is then highlighted in yellow.

To illustrate this, the small piece of code below calculates the variance of a series of data, which is displayed in the immediate window, just before the breakpoint:

```
Sub test()

Dim n%
Dim zoneVal As Range: Set zoneVal = Range([A1], [A1].End(xlDown))
n = zoneVal.Count
ReDim v!(n)
variance = 0

For i = 1 To n
    v(i) = zoneVal(i)
    variance = variance + v(i) ^ 2
Next i

vol = Sqr(variance / n) * 16
Debug.Print vol

vol = Sqr(variance / n) * 16
Debug.Print vol

End Sub
```

```
Immediate                    ☒
  0,137654561848794    ▲




                     ▼
◀ ||          ▶
```

In break mode, we type

$$n=n-1$$

inside the immediate window, following the value of the variance. To resume the code execution, we can press F5 or choose "Continue" to complete the runtime from the Run menu, or stepping through the code line by line (see below): the change in the value of n will be taken into account!

```
Sub test()

Dim n%
Dim zoneVal As Range: Set zoneVal = Range([A1], [A1].End(xlDown))
n = zoneVal.Count
ReDim v!(n)
variance = 0

For i = 1 To n
    v(i) = zoneVal(i)
    variance = variance + v(i) ^ 2
Next i

vol = Sqr(variance / n) * 16
Debug.Print vol

vol = Sqr(variance / n) * 16
Debug.Print vol

End Sub
```

```
Immediate                    ☒
  0,137654561848794    ▲
  n=n-1
  0,141426618105544


                     ▼
◀ ||          ▶
```

Stepping through the code From the beginning or after a breakpoint, it is possible to step through the program line by line. You can activate this by pressing the **F8** key from the start of the procedure execution, or from a toggle breakpoint. Pressing F8 causes VBA to execute each line one at a time, highlighting the next line of code in yellow.

If your (main) procedure calls another one, pressig F8 will cause VBA to step inside the called procedure and step through it line by line. You can use SHIFT+F8 to "Step Over" the procedure call, for the sake of time saving (for instance, if this external procedure populates a big matrix).

Locals Window When running a step-by-step execution of a procedure, it is very helpful to follow how the variables change in the course of the program execution. For this purpose, you can display the **Locals Window** by choosing it from the View menu. The Locals Window displays the **local** variables in a procedure and their values. To see the values taken by Global variables, you must:

- either display them with the Debug.Print statement into the immediate window
- or move the cursor over the variable you want to check.

CHAPTER 2

Mathematical Algorithms

2.1 INTRODUCTION

In this chapter, we will introduce a non-exhaustive set of numerical algorithms that play an essential part in the course of pricing programs:

- sorting algorithms
- implicit equation solving
- optimization (search for extrema)
- integration
- linear algebra.

The table below enumerates some of their contributions in quantitative finance:

Sorting algorithms	Search for extrema	Integration	Linear algebra
Value At risk Calibration	Calibration	Complex integrals Fourier/Laplace transforms	Numerical solutions Regression Principal Component Analysis Interpolation

2.2 SORTING LISTS

Data sorting aims at ordering huge amounts of numerical values recorded in financial databases or sampled by Monte-Carlo trials. In this section, we will introduce two popular sorting algorithms, **Shellsort** and **QuickSort**. The reader can refer to Knuth (1998) for more sorting methods.

2.2.1 Shell sort

This method was devised by Donald Shell (1959). The basic idea is to partition a large database into smaller subsets and to sort each separately, before sorting the entire set. The sorting method is called the **insertion method**, evoking the way a bridge player orders his deck of cards: it is efficient with rather short lists, or already sorted lists when they are placed end to end.

Sorting by insertion   This simple algorithm sorts one element of a list at a time. Every element is inserted at the correct position in an already sorted list. We start by sorting the two left-most elements of the list, then insert the third one, and proceed until we obtain the last element.

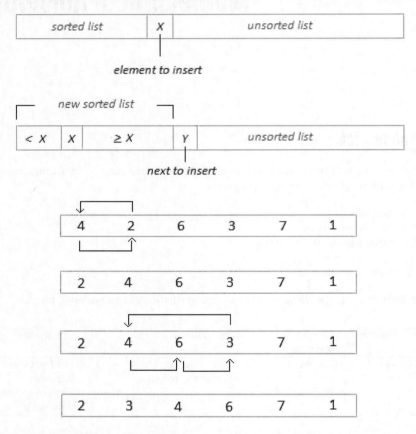

The VBA procedure **InsertSort** takes an array $t()$ as argument, and arranges it in ascending order.

```
Sub InsertSort(t!())

ReDim tt!(UBound(t))
tt = t

For n = 2 To UBound(t)
    x = t(n)
    i = 1

    Do While x < t(n - i)
        tt(n - i + 1) = t(n - i)
```

```
          tt (n - i)  = x
          t (n - i + 1) = tt (n - i + 1)
          t (n - i)  = tt (n - i)
          If i < n - 1 Then
               i = i + 1
          Else
               Exit Do
          End If
     Loop

Next n

End Sub
```

The way of partitioning the original list is the key to the method's efficiency. It is beyond the scope of this section to compare the average computation time needed for ordering the whole list with respect to this choice (specialists in this matter call it *time complexity*).

Different studies to date have shown that building subarrays with every n-th element of the list gives better results than dividing the array in intervals. For instance, consider the following set:

$$(x_1, x_2, x_3, x_4, x_5, x_6, x_7, x_8, x_9, x_{10}, x_{11}, x_{12}, x_{13}, x_{14}, x_{15})$$

Instead of dividing it into 3 adjacent subarrays

$$(x_1, x_2, x_3, x_4, x_5), (x_6, x_7, x_8, x_9, x_{10}), (x_{11}, x_{12}, x_{13}, x_{14}, x_{15})$$

the theory indicates you should rather build 4 subarrays with, e.g., every 4th element of the list

$$(x_1, x_5, x_9, x_{13}), (x_2, x_6, x_{10}, x_{14}), (x_3, x_7, x_{11}), (x_4, x_8, x_{12})$$

then sort each individually. The algorithm consists in joining these sorted subarrays and re-partitioning the array using a smaller gap, so as to obtain the smallest possible gap, i.e., 1.

Many gap sequences have been put forward to date: originally, Shell proposed

$$\left[\frac{N}{2}\right], \left[\frac{N}{4}\right], ..., \left[\frac{N}{2^k}, ..., 1\right]$$

For the purposes of our code implementation, we adopt a more recent gap sequence (Sedgewick, 1998):

$$4^k + 3.2^{k-1} + 1 \text{ and } 1, \text{ that is to say } 1, 8, 23, ...77$$

```
Public Function shellSort (v! ()) As Single ()

Dim n As Long: n = UBound (v)
ReDim w! (n)
ReDim tt! (n)

For i = 4 To 1 step -1
    M = 4 ^ (i) + 3 * 2 ^ (i - 1) + 1
    j = 1
    While j <= n - M
        k = 0
```

```
          While k * M + j <= UBound(v)
              w(k + 1) = v(k * M + j)
              k = k + 1
          Wend
          ReDim Preserve w!(k)
          Call InsertSort(w)

          For l = 0 To k - 1
              v(l * M + j) = w(l + 1)
          Next l
          j = j + 1
       Wend
       ReDim w(n)
Next i

Call InsertSort(v)

shellSort = v

End Function
```

2.2.2 Quick sort

Assume a list of n numerical values a_i, $i = 1,...,n$. The general idea of the quicksort method (Hoare, 1962) is to partition series of numerical data into two parts in relation to a **pivot**: lower values on the left, higher on the right. As a pivot, you can choose

- the medium index of the partition
- or the median
- or a random one.

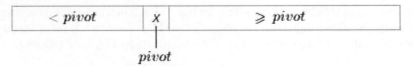

The algorithm proceeds like this: Starting with a list to be sorted in ascending order, create two sub-lists, separated by the so-called pivot. Values inferior to the pivot are moved down to the left side and inversely for higher values. Then, divide the sub-list on the left-hand side (values < pivot) again into two new sub-lists with respect to a new pivot. Continue until the leftmost series contains only the two absolute minima. Finally, switch the two values if they are unordered and proceed with the right adjacent sub-series:

1st call

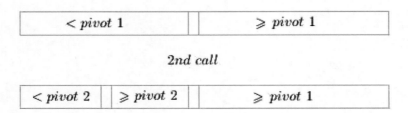

2nd call

. . .

Proceed till the left-hand side is fully arranged:

x_1	x_2	...	x_n		$\geqslant$ *pivot 1*

Then, sort the right-hand side values in the same way:

sorted list		$<$ *pivot$_n$*		$\geqslant$ *pivot$_n$*

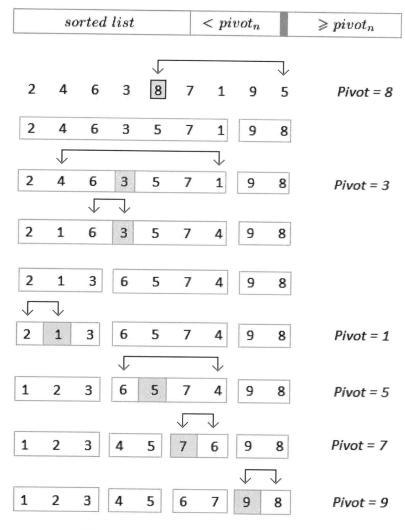

The scheme above illustrates the steps of a quicksort algorithm with a set of 9 integers, the pivot being always chosen in the middle of the remaining list.

```
Public Sub QuickSort(vArray!(), inLow As Long, inHi As Long)

    Dim pivot!
    Dim tmpswap!
    Dim tmplow  As Long
    Dim tmphi   As Long
```

```
    tmplow = inLow
    tmphi = inHi

    If inLow >= UBound(vArray) Then
       Exit Sub
    End If

    pivot = vArray((inLow + inHi)   2)

    While (tmplow <= tmphi)

       While (vArray(tmplow) < pivot And tmplow < inHi)
          tmplow = tmplow + 1
       Wend

       While (pivot < vArray(tmphi) And tmphi > inLow)
          tmphi = tmphi - 1
       Wend

       If (tmplow <= tmphi) Then
          tmpswap = vArray(tmplow)
          vArray(tmplow) = vArray(tmphi)
          vArray(tmphi) = tmpswap
          tmplow = tmplow + 1
          tmphi = tmphi - 1
       End If

    Wend

If (inLow <= tmphi) Then
    ReDim Preserve Rmax(UBound(Rmax) + 1)
    Rmax(UBound(Rmax)) = tmphi
    QuickSort(vArray,inLow,tmphi)
Else
```

The procedure is **recursive**, i.e., it is defined in terms of itself:

```
    ReDim Preserve Rmax(max(UBound(Rmax) - 1, 1))

    inLow = inHi + 1
    While inLow = Rmax(UBound(Rmax)) And inLow < UBound(vArray)
        inLow = inLow + 1
        ReDim Preserve Rmax(UBound(Rmax) - 1)
    Wend
    inHi = Rmax(UBound(Rmax))
    QuickSort(vArray,inLow,inHi)
End If

End Sub
```

2.3 IMPLICIT EQUATIONS

In finance, it is usual to encounter implicit equations to solve, i.e., to find the value X that satisfies

$$f(X) = target$$

or, equivalently,

$$g(X) = f(X) - target = 0$$

where f is most of the time differentiable and convex. As current examples, let us quote the calculation of bond yields and implied volatilities of options. In the common case where f is locally convex, the most straightforward method is the gradient-type method named after **Newton-Raphson**.

The idea is to approach the target, following the tangent line:

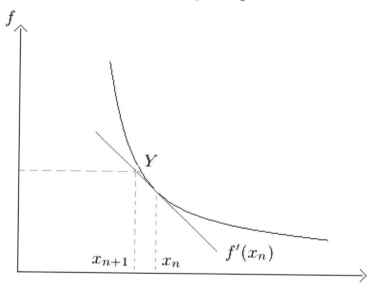

The sequence x_n satisfies the recursive formula

$$\frac{Y - f(x_n)}{x_{n+1} - x_n} = f'(x_n) \implies x_{n+1} = x_n + \frac{Y - f(x_n)}{f'(x_n)}$$

Code To initiate the sequence, we logically choose x_0 supposedly close to the target, for instance the last solution computed. Then, we build up the sequence until the error $|Y - f(x_n)|$ is considered tolerable. The pseudo-code looks like this:

```
x=[last result known]
y = f(x, [list of parameters])
 div_y = div_f(x, [list of parameters])
 While Abs(y - target) > [tolerable error]
 x = x + (target - y) / div_y
 y = f(x, [list of parameters])
 div_y = div_f(x, [list of parameters])
Wend
```

The slope of the tangent line, i.e., ***div***$_f$ may be calculated through derivation of f, or via $(f(x + \epsilon) - f(x - \epsilon))/(2\epsilon)$ to smooth the convexity effect. In the example below, we are trying to solve

$$\frac{5}{(1 + x)} + \frac{5}{(1 + x)^2} + \frac{105}{(1 + x)^3} = 102.75$$

This kind of computation is regularly carried out on bond portfolios for example. The initial value to start the algorithm is usually the solution of the very last computation. We assume that, at $D - 1$, the price of the bond was 102.35, which resulted in a 4.15% yield: this value will, thus, initiate the sequence:

```
Function bond(r!, c!, n%) As Single

For i = 1 To n
    bond = bond + c * 100 / (1 + r) ^ i
Next i
    bond = bond + 100 / (1 + r) ^ n

End Function
```

```
Function div_bond(r!, c!, n%) As Single
div_bond = (bond(r + 0.0001, c, n) - bond(r - 0.0001, c, n)) / 0.0002
End Function
```

```
Function yield_bond(targ!, x0!, c!, n%) As Single
```

   targ: target (102.75) x0: value to initiate the sequence (4.15%)

```
Dim r!: r = x0
    y = bond(r, c, n)
    div_y = div_bond(r, c, n)
    While Abs(y - targ) > 0.005
        r = r + (targ - y) / div_y
        y = bond(r, c, n)
        div_y = div_bond(r, c, n)
    Wend
yield_bond = r

End Function
```

2.4 SEARCH FOR EXTREMA

2.4.1 The Nelder-Mead algorithm

The Nelder-Mead algorithm is designed to find local minima of a given nonlinear function $f : \Re^n \to \Re$. The idea behind this heuristic method is to compare function values for a set of n+1 points (called *simplex*) of the $\Re^n$ space. Various test are performed on these values and, contingent upon their evaluations, the simplex may be distorted, expanded, or shrunk so as to narrow the gap between the worst vertex (i.e., the point where the image of f is maximum) and the center of gravity of the other vertices.

The principle is, after computation of f at every vertex, to discard the worst value and change it, thus transforming the simplex in such a way that the average value of $f(x_i)$ is lowered and iterate this until the center gets sufficiently close to a minimum.

In practice, we calculate the values taken by f at each vertex, sort these values in ascending order such that $f(x_m)$ and $f(x_{m-1})$ are the worst and second worst value, while $f(x_0)$ is the best. We then calculate the centroid x_c, average of the $m - 1$ best points.

Logically, we reckon the worst vertex x_h to represent the wrong side of the simplex, while the centroid x_c of the n other vertices represents the right side:

$$x_c = \sum_{i \neq h}^{n} \frac{x_i}{n}$$

Since we intend to sort a list of points, not only single values, we must, prior to the coding of the Nelder-Mead algorithm, create custom objects and customize the elementary arithmetic operations to handle them.

In a **class module**, we create the object type **Vector**, i.e., a class of objects that is represented by an array of coordinates:

```
Public nbEl%
Private mv!()

Public Property Get v(ByVal iI As Integer) As Single
ReDim Preserve mv(nbEl)
    If iI >= 0 And iI <= UBound(mv) Then
        v = mv(iI)
    End If
End Property

Public Property Let v(ByVal iI As Integer, ByVal vNewval As Single)
ReDim Preserve mv(nbEl)
    If iI >= 0 And iI <= UBound(mv) Then
        mv(iI) = vNewval
    End If
End Property
```

As an illustration, the code below finds the minimum of a function in $\mathfrak{R}^3$: the simplex is, then, a set of four Vector objects:

```
Sub Nelder()
simp(): the simplex of vertices
baseFunc: function to minimize
sumVec, moyVec, del, scalar, comp, shrink: basic arithmetic
operations on vectors
```

```
Sub Nelder()
Dim simp() As New vector
ReDim simp(4) As New vector
Dim i%

Dim sr As vector
Dim se As vector
Dim soc As vector
Dim sic As vector

For i = 1 To 4
    simp(i).nbEl = 3
```

```vba
      For j = 1 To 3
          simp(i).v(j) = 5 * Rnd()
      Next j
Next i

For m = 1 To 200

      simp = sort_vec(simp)
      Set sr = sum_vec(scalar(2, moy_vec(del(simp))), simp(4), -1)

      Select Case baseFunc(sr) 'less calls to BaseFunc speeds up the code
      (see CD)'

          Case baseFunc(simp(1)) To baseFunc(simp(3))
              simp = comp(del(simp), sr)

          Case Is < baseFunc(simp(1))
              Set se = sum_vec(scalar(2, sr), moy_vec(del(simp)), -1)

              If baseFunc(se) < baseFunc(sr) Then
                  simp = comp(del(simp), se)
              Else
                  simp = shrink(simp)
              End If

          Case baseFunc(simp(3)) To baseFunc(simp(4))
              Set soc = sum_vec(scalar(0.5, sr), scalar(0.5,
              moy_vec(del(simp))), 1)
              If baseFunc(soc) < baseFunc(sr) Then
                  simp = comp(del(simp), soc)
              Else
                  simp = shrink(simp)
              End If

          Case Is >= baseFunc(simp(4))
              Set sic = sum_vec(scalar(0.5, simp(4)), scalar(0.5,
              moy_vec(del(simp))), 1)
              If baseFunc(sic) < baseFunc(simp(4)) Then
                  simp = comp(del(simp), sic)
              Else
                  simp = shrink(simp)
              End If

      End Select

Next m

End Sub

Public Function sort_val(x!()) As Single()

Dim xmin!
ReDim xx!(UBound(x)), u!(UBound(x))
xx = x
For i = 1 To UBound(x)
    xmin = x(1)
    u(i) = 1
```

```
     For j = 2 To UBound(x)
          If x(j) < xmin Then xmin = x(j): u(i) = j
     Next j
     x(u(i)) = 10000000
Next i
For i = 1 To UBound(x)
    x(i) = xx(u(i))
Next i
sort_val = x
End Function
```

```
Public Function sort_vec(Vec() As Vector, n%) As Vector()

Dim vx!(), wx!()
ReDim vx!(n), wx!(n)

ReDim w(UBound(Vec)) As Vector

For i = 1 To n
        vx(i) = baseFunc(Vec(i), n)
    Next i
    wx = vx
    vx = sort_val(vx)
    For i = 1 To n
        j = 1
        While vx(i) <> wx(j)
            j = j + 1
        Wend
        Set w(i) = Vec(j)
    Next i

    sort_vec = w

End Function
```

Multiplication by a scalar

```
Public Function scalar(x!, vv As Vector) As Vector
Dim w As New Vector
w.nbEl = vv.nbEl
For i = 1 To w.nbEl
    w.v(i) = x * vv.v(i)
Next i
Set scalar = w
End Function
```

Addition of two vectors:

```
Public Function sum_vec(vv1 As Vector, vv2 As Vector, S%) As Vector
Dim w As New Vector
w.nbEl = vv1.nbEl
For i = 1 To w.nbEl
    w.v(i) = vv1.v(i) + S * vv2.v(i)
Next i
Set sum_vec = w
End Function
```

Calculation of the simplex center of gravity:

```
Public Function moy_vec(w() As Vector) As Vector

Dim vv As New Vector
vv.nbEl = w(1).nbEl

For i = 1 To vv.nbEl
    vv.v(i) = 0
    For j = 1 To UBound(w)
        vv.v(i) = vv.v(i) + w(j).v(i)
    Next j
    vv.v(i) = vv.v(i) / UBound(w)
Next i
Set moy_vec = vv
End Function
```

Removal of the last element in an array of vectors:

```
Public Function del(vv() As Vector) As Vector()
ReDim w(UBound(vv) - 1) As New Vector

For i = 1 To UBound(vv) - 1
    Set w(i) = vv(i)
Next i

del = w
End Function
```

To append one vector to an array:

```
Public Function comp(vv() As Vector, vvv As Vector) As Vector()
ReDim w(UBound(vv) + 1) As New Vector

For i = 1 To UBound(vv)
    Set w(i) = vv(i)
Next i
Set w(UBound(vv) + 1) = vvv

comp = w
End Function
```

To bring every vertex closer to the "best performer":

```
Public Function shrink(w() As Vector) As Vector()

ReDim ww(UBound(w)) As Vector

For i = 1 To UBound(w)
    Set ww(i) = sum_vec(w(1), scalar(0.5, sum_vec(w(i), w(1), -1)), 1)
Next i
shrink = ww

End Function
```

2.4.2 The simulated annealing

This probabilistic method is widely used to locate the global minimum of a function on a relatively large scale. Given a function $f(x_i, i = 1...n)$, let us assume that f admits d relative minima

$m_j \in \mathbb{R}^n, j = 1,...,d$. The algorithm consists in building a sequence of points that gradually get closer to an acceptable extremum.

Starting from an arbitrary point X_0, we draw n-dimensional random vectors (points in $\mathbb{R}^n$) driving the evolution of the sequence:

$$X_k \rightarrow X_k + \Delta_k \rightarrow \quad test \ of \ f(X_k + \Delta_k)$$

$$accepted \quad X_{k+1} = X_k + \Delta_k$$

$$rejected \quad X_{k+1} = X_k$$

$$\Delta_k = \begin{pmatrix} \Delta_k^1 \\ \vdots \\ \Delta_k^d \end{pmatrix} = \begin{pmatrix} \lambda_1 . \delta_{k1} \\ \vdots \\ \lambda_d . \delta_{kd} \end{pmatrix}$$

Δ_k is driven by uniform RVs λ_i with values in $[0, 1]$ and δ_{ki} are arbitrary constant increments: these increments must be consistent with the expected order of magnitude of $|X_k - m_i|$.

One condition to accept $X_{k+1} = X_k + \Delta_k$ is obviously that $f(X_k + \Delta_k) < f(X_k)$. However, this unique criterion leads us to a local minimum, not necessarily the absolute one.

To explore other minima, we must give X_k a chance to get out of the hole, even if $\Delta f = f(X_k + \Delta_k) - f(X_k) > 0$.

Let us call $X \in \mathbb{R}^n$, the point that navigates in search of the global minimum. At each step of the algorithm, X finds itself in one of these situations:

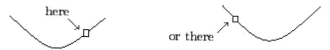

At an early stage of the process, X should be permitted to escape easily in order to visit other regions but, on the other hand, the deeper the hole, the higher the probability it corresponds to an absolute low. Therefore, the criterion to accept $X_{k+1} = X_k + \Delta_k$ when $f(X_k + \Delta_k) > f(X_k)$

- must be more restrictive as long as we move forward
- should take the amplitude $\delta f_k = f(X_k + \Delta_k) - f(X_k)$ as a driving factor.

Practically, at the n-th iteration, the algorithm goes like this

1. Generate n uniform RV λ_i and obtain a new point X_{k+1} in the neighborhood of X_k
2. Either $\Delta f < 0$, then $X_{k+1} = X_k + \Delta_k$ and proceed to the $(n + 1)$-th iteration.
3. Or $\Delta f > 0$, but give X a chance to move away by sampling a random uniform number U between 0 and 1: if $U < g(\Delta f, n)$ set $X_{k+1} = X_k + \Delta_k$

For the reasons given above, $g(x, y)$ must decrease when x and y increase. One of the most common forms of g is

$$g(\Delta f, n) = e^{-\Delta f / T(n)} \text{ with } T(n) \searrow \text{ when } n \nearrow .$$

This method is not 100% infallible in its first trial: achieving it depends on the choice of the initial point X_0 and of the increments δ_i. Since this algorithm converges quite rapidly, it is best to repeat the process N times with different parameters δ_i or initial values.

Below, we seek the minimum of a function in $\mathbb{R}$ which admits several local extrema with close minima. We repeat the algorithm with 11 different values for X_0 and, for each value of T, we shift X_k m times ($m = 100$ or 200):

$$f(x) = 10 * sin(50x) * sin(4x)$$

The graph below shows the image of f in the interval $[0.1, 1.1]$. The eleven initial values taken by X_0 are:

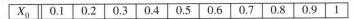

X_0	0.1	0.2	0.3	0.4	0.5	0.6	0.7	0.8	0.9	1

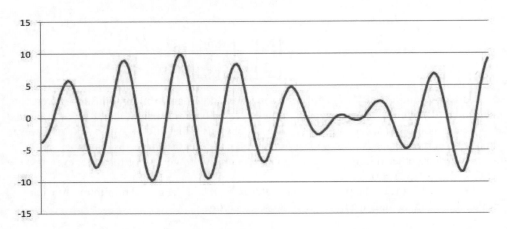

For the sake of simplicity, we have implemented the algorithm using the Excel function

Rnd()

to generate uniformly distributed numbers: in fact, practitioners commonly use in-house functions with better results (Chapter 4 addresses this issue). The results are given in the table below:

X_0	$m = 100$ $\delta = 0.2$ x	min	$m = 100$ $\delta = 0.1$ x	min	$m = 200$ $\delta = 0.2$ x	min	$m = 200$ $\delta = 0.1$ x	min
0	2.104	−8.453	−0.346	−9.824	−4.305	−9.977	−0.347	−9.824
0.1	−1.978	−9.972	−0.47	−9.502	−3.612	−9.512	−0.346	−9.824
0.2	4.304	−9.98	−0.914	−4.87	−2.67	−9.498	0.596	−6.877
0.3	−1.162	−9.98	−0.346	−9.824	5.938	−9.821	1.037	−8.449
0.4	−1.979	−9.973	1.287	−9.055	−2.796	−9.822	1.854	−9.054
0.5	1.979	−9.979	1.286	−9.032	1.162	−9.979	0.345	−9.813
0.6	3.488	−9.823	1.979	−9.979	1.162	−9.98	−0.594	−6.855
0.7	−2.795	−9.814	−0.347	−9.815	0.47	−9.505	0.22	−7.716
0.8	5.938	−9.816	2.546	−6.87	−0.346	−9.821	1.163	−9.98
0.9	−5.121	−9.977	1.162	−9.979	2.671	−9.514	2.103	−8.438
1	2.796	−9.823	1.287	−9.054	−1.162	−9.98	0.471	−9.512

Code The procedure **testSA()** tests the algorithm on the function $(fv(x) = 10sin(50x).sin(4x)$ $x = 0, 0.1,...,1)$:

```
Sub testSA()

Dim x!(10)
For i = 0 To 10
    x(i) = i / 10
Next i
Debug.Print algoSA("fv", x)
End Sub
```

The minima are stored in an array **MinVal**. The final result is the minimum of MinVal, calculated by **MinVec**:

```
Public Function algoSA(FuncName$, x!()) As Single  'function accept in CD'

ReDim MinVal!(UBound(x))
Dim z0!, z1!, dg!
Dim t!

For l = 0 To UBound(x)
    z0 = x(l): m = 2: t = 100 / m
    f0 = Application.Run(FuncName, z0)
    While t > 10 ^ (-1)

        For j = 1 To 100
            z1 = z0 + (0.5 - Rnd()) / 10
            f1 = Application.Run(FuncName, z1)
            dg = f1 - f0
            If accept(dg, t) Then z0 = z1: f0 = f1
        Next j

        m = m + 1
        t = 100 / m
    Wend
    MinVal(l) = Application.Run(FuncName, z0)
Next l

algoSA = MinVec(MinVal)

End Function

Public Function MinVec(v!()) As Single

MinVec = v(LBound(v))
For i = LBound(v) To UBound(v)
    If v(i) < MinVec Then MinVec = v(i)
Next i
End Function
```

2.5 LINEAR ALGEBRA

Matricial calculus plays a major role in statistics and financial topics since a large number of quantitative issues involve multiple assets and market data. Moreover, solving continuous time stochastic equations often proves to be too arduous, thus needing a discretization of time and space: at some point, a linear system has to be solved. We will encounter it in topics such as:

- Interpolation
- Regression
- Principal component analysis.

Before examining these matters, let us investigate the most usual matrix operations, i.e., **Matrix inversion** and **Matrix Pseudo-square roots**

2.5.1 Matrix inversion

Given a square matrix $[X]$, we seek $[A]$ such that

$$[A].[X] = [Id]$$

In the literature, we can find more than one method to invert a square matrix. Let us quote, for example:

- the **LU decomposition** method
- the **Gauss-Jordan elimination** method.

As a matter of fact, the LU decomposition (also called LU factorization) where **L** and **U** stand for Lower and Upper, is an appealing method since it factors the matrix to invert into a product of a lower triangular matrix and an upper one, before inverting them, resulting in a rather straightforward algorithm (see, e.g., Poole (2010)). Unfortunately, this method fails when there are some zeros on the diagonal (not a rare event in financial applications).

In this section, we opt for a basic version of the Gauss-Jordan algorithm.

Gauss-Jordan algorithm   In this section, we give up the square brackets ($A = [A]$). Assuming the following linear system to solve

$$A.X = Y \text{ (or equivalently } A.X = I.Y)$$

we seek to turn this problem into an upper triangular system, which is easier to solve. For this purpose, we perform row operations (linear combinations), so that, at the end, the leading coefficient, i.e., the leftmost non-zero element for each row, is on the diagonal (all the elements under the diagonal are zero).

Starting from

$$\begin{pmatrix} a_{1,1} & a_{1,2} & \cdots & a_{1,n} \\ a_{2,1} & a_{2,2} & \cdots & a_{2,n} \\ \vdots & \vdots & \cdots & \vdots \\ a_{n,1} & a_{n,2} & \cdots & a_{n,n} \end{pmatrix}$$

the 2nd row is replaced by $a_{2,1} * 1^{st}$ row $- a_{1,1} * 2^{nd}$ row

the 3rd row is replaced by $a_{3,1} * 1^{st}$ row $- a_{1,1} * 3^{rd}$ row

$$\vdots$$

the nth row is replaced by $a_{n,1} * 1^{st}$ row $- a_{1,1} * n^{th}$ row

Here, the leading term, called the **pivot**, is $a_{1,1}$, and at the end of this set of operations, A has been changed to

$$A^1 = \begin{pmatrix} a_{1,1} & a_{1,2} & \cdots & a_{1,n} \\ 0 & a_{2,1}a_{1,2} - a_{1,1}a_{2,2} & \cdots & a_{2,1}a_{1,n} - a_{1,1}a_{2,n} \\ 0 & a_{3,1}a_{1,2} - a_{1,1}a_{3,2} & \cdots & a_{3,1}a_{1,n} - a_{1,1}a_{3,n} \\ 0 & \vdots & \vdots & \vdots \\ 0 & a_{n,1}a_{1,2} - a_{1,1}a_{n,2} & \cdots & a_{n,1}a_{1,n} - a_{1,1}a_{n,n} \end{pmatrix}$$

We reinitiate the same kind of operations, starting from the third row, with a new pivot $= a_{2,1}a_{1,2} - a_{1,1}a_{2,2}$.

And again, until we obtain an upper triangular matrix T. In case the leading coefficient is beyond the diagonal, we swap two rows.

In a second step, the calculation of T^{-1} is straightforward.

Put into equations, all those operations are in fact matrix multiplications. For instance, the first one can be written

$$A^1 = \begin{pmatrix} 1 & 0 & 0 & \cdots & \cdots & 0 \\ a_{2,1} & -a_{1,1} & 0 & \cdots & \cdots & 0 \\ 0 & 0 & 1 & 0 & \cdots & 0 \\ \vdots & \vdots & \vdots & \vdots & \ddots & \vdots \\ 0 & \cdots & \cdots & \cdots & \cdots & 1 \end{pmatrix}.A$$

To recap: each transformation (+ calculation of T^{-1}) is a multiplication, resulting in

$$P.A = I, \text{ and, at the end, } P.A.X = P.I.Y = I.X \Longrightarrow P.I = A^{-1}$$

The Gaussian algorithm performs these operations, both on A <u>and</u> the identity matrix I, in order to get $P.I = A^{-1}$.

Code When dealing with matrix inversions, the use of **double precision** type variables is imperative: the argument is therefore declared as $v\#()$ (and passed ByRef !):

```
Function GaussJordan(v#()) As Double()

Dim n%: n = UBound(v, 1)

Dim Id#()
ReDim Id(n, n)
For i = 1 To n
    Id(i, i) = 1
Next i

For i = 1 To n - 1
    If v(i, i) = 0 Then
        l = 1
        While v(i + 1, i) = 0
            l = l + 1
        Wend
        For j = 1 To n
            temp1 = v(i, j): temp2 = Id(i, j)
```

```
            v(i, j) = v(i + 1, j): Id(i, j) = Id(i + 1, j)
            v(i + 1, j) = temp1: Id(i + 1, j) = temp2
        Next j
    End If
```

****

If v(i,i)<>0, piv is the regular pivot.

****

```
        piv = v(i, i)
        For K = 1 To n
            Id(i, K) = Id(i, K) / piv
            v(i, K) = v(i, K) / piv
        Next K

    For j = i + 1 To n
    piv = v(j, i)
        For K = 1 To n
            Id(j, K) = Id(j, K) - piv * Id(i, K)
            v(j, K) = v(j, K) - piv * v(i, K)
        Next K
    Next j
Next i

If v(n, n) <> 0 Then
    For i = 1 To n
            Id(n, i) = Id(n, i) / v(n, n)
    Next i
            v(n, n) = 1
End If

For i = 1 To n - 1
    For j = i To n - 1
        piv = v(i, j + 1)

        For K = 1 To n
            Id(i, K) = Id(i, K) - piv * Id(j + 1, K)
            v(i, K) = v(i, K) - piv * v(j + 1, K)
        Next K
    Next j
Next i

GaussJordan = Id

End Function
```

2.5.2 Cholesky decomposition

The Cholesky method is widely used to calculate the pseudo-square root of a positive sym-metrical matrix S in the form of a lower triangular matrix L thus verifying

$$L.L^\dagger = S$$

To exist, this matrix must be positive-definite. One necessary and sufficient condition for this is that all the **eigenvalues** of L must be **strictly positive**: their calculation is addressed in §2.5.5.

The Cholesky decomposition is rather straightforward. Denoting $(s_{i,j}) = S$

$$s_{i,j} = \sum_{k=1}^{\min(i,j)} l_{i,k} l_{j,k} \tag{2.1}$$

Since $s_{i,j} = s_{j,i}$ it suffices to solve 2.1 for $i \leq j$

$$l_{j,i} = \frac{1}{l_{i,i}} \left(s_{i,j} - \sum_{k=1}^{i-1} l_{i,k} l_{j,k} \right)$$

$$l_{i,i}^2 = s_{i,i} - \sum_{k=1}^{i-1} l_{i,k}^2$$

The equations above show that the system can be solved recursively, knowing the elements of the 1st column.

$$s_{1,1} = l_{1,1}^2 \implies l_{1,1} = \sqrt{s_{1,1}}$$

$$l_{1,1} l_{2,1} = s_{2,1} \implies l_{1,1} = \frac{s_{2,1}}{l_{1,1}}$$

$$\ldots \; l_{i,1} = \frac{s_{i,1}}{l_{1,1}}$$

Code

```
Public Function Cholesky(rho#(), n%) As Double()

Dim i%, j%, K%
Dim cumul: cumul = 0
ReDim trigo#(n - 1, n - 1)

For i = 1 To n - 1

    If i > 1 Then
        For K = 1 To i - 1
            cumul = cumul + trigo(K, i) * trigo(K, i)
        Next

        trigo(i, i) = Sqr(rho(i, i) - cumul)
        cumul = 0
    Else
        trigo(i, i) = Sqr(rho(i, i))
    End If

    For j = i + 1 To n - 1

        If i > 1 Then
            For K = 1 To i - 1
                cumul = cumul + trigo(K, i) * trigo(K, j)
            Next
```

```
            trigo(i, j) = (rho(i, j) - cumul) / trigo(i, i)
            cumul = 0
        Else
            trigo(i, j) = rho(i, j) / trigo(i, i)
        End If
    Next j

Next i

Cholesky = matTranspose(trigo)

End Function
```

The argument *n* in the function declaration seems quite redundant, since the matrix passed as argument and the lower triangular matrix derived from it are obviously of the same size. In fact, some programs in this book use a version of this function omitting this parameter (just replace *n* with *Ubound*(*rho*;1) in the body of the function).

The motivations for using both versions come from the Interest Rates Exotics algorithmic specificities. Without going into too much detail, a *n*-period long interest rate-related asset needs to sample $n-1$ forward rates, using an $(n-1)\times(n-1)$ correlation matrix: thus, to avoid any confusion in the duration of the asset, it seems worthwhile to mention explicitly *n* as parameter.

However, the call to use an alternative version of this Cholesky function, i.e., omitting the second argument, can also be found within some pieces of code in this book.

2.5.3 Interpolation

Given a series of known data points (x_i, y_i), we intend to build a function f estimating values at intermediate points x, within the range of the original series. This section will cover three current methods:

- linear
- polynomial
- cubic.

Linear interpolation   A quick and easy interpolation consists in building a piecewise function where every piece is linear. In other terms, intermediate points are linearly interpolated between two adjacent points. Given (x_i, y_i) and (x_{i+1}, y_{i+1}) as those two points, the interpolant is calculated by:

$$f(x) = f(x_i) + \frac{f(x_{i+1}) - f(x_i)}{x_{i+1} - x_i}.(x_{i+1} - x_i) \tag{2.2}$$

The VBA code divides into two steps:

- find the two immediate adjacent points
- apply equation (2.2) to find $f(x)$.

By convention, if the interpolation concerns a date "off limits" the solution is the closest value in the range.

```
Option base 1
Public Function interpol_Val(dx As Date, d() As Date, x#()) As Double

i = 1
While dx > d(i) And i <= UBound(x)
    i = i + 1
Wend

Select Case i
    Case 1
        interpol_Val = x(1)
    Case Ubound(x)+1
        interpol_Val = x(UBound(x))
    Case Else
        slop = (x(i) - x(i - 1)) / (d(i) - d(i - 1))
        interpol_Val = slop * (dx - d(i - 1)) + x(i - 1)
End Select

End Function
```

Polynomial interpolation   Given a series of n+1 data points (x_i, y_i), we search a polynom P of degree n such that $P(x_i) = y_i$ for all i. If $P(x)$ is in the form

$$P(x) = \sum_{i=0}^{n} a_i x^i = a_0 + a_1 x + \dots + a_n x^n,$$

we can rewrite $P(x_i) = y_i, i = 0,\dots,n$ in a matricial form

$$\begin{pmatrix} 1 & x_0 & x_0^2 & \dots & x_0^n \\ 1 & x_1 & x_1^2 & \dots & x_1^n \\ \cdot & \cdot & \cdot & \dots & \dots \\ \cdot & \cdot & \cdot & \dots & \dots \\ \cdot & \cdot & \cdot & \dots & \dots \\ 1 & x_n & x_n^2 & \dots & x_n^n \end{pmatrix} \begin{pmatrix} a_0 \\ a_1 \\ \cdot \\ \cdot \\ \cdot \\ a_n \end{pmatrix} = \begin{pmatrix} y_0 \\ y_1 \\ \cdot \\ \cdot \\ \cdot \\ y_n \end{pmatrix}$$

The matrix $[x_{i-1}^{j-1}]$ is known as the Vandermonde matrix and its determinant is

$$\prod_{i \neq j} (x_i - x_j)$$

which is non-zero since there are no doublons in the set of data. This matrix is regular, thus inversible:

$$\begin{pmatrix} a_0 \\ a_1 \\ \cdot \\ \cdot \\ \cdot \\ a_n \end{pmatrix} = [M]^{-1} . \begin{pmatrix} y_0 \\ y_1 \\ \cdot \\ \cdot \\ \cdot \\ y_n \end{pmatrix}$$

The inverse of M is the product $U^{-1}.L^{-1}$, where U^{-1} is an upper triangular matrix while L^{-1} is a lower one.

The elements $u(i,j)$ of U^{-1} are given by:

$$u(i,j) = 0 \qquad i > j$$

$$u(i,i) = 1$$

$$u(i,j) = u(i-1, j-1) - u(i,j-1)^*x_{j-1} \qquad i > j$$

The elements $l(i,j)$ of L^{-1} satisfy:

$$l(i,j) = 0 \qquad i < j$$

$$l(1,1) = 1$$

$$l(i,j) = \prod_{\substack{k=1 \\ k \neq j}}^{i} \frac{1}{x_j - x_k} \qquad i > j$$

```
Public Function Poly(vx#(), vy#()) As Double()

Dim n%: n = UBound(vx)
ReDim ml#(n, n), mu#(n, n)

mu(1, 1) = 1
For j = 2 To n
    mu(1, j) = -mu(1, j - 1) * vx(j - 1)
Next j
For i = 2 To n
    For j = i To n
        mu(i, j) = mu(i - 1, j - 1) - mu(i, j - 1) * vx(j - 1)
    Next j
Next i

ml(1, 1) = 1
For i = 2 To n
    For j = 1 To i
        ml(i, j) = 1
            For K = 1 To i
                If K <> j Then ml(i, j) = ml(i, j) * 1 / (vx(j) - vx(K))
            Next K
    Next j
Next i
Poly = MatMult(MatMult(mu, ml), vy)

End Function

Function Mdim(m!()) As Integer

On Error GoTo Dimension

 For DimNum = 1 To 3
    ErrorCheck = LBound(m, DimNum)
 Next DimNum
```

```
Dimension:
Mdim = DimNum - 1

End Function

Public Function MatMult(m1!(), m2!()) As Single()

Dim dim1%, dim2%
dim1 = Mdim(m1) : dim2 = Mdim(m2)

Dim res!()

Select Case dim1 * dim2

    Case 2
        ReDim res(UBound(m1, 1))
        For i = 1 To UBound(m1, 1)
            res(i) = 0
            For k = 1 To UBound(m1, 2)
                res(i) = res(i) + m1(i, k) * m2(k)
            Next k
        Next i

    Case 4
        ReDim res(UBound(m1, 1), UBound(m2, 2))
        For i = 1 To UBound(m1, 1)
            For j = 1 To UBound(m2, 2)
                res(i, j) = 0
                For k = 1 To UBound(m1, 2)
                    res(i, j) = res(i, j) + m1(i, k) * m2(k, j)
                Next k
            Next j
        Next i

End Select

MatMult = res

End Function
```

Cubic interpolation   Instead of one single high-degree polynomial to pass cross all the points, we are now looking for a function that is **piecewise cubic polynomial** and goes through all the points: practically, within the interval between two adjacent points, the function is polynomial of degree 3: the degree of the polynomials is to ensure the continuity of the first and second derivative at each node.

Given a set of n nodes (x_i, y_i) and $n - 1$ polynomials $P_i(x) = a_i x^3 + b_i x^2 + c_i x + d_i$, the interpolating function must satisfy $n + 3(n - 2)$ equations

$$n \ equations \begin{cases} f(x) = P_1(x) & x_1 \leq x < x_2 \\ f(x) = P_2(x) & x_2 \leq x < x_3 \\ f(x) = P_{n-1}(x) & x_{n-1} \leq x \leq x_n \\ P_i(x_i) = y_i \end{cases}$$

$$3(n-2) \ equations \begin{cases} P_1(x_2) = P_2(x_2) & \cdots & P_{n-2}(x_{n-1}) = P_{n-1}(x_{n-1}) \\ P'_1(x_2) = P'_2(x_2) & \cdots & P'_{n-2}(x_{n-1}) = P'_{n-1}(x_{n-1}) \\ P''_1(x_2) = P''_2(x_2) & \cdots & P''_{n-2}(x_{n-1}) = P''_{n-1}(x_{n-1}) \end{cases}$$

Total (**4n − 6**) equations

On the other hand, $n - 1$ cubic polynomials mean $(n - 1) \times 4 = $ (**4n- 4**) coefficients: the system above is just short of two equations. This issue can be fixed, imposing two conditions on the second derivatives at the endpoints. One common solution is the **natural splines** assumption which postulates:

$$P''_1(x_1) = 0 \qquad P''_{n-1}(x_n) = 0$$

$$6a_1 x_1 + 2b_1 = 0 \qquad 6a_{n-1}x_n + 2b_{n-1} = 0$$

For example, when $n = 3$, we get:

$$\begin{pmatrix} 6x_1 & 2 & 0 & . & . & . & . & 0 \\ x_1^3 & x_1^2 & x_1 & 1 & 0 & . & . & 0 \\ x_2^3 & x_2^2 & x_2 & 1 & 0 & . & . & 0 \\ 3x_2^2 & 2x_2 & 1 & 0 & -3x_2^2 & -2x_2 & -1 & 0 \\ 6x_2 & 2 & 0 & 0 & -6x_2 & -2 & 0 & 0 \\ 0 & . & . & 0 & x_2^3 & x_2^2 & x_2 & 1 \\ 0 & . & . & 0 & x_3^3 & x_3^2 & x_3 & 1 \\ 0 & . & . & 0 & 6x_3 & 2 & 0 & 0 \end{pmatrix} \begin{pmatrix} a_1 \\ b_1 \\ c_1 \\ d_1 \\ a_2 \\ b_2 \\ c_2 \\ d_2 \end{pmatrix} = \begin{pmatrix} 0 \\ y_1 \\ y_2 \\ 0 \\ 0 \\ y_2 \\ y_3 \\ 0 \end{pmatrix}$$

If the conditions on the endpoints change, only the first and last rows are to be modified. For instance, if we enforce

$$P''_1(x_1) = P''_1(x_2)$$

$$P''_{n-1}(x_n) = P''_{n-1}(x_{n-1}),$$

the matrix becomes

$$\begin{pmatrix} 6x_1 & 2 & 0 & 0 & -6x_2 & -2 & 0 & 0 \\ x_1^3 & x_1^2 & x_1 & 1 & 0 & . & . & 0 \\ x_2^3 & x_2^2 & x_2 & 1 & 0 & . & . & 0 \\ 3x_2^2 & 2x_2 & 1 & 0 & -3x_2^2 & -2x_2 & -1 & 0 \\ 6x_2 & 2 & 0 & 0 & -6x_2 & -2 & 0 & 0 \\ 0 & . & . & 0 & x_2^3 & x_2^2 & x_2 & 1 \\ 0 & . & . & 0 & x_3^3 & x_3^2 & x_3 & 1 \\ 6x_2 & 2 & 0 & 0 & -6x_3 & 2 & 0 & 0 \end{pmatrix}$$

To build **M**, we make a distinction between

1. the conditions to be met at both end of the x-coordinates, i.e., x_1 and x_n, (1)
2. the equations ensuring continuity at every node $x_2, x_3,...,x_{n-1}$ (2)

$$(1)\begin{cases} 6a_1x_1 + 2 = 0 \\ a_1x_1^3 + b_1x_1^2 + c_1x_1 + d_1 = y_1 \\ 6a_{n-1}x_n + 2 = 0 \\ a_{n-1}x_n^3 + b_{n-1}x_n^2 + c_{n-1}x_n + d_{n-1} = y_n \end{cases}$$

$$(2)\begin{cases} a_{i-1}x_i^3 + b_{i-1}x_i^2 + c_{i-1}x_i + d_{i-1} = y_i \\ a_ix_i^3 + b_ix_i^2 + c_ix_i + d_i = y_i \\ P'_{i-1}(x_i) - P'_i(x_i) = 0 \\ P''_{i-1}(x_i) - P''_i(x_i) = 0 \end{cases}$$

In matricial notation,

$$\underbrace{\begin{pmatrix} x_i^3 & x_i^2 & x_i & 1 & 0 & & . & & . & 0 \\ 3x_i^2 & 2x_i & 1 & 0 & -3x_i^2 & -2x_i & -1 & 0 \\ 6x_i & 2 & 0 & 0 & -6x_i & -2 & 0 & 0 \\ 0 & & . & . & 0 & x_i^3 & x_i^2 & x_i & 1 \end{pmatrix}}_{M_i} \begin{pmatrix} a_{i-1} \\ b_{i-1} \\ c_{i-1} \\ d_{i-1} \\ a_i \\ b_i \\ c_i \\ d_i \end{pmatrix} = \begin{pmatrix} y_i \\ 0 \\ 0 \\ y_i \end{pmatrix}$$

$$\begin{pmatrix} 6x_1 & 2 & 0 & 0 & \cdots & \cdots & \cdots & \cdots & \cdots & 0 \\ x_1^3 & x_1^2 & x_1 & 1 & 0 & \cdots & \cdots & \cdots & \cdots & 0 \\ & & M_2 & & & & & & & \\ & & & M3 & & & & & & \\ & & & & \searrow & & & & & \\ & & & & & M_{n-1} & & & & \\ 0 & \cdots & \cdots & \cdots & \cdots & 0 & x_n^3 & x_n^2 & x_n & 1 \\ 0 & \cdots & \cdots & \cdots & \cdots & 0 & 6x_n & 2 & 0 & 0 \end{pmatrix} \begin{pmatrix} a_1 \\ b_1 \\ c_1 \\ d_1 \\ \vdots \\ \vdots \\ \vdots \\ \vdots \\ a_{n-1} \\ b_{n-1} \\ c_{n-1} \\ d_{n-1} \end{pmatrix} = \begin{pmatrix} 0 \\ y_1 \\ y_2 \\ 0 \\ 0 \\ \vdots \\ \vdots \\ \vdots \\ 0 \\ y_{n-1} \\ y_n \\ 0 \end{pmatrix}$$

Written in a more concise form,

$$M \cdot A = Y \tag{2.3}$$

Code   We outline here below the steps of the interpolation process, then list the relevant VBA code. The data are retrieved from an array of abscissas [x] and an array of ordinates [y], and we seek to compute the array of coefficients A such that $A = M^{-1}.Y$:

1. Build block matrices M_i
2. Then, build M with the M_i blocks and complete with the first and last two lines (the boundaries of the range)
3. Then build Y from [y]
4. Invert M using the Gauss-Jordan algorithm and calculate A.

The benefit of this method is that A is computed once, and so doesn't need to be recalculated at each interpolation.

```
Public Function cubic(x#(),y#()) As Double()

Dim yCub#(): yCub = build_VectorY(y)
Dim xCub#(): xCub = buildM(x)
Dim w#(): w = GaussJordan(xCub)
Dim a#(): a = MatMult(w, yCub)
For i = 1 To UBound(a)
Debug.Print a(i)
Next i
cubic=a
End Function


Public Function build_VectorY(y#()) As Double()

ReDim temp#(4 * (UBound(y) - 1))
temp(1) = 0: temp(2) = y(1)
For i = 2 To UBound(y) - 1
    temp(4 * (i - 2) + 3) = y(i)
    temp(4 * (i - 2) + 4) = 0
    temp(4 * (i - 2) + 5) = 0
    temp(4 * (i - 2) + 6) = y(i)
Next i
temp(4 * (UBound(y) - 1) - 1) = y(UBound(y))
temp(4 * (UBound(y) - 1)) = 0
build_VectorY = temp

End Function


Public Function BlockM(x#) As Double()

Dim m#(4, 8)
For i = 1 To 4
    m(1, i) = x ^ (4 - i): m(4, 4 + i) = m(1, i)
Next i
For i = 1 To 3
    m(2, i) = (4 - i) * x ^ (3 - i): m(2, 4 + i) = -m(2, i)
Next i
    m(3, 1) = 6 * x: m(3, 2) = 2: m(3, 5) = -6 * x: m(3, 6) = -2

BlockM = m

End Function
```

```
Public Function buildM(x#()) As Double()

Dim n%: n = 4 * (UBound(x) - 1)

ReDim mat#(n, n)
ReDim m#(4, 8)

For K = 1 To UBound(x) - 2
    m = BlockM(x(K + 1))
    For i = 1 To 4
        For j = 1 To 8
            mat(4 * (K - 1) + 2 + i, 4 * (K - 1) + j) = m(i, j)
        Next j
    Next i
Next K

mat(1, 1) = 6 * x(1): mat(1, 2) = 2: mat(n, n - 3) = 6 * x(UBound(x)):
mat(n, n - 2) = 2
For i = 1 To 4
    mat(2, i) = x(1) ^ (4 - i): mat(n - 1, n - 4 + i) = x(4) ^ (4 - i)
Next i

 buildM = mat
End Function
```

Polynomial regression   In this section, we search the coefficients a_i of an m-degree polynomial that best fits a set of n data (x_i, y_i). Obviously, an $(n - 1)$-degree polynomial can do the job (see Interpolation above), but when the amount of data becomes too important, we seek to make a sort of *regression* with $m \ll n$. The optimal choice for m is somewhat subjective, the minimum suitable depending on the precision needed. Consider a polynomial:

$$\sum_{k=0}^{m} a_k X^{m-k}$$

The distance between the data and the polynomial curve is the least-square estimator:

$$L = \sum_{i=1}^{n} \left(\sum_{k=0}^{m} a_k x_i^{m-k} - y_i \right)^2$$

To find the coefficients a_k that minimize L, we solve:

$$\partial L / \partial a_0 = 0, \quad \partial L / \partial a_1 = 0, ..., \partial L / \partial a_m = 0$$

The system obtained:

$$\partial L / \partial a_0 : \quad \sum_{i=1}^{n} \left[\left(\sum_{k=0}^{m} a_k x_i^{m-k} - y_i \right) * x_i^m \right] = 0$$

$$\dots$$

$$\partial L / \partial a_j : \quad \sum_{i=1}^{n} \left[\left(\sum_{k=0}^{m} a_k x_i^{m-k} - y_i \right) * x_i^{m-j} \right] = 0$$

In matricial form:

$$
\begin{bmatrix}
\sum_{i=1}^{n} x_i^{2m} & \sum_{i=1}^{n} x_i^{2m-1} & \cdots & \sum_{i=1}^{n} x_i^{m} \\
\sum_{i=1}^{n} x_i^{2m-1} & \sum_{i=1}^{n} x_i^{2m-2} & \cdots & \sum_{i=1}^{n} x_i^{m-1} \\
\vdots & \vdots & \vdots & \vdots \\
\sum_{i=1}^{n} x_i^{m} & \sum_{i=1}^{n} x_i^{m-1} & \cdots & \sum_{i=1}^{n} x_i^{0} = n
\end{bmatrix}
\underbrace{\qquad}_{M}
\begin{bmatrix}
a_0 \\ a_1 \\ \vdots \\ a_m
\end{bmatrix}
=
\begin{bmatrix}
\sum_{i=1}^{n} y_i x_i^{m} \\
\sum_{i=1}^{n} y_i x_i^{m-1} \\
\vdots \sum_{i=1}^{n} y_i
\end{bmatrix}
$$

Then, we invert M to get $[A]$.

Code The following code describes a function taking a list of n points $data(i,j) = (x_i, y_i)$ and returning the coefficients of the polynom that goes through these points:

```
Function polyFit(data#(), m%)

Dim n%: n = m + 1

Dim v#(): ReDim v(n)
Dim u#(): ReDim u(2 * (n))
Dim a#()
Dim mat#(): ReDim mat(n, n)

For i = 1 To n
    v(i) = 0
    For j = 1 To UBound(dat, 1)
        v(i) = v(i) + data(j, 2) * data(j, 1) ^ (n - i)
    Next j
Next i

For i = 0 To 2 * m
    u(i) = 0
    For j = 1 To UBound(data, 1)
        u(i) = u(i) + data(j, 1) ^ i
    Next j
Next i

For i = 1 To n
    For j = 1 To m + 1
        mat(i, j) = u(2 * n - i - j)
    Next j
Next i

Dim invM#()
invM = GaussJordan(mat)
a = MatMult(invM, v)

polyFit = a

End Function
```

2.5.4 Integration

Two methods are studied in this section. Both are based on a subdivision of the domain of integration and a polynomial approximation of the function to integrate. In the first method, named after **Newton-Cotes**, subintervals $[x_i, x_{i+1}]$ are of equal length ($x_{i+1} - x_i = \Delta x$). In the second, called the **Gauss-Quadrature** method, they are not.

Newton-Cotes The accuracy of the method is supposed to incease with the number of subdivisions and the degree of the interpolating polynomials. For instance, the approximation of $f(x)$ with piecewise constants is obviously less accurate than with piecewise affine functions. As a matter of fact, this guesstimate is true as long as the number of points doesn't grow too much.

Depending on the degree of the approximation polynomials, the method is given different names: for each, the interpolation is done piecewise so that each needs a number of points equal to the degree of the polynomial $+1$.

Trapezoidal rule (affine)

$$\int_{x_1}^{x_n} f(x)\mathrm{d}x \simeq \sum_{i=1}^{n} \frac{\Delta x}{2}(f(x_i) + f(x_{i+1}))$$

Simpson's rule (degree 2)

$$\int_{x_1}^{x_n} f(x)\mathrm{d}x \simeq \sum_{i=1}^{(n-1)/2} \frac{\Delta x}{3}(f(x_{2i-1}) + 4f(x_{2i}) + f(x_{2i+1}))$$

Simpson's 3/8 rule (degree 3)

$$\int_{x_1}^{x_n} f(x)\mathrm{d}x \simeq \sum_{i=1}^{(n-1)/3} \frac{\Delta x}{8}(3f(x_{3i-2}) + 9f(x_{3i-1}) + 9f(x_{3i}) + 3f(x_{3i+1}))$$

Boole's rule (degree 4)

$$\int_{x_1}^{x_n} f(x)\mathrm{d}x \simeq \sum_{i=1}^{(n-1)/4} \frac{\Delta x}{45}(14f(x_{4i-3}) + 64f(x_{4i-2}) + 24f(x_{4i-1}) + 64f(x_{4i}) + 14f(x_{4i+1}))$$

Gauss-quadrature Consider a set of **orthogonal** polynomials ϕ_i of degree i, thus verifying $<\phi_i, \phi_j> \ = 0$ for $i \neq j$. In practice, the orthogonality must be defined with respect to an interval $[a, b]$ and a **weight function** $w(x)$, $w(x) > 0$ so as to comply with the condition

$$<\phi_i, \phi_j> \ = \int_a^b \phi_i(x)\phi_j(x)w(x)\mathrm{d}x = \delta_{i,j}\|\phi_i\|^2$$

The set of (ϕ_i) forms an **orthogonal basis** for polynomials of degree at most n. Therefore, any P_n can be expressed

$$P_n(x) = \sum_{i=0}^{n} \lambda_i \phi_i(x)$$

Given the orthogonality of the basis, any polynomial P_{n-1} of degree at most $n-1$ verifies

$$< P_{n-1}, \phi_n >$$

For instance, with respect to $[a, b] = [-1, 1]$ and for $w(x) = 1$, **Lagrange** polynomials $L_i(x)$ form an orthogonal basis. Given n points $(x_i, P_n(x_i))$ the orthogonal decomposition of Pn in (L_i) is

$$P_n(x) = \sum_{i=0}^{n} P_n(x_i)L_i(x)$$

(recalling that $L_i(x_j) = \delta_{i,j}$)

The starting point of the Gauss theorem is based on the orthogonality of L_i with any polynomial of degree inferior to i. Thus, given a polynomial P_{2n} of degree $2n$, the division of P_{2n} by L_{n+1} gives a remainder r_n

$$P_{2n}(x) = L_{n+1}(x)q_{n-1}(x) + r_n(x) \implies$$

$$\int_{-1}^{+1} P_{2n}\mathrm{d}x = \int_{-1}^{+1} r_n(x)\mathrm{d}x = \int_{-1}^{+1} \sum_{i=1}^{n} r_n(x_i)L_i(x)\mathrm{d}x = \sum_{i=1}^{n} w_i r_n(x_i)$$

$$w_i = \int_{-1}^{+1} L_i(x)\mathrm{d}x$$

If the interval $[-1, 1]$ is divided into $(n+1)$ abscissa chosen to be the *zeros of* $L_{n+1}(x)$

$$r_n(x_i) = P_{2n}(x_i) - L_{n+1}(x_i)q_{n-1}(x_i) = P_{2n}(x_i)$$

This equality works for any interpolating polynomial $P(X)$ of degree at most $2n$. Therefore, for any function f, continuous over $[-1, 1]$, we can approximate

$$\int_{-1}^{+1} f(x)\mathrm{d}x \simeq \sum_{i=1}^{n} w_i f(x_i)$$

where the nodes x_i are the **roots** of some series of orthogonal polynomials and w_i are the relevant weights, contingent on the properties of these polynomials. Among the most current ones, let us mention their reknowned authors **Legendre**, **Hermite**, and **Laguerre**. Each one applies to some form of integrand:

■ Legendre

$$\int_a^b f(u)\mathrm{d}u$$

- Hermite

$$\int_{-\infty}^{+\infty} e^{-u^2} f(u) du$$

- Laguerre

$$\int_{0}^{+\infty} e^{-u} f(u) du$$

The nodes and weights are not easy to determine, since the definition of these polynomials is recursive. Therefore, we made the choice to tabulate, for each polynomial basis, up to 32 values for w_i and x_i and to retrieve them when needed to compute some complex integral.

- Legendre polynomials

$$P_n(x) = \frac{1}{2^n} \sum_{i=0}^{n} \binom{n}{i}^2 (x-1)^{n-i} (x+1)^i$$

$$\int_{a}^{b} f(u) du = \frac{b-a}{2} \int_{-1}^{+1} f\left(\frac{b-a}{2} u + \frac{b+a}{2}\right) du$$

$$\simeq \frac{b-a}{2} \sum_{i=1}^{n} w_i f\left(\frac{b-a}{2} x_i + \frac{b+a}{2}\right)$$

- Hermite polynomials

$$P_n(x) = (-1)^n e^{x^2/2} \frac{d^n}{dx^n} (e^{-x^2/2})$$

- Laguerre polynomials

$$P_n(x) = \frac{e^x}{n!} \frac{d^n}{dx^n} (e^{-x} x^n)$$

Let us put this into practice and calculate the following integral:

$$\int_{0}^{+\infty} e^{-u/2} u \cos(u) du$$

First, rearrange it with an adequate change of variable $w = u/2$, in such a way as to recognize some familiar integral:

$$4 \int_{0}^{+\infty} e^{-w} w \cos(2w) dw$$

The integrand $x \cos(2x)$ is weighted by e^{-x}: we then retrieve an arbitrary number of nodes and weights from an Excel sheet named ... Worksheets("Laguerre") for instance.

A	B		
xL(i)	wL(i)		
0,047407181	0,121677895	21,32723616	2,899284354
0,249923917	0,283556883	24,3403367	3,170885114
0,614833454	0,446432427	27,60394795	3,395303559
1,143195826	0,61053213	31,14638178	3,676870349
1,836454555	0,776303479	34,95950705	3,852486285
2,696521875	0,94423329	39,13247348	4,491519612
3,725814508	1,114844706	43,59315526	4,568328055
4,927293766	1,288705377	48,52405304	5,252677916
6,304515581	1,466439233	53,82606265	5,68042054
7,861693371	1,648737336	59,7080521	6,094025615
9,603775575	1,836386201	66,17671986	6,810644646
11,53654838	2,030313492	73,44244847	7,739127743
13,66673787	2,231141586	81,73656266	8,94473403
16,00224311	2,441979687	91,55649532	10,87262965
18,55208542	2,659040432	104,1575231	15,02605417

```
Sub TestLaguerre()
Worksheets("Laguerre").Activate
Dim i%
Dim xL#(30), wL#(30)
For i = 1 To 30
    xL(i) = Cells(i, 1): wL(i) = Cells(i, 2)
    intLaguerre = intLaguerre + 4 * wL(i) * xL(i) * Cos(2 * xL(i))
Next i
Debug.Print intLaguerre

End Sub
```

2.5.5 Principal Component Analysis

In the financial derivatives industry, correlations between assets play a growing part since multi-asset instruments and interest rate exotics are gaining popularity. A Principal Component Analysis (PCA) aims to detect some kind of redundancy in the parameters measuring these correlations, in order to reduce the number of factors involved in the assets of dynamics and cut computation times. From the original list of factors, we tend to infer a smaller list made of **principal components**. For newcomers to this issue, we introduce the topic with a geometric analogy in the two-dimensional space (Euclidean plan).

The two-dimensional case   Let us consider a set of couples (xi,yi) made of n joint samples of the RVs X and Y, and denote:

$$\bar{x} = E(x) \text{ and } \bar{y} = E(y)$$

$$Cov(x, y) = E(xy) - E(x)E(y)$$

$$Var(x) = Cov(x, x)$$

We can give this set a geometric representation in the Euclidean plan, and obtain a cluster of points:

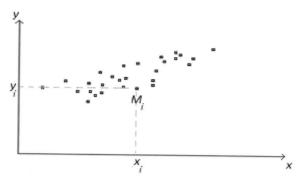

As a general rule, the points are not randomly spread. Some correlation between variables, figured by a straight line through the set of points, suggest a tendency in the joint evolution of X and Y.

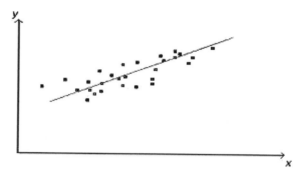

As a postulate, the line that best fits this relationship is obtained when the average square distance (or **quadratic distance**) between the line and the set of points is minimal.

Let us denote by $\vec{n} = (n_1; n_2)$ a unit vector perpendicular to this line named Δ: for some point M of Δ, the distance of $M_i(X_i; Y_i)$ to the line is:

$$|\overrightarrow{MM_i}.\vec{n}|$$

The center of gravity of the set (M_i) is defined as

$$\overrightarrow{OG} = \frac{1}{N} \cdot \sum_{i=1}^{N} \overrightarrow{OM_i}$$

Since G belongs to Δ,

$$d(G) = \frac{1}{N} \cdot \sum_{i=1}^{N} (\overrightarrow{GM_i}.\vec{n})^2 \qquad (2.4)$$

attains a **minimum** in G.

Setting $x_i^* = x_i - E(x)$, we can rewrite d as a sum of scalar products:

$$d = \sum_{i=1}^{N} (x_i^*.n_1 + y_i^*.n_2)^2 = \left(x_1^*.n_1 + y_1^*.n_2 \ , ..., \ x_N^*.n_1 + y_N^*.n_2 \right) . \begin{pmatrix} x_1^*.n_1 + y_1^*.n_2 \\ \vdots \\ x_N^*.n_1 + y_N^*.n_2 \end{pmatrix}$$

With matricial notations:

$$n = \begin{pmatrix} n_1 \\ n_2 \end{pmatrix} \qquad M = \begin{pmatrix} x_1^* \cdots x_N^* \\ y_1^* \cdots y_N^* \end{pmatrix}$$

Let us denote by H_i the orthogonal projection of M_i on Δ. Δ minimizes the quadratic distance iff

$$\sum_{i=1}^{N} \|\overline{H_i M_i}\|^2 = d = n^{\dagger}.(M.M^{\dagger}).n \text{ reach a } \mathbf{minimum}$$

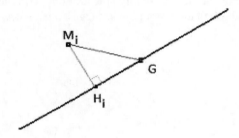

Since $\displaystyle\sum_{i=1}^{N} \|\overrightarrow{GH_i}\|^2 + d = \sum_{i=1}^{N} \|\overrightarrow{GM_i}\|^2$ (Pythagorus)

$\displaystyle\sum_{i=1}^{N} \|\overrightarrow{GH_i}\|^2$ is to be maximized.

In other words, for some unitary vector $\overrightarrow{t}(t_1, t_2)\|\Delta, t^{\dagger}.(M.M^{\dagger}).t$ is maximal.

$$\overrightarrow{GM_i} = \overrightarrow{GH_i} + \overrightarrow{H_i M_i} = x_1^{(i)}\overrightarrow{t} + x_2^{(i)}\overrightarrow{n}$$

t and n are called the **principal directions** of the distribution and the coordinates of M_i in $(G, t, \overrightarrow{n})$ are the **principal components**. Obviously, as $x_1^{(i)}$ accounts most in the data dispersion, it is inducted **first** principal component.

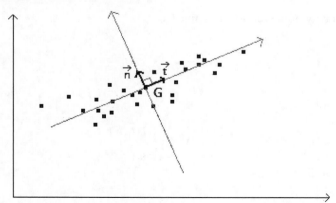

The _m_-dimension case Similarly, when $m \times N$ outcomes $x_{i,j}$ are observed on m-coordinates variables X_i,

$$M = \begin{pmatrix} x^*_{1,1} & \cdots & x^*_{1,N} \\ \vdots & \vdots & \vdots \\ x^*_{m,1} & \cdots & x^*_{m,N} \end{pmatrix}$$

The components of a unitary vector $\vec{u}\,(u_1, u_2, ..., u_m)$ showing the first principal direction must verify

$$\frac{\partial}{\partial u_i}\left(\frac{u^\dagger.(M.M^\dagger).u}{u^\dagger.u}\right) = 0, i = 1, ..., m \tag{2.5}$$

Developing $M.M^\dagger$ leads to an $m \times n$ matrix V that plays a prominent part in statistics:

$$V(i,j) = \sum_{k=1}^{m} x^*_{i,k}.x^*_{k,j} = m.\ \underbrace{Cov(X_i, X_j)}_{covariance\ matrix}$$

The system of m equations given in equation 2.5 becomes

$$\frac{u^\dagger.u.(2V.u) - (u^\dagger.V.u).(2u)}{(u^\dagger.u)^2} = 0$$

$$V.u = \frac{u^\dagger.V.u}{u^\dagger.u}u$$

Finally, u is an **eigenvector** of V, associated with the eigenvalue

$$\frac{u^\dagger.V.u}{u^\dagger.u}$$

Recall that, in algebra, an eigenvector u of a square-matrix V is a non-zero vector verifying

$$V.u = \lambda u$$

where λ is a non-zero scalar called **eigenvalue**.

Principal directions and eigenvectors Having found the first principal direction of the distribution, namely the eigenvector v_1, we can now rewrite

$$\overrightarrow{GM_i} = x_1^{(i)}.v_1 + y_i^{(i)}.v_2$$

where v_2 is the projection of $\overrightarrow{M_i}$ on a hyperplane ($m - 1$ dimension), orthogonal to v_1. Likewise, the same decomposition can be applied to $y_i.v2 = \overrightarrow{GM_i} - x_i.v_1$, giving rise to the **second principal direction** v_2, and its orthogonal projection $v_2^\perp$. Finally, in the orthonormal base $(G, v_1, v_2, ..., v_m)$,

$$\overrightarrow{GM_i} = x_1^{(i)}.v_1 + x_2^{(i)}.v_2 + ... + x_m^{(i)}.v_m$$

The next step consists in finding the coordinates of v_2, first principal direction of the projections of (M_i) such that

$$\overrightarrow{GM_i^*} = \overrightarrow{GM_i} - x_1^{(i)}.v_1 = x_2^{(i)}.v_2 + ... + x_m^{(i)}.v_m$$

Noticing that $x_1^{(i)} = \overrightarrow{GM}_i.v_1$, and setting

$$v_1 = \begin{pmatrix} v_1^{(1)} \\ v_2^{(1)} \\ \vdots \\ v_m^{(1)} \end{pmatrix}$$

$$M^{(2)} = M - \begin{pmatrix} \left(v_1^{(1)}x_{1,1}^* + v_2^{(1)}x_{2,1}^* + ... + v_m^{(1)}x_{m,1}^*\right).v_1^{(1)} & \cdots & \left(v_1^{(1)}x_{1,N}^* + v_2^{(1)}x_{2,N}^* + ... + v_m^{(1)}x_{m,N}^*\right).v_1^{(1)} \\ \vdots & \vdots & \vdots \\ \left(v_1^{(1)}x_{1,1}^* + v_2^{(1)}x_{2,1}^* + ... + v_m^{(1)}x_{m,1}^*\right).v_m^{(1)} & \cdots & \left(v_1^{(1)}x_{1,N}^* + v_2^{(1)}x_{2,N}^* + ... + v_m^{(1)}x_{m,N}^*\right).v_m^{(1)} \end{pmatrix}$$

In short,

$$M^{(2)} = M - v_1.v_1^\dagger.M$$

$$M^{(2)}.M^{(2)\dagger} = (M - v_1.v_1^\dagger.M).(M^\dagger - M^\dagger.v_1.v_1^\dagger) = V - v_1.v_1^\dagger.V$$

since

$$((v_1.v_1^\dagger).V)^\dagger = V.v_1.v_1^\dagger = \lambda_1.v_1.v_1^\dagger$$

$$((v_1.v_1^\dagger).V)^\dagger = (v_1.v_1^\dagger).V \leftrightarrow M^{(2)}.M^{(2)\dagger} = V - \lambda_1.v_1.v_1^\dagger$$

The eigenvalues of $V - \lambda_1.v_1.v_1^\dagger$ are $0, \lambda_2, \lambda_3,...$ where $|\lambda_2| > |\lambda_3| > ... > 0$. As a result, the first principal direction of $M^{(2)}$, v_2 is the eigenvector associated with λ_2: in other words, $|\lambda_2|$ is the maximum of $V - \lambda_1.v_1.v_1^\dagger$ absolute eigenvalues. To find out recursively all the λ_i, $i = 3,...,n$, we proceed as follows: knowing $\lambda_1, \lambda_2,...,\lambda_{i-1}$

- computation of $V^{(i)} = V - \sum_1^{i-1} \lambda_k.v_k.v_k^\dagger$
- solving $\lambda_i = \frac{u^\dagger.V^{(i)}.u}{u^\dagger.u}$

Algorithm for calculating eigenvalues Let λ_i be the eigenvalues of V, ranked in descending order with respect to their absolute values $|\lambda_1| > |\lambda_2| \geq |\lambda_3|...$. The set of eigenvectors v_i can serve as an orthogonal basis that represents any vector X:

$$X = \sum_{i=1}^m x_i.v_i \Longrightarrow V.X = \sum_{i=1}^m x_i.\lambda_i v_i \Longrightarrow V^n.X = \sum_{i=1}^m x_i.\lambda_i^n v_i$$

$$V^n.X = \lambda_1^n.\left(\sum_{i=1}^m x_i.\left[\frac{\lambda_i}{\lambda_1}\right]^n.v_i\right) \sim \lambda_1^n.x_1.v_1 \text{ as } n \to \infty$$

Consequently,

$$\frac{\|V^{n+1}.X\|}{\|V^n.X\|} \xrightarrow{n\to\infty} \lambda_1 \text{ for some } X.$$

Step 1(λ_1) From a random vector X, compute $Y = V.X$, then normalize $Y \rightarrow \frac{Y}{\|Y\|}$ and multiply $V.Y$.

Iterating this leads to building a sequence

$$Y_{n+1} = \frac{V.Y_n}{\|V.Y_n\|}.$$

that tends to the first principal factor, hence an eigenvector associated to the maximal eigenvalue (i.e., $|\lambda|$ max):

$$\frac{Y_n.V.Y_n^\dagger}{Y_n.Y_n^\dagger} \xrightarrow{n \rightarrow \infty} \lambda_1$$

Set an error target ϵ and proceed the iterations till

$$\|Y_{n+1} - Y_n\| < \epsilon$$

Finally, set

$$\upsilon_1 = Y_{n+1} \text{ and } \lambda_1 = \frac{\|V.Y_{n+1}\|}{\|Y_{n+1}\|}$$

recursion($\lambda_2,...,\lambda_m$) Redefine a random vector X and proceed identically with

$$V^{(2)} = V - \lambda_1.\upsilon_1.\upsilon_1^\dagger$$

$$...V^{(m)} = V^{m-1} - \lambda_{m-1}.\upsilon_{m-1}.\upsilon_{m-1}^\dagger$$

Code The following function **pseudo** takes a square matrix **v** as argument and computes the matrix **corr** each column of which consists of eigenvectors' coordinates. The array **lambda** contains the related eigenvalues.

```
Public Function pseudo(v!()) As Single()

Dim n%: n = UBound(v, 1)
ReDim EGmat!(n), x!(n), lambda!(n), corr!(n, n)

ReDim mat!(n, n)

For l = 1 To n

    For i = 1 To n
        EGmat(i) = Rnd()
    Next
    For k = 1 To 50
        For i = 1 To n
            x(i) = 0
            For j = 1 To n
                x(i) = x(i) + v(i, j) * EGmat(j)
            Next j
        Next i
        lambda(l) = x(1) / EGmat(1)
        For i = 1 To n
```

```
                EGmat(i) = x(i) / matNorm(x)
        Next i
    Next k
    For i = 1 To n
        If lambda(l) > 0 Then
            corr(i, l) = EGmat(i) * Sqr(lambda(l))
        Else
            corr(i, l) = 0
        End If
        Cells(i + 18, l) = corr(i, l)
    Next i

    For i = 1 To n
        For j = 1 To n
            v(i, j) = v(i, j) - lambda(l) * EGmat(i) * EGmat(j)
        Next j
    Next i
Next l
pseudo = corr
End Function
```

CHAPTER 3

Vanilla Instruments

3.1 DEFINITIONS

Financial assets may be roughly classified, according to the payoff, into three categories:

- Fixed income
- Derivatives
- Variable income.

The financial instruments presented in this book relate to assets with:

- predetermined cash flow payment dates
- revenues that can be modelized.

This excludes variable-income instruments, such as equities that bear random coupons: stocks will solely be accounted for as underlying assets involved in equity-related derivatives.

3.2 FIXED INCOME

For this class of assets, the calculation of the fair value is straightforward. Since cash flows and payment dates are predetermined at inception, the **present value** of the future flows is easily obtained, provided that a **relevant yield curve** is available for the calculation of the **discount factors**.

Let us denote by df_i these discount factors: the theoretical value of an asset paying n coupons $c_i, i = 1...n$ writes:

$$c_1.df(t_1) + c_2.df(t_2) + ... + c_n.df(t_n) = \sum_{i=1}^{n} c_i.df(t_i)$$

It is common to figure payments on a cash flow chart: each flow is represented by an arrow pointing either to a time line (inflows) or out of it (outflows). Practically, it implies that this kind of chart is drawn *from the point of view of one counterparty*. As an example, the n coupons received by an investor in a bond can be figured as below:

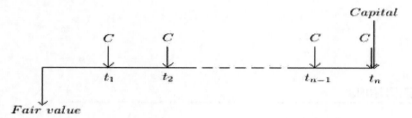

In a fair transaction, i.e., under market conditions, both counterparties are to be treated equally. As a result, for each counterparty, the inflows, present value must balance that of the outflows. For instance, the fair price of a fixed coupon bond is the present value of coupons C + capital redeemed:

$$- \text{Fair value} + \sum_{i=1}^{n} C.df(t_i) + Capital.df(t_n) = 0$$

In other words, the **net present value** of cash flow exchanges must be **zero**. Otherwise, a compensation balance must offset the difference:

$$\boxed{- \text{compensation balance} + \text{net present value} = 0}$$

Computing discount factors is an essential step in valuing fixed income assets, as is the choice of a relevant yield curve.

Interest rates can be retrieved from two sources of data:

- Prices of securities such as bonds
- Interbank market rates.

From the bond market, we can draw **zero-coupon yields**, from the interbank market, **swap rates**.

3.2.1 Bond market

There exists a one-to-one relation between discount factors and zero-coupon rates, i.e., discount rates of zero-coupon bonds.

$$df_t = \frac{1}{(1 + TZC_t)^t} \implies TZC_t = \left(\frac{1}{df_t}\right)^{(1/t)} - 1$$

Keep in mind that zero-coupon bonds, bearing no intermediate coupons, provide zero-coupon rates straight.

Government bond yields (TBonds in the US, Bunds, OATs, or BTPs for instance in the Euro monetary zone, Gilts in the UK, etc.) are assumed to provide the **benchmark curves** needed to price fixed-rate debt securities. In order to price private sector issues, investors retrieve zero-coupon rates from government bond market quotes. In a second step, they usually add spreads with regard to the issuer's rating, taking account of the bond maturity.

The problem is to extract rates from bond prices, i.e., to solve

$$\text{Bond price} = \sum_{i=1}^{n} C.df(t_i) + Capital.df(t_n)$$

Fixing this equation for a set of n bonds boils down to solving a linear system recursively. Practically, the objective is to find $df(t_n)$, knowing $df(t_1)$, $df(t_2)$, ... , $df(t_{n-1})$. The conditions required to obtain it are:

- for each bond maturing at t_n, there exists at least one bond maturing at t, such that

$$t_{n-1} < t < t_n$$

- the penultimate coupon is paid before t.

Actually, this condition is always met since government bonds are issued at least twice a year, and even more frequently in the US where bond coupons are paid semi-annually.

Algorithm To understand the basics of the method, let us start with a range of 4 bonds paying annual coupons, and maturing in 1, 2, 3, and 4 years. Obviously, in the real world, bond calculations are always performed between two coupon payment dates:

Issue	Maturity	Coupon	Mkt Price
Bond1	1	4%	101.46
Bond2	2	3%	100
Bond3	3	3.5%	101.46
Bond4	4	2%	94.55

$$101.46 = 4\mathbf{df(1)} + 100\mathbf{df(1)} = 104\mathbf{df(1)}$$

$$\implies \mathbf{df(1)} = 101.46/104$$

$$100 = 3df(1) + 103\mathbf{df(2)}$$

$$\implies \mathbf{df(2)} = (100 - 3df(1))/103$$

$$100.47 = 3.5df(1) + 3.5df(2) + 103.5\mathbf{df(3)}$$

$$\implies \mathbf{df(3)} = (100.47 - 3.5(df(1) + df(2)))/103.5$$

$$94.55 = 2(df(1) + df(2) + df(3)) + 102\mathbf{df(4)}$$

Finally

$$df(1) = 0.9756 \quad df(2) = 0.9425 \quad df(3) = 0.9058 \quad df(4) = 0.8716$$

$$TZC(1) = 2.5\% \quad TZC(2) = 3\% \quad TZC(3) = 3.35\% \quad TZC(4) = 3.5\%$$

Code   In the program below, the default lower bound is forced to 1.

```
Option Base 1
```

Bond prices and coupons, retrieved from an Excel sheet, were previously stored in **Bond-Price** and **Coupon** arrays: the dfs and TZCs are obviously stored in arrays of the same size.

```
Option Base 1
Dim nBonds%: nBonds = UBound(BondPrice)
ReDim df!(nBonds)
ReDim TZC!(nBonds)
```

Then, the discount factors (and TZCs) are computed recursively:

```
df(1) = BondPrice(1) / (100 * (1 + Coupon(1)))
For i = 2 To nBonds
    Num = BondPrice(i)
    For j = 1 To i - 1
        Num = Num - df(j) * 100 * Coupon(i)
    Next j
    df(i) = Num / (100 * (1 + Coupon(i)))
    TZC(i) = (1 / df(i) ^  (1 / i)) - 1
Next i
```

The sum of discounted coupons and redeemed capital, which the bond's investor is entitled to, is called the **dirty price**. On each payment date, the bond's payoff drops by the amount of the coupon; so does the dirty price. However, bonds are generally quoted as **clean prices**, i.e., excluding any interest that has accrued since the most recent coupon payment:

Clean Price = Dirty Price - Accrued Interest

Changes in clean prices, which are more stable, reflect market evolutions and are not affected by the specificity of coupons' schedules.

This accrued interest is calculated with respect to the day-count convention, usually an **actual/actual** (sometimes noted as act/act) basis: For instance, the accrued interest as of 06/11/2012 of a semi-annual 3% bond maturing on 15/04/2018 equals:

```
DateDiff("d", CDate("15/10/2012"), CDate("06/11/2012"))/
DateDiff("d", CDate("15/10/2012"), CDate("15/04/2013")) * 0.03
```

or, more concisely,

```
(CDate("06/11/2012") - CDate("15/10/2012")/ (CDate("15/04/2013") -
CDate("15/10/2012")* 0.03
```

Here below are displayed data retrieved from Tbond quotes as of 09/11/2012: the 1st column lists the maturity dates, the 2nd lists the coupon rates, and quotes are displayed in column 3.

We show, hereafter, the code of the function **BondValue**, extracting zero-coupons from market quotes, and pricing some fixed rate issue (zero-coupon yields are displayed on column 4).

Maturity	Coupon	Quote	Zero-coupon(computed)
31/01/2013	0.625	100.1172	0.104
15/04/2013	1.75	100.6953	0.137
30/09/2013	3.125	102.6016	0.197
15/03/2014	1.25	101.375	0.229
31/08/2014	2.375	103.8281	0.251
31/01/2015	2.25	104.3672	0.282
15/06/2015	0.375	100.1797	0.306
30/11/2015	1.375	103.0859	0.361
15/05/2016	5.125	116.3906	0.437
30/09/2016	3	109.7734	0.471
15/02/2017	4.625	117.3203	0.532
31/07/2017	2.375	108.2109	0.623
30/11/2017	2.25	107.9297	0.668
31/05/2018	2.375	108.8047	0.775
15/11/2018	3.75	117.2188	0.848
30/04/2019	1.25	101.9688	0.953
30/09/2019	1	99.8594	1.038
15/02/2020	3.625	117.875	1.12

The arguments passed to BondValue are:

BondQuotes: market quotes

BondCoup: coupons

BondMat: maturities

```
Function BondValue(mat As Date, coup!, _
                BondQuotes As Range, _
                BondCoup As Range, _
                BondMat As Range) As Single
Dim schedule() As Date, DFdates() As Date
' schedule: coupon dates  DFdates: Zero-coupon maturities
ReDim Dirty!(BondMat.Count)
ReDim DF!(1)
ReDim TZC!(1)

DF(0) = 1
ReDim DFdates(1): DFdates(0) = Date

For i = 1 To BondMat.Count
    c = BondCoup(i) / 2
    k = 1
    last = DateAdd("m", -6 * k, CDate(BondMat(i).Value))
```

```
    While last > Date
        k = k + 1
    Wend

    ReDim schedule(k)
    ReDim Preserve DF(i)
    ReDim Preserve TZC(i)
    ReDim Preserve DFdates(i)

    For j = 0 To k
        schedule(j) = DateAdd("m", 6 * j, last)
    Next j

    DFdates(i) = schedule(k)
    Dirty(i) = BondQuotes(i) + BondMat(i).Offset(0, 1) _
    / 2 * (Date - schedule(0)) / (schedule(1) - schedule(0))
    Num = Dirty(i)

    For j = 1 To k - 1
        Num = Num - c * cubicInterpol(schedule(j), DFdates, DF)
    Next j

    DF(i) = Num / 100 / (1 + c / 100)
    TZC(i) = (1 / DF(i)) ^ (365 / (schedule(k) - Date)) - 1

Next i

k = 1
last = DateAdd("m", -6 * k, CDate(mat))
While last > Date
    k = k + 1
    last = DateAdd("m", -6 * k, CDate(mat))
Wend
ReDim schedule(k)

For j = 0 To k
    schedule(j) = DateAdd("m", 6 * j, last)
Next j
Num = -coup / 2 * (Date - schedule(0)) / (schedule(1) - schedule(0))
For j = 1 To k - 1
    Num = Num + coup / 2 * cubicInterpol(schedule(j), DFdates, DF)
Next j

BondValue = Num + 100 * (1 + coup / 2 / 100) * cubicInterpol(schedule(k),
    DFdates, DF)

End Function
```

3.2.2 Interbank market

The swap curve   The interbank market refers to the market where banks extend loans and OTC derivatives one to another. Most of banks' needs are for (very) short-term resources: therefore, their refinancing costs are subject to floating benchmark rate (LIBOR...) changes.

To freeze these financing costs in the long run, they trade **I**nterest **R**ate **S**waps (IRS), by which they exchange floating interests for fixed interests.

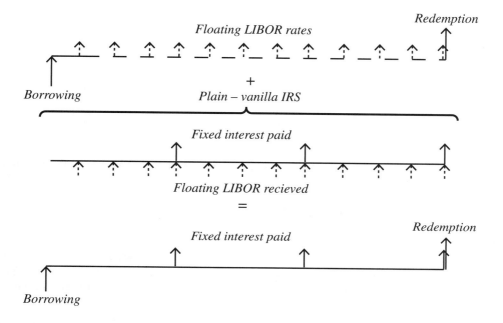

Only interest is exchanged in an IRS, not the principal. In the case where interest is paid in different currencies (e.g., **Currency swaps**), some currency risk at stake requires that the two counterparties exchange the notional in one currency for the equivalent amount in the other.

Some conventions of terminology are needed at this stage of the presentation:

- By default, a **swap** refers to an IRS.
- A counterparty is said to enter into a **paying** (resp. **receiving**) swap when he signs to pay **fixed** (resp. **floating**) interest.
- A **leg** refers to a payment schedule of either fixed (fixed leg) or floating (floating leg) coupons.

The easiest and also most cost-efficient way to borrow money in the long term is thus to enter into a revolving credit and enter simultaneously into a longer term swap. Practically, banks borrow overnight or at LIBOR (or EURIBOR) and "swap" it against a semi-annual or annual fixed rate: consequently, the swap curve may be considered as the benchmark of the medium/long-term yield curve.

For top rated financial institutions, this curve is of crucial importance, since any future cash has to be discounted using this curve.

Discount factors Now, we can derive discount factors on the medium/long-term interbank market straight from a par swap curve. In other words, given $r_1, r_2, \ldots, r_N$, the swap rates that apply to IRS maturing in 1, 2,...,N years, 1 unit borrowed over a period of m years produces m annual interest r_m and full capital redemption on the maturity date.

$df_1, df_2, \ldots, df_m$ are calculated recursively:

$$df_1 = \frac{1}{1 + r_1}$$

$$(1 - r_2 df_1) = (1 + r_2)df_2$$

$$\vdots$$

$$1 - r_m \sum_{i=1}^{m-1} df_i = (1 + r_m)df_m$$

Below, we display the code of a procedure termed **initDF** that retrieves a yield curve built with:

- the money-market rates for less than 9-month maturities
- the swap curve from one year up to 10 years.

Notice that this source of data is arbitrary, i.e., not the official money-market curve: in any case, it makes no difference in terms of algorithm. For the sake of simplicity, value dates and non-business days will be ignored. By convention, we will apply the money-market convention up to 9 months and bond-basis one beyond this date.

```
Sub initDF()

Sheets("Rates").Activate

Dim tenor As Range: Set tenor = Range([C4], [C4].End(xlDown))
ReDim DF(tenor.Count)

Dim i%: i = 0
For Each cell In tenor
    Select Case cell
        Case Is < DateAdd("yyyy", 1, [A2])
            DF(i) = 1 / (1 + (cell - [A2]) / 360 * cell.Offset(0, 1) / 100)
        Case DateAdd("yyyy", 1, [A2]) To DateAdd("yyyy", 10, [A2])
            If cell = DateAdd("yyyy", 1, [A2]) Then
                DF(i) = 1 / (1 + cell.Offset(0, 1) / 100): sumDF = DF(i)
            Else
                DF(i) = (1 - sumDF * cell.Offset(0, 1) / 100) /
                (1 + cell.Offset(0, 1) / 100)
                sumDF = sumDF + DF(i)
            End If
    End Select
    i = i + 1
Next cell

End Sub
```

Maturity	Rate	Maturity	Rate
1D	0.75	3y	1.9
1m	0.9	4y	2.1
2m	1.05	5y	2.3
3m	1.25	6y	2.45
6m	1.4	7y	2.6
9m	1.5	8y	2.725
1y	1.575	9y	2.805
2y	1.75	10y	2.9

3.3 VANILLA DERIVATIVES

3.3.1 Forward contracts

A forward contract is a transaction by which two counterparties agree on conditions of a contract whose settlement or starting date has been postponed to a predetermined future date. A very popular contract of this kind is the **FRA** (**F**orward **R**ate **A**greement).

The FRA An FRA is quite similar to a loan/borrowing starting on a future date, at a pre-established interest rate. **Buying** (resp. *selling*) a contract means **borrowing** (resp. *lending*), the FRA rate acting as the borrowing rate. We can guess that the FRA buyer anticipates or hedges against a rate rise.

Actually, the FRA transaction is not physically settled, i.e., there is no commitment to exchange principals. On the expiry date, some benchmark rate, usually LIBOR, is fixed. The difference

$$\text{Reference ("Benchmark") rate - FRA rate}$$

determines which position, long or short, is profitable. Practically, if Δt denotes the duration of the borrowing contract (i.e., the underlying asset of the FRA contract), the buyer will receive

$$\text{Contract Nominal} * \frac{(\textit{Benchmark rate} - \textit{FRA rate}) * \Delta t}{(1 + \textit{Benchmark rate} * \Delta t)}$$

By way of example, assuming an FRA written on 6-mth EURIBOR, struck at 4%: at expiration, if the EURIBOR fixes at 3.5%, the buyer of the FRA will receive

$$\text{Nominal amount} \frac{(3.5\% - 4\%)/2}{(1 + 3.5\%/2)} = -0.2457\%$$

In fact, the buyer will pay 0.2457% of the contract nominal to the seller.

At any given time, the fair price of the FRA must reflect the theoretical rate of the forward borrowing contract: "theoretical" means that, under market conditions, the deal gives no advantage to one specific counterparty. The calculation of this rate is quite straightforward.

Let us denote by $Fwd(t)$, this rate, called the **forward interest rate**, over the period $(t, t + \Delta t]$. It makes no difference whether one:

1. borrows over a period $(0, t + \Delta t]$ or
2. borrows over a period $(0, t]$ and then refunds capital + interest over $(t, t + \Delta t]$.

To put it mathematically,

$$1/df(t + \Delta t) = 1/df(t + \Delta t)(1 + Fwd(t)\Delta t)$$

$$1 + Fwd(t)\Delta t = \frac{df_t}{df_{t+\Delta t}}$$

The forward rate is often improperly called the FRA rate.

The forward exchange rate   In a **forward exchange** transaction, two counterparties agree to exchange one currency for another at a future date, under predetermined conditions. In contrast, in a **spot transaction**, the settlement takes place (almost) immediately, actually at D+2.

Let us consider the example of an agent selling USD forward against EUR. On settlement, he pays some amount denominated in USD and receives some other in EUR, the **forward exchange rate** being the ratio between those amounts. It is just as if he were paying off a loan in USD and receiving, on the other side, some reimbursement in EUR. This forward transaction seems to boil down to a treasury operation in two currencies, except that there is no capital exchanged at inception. This can be solved by entering into a spot transaction that neutralizes the initial flows of capital.

The diagram below describes the loan/borrowing + spot transactions

$$
\begin{array}{|ccc|}
\hline
+100 * S * \dfrac{1 + r_e t}{1 + r_\$ t} & & -100 \\
& & \\
(3) \downarrow & & (1) \uparrow \\
& & \\
-\dfrac{100}{1 + r_\$ t} * S & \xleftarrow{(2)} & +\dfrac{100}{1 + r_\$ t} \\
\hline
\end{array}
$$

More precisely, the agent:

1. borrows $100/(1 + r_\$ t)$ USD ($r_\$$: borrowing rate)
2. sells this amount against EUR at the spot rate S
3. lends the capital $100 * S/(1 + r_\$ t)$ in EUR (r_e: lending rate).

Instead of entering into three operations, which could involve more transaction costs and counterparty risks, our agent may choose to enter into one single deal with some market-maker buying dollars forward vs euros. To be fair, the price offered by the market-maker, let us denote it X, must be close to the theoretical parity of exchange:

$$S * \frac{1 + r_e t}{1 + r_\$ t}$$

If market and theoretical prices differ significantly, there is a winner and a loser. For instance, if the price offered by the market-maker is too high, the agent can turn the deal in his advantage, i.e., hedge his position by:

1. borrowing $100 * S/(1 + r_\$ t)$ in EUR
2. selling this amount against USD
3. lending $100/(1 + r_\$ t)$ USD.

In the end, the agent will have realized a theoretical profit (excluding any friction cost) of

$$X - S * \frac{1 + r_e t}{1 + r_\$ t}$$

without any investment at inception. This strategy is called **arbitrage**. As a general rule, similar assets must be set at similar prices, to avoid arbitrage opportunities. In the real world, perfect arbitrage transactions are almost impossible, given market efficiency (the information is shared almost at the speed of the light). Nowadays, an arbitrage is a strategy potentially profitable with a rather low residual risk, and no capital commitment.

3.3.2 Swaps

As we pointed out earlier, the two parties in a swap contract agree to exchange interest cash flows. Most of the time, one pays a fixed interest while the other pays a floating one. However, numerous varieties have emerged since the early period.

The goal of this section is not to plow through all these varieties – Chapter 8 will fix some exotics among them – but just to investigate the most common methods to cope with the pricing of fixed-for-floating plain-vanilla swaps.

The backing method   As the calculation of the floating leg's present value is the most delicate issue, the idea is to back the initial swap (A) with another swap (B) in order to balance, and thus neutralize, the floating leg of A. Under market conditions, the net present value of B is theoretically 0: therefore

A market value + B market value = A market value

Let us illustrate this with the example of a 4.5-year fixed-rate payer swap: B is indeed a fixed-receiver swap. We assume that:

- A bears an annual 2.5% fixed rate
- the floating rate is semi-annual
- the market data are those of §3.2.2.

Since the calculation date is a fixing date, both floating legs (from A and B) match perfectly. To simplify, we calculate the theoretical 4.5-year market rate by means of a linear interpolation, which yields $(2.3\% + 2.1\%)/2 = 2.2\%$. Since the first period is broken, only half of the $2.2\% = 1.1\%$ is received. The resulting cash flow diagram is displayed below:

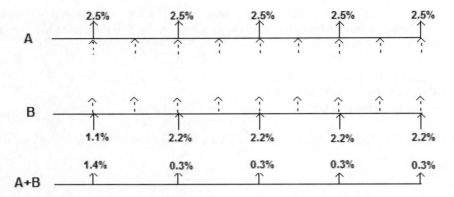

To complete the calculation, all we have to do is discount the net flows, i.e.,

$$PV = 1.4\% df_{6m} + 0.3\% \sum_{i=1}^{4} df_{i+0.5}$$

The "leg by leg" method The most common method consists in discounting both legs separately:

$$\text{Net swap value} = \text{fixed leg PV} - \text{floating leg PV}$$

Suppose an m-year swap where party A pays an annual rate R on a nominal N and receives the quarterly LIBOR rate. The fixed leg PV is obtained via $df_1, df_2,\dots$ derived from the par swap rates:

$$\text{fixed leg PV} = N \sum_{i=1}^{m} df_i.R$$

At this stage, theoretical forward rates are needed in order to price the floating leg PV. As previously established, they are given by:

$$1 + \boldsymbol{fwd_i}(t_{i+1} - t_i) = \frac{df_i}{df_{i+1}} \Longrightarrow \boldsymbol{fwd_i} = \left(\frac{df_i}{df_{i+1}} - 1 \right) . \frac{1}{(t_{i+1} - t_i)}$$

The floating leg is thus given by:

$$N \sum_{j=0}^{4m-1} fwd_j(t_{j+1} - t_j).df_{(j+1)}$$

$$\text{float leg} = N \sum_{j=0}^{4m-1} (df_j - df_{(j+1)}) = df_0 - df_m = 1 - df_m$$

When the fixed rate R fits the par swap m-year rate,

$$1 - df_m = R \sum_{i=1}^{m} df_i$$

$$\text{Net swap value} = 0$$

Broken periods In real life, the net value of a swap is to be calculated between two payment dates, as we need to fix the valuation of swaps with **broken periods** (we tackled one trivial example in § 3.2.2 *Backing method*). Here we develop the general case, with some numerical application. Let us fix the issue with the example of a swap on which the fixed rate payer (party A):

- receives EURIBOR 6m
- pays an annual rate of 3%

to party B.

The swap is set to have a 3-year and 3-month tenor (see diagram)

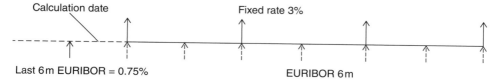

Party A is then committed to pay a full interest of 3% in 3 months while party B has to pay EURIBOR calculated for the period between the last and next fixings (one semester)on the same date. Beyond this date, a residual swap still runs over 3 years. To recap, the value of this swap is the sum of:

- the present value of net cash flows due in 3 months, i.e.,

$$(3\% - 0.75\%/2).df_{1/4}$$

- the value of a 3-year swap starting in 3 months, i.e., a **forward swap**.

To achieve this calculation:

- The fixed cash flows are interpolated between adjacent values of the **df** curve. For instance, the first payment, due in one year and 3 months, is discounted using df_1 and df_2:

$$\text{fixed leg} = 3\%.(df_{1+1/4} + df_{2+1/4} + df_{3+1/4})$$

- the floating leg PV does not include the next EURIBOR flow, that is to say

$$\text{floating leg} = N \sum_{j=1}^{12} (df_{j/4} - df_{(j+1)/4}) = df_{1/4} - df_{3+1/4}$$

Finally, the net value of the swap is, for the fixed leg receiver

$$(3\% - 0.75\%/2).df_{1/4} + 3\%.(df_{1+1/4} + df_{2+1/4} + df_{3+1/4}) - (df_{1/4} - df_{3+1/4}), \text{ or}$$

$$3\%.(df_{1/4} + df_{1+1/4} + df_{2+1/4} + df_{3+1/4}) - (1 + 0.75\%/2)df_{1/4} + df_{3+1/4}$$

Code   We list below the code of a function **ValSwap** taking as arguments:

- the swap nominal
- the fixed rate and last fixing of EURIBOR
- the frequency of fixed and floating interests
- the tenor (maturity).

```
Function ValSwap(Nom!, Rate!, LastEur!, freqFix$, freqFloat$, tenor As Date)

Dim pFix%: pFix = convFreq(freqFix)
Dim pFloat%: pFloat = convFreq(freqFloat)

Dim d As Date: d = tenor

Dim fixLeg!: fixLeg = 0
Dim floatLeg!: floatLeg = 0

i = 1
While d > Date
    fixLeg = fixLeg + Nom * Rate * cubicInterpol(d, stdDF, DF)
    d = DateAdd("m", -i * pFix, tenor)
    i = i + 1
Wend

i = 1
While d > Date
    d = DateAdd("m", -i * pFloat, tenor)
    i = i + 1
Wend
floatLeg = Nom * ((1 + LastEur * pFloat / 12) *
    cubicInterpol(adddate("m", pFloat, d), stdDF, DF) -
    cubicInterpol(tenor, stdDF, DF))

ValSwap = fixLeg - floatLeg

End Function


Function convFreq(f$) As Integer
Select Case f

    Case "annual"
        convFreq = 12
    Case "semi"
        convFreq = 6
    Case "quarter"
        convFreq = 3

End Select
End Function
```

The floating rate reference depends on the periodicity of cash flows. For instance, when payments are due every quarter, the floating rate will be a 3-month IBOR. On the fixed leg (fixed rate payments schedule), the frequency depends on domestic conventions. For instance, it is annual in the Euro zone.

Forward swaps Forward IRS play a prominent role among interest rate derivatives since they serve as swaptions' underlying asset (see Chapter 6). Given a forward swap starting at a future date t_m and terminating at t_{m+n} (i.e. n fixed rate cash flows):

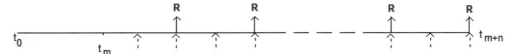

To simplify, let us state

$$t_{m+j+1} - t_{m+j} = \tau \;\; \forall j (n/\tau = p \;\; \text{floating rate fixings})$$

Fixed leg: $\sum_{j=1}^{n} R.df_{m+j}$

Floating leg: $\sum_{j=0}^{p-1} fwd_{m+j}.\tau.df_{m+j+1}$

Since

$$fwd_{m+j}.\tau = \frac{df_{m+j}}{df_{m+j+1}} - 1$$

Floating leg: $df_m - df_{m+n}$

$$R = \frac{df_m - df_{m+n}}{\sum_{j=1}^{n} df_{m+j}}$$

3.3.3 Bond futures

A bond future is an exchange-traded forward contract which requires the physical delivery of a bond on settlement date. The underlying asset is a **notional** bond, thus not deliverable, but used as *numeraire* to obtain real deliverable issues. The choice of the bond to be delivered is entrusted to parties with short positions (bond sellers). Thus, the ratio of delivery on settlement date should amount to:

$$f = \frac{Notional\ price}{Delivrable\ price}$$

with

$$1 \text{ future contract} = 1 \text{ notional bond} = f * \text{deliverable bond}$$

In the CBOT, the notional bond bears a coupon of 6% with a minimum maturity of 15 years. Logically, the number of deliverable bonds for each contract should be known only at the time of settlement: however, the practical choice made by the clearing house was to pre-establish this ratio, making it in some sense approximative. Concretely, a **conversion factor** is calculated by the clearing house for each of the deliverable bonds. Since these factors don't reflect the accurate ratio, one might foresee arbitrage opportunities. In fact, one bond known as **cheapest-to-deliver** is almost automatically chosen.

To find out the conversion factor, the rule is to discount the coupons and principal of a deliverable bond using the coupon rate of the notional (6%). As an illustration, we show below the list of deliverable Bunds (German government bonds) for the Eurex Bund Future March 2013 expiry and their conversion factors. These bonds have a maturity of between 8.5 and 10.5 years and the discount rate (notional coupon) is also 6%:

Deliverable bond ISIN	Coupon rate (%)	Maturity date	Conversion factor
DE0001102309	1.50	15/02/2023	0.670316
DE0001135465	2.00	04/01/2022	0.732026
DE0001135473	1.75	04/07/2022	0.703119
DE0001135499	1.50	04/09/2022	0.681447

The official formula to find the conversion factors is somewhat intricate. We are going to use the following simplified formula:

$$100 \; C.F. = \sum_{i=0}^{n-1} \frac{c.(t_{i+1}-t_i)/Basis_i}{(1+6\%)^{\sum_{j=0}^{i}(t_{i+1}-t_i)/Basis_j}} + \frac{100}{(1+6\%)^{\sum_{j=0}^{n-1}(t_n-t_{n-1})/Basis_j}}$$

$$t_0 = Settlement\ Date$$

$$c = coupon$$

```
Public Function cf(c!, tenor As Date, settle As Date) As Single

Dim n%: n = 0
Dim t() As Date
t = BondFutDates(tenor, settle, "12m")

For i = 0 To UBound(t)
    Debug.Print t(i)
Next i

ReDim p!(UBound(t)), coup!(UBound(t) - 1)

For i = 0 To UBound(t) - 1
    If isLeapPeriod(t(i), t(i + 1)) Then
        coup(i) = c * (t(i + 1) - t(i)) / 366
    Else
        coup(i) = c * (t(i + 1) - t(i)) / 365
    End If
Next i

cf = 0

If isLeapPeriod(settle, t(1)) Then
    p(0) = (t(0) - settle) / 366: accrued = c * (settle - t(0)) / 366
```

```
Else
    p(0) = (t(0) - settle) / 365: accrued = c * (settle - t(0)) / 365
End If

For i = 0 To UBound(t) - 1
    If isLeapPeriod(t(i), t(i + 1)) Then
        p(i + 1) = p(i) + (t(i + 1) - t(i)) / 366
    Else
        p(i + 1) = p(i) + (t(i + 1) - t(i)) / 365
    End If
    cf = cf + coup(i) / (1.06 ^ (p(i + 1)))
Next i

cf = cf + 100 / (1.06 ^ (p(i))) - accrued
End Function

Public Function BondFutDates(tenor As Date, fut As Date, period$) As Date()

Dim d As Date: d = tenor
Dim n As Long: n = 0
Dim i As Long

Dim tempDates() As Date

Dim f%: f = CInt(Left(period, Len(period) - 1))
Dim m%: m = Fix(DateDiff("m", Date, tenor) / f)

ReDim tempDates(m) As Date

While d > fut
    tempDates(m - n) = d
    n = n + 1
    d = DateAdd("m", -f * n, tenor)
Wend
tempDates(0) = d

For i = 0 To m
    While Weekday(tempDates(i)) = 7 Or Weekday(tempDates(i)) = 1
        tempDates(i) = tempDates(i) + 1
    Wend
Next i

BondFutDates = tempDates

End Function

Public Function isLeapPeriod(d1 As Date, d2 As Date) As Boolean


If DateDiff("d", d1, DateAdd("m", 12, d1)) >= 366 _
Or DateDiff("d", DateAdd("m", -12, d2), d2) >= 366 _
Then isLeapPeriod = True

End Function
```

3.4 OPTIONS BASICS

3.4.1 Brownian motion

Throughout this book, all the models investigated will include one stochastic term called the **Wiener process**, a specific case of the wider class of **Levy processes**. Within the equations describing the assets' dynamics, this term is denoted by

$$\mathrm{d}w_t \ (\text{or } \mathrm{d}B_t)$$

In a first attempt, we can define this time-continuous stochastic increment as the limit, when $\Delta t \to 0$ of the normally distributed random variable Δw_t, given that

$$\Delta w_t \equiv N(0, \Delta t)$$

The corresponding density function is

$$f_t(u) = Exp\left(-\frac{u^2}{2.t}\right) / \sqrt{2.\pi.t}$$

where 0 denotes the expected value and Δt the variance of the process. However, the limit of Δw_t when Δt tends to 0 does not make sense, since it is not deterministic: we ought to specify the convergence mode (law, probability,...).

By the way, the complete definition of the Wiener process w_t includes the following properties:

1. $w(t = 0) = 0$
2. w_t is (simply) continuous for every t **with probability 1**
3. for $0 < s < t$, the increments $w_t - w_s$ are independent and follow a standard normal distribution

$$\mathbb{E}(w_t - w_s) = 0 \quad \mathbb{E}([w_t - w_s]^2) = t - s \tag{3.1}$$

To price contingent claims written on an asset X_t, we ought to put some probability on events such as

$$P(X_t \in [a, b]/X_s = x, \ s < t)$$

or

$$P(X_s < y \text{ and } X_t > z/X_0 = x, \ s < t)$$

Given t, the probability space associated with X_t, i.e., the triplet $(\Omega, \mathcal{F}, P)$ where

1. Ω is the set of all elementary events ($X_t \in [x, x + \mathrm{d}x]$)
2. $\mathcal{F}$ is the σ-algebra of all the subsets of ω, i.e., closed under (countably many) set operations (union, intersection, or complement).
3. P is the probability measure associated with any event of $\mathcal{F}$

is contingent on the probability space of w_t. As a matter of fact, the set of events in question is the **Borel set**, i.e., the σ-algebra built with intervals in $\mathbb{R}$, and the probability measure is given by equation (3.1).

Moreover, since all the events that occurred before $s < t$, regarded as the information available at s, are included in the set of events generated by w_t, the continuous sequence of σ-algebras generated by the process over $[0, t]$ is then **increasing**: it is currently named **filtration of the Brownian motion**, referring to the model of random walk where the increments are normally distributed, and denoted $\mathcal{F}_t$.

Returning to our asset, we expect that every outcome of X_t derives from one subset of $\mathcal{F}_t$: this is the case when X_t is an $\mathcal{F}_t$-**adapted** process. If we regard X as a function mapping w with the price of the asset, it means that this function is $\mathcal{F}_t$-measurable.

Ex: Given that X_t is an $\mathcal{F}_t$-adapted process: any process defined by the following dynamics

$$\alpha(X_t, t)dt + \beta(X_t, t)dw_t$$

where $\alpha : \Omega * \mathbb{R}^+ \mapsto \mathbb{R}$ and $\beta : \Omega * \mathbb{R}^+ \mapsto \mathbb{R}$ are continuous, is also $\mathcal{F}_t$-adapted.

3.4.2 Ito integral

Let us consider the seminal dynamics:

$$dX_t = \alpha(X_t, t)dt + \beta(X_t, t)dw_t \tag{3.2}$$

$$X_t - X_0 = \int_0^t \alpha ds + \int_0^t \beta dw_s$$

raises the question of how to deal with $\int_0^t \beta dw_s$ where the infinitesimal increment is stochastic. This sort of integral in which the integrand is $\mathcal{F}_t$ – adapted is known as an **Ito integral**.

The Ito integral is constructed as a limit of

$$\int_t^T \phi_f dw$$

where ϕ_f is piecewise constant (thus behaving like a discrete RV) on a subdivision $(t_0, t_1, \ldots, t_i, t_{i+1}, \ldots, t_n)$, i.e., a sum of $\mathcal{F}_{w_i}$-measurable **elementary functions**:

$$\int_{t_0}^{t_n} \phi_f dw = \sum_{i=0}^{n-1} \mathbb{1}_{(t_i, t_{i+1}]} \phi_f(w_{t_i}) \Delta w_{t_i} \text{ (see Oksendal (2000))}.$$

Beside the linearity properties of deterministic integrals, Ito integrals have two remarkable features:

1. $\mathbb{E}\left(\int f dw\right) = 0$

2. $\mathbb{E}\left[\left(\int f dw\right)^2\right] = \mathbb{E}\left[\int f^2 dt\right]$ (Isometry property)

Ex: As an illustration, let us consider the trivial case where $\phi_f(w_{t_i}) = x_i \in \mathbb{R}$ and $\Delta t_i = t_{i+1} - t_i = \tau$. then

$$\mathbb{E}\left[\left(\int f \mathrm{d}w\right)^2\right] = \mathbb{E}\left[\left(\sum_{i=0}^{n-1} x_i \Delta w_i\right)^2\right]$$

As a result of the independence between increments

$$\mathbb{E}(\Delta w_i \Delta w_j) = \delta_{i,j}\tau$$

Finally,

$$\mathbb{E}\left[\left(\sum_{i=0}^{n-1} x_i \Delta w_i\right)^2\right] = \sum_{i=0}^{n-1} x_i^2 \tau = \mathbb{E}\left[\int f^2 \mathrm{d}t\right]$$

3.4.3 Ito formula

Previously, we have put into practice the calculation of an Ito integral with the trivial example of a deterministic constant by piecewise process. Things are a bit more delicate when the integrand is a time-continuous process, especially a stochastic one. For instance: would w be deterministic, the Riemann integral

$$\int_0^t w \mathrm{d}w = \frac{1}{2}(w(t)^2 - w(0)^2)$$

is straightforward, standing on the derivability of w^2.

By definition, a Brownian motion w_t is **nowhere-differentiable** with probability 1, which indicates that the rules are to be changed. As a matter of fact, we are prone to estimate $\mathrm{d}(w_t^2)$ as the limit (the mode of convergence is then to be clarified) of

$$(w_t + \Delta w_t)^2 - w_t^2 = 2w_t \Delta w_t + \Delta w_t^2$$

when $\Delta t \to 0$. In practice, we need to find the **limit** of $2w_t \Delta w_t + \Delta w_t^2$ with **probability 1**. To achieve this concisely and "comfortably", we are going to play fast and loose with sound mathematics: for rigorous proofs, see Karatzas and Shreve (1991) and Ito (1944).

First, assume a C^2, bounded function $f : \mathbb{R} \times \mathbb{R}^+ \mapsto \mathbb{R}$. Let us also assume that the first and second partial derivatives of f with respect to X and t are bounded. A Taylor expansion around (X, t) gives

$$\Delta f(X, t) = f'_x \Delta X + f'_t \Delta t + \frac{1}{2}(\underbrace{f''_x \Delta X^2}_{(1)} + 2\underbrace{f''_{x,t} \Delta X \Delta t}_{(2)} + \underbrace{f''_t \Delta t^2}_{(3)}) + \mathcal{O}^3(\Delta X, \Delta t)$$

First, it is clear that (2) is negligible with respect to the first derivatives as $\Delta t \to 0$.

To proceed with (1), let us recall that the Ito integral

$$\Delta X = \int\limits_{t}^{t+\Delta t} \alpha(X_s, s)ds + \beta(X_s, s)dw_s$$

is built as the limit of a sum of elementary functions:

■ $\sum\limits_{i} \alpha_i(w)\mathbb{1}_{(t_i, t_{i+1}]}\Delta t_i \rightarrow \int\limits_{t}^{t+\Delta t} \alpha(X_s, s)ds = I_\alpha$

■ $\sum\limits_{i} \beta_i(w)\mathbb{1}_{[t_i, t_{i+1}[}\Delta w_i \rightarrow \int\limits_{t}^{t+\Delta t} \beta(X_s, s)dw_s = I_\beta$

Setting $\Delta t_i = \Delta t/n$ for Δt arbitrarily low, we calculate the expression

$$\mathbb{E}\left[[\Delta X - \underbrace{(\sum\limits_{i} \alpha_i(w)\mathbb{1}_{(t_i, t_{i+1}]}\Delta t_i + \sum\limits_{i} \beta_i(w)\mathbb{1}_{[t_i, t_{i+1}[}\Delta w_i)]^2}_{J} \right] \tag{3.3}$$

which, by definition, tends to 0 as $n \rightarrow \infty$. The key point in the following sketch of a proof is that we can decide "ad libitum" to give arbitrary low values to Δt and make n rise to infinity.

When developing equation (3.3) it appears that the quadratic term in $\Delta w_i \Delta w_j$ is to play a prominent role compared to $(\Delta t_i)^2$ and $\Delta t_i \Delta w_i$, based on the convergence

$$\lim\limits_{n \rightarrow \infty} \sum\limits_{i=1}^{n} (\Delta w_i)^2 = \Delta t$$

Given $\mathbb{E}(\Delta w_i \Delta w_j) = \delta_{i,j}\Delta t$,

$$\mathbb{E}\left([\sum\limits_{i} \beta_i(w)\mathbb{1}_{[t_i, t_{i+1}[}\Delta w_i]^2 \right) = \mathbb{E}\left(\sum\limits_{i} \mathbb{1}_{[t_i, t_{i+1}[}[\beta_i(w)\Delta w_i]^2 \right)$$

From the continuity of $\beta(X, t)$, we draw

$$\mathbb{E}\left(\sum\limits_{i} \mathbb{1}_{[t_i, t_{i+1}[}[\beta_i(w)\Delta w_i]^2 \right) \rightarrow \mathbb{E}\left[\beta(X_t, t)^2 \underbrace{\sum\limits_{i} (\Delta w_i)^2)}_{\Delta t} \right] = \beta(X_t, t)^2\Delta t$$

as Δt tends to 0.

Also, the properties of the Ito integral state that

$$\mathbb{E}\left(\int_t^{t+\Delta t} \beta(X_s, s)\mathrm{d}w_s\right) = 0$$

$$\mathbb{E}\left(\left[\int_t^{t+\Delta t} \beta(X_s, s)\mathrm{d}w_s\right]^2\right) = \mathbb{E}\left(\int_t^{t+\Delta t} \beta(X_s, s)^2\mathrm{d}s\right)$$

Moreover, it is quite obvious that $\mathbb{E}(I_\alpha^2)$ and $\mathbb{E}(I_\alpha I_\beta)$ are negligible compared to $\mathbb{E}(I_\beta^2)$ (so is $\mathbb{E}(\Delta X.J)$):

$$\mathbb{E}([\Delta X]^2) \rightarrow \mathbb{E}\left(\int_t^{t+\Delta t} \beta(X_s, s)^2\mathrm{d}s\right) \text{ as } \Delta t \text{ tends to } 0.$$

And, finally,

$$(3.3) \rightarrow \mathbb{E}([\Delta X]^2 - \beta(X_t, t)^2\Delta t) \rightarrow 0$$

From $f_t''\Delta t^2 \ll f_x''\Delta X^2$, we can conclude:

$$\Delta f(X_t, t) = f_x'\Delta X + f_t'\Delta t + \frac{1}{2}f_x''\beta(X_t, t)^2\Delta t + \mathcal{O}(\Delta X\Delta t, \Delta t^2) \qquad (3.4)$$

We now introduce the probabilistic definition of the inner product:

$$< \mathrm{d}X_t, \mathrm{d}Y_t > \ = \mathbb{E}(\mathrm{d}X_t\mathrm{d}Y_t)$$

Equation (3.4) can be now reformulated:

$$\mathrm{d}f(X, t) = f_x'\mathrm{d}X + f_t'\mathrm{d}t + \frac{1}{2}f_x'' < \mathrm{d}X, \mathrm{d}X >$$

If we just go back to the case of $\int w\mathrm{d}w$:

$$\mathrm{d}(w_t^2) = 2w\mathrm{d}w_t + 2.\frac{1}{2}\mathrm{d}t$$

$$\int_0^t w_s\mathrm{d}w_s = \frac{1}{2}(w_t^2 - t)$$

Integration by parts Let us consider two correlated assets X_t and Y_t: to lighten the text, $\alpha_x(_y)$ and $\beta_x(_y)$ stand for $\alpha_x(X_t, t)$ etc.

$$dX_t = \alpha_x\mathrm{d}t + \beta_x\mathrm{d}w_x$$
$$dY_t = \alpha_y\mathrm{d}t + \beta_y\mathrm{d}w_y$$

By definition of the linear correlation

$$\rho_{x,y} = \frac{Covar(dX, dY)}{\sqrt{Var(dX)}\sqrt{Var(dY)}}$$

$$= \frac{<dX, dY>}{\beta_x\sqrt{dt}\beta_y\sqrt{dt}}$$

$$<dX, dY> = \beta_x\beta_y\rho_{x,y}dt$$

Applying the Ito formula to $(X_t + Y_t)^2$ and $(X_t^2 + Y_t^2)$ (see Lamberton and Lapeyre, 1997):

$$d[(X_t + Y_t)^2] = 2(X_t + Y_t)d(X_t + Y_t) + \frac{1}{2}2 < d(X_t + Y_t), d(X_t + Y_t) >$$

$$d(X_t^2 + Y_t^2) = 2X_t dX_t + <dX_t, dX_t> + 2Y_t dY_t + <dY_t, dY_t>$$

$$d[(X_t + Y_t)^2] - d(X_t^2 + Y_t^2) = 2d(X_tY_t)$$

$$= 2(Y_t dX_t + X_t dY_t) + 2 < dX_t, dY_t >$$

$$d(X_tY_t) = Y_t dX_t + X_t dY_t + <dX_t, dY_t >$$

3.4.4 Black–Scholes basic model

The seminal form of the models ruling the behavior of volatile assets, in the absence of "jumps", is the diffusion equation:

$$\frac{dS}{S} = \mu(S, t).dt + \sigma(S, t).dw_t \qquad (3.5)$$

where dw is a standard Brownian.

In this equation, $\sigma(S, t)$ exhibits the **volatility** of the asset, while $\mu(S, t)$ stands for the **mean instantaneous rate** of return.

In order to solve (3.5), we will apply the Ito formula to

$$f(S) = Log(S)$$

$$dLog(S) = \frac{dS}{S}dS + \frac{1}{2}\left(\frac{-1}{S^2}\right) * \sigma(S, t)^2 S^2 dt$$

$$dLog(S) = \left(\mu(S, t) - \frac{1}{2}\sigma^2(S, t)\right)dt + \sigma(S, t).dw$$

$$S = Exp\left(\int_0^t (\mu(S, u) - \frac{1}{2}\sigma^2(S, u))du + \int_0^t \sigma(S, u)dw\right)$$

When $\mu(S, t)$ and $\sigma(S, t)$ are constant,

$$S = Exp\left(\left(\mu - \frac{1}{2}\sigma^2\right)t + \sigma w_t\right)$$

3.4.5 Risk-neutral probability

One objective method to price an asset consists in:

- assuming some probability distribution, designed for complying with possible scenarios and their likelihood, regarding the future of the asset;
- postulating that the mathematical expectation best reflects the fair price: in fact, it is mere economic logic.

Replacing $\mu(S, t)$ by the instantaneous riskless rate r in (3.5), and solving

$$\frac{dS}{S} = r.dt + \sigma(S, t).dw_t \qquad (3.6)$$

leads to

$$S_t = S_0 Exp\left(rt - \int_0^t \frac{\sigma_s^2}{2}ds + \int_0^t \sigma_s dw_s\right)$$

provided that w_t is a standard Brownion motion.

Moreover, it is easy to establish that $\mathbb{E}(S_t) = S_0 e^{rt}$, which, actually, yields the **forward price** at t.

As a general rule, the probability under which the mathematical expectation of some payoff $f(S_t)$ reflects its market price, i.e., the fair value of the asset, is called **risk-neutral probability**.

More specifically, the mean expected payoff at t must be discounted to give the fair price (present value) as of $t = 0$

$$\text{Fair price} = \mathbb{E}(e^{-rt} f(S_t)) = e^{-rt}\mathbb{E}(f(S_t)) \ (r \text{ being constant})$$

3.4.6 Change of probability

In what follows, and for reasons of conciseness, the theory applies to the simplified model of equation (3.6): in any case, this holds for a larger framework as well.

Assume the "drifted" process

$$b_t = w_t + \alpha t$$

Replacing w_t in equation (3.6):

$$\frac{dS}{S} = (r - \alpha\sigma)dt + \sigma.db_t$$

The stochastic term db_t in the dynamics of S_t is, obviously, not a standard Brownian under the original risk-neutral measure.

Suppose now that, instead of describing the dynamics under this measure, we want to describe it using a different, but equivalent, probability. Notice, first, that two probability measures P and Q in a space $(\Omega, \mathcal{A})$ are equivalent when each of them is **absolutely continuous** with respect to the other, i.e., whatever the event A of the common σ-algebra,

$$P(A) = 0 \Longrightarrow Q(A) = 0$$

A theorem, named after **Radon, Nikodym** and **Lebesgue**, states that, if Q is absolutely continuous with respect to P, then there exists a measurable function $f : \Omega \mapsto \mathbb{R}^+$ such that

$$\forall A \in \mathcal{A} \ Q(A) = \int_A f.dP(w)$$

and the reverse is obviously also true. f is called the **density of Radon-Nikodym** of Q with respect to P and denoted dQ/dP (for a comprehensive study of this matter, see Zaanen (1996)). Let us consider, then, some probability Q, equivalent to the risk-neutral measure P and a density of the form

$$dQ/dP = e^{-\alpha u - 1/2\alpha^2 t}$$

The density function of b_t under Q is written

$$\frac{dQ}{du}(b_t \in du) = \frac{dQ}{dP} \cdot \frac{dP}{du}(b_t \in du)$$

$$= e^{-\alpha u - 1/2\alpha^2 t} \frac{dP}{du}(w_t \in du - \alpha t)$$

$$= \frac{e^{-u^2/2t}}{\sqrt{2\pi t}}$$

As a result, b_t is a standard Brownian under Q. Therefore, it is equivalent to say:

- the dynamics of S_t under P is

$$\frac{dS}{S} = r.dt + \sigma.dw_t$$

  where w_t is a P-standard Brownian
- the dynamics of S_t under Q is

$$\frac{dS}{S} = (r - \alpha\sigma).dt + \sigma.dw_t$$

  where w_t is a Q-standard Brownian.

This result holds not only for α constant but can be generalized (**Girsanov theorem**) to $\mathcal{F}_t$-adapted processes α_t verifying the Novikov condition:

$$\mathbb{E}^P \left[Exp \left(\frac{1}{2} \int_0^t \alpha_s^2 ds \right) \right] < \infty$$

In turns out that this natural measure is not so commonly used in quantitative finance. In particular, when dealing with interest rate-related assets where r_t is stochastic, the solving of

$$\mathbb{E}(e^{-\int r_s ds} f(S_t))$$

becomes an intricate issue under this measure.

At first sight, the benefit drawn from a change of measure is not intuitive: it will be more obvious when dealing with payoffs such as **barrier options** or **interest rate exotics**. However, the technique is more or less always the same.

3.4.7 Martingale and numeraires

The martingale property Returning to the drifted process:

$$b_t = w_t + \alpha t$$

if we set $\alpha = \frac{r}{\sigma}$, the dynamics of S_t under Q reduce to

$$\frac{dS}{S} = \sigma.db_t$$

Recalling the Ito integral property (see §3.4.1)

$$\mathbb{E}\left(\int S_t\sigma.db_t\right) = 0$$

In other words,

$$\mathbb{E}(S_t) = S_0 \tag{3.7}$$

This property is called **a martingale** property: it holds for every date in the future, that is to say:

$$\mathbb{E}(S_T/\mathcal{F}_t) = S_t$$

The converse is also true in a broader context. This remarkable result is the main issue of the **martingale representation theorem**: for S_t to be a martingale, there must exist an $\mathcal{F}_t$-adapted process $g(s, w)$ such that

$$S_t = S_0 + \int\limits_0^t g(s, w)\mathrm{d}w_s$$

with the condition that S_t is square integrable:

$$\mathbb{E}^P\left(\int\limits_0^t S_u^2\mathrm{d}u\right) < \infty$$

This theorem is usually invoked to characterize martingales as **driftless** processes. This property is widely used to price interest rate derivatives.

Current numeraires A **numeraire** is a **non-dividend paying asset** (see Brigo and Mercurio, 2006) that can serve as a unit in which all other assets can be denominated: in other words, it normalizes all other assets with respect to it.

For instance, returning to the density (§3.4.6):

$$dQ/dP = e^{-\alpha w - 1/2\alpha^2 t} = 1/e^{\alpha w + 1/2\alpha^2 t}$$

From the Ito formula:

$$d(e^X) = e^X dX + e^X \frac{1}{2} < dX, dX >$$

Applied to $X = -(\alpha w + 1/2\alpha^2 t)$, it yields

$$d(e^X) = -\alpha e^X dw$$

from which it emerges that dQ/dP can be regarded as a numeraire which, in addition, is a P-martingale (driftless process). We are now going to introduce one specific numeraire that plays a crucial role in interest rate-related assets, called the **forward martingale measure**. Actually, common sense dictates that there should exist one probability under which the price of any future asset, settled precisely at this future date T, is equal to the expected value of this asset at t. Denoting by Q_T this measure, X_t the price of the spot asset, settled at t, F_T the future theoretical price, F_t the price of this future settled at t

$$F_T = X_t \frac{1}{B(t, T)} = \mathbb{E}^{Q_T}(X_T / \mathcal{F}_t)$$

Given $B(T, T) = 1$, we conclude:

$$\frac{X_t}{B(t, T)} = \mathbb{E}^{Q_T}(\frac{X_T}{B(T, T)} / \mathcal{F}_t)$$

Therefore, under Q_T, the price of any asset normalized by the numeraire $B(t, T)$ (zero-coupon bond) is a martingale.

Another remarkable proposition, thanks to Geman, El Karoui, and Rochet (1995), states that, given some numeraire N, if there exists a numeraire X and a probability measure Q^X (the Forward martingale measure for instance) such that any traded asset normalized by X is a martingale under Q^X, then there exists a probability measure Q^N under which any *attainable claim* normalized by N is a martingale under Q^N.

"Attainable claim" designates some asset that can be perfectly hedged with liquid traded assets, or, to put it differently, can be replicated by a **self-financing strategy**. Without going into technicalities, a self-financing strategy is a strategy continuously hedged, where each hedging transaction is financed: no transaction except (delta-)hedge and refinancing is initiated.

An example of an attainable claim is the European-style option, provided that the volatility remains constant.

Among the most usual numeraires, let us quote the **swap probability measure** whose related numeraire is

$$\sum_{i=1}^{n} B(t, T_i)$$

Under this measure, the attainable claim

$$1 - B(t, T_n)$$

normalized by the swap numeraire, i.e., the **swap market price** (see §3.3.2), is a martingale
asset

$$SW(t, T_n) = \frac{1 - B(t, T_n)}{\displaystyle\sum_{i=1}^{n} B(t, T_i)}$$

Both forward and swap numeraires are unavoidable when pricing interest rate derivatives
where the discount factor $Exp(- \int r_s ds)$ is stochastic. Finally, when we use the Ito formula
on

$$\frac{Y_t}{X_t}$$

given

$$dY_t = \alpha_t^y dt + \sigma_t^y dw_t^y$$

$$dX_t = \alpha_t^x dt + \sigma_t^x dw_t^x$$

the resulting volatility of Y_t/X_t, is

$$\sigma_t^{y/x} = \sigma_t^y$$

The volatility of the asset is preserved by a change of numeraire.

3.4.8 European-style options pricing

An option is a **conditional asset**, giving the right, not the obligation, to enter into a financial
transaction under conditions that are predetermined at inception. This right may be exercised:

- on a <u>unique date</u>, i.e., the expiry date of the option: we call it a **European**-style option;
- at any time before expiration, which corresponds to the **American** style;
- at some anniversary dates: **Bermudan** style.

The terms of an option are thus:

- the underlying asset (exchange rate, equity index future, commodity, etc.)
- the expiry date
- the nominal involved
- the exercise price, or **strike**.

If we postulate that $\mu = r$ is constant and $\sigma(S, t) = \sigma(t)$ is deterministic, we obtain the formula
given in §3.4.5:

$$S_t = S_0 Exp\left(rt - \int_0^t \frac{\sigma_s^2}{2} ds + \int_0^t \sigma_s dw_s\right)$$

Moreover, stating $\sigma_t = \sigma = $ constant, we can infer the price of a European call struck at K:

$$\mathbb{E}(e^{-rt}[S_t - K]^+) = e^{-rt} \int_{-d_2}^{+\infty} [S_0 Exp\left((r - \sigma^2/2)t + \sigma\sqrt{t}u\right) - K]\frac{1}{\sqrt{2\pi}} e^{-u^2/2} du$$

$$= S_{0t}N(d_1) - Ke^{-rt}N(d_2)$$

where

$$d_1 = \frac{Ln(S_0/K) + (r + \sigma^2/2)t}{\sigma\sqrt{t}} \qquad d_2 = d_1 - \sigma\sqrt{t}$$

$$N(x) = \frac{1}{2\pi} \int\limits_{-\infty}^{x} e^{-u^2/2} du$$

A bit of terminology: let us call **intrinsic value (IV)**, the difference

- $Max(Se^{rt} - K, 0)$ for a European call
- $Max(K - Se^{rt}, 0)$ for a European put.

A European-style option (for American-style options, change Se^{rt} for S) is said to be:

- **In-the-money** when IV>0
- **Out-of-the-money** when IV=0
- **At-the-money** (ATM): used to designate options where strike = spot price (American-style) or strike = future price (European-style).

3.5 FIRST GENERATION EXOTIC OPTIONS

In this section, we study some "first generation exotic" assets, i.e., contingent claims with path-dependent payoffs or depending on another asset. The exotic derivatives investigated here have in common that they are priced analytically (without the aid of numerical solutions).

3.5.1 Barrier options

A barrier option is a regular option with restrictive clauses. More precisely, the option may or may not be exercised provided that the underlying asset has or has not reached a predetermined level (the *barrier*) before expiration date.

Therefore, a barrier option can be:

- a call or a put;
- activated when the barrier is reached (knocked in) or desactivated (knocked out);
- **up** or **down**, according to whether the spot price has to move up or down to reach the barrier.

Knock-in and knock-out options are complementary:

$$K.I. \text{ option} + K.O. \text{ option} = \text{Regular option}$$

As an example, the payoff of a **put up & in** struck at T, is

$$1_{max(S_t)>Bar,t\leq T} \; Max(K - S_T, 0)$$

Bar standing for the barrier level. The fair value of this instrument is, for r constant

$$e^{-rT}[K.\mathbb{E}(1_{max(S_t)>Bar,S_T<K}) - \mathbb{E}(1_{max(S_t)>Bar,S_T<K}S_T)]$$

The Brownian case   If we take a look at the first term of the formula

$$\mathbb{E}(1_{Max(S_t)>Bar,S_T<K}) = P(Max(S_t) > Bar, S_T < K)$$

when the asset price follows a pure brownian motion w_t, there is no difficulty in solving the above equation, thanks to the symmetry of w_t paths. This feature is illustrated in the diagram below, displaying the path followed by w_t starting from some point y at s, and the "shadow" path (dotted curve) obtained by reflection about the level y. Each path and its mirrored one have the same probability.

Given two arbitrary values x and y such that $x \leq y$ (x is supposed to play the role of the strike and y that of the barrier), setting $w_t - w_s = w_{t-s}$,

$$P(w_{t-s} > a) = P(w_{t-s} < -a) \; \forall a$$
$$\Rightarrow P(w_T \leq x, w_s = y) = P(w_T \geq 2y - x, w_s = y)$$

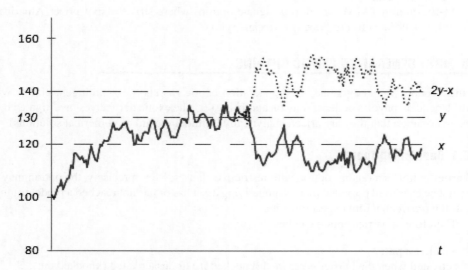

As a consequence, if we denote by $M_w(0, T)$ the maximum attained by w_t between $t = s$ and $t = T$,

$$P(w_T \leq x, M_w(0, T) \geq y) = P(w_{T-s} \geq 2y - x, M_w(0, T) \geq y)$$
$$= P(w_{T-s} \geq 2y - x)$$

Thus,

$$\mathbb{E}(1_{Max(w_t)>y, \; t \leq T, \; w_T < x}f(w_T)) = \mathbb{E}(1_{w_T>2y-x} \; f(2y - w_T)) \qquad (3.8)$$

Returning to the Put up & in:

$$PutUI(K, T) = \mathbb{E}(1_{w_T>2Bar-K} \; w_T - (2Bar - K)) = Call \, (2Bar - K, T)$$

Brownian with drift The reflection principle does not hold for a process with drift since upward and downward paths do not have the same probability:

$$P(w_t + \mu.t < -a) \neq P(w_t + \mu.t > +a) \tag{3.9}$$

Therefore, we are going to achieve some change of probability measure in order to turn the process with drift into a driftless one under another measure Q (as in §3.4.6). To that end, let us define $w_t' = w_t + \mu t$ and state:

$$dQ/dP = e^{-\mu w - \mu^2 t/2}$$

As a first step, this will help to solve

$$\mathbb{E}^P(1_{Max(S_t)>Bar,S_T<K}) \tag{3.10}$$

First, we set

$$X_t = \frac{1}{\sigma} Ln \frac{S_t}{S_0} \qquad k = \frac{1}{\sigma} Ln \frac{K}{S_0}$$

$$H = \frac{1}{\sigma} Ln \frac{Bar}{S_0} \qquad \lambda = \frac{\mu - \sigma^2/2}{\sigma}$$

$$\mathbb{E}^P(1_{Max(S_t)>B,S_T<K}) = \mathbb{E}^P(1_{Max(X_t)>H,X_T<k})$$

We will use successively two changes of measure:

1. $P \to Q$, $\quad \frac{dQ}{dP} = e^{-\lambda w_t - (\lambda^2/2)t}$ $\quad (B_t = w_t + \lambda t$ Brownian under $Q)$
2. $Q \to \tilde{Q}$, $\quad \frac{d\tilde{Q}}{dQ} = e^{-\lambda B_t - (\lambda^2/2)t}$ $\quad (\tilde{B}_t = B_t + \lambda t$ Brownian under $\tilde{Q})$

$$\mathbb{E}^Q(\square) = \mathbb{E}^P\left(\frac{dQ}{dP}\square\right) \iff \mathbb{E}^P(\square) = \mathbb{E}^Q\left(\frac{dP}{dQ}\square\right) = \mathbb{E}^Q\left(1/\frac{dQ}{dP}\square\right)$$

First change

$$\mathbb{E}^P(1_{Max(X_t)>H,X_T<k}) = \mathbb{E}^Q(e^{\lambda w_T + (\lambda^2/2)T} 1_{Max(X_t)>H,X_T<k})$$

$$= \mathbb{E}^Q(e^{\lambda B_T - (\lambda^2/2)T} 1_{Max(X_t)>H,X_T<k})$$

$$= \mathbb{E}^Q(e^{\lambda B_T - (\lambda^2/2)T} 1_{Max(B_t)>H,B_T<k})$$

In fact, $X_t = \frac{1}{\sigma} Ln \frac{S_t}{S_0} = w_t + \lambda t$
From equation 3.8,

$$\mathbb{E}^Q(e^{\lambda B_T - (\lambda^2/2)T} 1_{Max(B_t)>H,B_T<k}) = \mathbb{E}^Q(e^{\lambda(2H-B_T) - (\lambda^2/2)T} 1_{B_T>2H-k})$$

Second change

$$\mathbb{E}^Q(e^{-\lambda B_T - (\lambda^2/2)T} 1_{B_T > 2H - k}) = \mathbb{E}^{\tilde{Q}}(e^{\lambda B_T + (\lambda^2/2)T} e^{-\lambda B_T - (\lambda^2/2)T} 1_{B_T > 2H - k})$$

$$= \mathbb{E}^{\tilde{Q}}(1_{\tilde{B}_T - \lambda T > 2H - k})$$

Thus:

$$\mathbb{E}^P(1_{Max(S_t) > Bar, S_T < K}) = e^{2\lambda H} P^{\tilde{Q}}(\tilde{B}_T > 2H - k + \lambda T)$$

$$= e^{2\lambda H} N((-2H + k - \lambda T)/\sqrt{T})$$

To recap:

$$PutUI(K, T) = e^{-rT}.\mathbb{E}^P(1_{Max(S_t) > Bar, S_T < K}(K - S_T))$$

$$= UI_1 + UI_2$$

$$UI_1 = e^{-rT}.K.e^{2\lambda H} N((-2H + k - \lambda T)/\sqrt{T})$$

$$UI_2 = -e^{-rT}\mathbb{E}^P(S_T.1_{Max(S_t) > Bar, S_T < K})$$

$$= -e^{-rT}\mathbb{E}^P\left(S_0 e^{(\mu - \sigma^2/2)T + \sigma w_T}.1_{Max(S_t) > Bar, S_T < K}\right)$$

A last change $P \to \hat{Q}$, $\frac{d\hat{Q}}{dP} = e^{\sigma w_t - (\sigma^2/2)t}$ ($\hat{w}_t = w_t - \sigma t$ is a $\hat{Q}$)-brownian.

$$UI_2 = e^{(\mu - r)T} S_0 \mathbb{E}^{\hat{Q}}((1_{Max(S_t) > Bar, S_T < K})$$

$$UI_2 = e^{(\mu - r)T} S_0 \hat{Q}(Max(S_t) > Bar, S_T < K)$$

The new expression of S is

$$S = S_0 e^{(\mu \boxed{+} \sigma^2/2)t + \sigma \hat{w}_t}$$

The analogy with the expression of S_t under P leads us to shift $\lambda = \frac{\mu - \sigma^2/2}{\sigma}$ for $\hat{\lambda} = \frac{\mu \boxed{+} \sigma^2/2}{\sigma}$

$$UI_2 = e^{(\mu - r)T} S_0.e^{2\hat{\lambda} H} N((-2H + k - \hat{\lambda}T)/\sqrt{T})$$

Finally,

$$PutUI = e^{-rT}.K.e^{2\lambda H} N((-2H + k - \lambda T)/\sqrt{T}) - e^{(\mu - r)T} S_0.e^{2\hat{\lambda} H} N((-2H + k - \hat{\lambda}T)/\sqrt{T})$$

Below, we show a compilation of barrier option pricing formulae, that aims to cover all the possible situations, and their coding: these formulae are drawn from (Hull, 1997).

Calls There are three possibilities:

- **Call down & in with Bar<K**

$$c_{di} = S_0 e^{(\mu - r)t} (Bar/S_0)^{2\lambda} N(y) - K e^{-rt} (Bar/S_0)^{2\lambda - 2} N(y - \sigma\sqrt{t})$$

with

$$\lambda = \frac{\mu + \sigma^2/2}{\sigma^2} \qquad y = \frac{Ln[Bar^2/(SK)]}{\sigma\sqrt{T}}$$

- **call down & in with Bar>K**

$$c_{di} = c - c_{do}, \text{ where}$$

$$c_{do} = S_0 N(x_1)e^{(\mu-r)t} - Ke^{-rt}N(x_1 - \sigma\sqrt{t})$$

$$\qquad - S_0 e^{(\mu-r)t}(Bar/S_0)^{2\lambda}N(y_1) + Ke^{-rt}(Bar/S_0)^{2\lambda-2}N(y_1 - \sigma\sqrt{t})$$

$$x_1 = \frac{Ln(S_0/Bar)}{\sigma\sqrt{t}} + \lambda\sigma\sqrt{t} \qquad y_1 = \frac{Ln(Bar/S_0)}{\sigma\sqrt{t}} + \lambda\sigma\sqrt{t}$$

- **call up & in with Bar>K** (when Bar<K, call up & in=regular call)

$$c_{ui} = S_0 N(x_1)e^{(\mu-r)t} - Ke^{-rt}N(x_1 - \sigma\sqrt{t}) - S_0 e^{(\mu-r)t}(Bar/S_0)^{2\lambda}(N(-y) - N(-y_1))$$

$$\qquad + Xe^{-rt}(Bar/S_0)^{2\lambda-2}(N(-y + \sigma\sqrt{t}) - N(-y_1 + \sigma\sqrt{t})$$

Puts There are three possibilities as for calls (when Bar>K, put down & in=regular put):

- **Put down & in with Bar<K**

$$p_{di} = -S_0 N(-x_1)e^{(\mu-r)t} + Ke^{-rt}N(-x_1 + \sigma\sqrt{t})$$

$$\qquad + S_0 e^{(\mu-r)t}(Bar/S_0)^{2\lambda}(N(y) - N(y_1))$$

$$\qquad - Ke^{-rt}(Bar/S_0)^{2\lambda-2}(N(y - \sigma\sqrt{t}) - N(y_1 - \sigma\sqrt{t}))$$

- **put up & in with Bar>K**

$$p_{ui} = -S_0(Bar/S_0)^{2\lambda}e^{(\mu-r)t}N(-y) + Ke^{-rt}(Bar/S_0)^{2\lambda-2}N(-y + \sigma\sqrt{t})$$

- **put up & in with Bar<K**

$$p_{ui} = p - p_{uo}, \text{ where}$$

$$p_{uo} = -S_0 N(-x_1)e^{(\mu-r)t} + Ke^{-rt}N(-x_1 + \sigma\sqrt{t})$$

$$\qquad + S_0 e^{(\mu-r)t}(Bar/S_0)^{2\lambda}N(-y_1) - Xe^{-rt}(Bar/S_0)^{2\lambda-2}(N(-y_1 + \sigma\sqrt{t})$$

Code Below, we display the generic function OptBar that, in addition to the usual parameters, S, K, σ, r, and t, takes the following string-type arguments:

- **c** or **p** (call or put)
- **dn** or **up** (down or up)
- **in** or **out**.

We assume no coupon is paid from the asset, so that $\mu = r$. Otherwise, assume that $\mu = r - d$, where d denotes the continuous coupon rate, although this does not make much sense when approaching the coupon payment date.

```vba
Public Function OptBar(c_p As String, d_u$, i_o$ ,S#, K#, Bar#, vol#, r#, t#)
As Double

Dim lbda#: lbda = (r + vol ^ 2 / 2) / vol ^ 2
Dim y#: y = Log(Bar ^ 2 / (S * K)) / vol / Sqr(t) + lbda * vol * Sqr(t)

Dim x1#: x1 = Log(S / Bar) / vol / Sqr(t) + lbda * vol * Sqr(t)
Dim y1#: y1 = Log(Bar / S) / vol / Sqr(t) + lbda * vol * Sqr(t)

Dim din#, dout#, uin#, uout#

Select Case c_p
    Case "c"
        Select Case d_u
            Case "d"
                If Bar < K Then
                    din = S * (Bar / S) ^ (2 * lbda) * norm(y) - _
                    K * Exp(-r * t) * (Bar / S) ^ (2 * lbda - 2) * _
                    norm(y - vol * Sqr(t))
                    dout = -din + call_BS(S, K, vol, r, t)
                End If

                If Bar > K Then
                    dout = S * norm(x1) - K * Exp(-r * t)
                        * norm(x1 - vol * Sqr(t)) _
                        - S * (Bar / S) ^ (2 * lbda) * norm(y1) _
                        + K * Exp(-r * t) * (Bar / S) ^ (2 * lbda - 2) * _
                        norm(y1 - vol * Sqr(t))
                    din = -dout + call_BS(S, K, vol, r, t)
                End If
                If i_o = "in" Then OptBar = din
                If i_o = "out" Then OptBar = dout

            Case "u"
                If Bar < K Then
                    uin = call_BS(S, K, vol, r, t): uout = 0
                End If

                If Bar > K Then
                    uin = S * norm(x1) - K * Exp(-r * t) *
                    norm(x1 - vol * Sqr(t)) _
                        - S * (Bar / S) ^ (2 * lbda)
                        * (norm(-y) - norm(-y1)) _
                        + K * Exp(-r * t) * (Bar / S) ^ (2 * lbda - 2) * _
                            (norm(-y + vol * Sqr(t)) - norm(-y1 + vol * 
                            Sqr(t)))
                    uout = -uin + call_BS(S, K, vol, r, t)
                End If
                If i_o = "in" Then OptBar = uin
                If i_o = "out" Then OptBar = uout
        End Select
```

```
        Case "p"
            Select Case d_u
                Case "d"
                    If Bar < K Then
                        din = -S * norm(-x1) + K * Exp(-r * t)
                             * norm(-x1 + vol * Sqr(t)) _
                             + S * (Bar / S) ^ (2 * lbda) * (norm(y) - norm(y1)) _
                             - K * Exp(-r * t) * (Bar / S) ^ (2 * lbda - 2) * _
                             (norm(y - vol * Sqr(t)) - norm(y1 - vol * Sqr(t)))
                        dout = -din + put_BS(S, K, vol, r, t)
                    End If

                    If Bar > K Then
                        din = put_BS(S, K, vol, r, t): dout = 0
                    End If
                    If i_o = "in" Then OptBar = din
                    If i_o = "out" Then OptBar = dout

                Case "u"
                    If Bar < K Then
                        uout = -S * norm(-x1) + K * Exp(-r * t)
                             * norm(-x1 + vol * Sqr(t)) _
                             + S * (Bar / S) ^ (2 * lbda) * norm(-y1) _
                             - K * Exp(-r * t) * (Bar / S) ^ (2 * lbda - 2)
                                  * norm(-y1 + vol * Sqr(t))
                        uin = -uout + put_BS(S, K, vol, r, t)
                    End If

                    If Bar > K Then
                        uin = -S * (Bar / S) ^ (2 * lbda) * norm(-y) _
                            + K * Exp(-r * t) * (Bar / S) ^ (2 * lbda - 2)
                              * norm(-y + vol * Sqr(t))
                        uout = -uin + put_BS(S, K, vol, r, t)
                    End If
                    If i_o = "in" Then OptBar = uin
                    If i_o = "out" Then OptBar = uout

            End Select
        End Select

End Function

Public Function norm(x#) As Double
norm = WorksheetFunction.NormSDist(x)
End Function


****************************************************
```

call_BS and put_BS are regular European options prices.

```
****************************************************

Public Function call_BS(S#, K#, vol#, r#, t#) As Double

Dim d1#, d2#
d1 = (Log(S / K) + (r + vol ^ 2 / 2) * t) / vol / Sqr(t)
d2 = d1 - vol * Sqr(t)
```

```
call_BS = S * norm(d1) - K * Exp(-r * t) * norm(d2)

End Function

Public Function put_BS(S#, K#, vol#, r#, t#) As Double

Dim d1#, d2#
d1 = (Log(S / K) + (r + vol ^ 2 / 2) * t) / vol / Sqr(t)
d2 = d1 - vol * Sqr(t)

put_BS = call_BS(S, K, vol, r, t) - (S - K * Exp(-r * t))

End Function
```

3.5.2 Quanto options

A quanto option is an option denominated in one currency but settled in another currency. An example of a quanto option is a call on the EuroStoxx 50 index (a Euro denominated asset), settled in USD. The final payoff

$$Max(EuroStoxx50(t)\text{-}Strike,0)$$

will be paid, in this case, in USD instead of EUR. This class of instruments is sought after by foreign investors looking for protection against exchange rate fluctuations.

To put a price on this exotic instrument, let us now consider a call option struck at K on an asset denominated in USD, bought by an investor from the Euro zone.

Let us denote by $\mathbf{S_t}$, the price of the "foreign" asset and by $\mathbf{X_t}$, the **exchange rate**, i.e., the number of EUR units per unit of USD.

On the expiry date, if the option's seller agreed to pay

$$Max(S_t - K, 0)/\mathbf{X_t} \text{ in USD}$$

instead of

$$Max(S_t - K, 0),$$

the buyer could change this payoff in the spot market to obtain

$$Max(S_t - K, 0)/X_t * X_t = Max(S_t - K, 0) \text{ EUR}$$

and get rid of the currency risk. We can then give a formal expression of the quanto call:

$$e^{-r_\$ t}\mathbb{E}(Max(S_t - K, 0)/X_t) \text{ in USD},$$

or, equivalently,

$$e^{-r_\$ t}. \underbrace{X_0}. \mathbb{E}(Max(S_t - K, 0)/X_t) \text{ in EUR}$$

The theoretical expression of X_t derives from the following dynamics of the foreign exchange rate:

$$dX_t = X_t((r_d - r_f)dt + \sigma_x dw_x) \tag{3.11}$$

r_d stands for the **domestic** interest rate (in our example $r_d = r_e$ and r_f is the **foreign** interest rate ($r_\$$).

In fact, recall (§3.3.1) that the forward exchange rate at t, given the spot rate X_0 at $t = 0$ and both interest rates r_d and r_f, is written:

$$X_0 * \frac{1 + r_d t}{1 + r_f t} \tag{3.12}$$

Without arbitrage opportunities, X_t is also the expected value at t of the exchange rate, i.e., $\mathbb{E}(X_t)$: in the BS framework, given

$$dX_t = \mu dt + \theta_x dw_x$$

$$\mathbb{E}(X_{t+dt}/X_t) = \mu dt$$

To obtain μ, we simply take the first order terms while differentiating (3.12), which yields

$$\mu dt \simeq X_t(r_d - r_f)dt$$

Setting $\theta_x = \sigma_x X_t$, we land on equation (3.12). After integration:

$$X_t = X_0.e^{(r_e - r_\$ - \sigma_x^2/2)t + \sigma_x w_x}$$

The theoretical price of the European quanto call is now written (in EUR):

$$Call(K,t) = e^{-r_\$ t}.\mathbb{E}^P(Max(S_0.e^{(r_\$ - \sigma_s^2/2)t + \sigma_s w_s} - K, 0).e^{(r_\$ - r_e + \sigma_x^2/2)t - \sigma_x w_x})$$

$$= e^{-r_e t}.\mathbb{E}^P(Max(S_0.e^{(r_\$ - \sigma_s^2/2)t + \sigma_s w_s} - K, 0).e^{(\sigma_x^2/2)t - \sigma_x w_x})$$

Let us denote by $\rho_{x,s}$ the correlation coefficient, i.e.:

$$\rho_{x,s} dt = \; < dw_x, dw_s >$$

By definition:

$$< dw_s - \rho_{x,s} dw_x, dw_x > \; = 0$$

As a matter of fact

$$w^* = (w_s - \rho_{x,s} w_x)/\sqrt{1 - \rho_{x,s}^2}$$

is a standard Brownian motion uncorrelated with w_x.

Let us simplify $\rho_{x,y} = \rho$. We can then rewrite the payoff, replacing w_s by $\rho_{x,s} w_x + \sqrt{1 - \rho_{x,s}^2} w^*$ in the expression of S_t:

$$Call(K,t) = e^{-r_e t}.\mathbb{E}^P(Max(S_0.e^{(r_\$ - \sigma_s^2/2)t + \sigma_s(\rho w_x + \sqrt{1-\rho^2} w^*)} - K, 0).e^{(\sigma_x^2/2)t - \sigma_x w_x})$$

The factor $e^{(\sigma_x^2/2)t - \sigma_x w_x}$ which indicates that the numeraire chosen is the foreign currency unit exhibits a density of probability:

$$e^{(\sigma_x^2/2)t - \sigma_x w_x} = e^{\sigma_x^2} * e^{-(\sigma_x^2/2)t - \sigma_x w_x} = e^{\sigma_x^2} * \frac{dQ}{dP}$$

Q is therefore the probability measure under which

$$w_x^* = w_x + \sigma_x t$$

is a standard Brownian. Given $dP/dQ = e^{(\sigma_x^2/2)t + \sigma_x w_x}$, so that

$$\mathbb{E}^P(\square) = \mathbb{E}^Q(dP/dQ\square)$$

the option price is written:

$$e^{(-r_e + \sigma_x^2)t}\mathbb{E}^Q(Max(S_0.e^{(r_\$ - \sigma_s^2/2 - \rho\sigma_s\sigma_x)t + \sigma_s(\rho w_x^* + \sqrt{1-\rho^2}w^*)} - K, 0)$$

Being uncorrelated with w_x^*, the properties of w_x as a standard Brownian motion are preserved along with the change of probability. So we can set

$$w^{**} = \rho w_x^* + \sqrt{1 - \rho^2}w^*$$

Introducing w^{**} in the payoff formula, we are close to finalizing the pricing: indeed, the payoff expression

$$e^{(-r_e + \sigma_x^2)t}\mathbb{E}^Q(Max(S_0.e^{(r_\$ - \sigma_s^2/2 - \rho\sigma_s\sigma_x)t + \sigma_s w^{**}} - K, 0)$$

is analogous to a plain-vanilla European call struck at K, i.e.,

$$e^{-rt}\mathbb{E}^Q(Max(S_0.e^{(r - \sigma_s^2/2)t + \sigma_s w^{**}} - K, 0)$$

provided that

- r is replaced by $r_\$ - \rho\sigma_s\sigma_x$
- the whole expression is multiplied by $e^{r_\$ - r_e - (\rho\sigma_s\sigma_x + \sigma_x^2)t}$

and setting

$$d1 = \frac{Ln(S_0/K) + (r_\$ - (\rho\sigma_s\sigma_x + \sigma_s^2/2)t}{\sigma_s\sqrt{t}}$$

$$d2 = d1 - \sigma_s\sqrt{t}$$

$$\text{Call(K,t)} = e^{(-r_e + \sigma_x^2)t}(e^{(r_\$ - \rho\sigma_s\sigma_x)t}S_0 N(d1) - KN(d2))$$

The same rationale leads to:

$$\text{Put(K,t)} = e^{(-r_e + \sigma_x^2)t}(KN(-d2) - e^{(r_\$ - \rho\sigma_s\sigma_x)t}S_0 N(-d1))$$

CHAPTER 4

Numerical Solutions

This chapter handles common numerical methods used in finance to tackle path-dependent contingent claims and multi-asset instruments. Most of them consist in transferring a continuous-time valuation issue into a discrete time one, which is more tractable. Here is a list of problems solved by discretization of time: American-style options, early termination issues, exotic contingent claims, basket options...

We will review successively:

1. finite differences
2. binomial and trinomial trees
3. Monte-Carlo scenarios
4. simulation and regression.

At the end of this chapter, we will develop a recipe to price double-barrier options as a series of single barriers: the benefit of this method is that it allows stochastic volatility models to be taken into account when pricing a double-barrier.

4.1 FINITE DIFFERENCES

4.1.1 Generic equation

The rationale is to find close solutions to differential equations, using finite differences to approximate derivatives. This method applies to contingent claims satisfying the following generic equation, in a **complete market** (in which every contingent claim can be perfectly hedged with liquid assets):

$$\frac{\partial x}{\partial t} + rS\frac{\partial x}{\partial S} + \frac{1}{2}\frac{\partial^2 x}{\partial^2 S}\sigma^2 S^2 = rx \tag{4.1}$$

To justify this equation, let's consider the matter from the market-maker's point of view. In theory, this portfolio must be **self-financing**. Concretely, it means that the changes in the values of the contingent claim + the hedge must be balanced by the funding cost of the book between t and $t + dt$.

Let us clarify each element of the formula:

- change in the derivative's value (straight application of Ito's formula)

$$dx = \frac{\partial x}{\partial t}dt + \frac{\partial x}{\partial S}dS + \frac{1}{2}\frac{\partial^2 x}{\partial^2 S}\sigma^2 S^2 dt$$

- change in the hedge value

$$-\frac{\partial x}{\partial S}dS$$

- funding of the derivative

$$-rxdt$$

- funding of the hedge

$$+r\frac{\partial x}{\partial S}dt$$

The self-funding of this portfolio imposes

$$dx - \frac{\partial x}{\partial S}dS - rxdt + r\frac{\partial x}{\partial S}dt = 0 \Rightarrow (4.1)$$

4.1.2 Implementation

To build the grid, time to maturity is divided into n equal periods $\Delta t = t/n$.

We choose a reasonably wide range of possible values for the asset price on either side of the current price. In that context, *reasonable* means that the probability of reaching values beyond the limits is considered arbitrarily negligible.

Let us start with m values ranging from 0 to S_m, with $0 < S < m\Delta S$. $(n + 1) * (m + 1)$ nodes build up the grid. At each node, the derivative price is written:

$$x(i, j) = x(i\Delta t, j\Delta S)$$

Change of variable Define $y = ln(S/S_0)$. Equation (4.1) becomes:

$$\frac{\partial x}{\partial t} + \left(r - \frac{\sigma^2}{2}\right)\frac{\partial x}{\partial y} + \frac{1}{2}\frac{\partial^2 x}{\partial^2 y}\sigma^2 = rx \qquad (4.2)$$

The approximation of $\partial x/\partial t$ is straightforward:

$$\frac{\partial x}{\partial t} \simeq \frac{(x(i + 1, j) - x(i, j))}{\Delta t}$$

In fact, the discretization of $\partial x/\partial y$ can be carried out in different manners. First, in order to smoothe the **convexity** effect, i.e., the asymmetric impact of $\pm \Delta y$ on x, we state:

$$\frac{\partial x}{\partial y} = \frac{(x(., j + 1) - x(., j - 1))}{2\Delta y}$$

Moreover,

1. Either we infer $\Delta x / \Delta y$ at $t = i\Delta t$, i.e.,

$$\frac{\partial x}{\partial y} = \frac{(x(i, j+1) - x(i, j-1))}{2\Delta y}$$

This approach leads to a linear system that requires a matrix inversion

$$\begin{pmatrix} x_{n,0} \\ \vdots \\ x_{n,m} \end{pmatrix} = \mathcal{M} \begin{pmatrix} x_{0,0} \\ \vdots \\ x_{0,m} \end{pmatrix} \Rightarrow \begin{pmatrix} x_{0,0} \\ \vdots \\ x_{0,m} \end{pmatrix} = \mathcal{M}^{-1} \begin{pmatrix} x_{n,0} \\ \vdots \\ x_{n,m} \end{pmatrix}$$

or

2. We may also derive directly from backward induction, i.e.,

$$\frac{\partial x}{\partial y} = \frac{(x(i+1, j+1) - x(i+1, j-1))}{2\Delta y}$$

From equation (4.1), this form leads to an explicit relationship for $x(i,.)$, knowing $x(i+1,.)$, called **backward induction**. In contrast to the first method, called **implicit**, this one is easier to implement, though less robust.

Implicit method Substituting

$$\frac{\partial x}{\partial y} = \frac{(x(i, j+1) - x(i, j-1))}{2\Delta y}$$

$$\frac{\partial^2 x}{\partial y^2} = \frac{(x(i, j+1) + x(i, j-1) - 2x(i, j))}{2\Delta y^2}$$

into equation (4.2) leads to:

$$x(i+1, j) = a \; x(i, j-1) + b \; x(i, j) + c \; x(i, j+1)$$

with

$$a = \frac{\Delta t}{2\Delta y}(r - \sigma^2/2) - \frac{\Delta t}{2\Delta y^2}\sigma^2$$

$$b = 1 + \frac{\Delta t}{\Delta y^2}\sigma^2 + r\Delta t$$

$$c = -\frac{\Delta t}{2\Delta y}(r - \sigma^2/2) - \frac{\Delta t}{2\Delta y^2}\sigma^2$$

This equation concerns interior points of the grid (i.e., for $j > 0$ and $j < m$). The nodes at the bounds $x(i, 0)$ and $x(i, m)$ are contingent on the payoff. For European calls or puts, these values must equal the intrinsic value. As a general rule, when the range $[S_{min}, S_{max}]$ is chosen to be sufficiently wide, we may impose

$$x(i+1,0) = b * x(i,0) + c * x(i,1)$$

$$x(i+1,m) = a * x(i,m-1) + b * x(i,m)$$

In matricial notation,

$$A.X^{(i)} = X^{(i+1)}$$

$$
\begin{pmatrix}
b & c & 0 & & \cdots & \cdots & 0 \\
a & b & c & 0 & \cdots & \cdots & 0 \\
0 & a & b & c & \cdots & \cdots & 0 \\
\vdots & \vdots & \vdots & \vdots & \vdots & \vdots & \vdots \\
0 & \cdots & 0 & a & b & c & \vdots \\
0 & \cdots & \cdots & \cdots & 0 & a & b
\end{pmatrix}
\begin{pmatrix}
x(i,0) \\
x(i,1) \\
\vdots \\
x(i,j) \\
\vdots \\
x(i,m)
\end{pmatrix}
=
\begin{pmatrix}
x(i+1,0) \\
x(i+1,1) \\
\vdots \\
x(i+1,j) \\
\vdots \\
x(i+1,m)
\end{pmatrix}
$$

The array $x(n, j)$ on the expiration date is populated according to the final payoff (e.g., the intrinsic values in the case of options):

$$X^{(n-1)} = A^{-1}.X^{(n)} \Rightarrow X^{(n-2)} = A^{-1}.X^{(n-1)}$$

$$= [A^{-1}]^2.X^{(n)}$$

$$X^{(0)} = [A^{-1}]^n.X^{(n)}$$

We choose to compute $[A^{-1}]^n$ instead of inverting $[A^n]^{-1}$, which gives more robust solutions.

Code Let us first implement a plain-vanilla 6-mth at-the-money European call. For this application, we set:

$$S = K(strike) = 100, \quad \sigma = 25\%, \quad r = 3\%$$

Arbitrarily, without loss of generality, $n = m$. Given the volatility and the maturity, it looks reasonable to set:

$$S_{min} = 0.5S \quad \text{and} \quad S_{max} = 2S$$

Thus:

$$\Delta y = Ln(4)/n \quad \text{and} \quad \Delta t = 0.5/n$$

The code below uses the Gauss-Jordan algorithm to compute A^{-1}.
For $n = 100$, we obtain a price of 7.78, and 7.767 for $n = 200$: Black–Scholes analytical formula gives a price of 7.76.

```
Sub testDiffFin()

Dim t#, vol#, S#, r#, k#
t = 0.5
vol = 0.25
S = 100: k = 100
```

```
r = 0.03

Dim y!: y = 0

Dim n#: n = 200
Dim dt!: dt = t / n

Dim ymin!, ymax!

ymin = Log(0.5)
ymax = Log(2)
Dim dy!: dy = Log(4) / n

Dim a#, b#, c#
a = dt * (r - vol ^ 2 / 2) / 2 / dy - dt / 2 / dy ^ 2 * vol ^ 2
b = 1 + dt / dy ^ 2 * vol ^ 2 + r * dt
c = -dt / 2 / dy * (r - vol ^ 2 / 2) - dt / 2 / dy ^ 2 * vol ^ 2

ReDim mat#(n, n)
ReDim mat2#(n, n)
ReDim mat3#(n, n)

mat(1, 1) = b
mat(1, 2) = c

For i = 2 To n - 1
    mat(i, i - 1) = a
    mat(i, i) = b
    mat(i, i + 1) = c
Next i

mat(n, n - 1) = a
mat(n, n) = b

For i = 0 To n
    mat2(i, i) = 1
Next i

mat3 = GaussJordan(mat)
ReDim v#(n), x#(n)
For i = 0 To n
    x(i) = ymin + i * dy
    v(i) = max(S * Exp(x(i)) - k, 0)
Next i

For i = 1 To n
    v = MatMult(mat3, v)
'    v(n) = 50
Next i

v = MatMult(mat3, v)
For i = 0 To n
    Cells(i + 1, n + 4) = v(i)
Next i

End Sub
```

As a recursive algorithm, the finite difference method is perfectly suited to American-style options. In particular, this method is favored when tackling **double-barrier** issues that are hardly handled with other numerical procedures.

Let us recall that a double-barrier option is a knock-in (or knock-out option) with one barrier down <u>and</u> one barrier up.

The code below deals with the pricing of a 6-mth European call ATM (at-the-money), knocked out at 80% and 125% of the spot price. The K.O. levels are denoted n_1 and n_2 in the program.

```vba
Sub testDiffFin2Bar()

Dim t#, vol#, S#, r#, k#
t = 0.5
vol = 0.25
S = 100: k = 100
r = 0.01

Dim y!: y = 0

Dim n#: n = 200
Dim dt!: dt = t / n

Dim ymin!, ymax!

ymin = Log(0.5)
ymax = Log(2)

Dim dy!: dy = Log(4) / n

Dim Bmin!, Bmax!
Bmin = 80
Bmax = 125

Dim n1%, n2%
n1 = Int(Log(2 * Bmin / S) * n / Log(4))
n2 = Int(Log(2 * Bmax / S) * n / Log(4))

Dim a#, b#, c#
a = dt * (r - vol ^ 2 / 2) / 2 / dy - dt / 2 / dy ^ 2 * vol ^ 2
b = 1 + dt / dy ^ 2 * vol ^ 2 + r * dt
c = -dt / 2 / dy * (r - vol ^ 2 / 2) - dt / 2 / dy ^ 2 * vol ^ 2

ReDim mat#(1 To n, 1 To n)
ReDim mat2#(1 To n, 1 To n)
ReDim mat3#(1 To n, 1 To n)

mat(1, 1) = b
mat(1, 2) = c

For i = 2 To n - 1
    mat(i, i - 1) = a
    mat(i, i) = b
    mat(i, i + 1) = c
Next i
```

```
mat(n, n - 1) = a
mat(n, n) = b

For i = 1 To n
    mat2(i, i) = 1
Next i

mat3 = GaussJordan(mat)
ReDim v#(n), x#(n)
For i = n1 To n2
    x(i) = ymin + i * dy
    Cells(i, n + 5) = Exp(x(i))
    v(i) = max(S * Exp(x(i)) - k, 0)
    Cells(i, n + 2) = v(i)
Next i

For i = 1 To n
    v = MatMult(mat3, v)
```

****

Here, the values v(i) of the asset are put to 0, for i=n_1 or i=n_2.

****

```
    v(n1) = 0
    v(n2) = 0
Next i

v = MatMult(mat3, v)
For i = 1 To n
    Cells(i, n + 4) = v(i)
Next i

End Sub
```

Explicit method

$$\frac{\partial x}{\partial y} = \frac{(x(i+1, j+1) - x(i+1, j-1))}{2\Delta y}$$

$$\frac{\partial^2 x}{\partial y^2} = \frac{(x(i+1, j+1) + x(i+1, j-1) - 2x(i+1, j))}{2\Delta y^2}$$

leads to

$$x(i, j) = a^* \; x(i+1, j-1) + b^* \; x(i+1, j) + c^* \; x(i+1, j+1)$$

with

$$a^* = \frac{1}{1 + r\Delta t} \left(-\frac{\Delta t}{2\Delta y}(r - \sigma^2/2) + \frac{\Delta t}{2\Delta y^2}\sigma^2 \right)$$

$$b^* = \frac{1}{1 + r\Delta t} \left(1 - \frac{\Delta t}{\Delta y^2}\sigma^2 \right)$$

$$c^* = \frac{1}{1 + r\Delta t} \left(\frac{\Delta t}{2\Delta y}(r - \sigma^2/2) + \frac{\Delta t}{2\Delta y^2}\sigma^2 \right)$$

4.2 TREES

4.2.1 Binomial trees

Consider the instantaneous return of an asset between t and $t + dt$:

$$\frac{dS}{S} = \mu(S, t)dt + \sigma(S, t)dw$$

In its most simplified version:

$$\frac{dS}{S} = \mu dt + \sigma dw \Rightarrow S = S_0 e^{((\mu - \sigma^2/2)t + \sigma \Delta w_t)}$$

Given the stationary independent increments

$$w_t - w_0 = w_{t+u} - w_u,$$

this model highlights the mutual independence of changes:

$$Ln(S_{\Delta t}) - Ln(S_0) = Ln(S_{\Delta t}/S_0)$$
$$= Ln(S_{\Delta t + u}/S_u)$$

providing a sufficient condition to apply the central limit theorem. With a reasonably high number of time-steps, $w_t - w_0$, and consequently $LnS_t - LnS_0$, can be approximated (in law) by a sum of independent discrete variables:

$$LnS_t - LnS_0 = \sum_{i=1}^{n} [LnS_{i\Delta t} - LnS_{(i-1)\Delta t}]$$

For the sake of simplicity, we choose (as everyone does) a Bernouilli variable with two opposite outcomes: one increase x^+ and one fall x^-. Since the Gaussian distribution is fully determined by the first two moments, we can state an arbitrary relation between x^+ and x^- and find out the Bernouilli probability p and x^+ that meet these moments. For the purposes of symmetry, we assume:

$$x^+ = -x^-$$

Since w_t is normal, $Var(\sigma w_t) = \sigma^2 t$. Thus, given that $t = n.\Delta t$:

$$\sigma^2 t = \sum_{i=1}^{n} p(x^+)^2 + (1 - p)(x^-)^2 = \sum_{i=1}^{n} (x^+)^2$$
$$= n.\sigma^2 \Delta t \Rightarrow x^+ = \sigma \sqrt{\Delta t}$$

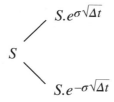

The no-arbitrage condition requires the following equation:

$$S = e^{-\mu\Delta t}.(pSe^{\sigma\sqrt{\Delta t}} + (1-p)Se^{-\sigma\sqrt{\Delta t}})$$

$$\Rightarrow p = \frac{e^{\mu\Delta t} - e^{-\sigma\sqrt{\Delta t}}}{e^{\sigma\sqrt{\Delta t}} - e^{-\sigma\sqrt{\Delta t}}}$$

Building the tree Given the maturity t of the instrument, we have to choose the time-step of the lattice, i.e., n such that $\Delta t = t/n$. At each step, the asset price is assumed to move up by a factor $u = e^{\sigma\sqrt{\Delta t}}$ or down by a factor $d = e^{-\sigma\sqrt{\Delta t}}$. Since $u.d = d.u = 1$, the number of nodes (also the number of possible asset prices) is $1 + 2 + 3 + ... + n$, the tree is said to be *recombining*:

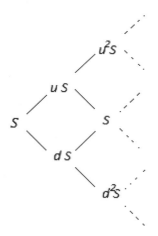

On the expiration date, asset prices are $u^n S, u^{n-1}dS, \ u^{n-2}d^2S,..., \ u^{n-i}d^iS,..., \ d^nS$, i.e.,

$$Se^{(2n-i)\sigma\sqrt{\Delta t}}$$

Algorithm From the values of a contingent claim:

$$X = f(n\Delta t, S_{n\Delta t})$$

at maturity, (the intrinsic value in the case of options), we infer the values at time $(n-1)\Delta t, (n-2)\Delta t,...$ through backward induction, until $t = 0$, using the no-arbitrage condition:

$$X(i.\Delta t, S) = e^{-\mu\Delta t} * [p.X((i+1)\Delta t, \mathbf{u}.S) + (1-p).X((i+1)\Delta t, \mathbf{d}.S)]$$

One substantial benefit of the binomial lattice is to incorporate coupon payments or additional conditions to the basic recursive formula. For instance, this feature suits quite well for pricing structured issues such as convertible bonds.

Convertible bonds   These bonds, mainly issued by corporates, are **hybrid** instruments that combine a regular revenue, commonly a fixed coupon, and the right to convert it into the issuer's shares, provided some conditions are met. The terms of a CB (popular acronym for Convertible **B**ond) are:

- the nominal, coupon, coupon periodicity and maturity, just as a regular fixed-rate bond;
- the date from which the bondholder has the right to convert the issue into a specified number of shares (**parity**);
- some additional clauses, such as:
  - **put** clause, giving the holder the right to demand early redemption at a guaranteed price.
  - **call** clause, giving the issuer the right to call the bond back at a specified price (**hard call**) or contingent on the equity market quote (**soft call**).

As a practical example of the binomial tree recursive procedure, we consider a CB at par (nominal=100) with an annual coupon. To simplify, the issue does not bear any additional clause (call or put). The arguments of the pricing function **CBprice** are:

- **tenor**, **c**, and **par** that stand for the maturity of the bond, the fixed coupon, and the parity of exchange;
- **S**, **vol**, and **r** that stand for the spot equity price, the volatility, and the riskless instantaneous rate.

```
Function CBprice(tenor As Date, c!, par!, S!, vol!, r!) As Single

ReDim CouponStd&(Int(tenor - Date) / 365 + 1)
Dim i%, j%

i = 0
While DateAdd("yyyy", -i, tenor) - Date > 0
    i = i + 1
Wend

Dim nCoup%: nCoup = i
ReDim CouponStd&(nCoup - 1)

For j = 0 To i - 1
    CouponStd(j) = tenor - DateAdd("yyyy", -j, tenor)
Next j

ReDim CouponAlgo&(i)
```

```
*****************************************************
```
The array named CouponAlgo lists the coupon payment dates (actually in rounded fractions of years).
```
*****************************************************

Dim n&: n = 500
CouponAlgo(0) = 0
Dim step!: step = (tenor - Date) / n

i = 1: j = 0
While CouponAlgo(i) < tenor - Date And i < nCoup
    j = j + 1
    If Int(j * step) >= CouponStd(i) Then
        CouponAlgo(i) = Int(j)
        If i < nCoup Then i = i + 1
    End If
Wend

ReDim cTemp&(nCoup - 1)
For i = nCoup - 1 To 0 Step -1
    cTemp(i) = n - CouponAlgo(nCoup - 1 - i)
Next i
For i = 0 To nCoup - 1
    CouponAlgo(i) = cTemp(i)
Next i

Dim t!: t = WorksheetFunction.YearFrac(Date, tenor)
ReDim CBval!(n, n)

Dim flowCoupon%

Dim u!, d!
u = Exp(vol * Sqr(t / n)): d = 1 / u

Dim p!: p = (Exp(r * t / n) - d) / (u - d)

For i = 0 To n
    CBval(n, i) = max(100 * (1 + c), par * S * u ^ (i) * d ^ (n - i))
Next i
flowCoupon = nCoup - 2
```

```
*****************************************************
```
flowCoupon is the index signaling one coupon due.
```
*****************************************************

For j = n - 1 To 0 Step -1
    If flowCoupon > -1 Then
        If j < CouponAlgo(flowCoupon) Then Coupon = 100 * c: _
        flowCoupon = flowCoupon - 1
    End If
    For i = 0 To j
        CBval(j, i) = Exp(-r * t / n) * _
        (p * CBval(j + 1, i + 1) + (1 - p) * CBval(j + 1, i)) + Coupon
        If CBval(j, i) < par * S * u ^ (i) * d ^ (j - i) Then
            CBval(j, i) = par * S * u ^ (i) * d ^ (j - i)
        End If
```

```
    Next i
    Coupon = 0
Next j

CBprice = CBval(0, 0)

End Function
```

4.2.2 Trinomial trees

The building of a trinomial tree adds a third branch at each node, thus bringing some refinement to the algorithm

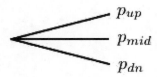

To match approximately the expectation and standard deviation, Hull (1997) suggests the following probability values:

$$p_{dn} = -\sqrt{\frac{\Delta t}{12\sigma^2}}\left(\left(r - \frac{\sigma^2}{2}\right) + 1/6\right.$$

$$p_{mid} = 2/3$$

$$p_{up} = \sqrt{\frac{\Delta t}{12\sigma^2}}\left(\left(r - \frac{\sigma^2}{2}\right) + 1/6\right.$$

$$u = e^{\sigma\sqrt{3\Delta t}}$$

$$d = 1/u$$

4.3 MONTE-CARLO SCENARIOS

Suppose n occurences $Z_1, Z_2,...,Z_n$ from a random sampling of a variable Z, assuming the samplings are independent. Let us count variates that fall in the interval $[a, a + \Delta a]$ and denote their number by $N(a, a + \Delta a)$. For a sufficiently large number of trials n, $N(a, a + \Delta a)/n$ is an unbiased estimator of $Prob(a < Z < a + \Delta a)$, i.e., the value obtained from the theoretical distribution of Z.

Let us consider $[a, b]$, a domain of possible inputs for Z, and divide this range into m intervals of equal lengths $(b - a)/m$:

$$[a + j(b - a)/m, a + (j + 1)(b - a)/m], \quad j = 0, 1,...,m - 1$$

After sorting the set of Z_i in ascending (or descending) order, we store variates according to the range to which they belong.

Let us denote by N_j the amount of variates falling in $\Delta_j = [a + j(b-a)/m, a + (j+1)(b-a)/m]$, where f is a Z-dependent function, and M_j and m_j the max and the min attained by $f(Z)$ in each interval:

$$\sum_{j=1}^{m-1} N_j.min(f(Z_i)) < \sum_{i=1}^{n} f(Z_i) < \sum_{j=1}^{m-1} N_j.Max(f(Z_i))$$

Provided that f is continuous in the closed set $[a, b]$,

$$Max(f(Z_i)) - min(f(Z_i)) \xrightarrow[m \to \infty]{} 0$$

the distance $M_j - m_j$ shrinks when m increases so that M_j (resp m_j) gets closer and closer to the mean value $\bar{f}_j$ of f in Δ_j. As a result:

$$\frac{1}{n}\sum_{i=1}^{n} f(Z_i) \to \sum_{j=1}^{m-1} \frac{N_j}{n}\bar{f}_j \approx \sum_{j=1}^{m-1} P(Z \in \Delta_j)\bar{f}_j \approx E(f)$$

We can then approach the fair value of an asset (no-arbitrage principle), i.e.,

$$\int_a^b e^{-rt}f(S(Z_t))dP(Z_t)$$

by

$$e^{-rt}\frac{1}{n}\sum_{i=1}^{n} f(Z_i(t))$$

for r constant.

A Monte-Carlo method to approximate an asset value $S(Z_t)$ consists in n trials of Z_t and the calculation of the average of outcomes $S(Z_i)$. To achieve this, we need to generate computationally random variates satisfying some chosen distribution. This delicate issue boils down to generating uniform variates between 0 and 1, and finding the inverse of a function. In fact, given a uniform variable U, if, for any outcome u, we compute $x = F^{-1}(u)$ where F is the cumulative distribution of Z:

$$P(x < a) = P(F^{-1}(u) < a) = P(u < F(a)) = F(a)$$

4.3.1 Uniform number generator

The easiest way to start a Monte-Carlo algorithm is to use the VBA generator of uniform variates

Rnd()

Like most system generators, Rnd()is not reliable if accuracy is your number 1 concern. On the other hand, its use allows quick albeit rough approximations. Actually, this VBA native function will be frequently invoked in this book for this very reason.

Quite a lot of generators have been developed over the past 50 years. As a matter of fact, since the samples of a random number generator are produced through algorithms, they may be considered at best as **pseudo**-random. In this section, we present just a few of them, probably those which are easiest to implement: It is beyond the scope of this book to give an exhaustive presentation of the state-of-the-art in that matter.

A second failure is the lack of homogeneity when the generator fills the interval $[0, 1]$ unevenly. It means that you need a lot of samples to obtain a typical set of uniform variates. As a consequence, quants often favour homogeneity over randomness and store series of data that will be used as a whole in the payoff calculations.

Congruential method   The sequence is defined recursively, through a simple linear congruence:

$$U_n = a * U_{n-1} \bmod m$$

Such generators, needing reduced memory, have the bad reputation of being self-correlated. However, a good choice, according to Jackel (2002), is:

$$U_0 = 1, \quad a = 5^{17}, \quad m = 2^{40}$$

A difficulty arises when applying the **Mod** VBA function that does not perform correctly for long integers higher than 2^{32}.

For instance, to generate 1000 variates $v(i)$, i=1,..,1000, we use a circuitous computation:

$$a * U_{n-1} \bmod m = U_{n-1} * a - Int(U_{n-1} * a/m) * m$$

```
ReDim u#(1000), v#(1000)
u(0) = 1
dim i%
For i = 1 To 1000
    u(i) = u(i - 1) * 5^17 - Int(u(i - 1) * 5^17 / 2 ^ 40) * 2 ^ 40
    v(i) = u(i) / 2 ^ 40
Next i
```

KISS generator   To enhance the congruential method and produce higher sequence periods, (L'Ecuyer, 1994) and Marsaglia (Marsaglia, 1984), developed an algorithm combining congruences and *bit-shifting*. There are no VBA functions equivalent to C left shift $a < < n$ and right shift $a > > n$. The same results can be obtained with power operators:

$$a < < n \ = a * 2^n \quad a > > n = Int(a/2^n)$$

Many versions of KISS generators have been proposed. The following is one that can be implemented in a 32-bit engine.

The mathematical symbol for **Xor** is $\oplus$

$$1 \oplus 1 = 0 \quad 0 \oplus 1 = 1 \quad 0 \oplus 0$$

```
y = y Xor y * 2 ^ 5: y = y Xor y / 2 ^ 7: y = y Xor y * 2 ^ 22

    t = z + w + c
    z = w
```

```
c = t < 0
w = t And 2147483647: x = x + 1411392427
random_number = x + y + w
```

The arithmetic above is carried out modulo 2^{32}, e.g.,

$$a < \; < n = a * 2^n - Int(a * 2^n / 2^{32}) * 2^{32}$$

Some arguments may exceed 2^{32}, which makes VBA bitwise operators such as *And* or *Xor* inadequate.

First, noticing that $2147483647 = 2^{31} - 1$ or $\underbrace{(111....111)}_{31 \; times}$

$$t \; And \; 2147483647$$

is equivalent to

$$t \; \& \; 2147483647$$

then

$$w = t - Int(t/2\textasciicircum 31).2\textasciicircum 31 \; And \; 2147483647$$

Secondly, a function xor_VBA has been developed to replace the failing Xor function. The idea is to split the arguments into 16 bit integers and apply Xor to the segments obtained:

```
Public Function xor_VBA(x#, y#) As Double

Dim z#: z = max(x, y)
xor_VBA = 0

If max(x, y) < 2 ^ 32 Then
    xor_VBA = x Xor y

Else
    alpha = Int(Log(z) / 15 / Log(2))

ReDim ux#(alpha + 1)
ReDim uy#(alpha + 1)

For i = 1 To alpha + 1
    ux(i) = Int(x / 2 ^ (15 * (i - 1))) - Int(x / 2 ^ (15 * i))
* 2 ^ 15 + 2 ^ 15
    uy(i) = Int(y / 2 ^ (15 * (i - 1))) - Int(y / 2 ^ (15 * i))
* 2 ^ 15 + 2 ^ 15

    xor_VBA = xor_VBA + (ux(i) Xor uy(i)) * 2 ^ ((i - 1) * 15)
Next i

End If

If x = 0 Or y = 0 Then
    xor_VBA = max(x, y)
End If

End Function
```

x, y, z, c, and w are seed values in the interval $[1, 2^{32} - 1]$.

```
Dim y#: y = 234567891
Dim z#: z = 345678912
Dim c#: c = 0
Dim x#: x = 123456789
Dim w#: w = 456789123

Dim ran#(10000)

For j = 1 To 10000

    y = xor_VBA(y, (y * 2 ^ 5 - Int(y * 2 ^ 5 / 2 ^ 32) * 2 ^ 32))
    y = xor_VBA(y, Int(y / 2 ^ 7))
    y = xor_VBA(y, (y * 2 ^ 22 - Int(y * 2 ^ 22 / 2 ^ 32) * 2 ^ 32))

    t = z + w + c - Int((z + w + c) / 2 ^ 32) * 2 ^ 32
    z = w
    c = t < 0

    w = (t - Int(t / 2 ^ 31) * 2 ^ 31) And 2147483647

    x = x + 1411392427 - Int((x + 1411392427) / 2 ^ 32) * 2 ^ 32

    ran(j) = (x + y + w - Int((x + y + w) / 2 ^ 32) * 2 ^ 32) / 2 ^ 32

Next j
```

Law discrepancy numbers: the Van der Corput method   Sequences of law discrepancy numbers are built so as to fill evenly a range of values. These series are called **quasi-random**. As congruences, they mimic randomness but methodically target the gaps to be filled.

The idea of Van der Corput is to reverse the representation of a rising sequence of natural numbers in order to obtain values in the unit interval: the numbers obtained form a dense set in [0,1]. For instance, in base 2

$$13_{10} = 1101_2$$

$$1101 \circlearrowleft 1011$$

$$1101 \rightarrow 0.1011_2 = 1.2^{-1} + 0.2^{-2} + 1.2^{-3} + 1.2^{-4} = 0.6875_{10}$$

For some integer k, in base 2,

$$k = b_j(k)2^j + b_{j-1}(k)2^{j-1} + ... + b_0(k)$$

the Van der Corput transformation gives

$$\phi(k) = b_0(k)2^{-1} + b_1(k)2^{-2} + ... + b_j(k)2^{-(j+1)}$$

In base 2, it is easy to verify that $\phi(k)$ and $\phi(k + 1)$ are alternatively superior and inferior to $\frac{1}{2}$ and, when $k \rightarrow \infty$, $\phi(k)$ fill the interval [0, 1).

The code listed below generates 5000 variates in **base 3**: the algorithm proceeds by:

1. representing 1,2,3,...,5000 in base 3
2. reversing the order of the powers and changing their signs.

```
Dim base%: base = 3
Dim VDC!(5000)

For m = 1 To 5000

    x = m
    n = 0: j = 0
    While x <> 0
        i = 0
        While base ^ (i) <= x
            i = i + 1
        Wend

        If n = 0 Then n = i - 1: ReDim a%(n)
        a(n - j) = Int(x / base ^ (n - j))
        x = x - a(n - j) * base ^ (n - j): j = j + 1

    Wend
    i = 1
    y = 0
    For K = 0 To n
        y = y + a(K) * base ^ (-i)
        i = i + 1
    Next K

    VDC(m) = y
Next m
```

Sobol numbers This method, based on low-cost computing bitwise recursive operations such as $\oplus$, generates n-dimensional law discrepancy sequences. Today, this method is very popular to fix valuations of multi-asset instruments or yield curve derivatives that need to generate n vectors of independent uniformly distributed coordinates. Let us denote d as the dimension of each generated vector: practically, we intend to fill randomly the unit hypercube

$$[0, 1]^d$$

Basically, the Sobol algorithm extends the Van der Corput method in base 2, to several dimensions.

Recall, from above, that the Van der Corput transformation of any integer k is written:

$$\phi(k) = b_0(k)2^{-1} + b_1(k)2^{-2} + \dots + b_j(k)2^{-(j+1)}$$

given the binary expansion $(b_j(k))$ of k. Put matricially, this yields:

$$\phi(k) = \sum_{i=0}^{j} v_i(k), \quad \text{with}$$

$$\mathbf{v} = \begin{pmatrix} 2^{-(j+1)} & 0 & \cdots & 0 & 0 \\ 0 & 2^{-j} & \cdots & 0 & 0 \\ \vdots & \vdots & \vdots & \vdots \\ 0 & 0 & \cdots & 2^{-2} & 0 \\ 0 & 0 & \cdots & 0 & 2^{-1} \end{pmatrix} \begin{pmatrix} b_j(k) \\ b_{j-1}(k) \\ \vdots \\ b_1(k) \\ b_0(k) \end{pmatrix}$$

or

$$\left(2^{-(j+1)}, 2^{-j}, \cdots, 2^{-1}\right).I. \begin{pmatrix} b_j(k) \\ b_{j-1}(k) \\ \vdots \\ b_1(k) \\ b_0(k) \end{pmatrix} \tag{4.3}$$

The idea is to generate d sequences (x_k^l), $l = 1,...,d$, using a different matrix V^l for each sequence, i.e., changing I for V^l, and perform (4.3) **mod 2** so that

$$x_k^l = \left(2^{-(j+1)}, 2^{-j}, \cdots, 2^{-1}\right).V^l. \begin{pmatrix} b_j(k) \\ b_{j-1}(k) \\ \vdots \\ b_1(k) \\ b_0(k) \end{pmatrix}$$

Denoting by $v_j^l = \left(2^{-(j+1)}, 2^{-j}, \cdots, 2^{-1}\right).V^l(b_j)$, we can put it more concisely:

$$x_k^l = v_1^l b_0(k) \oplus v_2^l b_1(k) \oplus ... \oplus v_j^l b_{j-1}(k) \tag{4.4}$$

The size of the square matrix $V_l(n, n)$ obviously depends on the cardinal N of the set of samples:

$$n = Int\left(\frac{Ln(N)}{Ln(2)}\right) + 1$$

To build V_l so that every sequence x_k^l meets the low discrepancy and mutual independence criteria, Sobol introduced a recursive algorithm based on some odd integer whose binary expansion provides the coefficients of a **primitive polynomial**: by *primitive*, we mean that the order of the polynomial, given its degree n_k, must be $2^{n_k} - 1$. By definition, the order of a polynomial is the smallest positive integer q for which $P(x)$ divides $x^q - 1$.

For instance:

$$1 + x + x^2 \text{ is primitive.}$$

By contrast, $1 + x + x^2 + x^3$ is not primitive, since

$$(x^3 + x^2 + x + 1).(x + 1) = x^4 + 2x^3 + 2x^2 + 2x + 1 \equiv x^4 + 1 \quad \text{mod} \quad 2$$

To detail the method, let us focus on one coordinate and denote by n the degree of the polynomial:

$$P(x) = x^n + c_1 x^{n-1} + ... + c_{n-1} x + 1 \quad (c_i = 0 \text{ or } 1)$$

From the coefficients c_i, we derive a recurrence relation that will provide the elements of each column of V:

$$m_j = \frac{1}{2^j}\left(2c_1 m_{j-1} \oplus 2^2 c_2 m_{j-2} \oplus \dots \oplus 2^{n-1} c_{n-1} m_{j-n+1} \oplus 2^n m_{j-n} \oplus m_{j-n}\right)$$

For instance, to generate 100 uniform variates, V must count $Int[Ln(100)/Ln(2)] + 1] = 7$ columns, i.e., 7 values $m_1, m_2, \dots, m_7$ need to be calculated. If we assume the primitive polynomial to be of degree 4, then 4 values $m_1, \dots, m_4$ are to be chosen arbitrarily to initiate the sequence m_j: these initial values must in any case be <u>odd and inferior to 2^j</u>.

Once the m_j are known, their binary fraction representation is to populate the j-th column of V. As an illustration, let us state:

$$P(x) = x^3 + x + 1$$

$$m_1 = 1 \quad m_2 = 1 \quad m_3 = 3$$

then

$$m_4 = \frac{1}{2^4}(2 * 0 * m_3 \oplus 2^2 * 1 * m_2 \oplus 2^3 * m_1 \oplus m_1)$$

$$= \frac{1}{2^4}(4 \oplus 8 \oplus 1) = \frac{1}{2^4} * \begin{matrix}1\\0\\0\\1\end{matrix} = 0.1101$$

The 4-th column of the $7 * 7$ matrix V is then written as:

$$v_{.,4} = \begin{pmatrix}1\\0\\1\\1\\0\\0\\0\end{pmatrix}$$

To recap, given (b_k) the binary representation of k,

$$x_k = (2^{-1}, 2^{-2}, \dots, 2^{-7}).V.(b_k)$$

The power of V to generate uniformly distributed variates x_k results from the specific primitive polynomial's properties in the finite field (Galois field) where operations are carried out modulo 2. A comprehensive presentation of these fields can be found in Lidl and Niederreiter (1996).

The recurrence greatly simplifies if the binary representation of k is replaced by its **Gray code** representation $g(k)$(see Antonov and Saleev (1979)) By definition

$$g(k) = k \oplus Int(k/2)$$

This transformation is obtained simply by adding (in the sense of $\oplus$) k with its right-shifted representation. For instance, the Gray code of 101 is

$$101 \oplus 010 = 111$$

It is easy to verify (just write the polynomial representation of k) that this transformation is unique, and therefore operates a permutation in the sequence

$$k_1 \neq k_2 \Rightarrow g(k_1) \neq g(k_2)$$

Since the representations of k and $k + 1$ differ in only one bit, let's say the l-th one, we can rewrite equation (4.4) as follows:

$$x_k = v_1 g_0(k) \oplus v_2 g_1(k) \oplus ... \oplus v_j g_{j-1}(k)$$

$$\Rightarrow x_{k+1} = v_1 g_0(k) \oplus v_2 g_1(k) \oplus ... \oplus v_l(g_{l-1}(k) \oplus 1) \oplus ... \oplus v_j g_{j-1}(k)$$

$$= x_k \oplus v_l$$

The l-th bit that makes the difference can easily be calculated:

$$l = \frac{Ln(g(k + 1) - g(k))}{Ln(2)}$$

To generate n values of a d-dimension vector, the function Sobol retrieves the following parameters from Excel sheet "SobolParam":

- Col A $\rightarrow$ d=vecteur dimension
- Col B $\rightarrow$ s=order of the primitive polynomial
- Col C $\rightarrow$ a=an integer figuring the coordinates of the polynomial $P(x)$
- Col D $\rightarrow$ m_i=a list of arbitrary direction numbers that determine the recurrence relation.

Precisely, the polynomial coefficients are given by the binary representation of

$$2^s + 2a + 1$$

For instance, given $d = 10$, and $s = 5$,

$$a = 7 \rightarrow 2^5 + 2.7 + 1 = 100000_2 + \underbrace{1110_2}_{2a} + 1 = 101111_2$$

Then

$$P(x) = 1.x^5 + 0.x^4 + 1.x^3 + 1.x^2 + 1.x + 1$$

Data regarding primitive polynomials and direction numbers listed above, as well as the algorithm from which the following VBA code derives, come from the web site (Joe and Kuo). For more details on this algorithm and more, see Joe and Kuo (2003), (2008).

d	s	a	m_i						
2	1	0	1						
3	2	1	1	3					
4	3	1	1	3	1				
5	3	2	1	1	1				
6	4	1	1	1	3	3			
7	4	4	1	3	5	13			
8	5	2	1	1	5	5	17		
9	5	4	1	1	5	5	5		
10	5	7	1	1	7	11	19		
11	5	11	1	1	5	1	1		
12	5	13	1	1	1	3	11		
13	5	14	1	3	5	5	31		
14	6	1	1	3	3	9	7	49	
15	6	13	1	1	1	15	21	21	
16	6	16	1	1	1	13	27	49	
17	6	19	1	1	1	15	7	5	
18	6	22	1	1	1	15	13	25	
19	6	25	1	5	5	5	19	61	
20	7	1	1	7	7	11	23	15	103
21	7	4	1	7	7	13	13	15	69
22	7	7	1	3	3	13	7	35	63
23	7	8	1	5	5	9	1	25	53
24	7	14	1	1	1	13	9	35	107
25	7	19	1	1	1	5	27	61	31
26	7	21	1	5	5	11	19	41	61
27	7	28	1	5	5	3	3	13	69
28	7	31	1	7	7	13	1	19	1
29	7	32	1	7	7	5	13	19	59
30	7	37	1	3	3	9	25	29	41
31	7	41	1	5	5	13	23	1	55
32	7	42	1	7	7	3	13	59	17
33	7	50	1	1	1	3	5	53	69
34	7	55	1	5	5	5	23	33	13
35	7	56	1	7	7	7	1	61	123
36	7	59	1	7	7	9	13	61	49
37	7	62	1	3	3	5	3	55	33

```
Public Function Sobol(n As Long, d%) As Double()

ReDim valRand#(n, d), unif#(n, d)

Dim s%, a%, m%(), i As Long
Dim p%: p = Int(Log(n) / Log(2))
ReDim v#(p + 1)

For i = 1 To p
    v(i) = 2 ^ (32 - i)
Next i

valRand(0, 0) = 0: unif(0, 0) = 0
```

```vba
For i = 1 To n
    valRand(i, 0) = xor_VBA(valRand(i - 1, 0), v(GrayC(i - 1)))
    unif(i, 0) = valRand(i, 0) / 2 ^ 32
Next i

Sheets("SobolParam").Activate

For l = 1 To d - 1

    s = Cells(2 + l, 2): a = Cells(2 + l, 3)

    ReDim m(s)
    For j = 1 To s
        m(j) = Cells(2 + l, 3 + j)
    Next j

    For i = 1 To s
        v(i) = m(i) * 2 ^ (32 - i)
    Next i

    Dim z#
    For i = s + 1 To p
        z = v(i - s)
        For j = 1 To s
            z = Int(z / 2)
        Next j
        v(i) = xor_VBA(v(i - s), z)
        For K = 1 To s - 1
            z = a
            For j = 1 To s - 1 - K
                z = Int(z / 2)
            Next j
            v(i) = xor_VBA(v(i), (z Mod 2) * v(i - K))
        Next K
    Next i

    valRand(0, l) = 0: unif(0, l) = 0

    For i = 1 To n
        valRand(i, l) = xor_VBA(valRand(i - 1, l), v(GrayC(i - 1)))
        unif(i, l) = valRand(i, l) / 2 ^ 32
    Next i

Next l
Sobol = unif

End Function

Public Function GrayC(ByVal n#) As Integer

Select Case (n Mod 2)
    Case 0
        GrayC = 1
    Case 1
        Dim nBin%(): nBin = decbin(n)
        ReDim Preserve nBin(UBound(nBin) + 1)
```

```
        nBin(UBound(nBin)) = 0
        i = 0
        While nBin(i) <> 0
            i = i + 1
        Wend
        GrayC = i + 1
```

End Select

End Function

4.3.2 From uniform to Gaussian numbers

Recalling that, if u is a uniform variate, $x = F^{-1}(u)$ is Gaussian with

$$F(a) = P(x < a) = \frac{1}{2\pi} e^{-a^2/2}$$

Using VBA function *NormSInv(u)* is the most straightforward way to draw a Gaussian sequence from a uniform one, but rather computationally expensive. Instead, the rather fast algorithm devised by Acklam (2003) divides the computation time roughly by 5. The related code is given below:

```
Public Function Acklam(p#) As Double

Dim a#(6), b#(5), c#(6), d#(4)

a(1) = -39.6968302866538
a(2) = 220.946098424521
a(3) = -275.928510446969
a(4) = 138.357751867269
a(5) = -30.6647980661472
a(6) = 2.50662827745924

b(1) = -54.4760987982241
b(2) = 161.585836858041
b(3) = -155.698979859887
b(4) = 66.8013118877197
b(5) = -13.2806815528857

c(1) = -7.78489400243029E-03
c(2) = -0.322396458041136
c(3) = -2.40075827716184
c(4) = -2.54973253934373
c(5) = 4.37466414146497
c(6) = 2.93816398269878

d(1) = 7.78469570904146E-03
d(2) = 0.32246712907004
d(3) = 2.445134137143
d(4) = 3.75440866190742

    p_low = 0.02425
    p_high = 1 - p_low
```

```
If p < p_low Then
  q = Sqr(-2 * Log(p))
  Acklam = (((((c(1) * q + c(2)) * q + c(3)) * q + c(4))
* q + c(5)) * q + c(6)) / _
         ((((d(1) * q + d(2)) * q + d(3)) * q + d(4)) * q + 1)
  End If

If p_low <= p And p <= p_high Then
  q = p - 0.5
  r = q * q
  Acklam = (((((a(1) * r + a(2)) * r + a(3)) * r + a(4))
* r + a(5)) * r + a(6)) * q / _
         (((((b(1) * r + b(2)) * r + b(3)) * r + b(4)) * r + b(5)) * r + 1)
  End If

If p_high < p Then
  q = Sqr(-2 * Log(1 - p))
  Acklam = -(((((c(1) * q + c(2)) * q + c(3)) * q + c(4))
* q + c(5)) * q + c(6)) / _
         ((((d(1) * q + d(2)) * q + d(3)) * q + d(4)) * q + 1)
  End If

  End Function
```

Box-Müller method　Let us denote $x(u, v)$ and $y(u, v)$, both functions of two independent uniform variables u and v in the unit interval. Since the density function of u (resp. v) is equal to 1, the joint distribution of x and y is given by the **Jacobian**:

$$f(x, y) = \left| \frac{\partial(u, v)}{\partial(x, y)} \right| . 1 = \frac{\partial u}{\partial x} \frac{\partial v}{\partial y} - \frac{\partial u}{\partial y} \frac{\partial v}{\partial x}$$

It is easy to verify that, given

$$x = \sqrt{-2Ln(u)} * sin(2\pi v) \quad \text{and} \quad y = \sqrt{-2Ln(u)} * cos(2\pi v)$$

$$u = e^{-(x^2+y^2)/2} \quad \text{and} \quad v = \frac{1}{2\pi} Arctg(x/y)$$

$$f(x, y) = \frac{1}{\sqrt{2\pi}} e^{-x^2/2} . \frac{1}{\sqrt{2\pi}} e^{-y^2/2}$$

Thus, u and v generate two independent Gaussian variates: this method is called the **Box-Müller** method, named after George Box and Melvin Müller. Coupling Van der Corput sequences can then produce Gaussian series. This is precisely what **Halton sequences** are dealing with, pairing up uniform numbers issued from Van der Corput sequences using **prime numbers** as bases. As a consequence, Gaussian sequences can be obtained:

- from pseudo-random series with changing seed values, or
- law discrepancy sequences using two or more bases.

As an example, we show below a procedure valuing a European call option using a Halton sequence of 5000 pairs built up from prime number **bases 3 and 5**.

Having noticed some correlation bias on the first elements of the sequence, the first 20 entries have been deliberately dropped:

```
Const PI=3.14159
Sub Halton()

Dim base%(2), Halt!(5000, 1 To 2)
base(1) = 3: base(2) = 5

Dim y#
For m = 20 To 5019

    For l = 1 To 2
        x = m
        n = 0: j = 0
        While x <> 0
            i = 0
            While base(l) ^ (i) <= x
                i = i + 1
            Wend

            If n = 0 Then n = i - 1: ReDim a%(n)
            a(n - j) = Int(x / base(l) ^ (n - j))
            x = x - a(n - j) * base(l) ^ (n - j): j = j + 1

        Wend
        i = 1
        y = 0
        For K = 0 To n
            y = y + a(K) * base(l) ^ (-i)
            i = i + 1
        Next K

        halt(m - 19, l) = y
    Next l
Next m

r = 0
vol = 0.3
t = 1
po = 0

For i = 1 To 5000
    b = Sqr(-2 * Log(halt(i, 1))) * Cos(2* PI * halt(i, 2))
    po = po + max(100 * Exp((r - vol ^ 2 / 2) * t + vol * Sqr(t)*b) - 100, 0)
Next i

Debug.Print po / 5000
End Sub
```

4.4 SIMULATION AND REGRESSION

As previously emphasized, Monte-Carlo techniques are optimal to evaluate path-dependent or multi-asset instruments since any asset price can be known at every reset date, for a given scenario. When the instrument is callable, i.e., can be terminated before the final term, bi(tri)nomial trees or finite differences techniques are then commonly addressed. Recall that the decision to terminate a callable instrument before expiration at time t depends on the maximum between the intrinsic value at t and the payoff expected from continuation. In the binomial-tree approach, the calculation is straightforward:

$$\mathbf{E}(S_{i+1}|S_{i,j}) = pS_{i+1,j+1} + (1-p)S_{i+1,j} \tag{4.5}$$

The resulting value of the instrument at node (i, j) is given by

$$Z(i, j) = e^{-r\Delta t}Max(\text{Intrinsic Value}(S_{i,j}, t_i), \mathbf{E}(S_{i+1}|S_{i,j}))$$

In this section, we show how simulations can also be used to price American-style options and, more generally, instruments with early termination provisions.

Basically, the idea is to use the backward induction method on a set of *simulated* values, instead of *fixed* values preset at each node of a grid (finite differences) or a tree. For this purpose, we start by generating N scenarios of an asset price at time $t_1, t_2, ..., t_p$ and store them into an array $S(i, j)i = 1, ..., N$, and $j = 1, ..., p$.

Knowing the payoffs *realized ex post* (i.e., at time t_j, $j = i + 1, ..., p$) for a given $S_{i,j}$, we try to find out an analytical expression of $\mathbf{E}(S_{i+1}|S_i)$ (the *early termination boundary*). This relationship is obtained by regressing these payoffs on functions aimed at fitting $\mathbf{E}(S_{i+1}|S_i)$.

Practically, given an i-th scenario and p calculation dates t_j, we set

$$S(i, j) : \text{spot price of the asset at} \quad t_j$$

$$V(i, j) : \text{intrinsic values at} \quad t_j$$

$$Z(i, j) : \text{the early exercise payoff}$$

$Z(i, j) = V(i, j)$ when the exercise becomes effective.

We start from the expiry date t_p and compute $Z(i, p) = V(i, p)$ for all i, since there is no continuation possible after t_p. Then, we proceed backward, from t_{p-1} to t_1. At each step (i.e., on t_j), and for all i:

1. Populate an array $X(k)$ of asset prices when $V(k, j) > 0$: $X(k) = S_{k,j}$, $k = 1, ..., n_k \le n$.
2. Regress these data with the array $Y(k)$ filled with $Z(k, j+1)$, i.e., the payoff expected from continuation, discounted by $e^{-r\Delta t}$. The regression function f is currently a combination of monomials or Legendre polynomials:

$$y(t_k) = f(e^{-r\Delta t}x(t_k)) = e^{-r\Delta t}\mathbf{E}(Z(k+1, j)|Z(k, j))$$

3. Set $Z(k, j) = Max(V(k, j), f(X(k)))$.

When an early termination option falls out, the payoffs once computed from backward induction are put to zero. For a given scenario, the algorithm must register the most recent exercise date (if any) and *erase the later ones*. This is done via an array U where $U(i, j) = 1$ if an exercise came about at t_j of the i-th scenario: otherwise $U(i, k) = 0$ for $k \ne j$. As an example, let us price an American 2-yr at-the-money put. We adopt a subdivision of four semi-annual calculation dates. Both spot and strike prices are set equal to 100.

The price of the option is obtained by computing the mean present value of the flows, i.e.:

$$\frac{0.956 * 29.2 + 0.942 * 36.3 + 0.9852 * 26.4 + ...}{12} = 14.41$$

Below (in Figures 4.1 to 4.4), in-the-money asset prices at any intermediate step $(1...p-1)$ are framed. In-the-money prices on the expiration date (final step p) are bolded: the corresponding intrinsic values will be discounted to serve as payoffs expected from continuation and be regressed with asset prices when an early exercise is conceivable.

$S(i,0)$	$S(i,1)$	$S(i,2)$	$S(i,3)$	$S(i,4)$
100	91.9	100.6	70.8	70.5
100	105	101.6	120.2	120.1
100	110.1	111.2	85.3	63.7
100	73.6	101.6	108.8	126.6
100	140.1	124.1	127	114.7
100	83.2	97.1	114	99
100	109.8	106.1	56.1	56
100	103.8	139.9	201.4	223.6
100	102.3	98.7	95.9	124.3
100	103.1	75.8	81.2	86
100	77.4	67.8	54.4	67.8
100	105.7	110.7	111.4	121.7

FIGURE 4.1   Scenarios

$S(i,0)$	$S(i,1)$	$S(i,2)$	$S(i,3)$	$S(i,4)$	$Z(i,4)$
100	91.9	100.6	70.8	**70.5**	29.5
100	105	101.6	120.2	120.1	0
100	110.1	111.2	85.3	**63.7**	36.3
100	73.6	101.6	108.8	126.6	0
100	140.1	124.1	127	114.7	0
100	83.2	97.1	114	**99**	1
100	109.8	106.1	56.1	**56**	44
100	103.8	139.9	201.4	223.6	0
100	102.3	98.7	95.9	124.3	0
100	103.1	75.8	81.2	**86**	14
100	77.4	67.8	54.4	**67.8**	32.2
100	105.7	110.7	111.4	121.7	0

X	Y	f	$f(X)$	Exercise
70.8	29.5 * 0.9852 = 29.06		26.67	Yes
85.3	36.3 * 0.9852 = 35.76		21.04	No
56.1	44 * 0.9852 = 43.35		34.77	Yes
95.9	0 * 0.9852 = 0	$-0.00184x^3 + 0.396x^2 - 28.481x + 711.13$	-1.09	Yes
81.2	14 * 0.9852 = 13.79		24.36	No
54.4	32.2 * 0.9852 = 31.72		37.45	Yes

FIGURE 4.2   (p-1)-th step

	$S(i,0)$	$S(i,1)$	$S(i,2)$	$Z(i,3)$	$Z(i,4)$	
	100	91.9	100.6	29.2	0	
	100	105	101.6	0	0	
	100	110.1	111.2	0(35.76)	36.3	
	100	73.6	101.6	0	0	
	100	140.1	124.1	0	0	
	100	83.2	97.1	0(0.985)	1	
	100	109.8	106.1	43.9	0	
	100	103.8	139.9	0	0	
	100	102.3	98.7	4.1	0	
	100	103.1	75.8	0(13.79)	14	
	100	77.4	67.8	45.6	0	
	100	105.7	110.7	0	0	

X	Y	f	$f(X)$	Exercise
97.1	0.9852 * 0.9852 = 0.971		−0.847	Yes
98.7	4.1 * 0.9852 = 4.04	$0.113x^2 - 20.17x^2 + 892.25$	2.28	No
75.8	13.79 * 0.9852 = 13.59		12.62	Yes
67.8	45.6 * 0.9852 = 44.93		44.17	No

FIGURE 4.3 (p-2)-th step

	$S(i,0)$	$S(i,1)$	$Z(i,2)$	$Z(i,3)$	$Z(i,4)$
	100	91.9	0(28.77)	29.2	0
	100	105	0	0	0
	100	110.1	0(35.23)	0(35.76)	36.3
	100	73.6	0	0	0
	100	140.1	0	0	0
	100	83.2	2.9	0	0
	100	109.8	0(43.25)	43.9	0
	100	103.8	0	0	0
	100	102.3	0(4.04)	4.1	0
	100	103.1	14.2	0	0
	100	77.4	0(44.93)	45.6	0
	100	105.7	0	0	0

X	Y	f	$f(X)$	Exercise
91.9	0.9852 * 28.77 = 28.34		24.3	No
73.6	0 * 0.9852 = 0	$-0.0225x^2 + 4.34x^2 - 184.51$	13.03	Yes
83.2	2.9 * 0.9852 = 2.86		20.83	No
77.4	44.93 * 0.9852 = 44.27		16.61	Yes

FIGURE 4.4 (p-3)-th step

$S(i,0)$	$Z(i,1)$	$Z(i,2)$	$Z(i,3)$	$Z(i,4)$
100	0	0	29.2	0
100	0	0	0	0
100	0	0	0	36.3
100	26.4	0	0	0
100	0	0	0	0
100	0	2.9	0	0
100	0	0	43.9	0
100	0	0	0	0
100	0	0	4.1	0
100	0	14.2	0	0
100	22.6	0	0	0
100	0	0	0	0

Code The pricing of an at-the-money 1-yr American put on a non-coupon-bearing asset is listed below. The spot and the strike prices are set equal to 100. We choose a time-step of $\Delta t = t/50$ and 50 000 paths.

```
Sub LSM() 'put

Dim r#: r = 0.04
Dim vol#: vol = 0.3
Dim t#: t = 1
Dim spot#: spot = 100

Dim n As Long, p#
n = 50000: p = 50

ReDim fx#(n, p), s#(n, p), ef%(n, p)

Dim x#(), y#(), reg#()
ReDim x#(n), y#(n)

For i = 1 To n
    s(i, 0) = spot
    For j = 1 To p
        s(i, j) = s(i, j - 1) * Exp((r - vol ^ 2 / 2) * t / p + gauss()
* Sqr(t / p) * vol)
    Next j
Next i

    For i = 1 To n
        If s(i, p) < spot Then fx(i, p) = spot - s(i, p): ef(i, p) = 1
Else fx(i, p) = 0
    Next i

For l = p - 1 To 1 Step -1

    c = 1
```

```
    For i = 1 To n
        If s(i, 1) < spot Then x(c) = s(i, 1): y(c) = fx(i, 1 + 1)
* Exp(-r * t / p): ef(i, 1) = 1: c = c + 1
    Next i
    ReDim Preserve x(c - 1)
    ReDim Preserve y(c - 1)

    reg = regression(x, y, 3)
    a1 = reg(1): a2 = reg(2): a3 = reg(3): a4 = reg(4)

    For i = 1 To n
        fx(i, 1) = fx(i, 1 + 1) * Exp(-r * t / p)
        If ef(i, 1) = 1 Then
            If a1 * s(i, 1) ^ 3 + a2 * s(i, 1) ^ 2 + a3 * s(i, 1)
+ a4 < spot - s(i, 1) Then
                fx(i, 1) = spot - s(i, 1)
                For m = 1 + 1 To p
                    ef(i, m) = 0
                Next m
            Else
                ef(i, 1) = 0
            End If
        End If
    Next i

    ReDim x(n)
    ReDim y(n)

Next 1

po = 0
For i = 1 To n
    For j = 1 To p
        po = po + ef(i, j) * (spot - s(i, j)) * Exp(-r * j * t / p)
    Next j
Next i

End Sub
```

4.5 DOUBLE-BARRIER ANALYTICAL APPROXIMATION

This intuitive and easy to implement method is taken from a paper by E. G. Haug (1999). The intuition behind this method is that one can approximately hedge a double-barrier option with a series of single-barrier options.

Let us assume that we seek to hedge a short double knock-in position, involving a lower barrier L and an upper one U. As a first step, we are naturally pushed to buy two single options, up & in at U and down & in at L. The problem arises when both barriers are touched: as a result, we are long one option. Our hedge cost us too much.

As a second step, we can imagine hedging by selling two other options that are activated when both barriers are touched. Let's take an example and consider a double knock-in call, strike K. Let us denote:

1. $C_{di}(S, K, L)$: Call down-in, barrier L
2. $C_{ui}(S, K, U)$: Call up-in, barrier U
3. $C_{dui}(S, K, U, L)$: Call **first** down **then** up-in
4. $C_{udi}(S, K, U, L)$: Call **first** up **then** down-in.

If zero, one, or two barriers are touched, the position is perfectly hedged. If the spot hits successively U, then L, then U again, we are short $C_{dui}(S, K, U, L)$. Inversely, if the spot hits L, then U, then L again, we are short $C_{udi}(S, K, U, L)$. In any case, the probability of this event tends to be negligible, but, to approach the perfect hedging, we might be tempted to buy two other options, respectively a call down then up then down and in, and a call up then down then up and in.

The point is now to give a theoretical price to these exotic calls. Let us start with $C_{dui}(S, K, U, L)$. The **Put-Call transformation** relationship will give us a precious insight.

Bjerksund and Stensland (1993) have shown that American calls and puts were linked by the following equation:

$$C(S, K, \tau, r, b, \sigma) = P(K, S, \tau, r - b, -b, \sigma) \tag{4.6}$$

where r denotes the risk free rate and b, the cost of carry. If the asset pays no intermediate coupon and no repo rate is accounted for, $r = b$:

$$C(S, K, \tau, r, r, \sigma) = P(K, S, \tau, 0, -r, \sigma)$$

This naturally holds for European options. Now, noticing that

$$Max(S - K, 0) = \frac{K}{S} Max\left(\frac{S^2}{K} - S, 0\right)$$

we can rewrite the Put-Call relationship:

$$C(S, K, \tau, r, r, \sigma) = \frac{K}{S} P\left(S, \frac{S^2}{K}, \tau, 0, -r, \sigma\right)$$

From now on and for the sake of more readable formulae, we will not mention r and σ in the expressions of calls and puts. In practice:

$$C(S, K) = C(S, K, \tau, r, b, \sigma)$$

$$P(S, K) = P(S, K, \tau, 0, -r, \sigma)$$

We can extend the scope of this equation to barrier options, e.g., up-and-in calls and down-and-in puts, for instance, provided that some symmetry involving strikes and barriers is respected. In (4.7), the strike of the put plays the role of the spot in the call and vice versa. So, what matters is that the distance between the strike remains the same for the call and the put, that is to say:

$$Ln\left(\frac{H}{K}\right) = Ln\left(\frac{S}{L}\right)$$

Applying the Put-Call transformation yields:

$$C_{ui}(S, K, U) = P_{di}(K, S, \frac{SK}{U}) = \frac{K}{S} P_{di}\left(S, \frac{S^2}{K}, \frac{S^2}{U}\right) \tag{4.7}$$

Suppose you sell $C_{dui}(S, K, L, U)$ (i.e., first down then up-and-in call) to hedge a double-knock-in option. If the spot reaches L in the course of the option's life, $C_{dui}(S, K, L, U)$ becomes a "vanilla" up-and-in call whose price is $C_{ui}(L, K, U)$. From equation (4.7), we draw that:

$$C_{ui}(L, K, U) = \frac{K}{L} P_{di}\left(L, \frac{L^2}{K}, \frac{L^2}{U}\right) \tag{4.8}$$

The interesting thing in the relation above is that the barrier of the put, i.e., $L^2/U <$ is lower than L. Practically, it means that:

- As long as L has not been reached, both the call and the put in equation (4.8) are actually worthless.
- If the spot hits L, the price of the up-and-in call equals the price of the put down and in. Both can be sold at the same price then.

From the above, we conclude that our exotic call can be hedged by a single down-and-in put since, when the lower barrier is hit, one can buy the call back and sell the hedging put at the same cost. Moreover:

$$C_{dui}(S, K, L, U) = \frac{K}{L} P_{di}\left(S, \frac{L^2}{K}, \frac{L^2}{U}\right)$$

The same reasoning applies when the upper barrier is hit first.

$$C_{udi}(S, K, L, U) = \frac{K}{U} P_{ui}\left(S, \frac{U^2}{K}, \frac{U^2}{L}\right)$$

If U then L, then U again are hit (or L then U then L), unfortunately we stay short of a call. To complete the hedge, we should buy one call C_{dudi} and one call C_{udui}, whose prices are derived from P_{dui} and P_{udi}, themselves deriving from C_{di} and C_{ui}. Finally, we could build a perfect hedge with an infinite series of single-barrier options, but, provided the barriers are not too close *and* the time to maturity not too long, four terms work fine. Otherwise, Haug has shown that, in the case of narrow barriers, the probability of hitting the barrier was so high that the double knock-in price was close to the plain-vanilla call (resp. put) price.

Below, we display the double knock-in call and put prices, approximated by the first four terms of the series:

$$C_i(S, K, L, U) \simeq \ Min \ [C(S, K),$$

$$C_{ui}(S, K, U) + C_{di}(S, K, L)$$

$$- \frac{K}{U} P_{ui}\left(S, \frac{U^2}{K}, \frac{U^2}{L}\right) - \frac{K}{L} P_{di}\left(S, \frac{L^2}{K}, \frac{L^2}{U}\right)$$

$$+ \frac{U}{L} C_{di}\left(S, \frac{L^2 K}{U^2}, \frac{L^3}{U^2}\right) + \frac{L}{U} C_{ui}\left(S, \frac{U^2 K}{L^2}, \frac{U^3}{L^2}\right)$$

$$- \frac{LK}{U^2} P_{ui}\left(S, \frac{U^4}{L^2 K}, \frac{U^4}{L^3}\right) - \frac{UK}{L^2} P_{di}\left(S, \frac{L^4}{U^2 K}, \frac{L^4}{U^3}\right)$$

$$+ \frac{U^2}{L^2} C_{di}\left(S, \frac{L^4 K}{U^4}, \frac{L^5}{U^4}\right) + \frac{L^2}{U^2} C_{ui}\left(S, \frac{U^4 K}{L^4}, \frac{U^5}{L^4}\right)]$$

$$P_i(S, K, L, U) \simeq \text{Min } [P(S, K),$$

$$P_{ui}(S, K, U) + P_{di}(S, K, L)$$

$$- \frac{K}{U} C_{ui}\left(S, \frac{U^2}{K}, \frac{U^2}{L}\right) - \frac{K}{L} C_{di}\left(S, \frac{L^2}{K}, \frac{L^2}{U}\right)$$

$$+ \frac{U}{L} P_{di}\left(S, \frac{L^2 K}{U^2}, \frac{L^3}{U^2}\right) + \frac{L}{U} P_{ui}\left(S, \frac{U^2 K}{L^2}, \frac{U^3}{L^2}\right)$$

$$- \frac{LK}{U^2} C_{ui}\left(S, \frac{U^4}{L^2 K}, \frac{U^4}{L^3}\right) - \frac{UK}{L^2} C_{di}\left(S, \frac{L^4}{U^2 K}, \frac{L^4}{U^3}\right)$$

$$+ \frac{U^2}{L^2} P_{di}\left(S, \frac{L^4 K}{U^4}, \frac{L^5}{U^4}\right) + \frac{L^2}{U^2} P_{ui}\left(S, \frac{U^4 K}{L^4}, \frac{U^5}{L^4}\right)]$$

CHAPTER 5

Monte-Carlo Pricing Issues

Monte-Carlo techniques may be fairly considered as the easiest way to deal with multi-asset or path-dependent payoffs. In the first section of this chapter, a method for sampling a set of correlated assets under the multivariate Gaussian model will be developed. In the second section, we will investigate some techniques to reduce the variability of simulation outputs, whatever the payoff.

5.1 MULTI-ASSET SIMULATION

5.1.1 The correlations issue

Higher dimensionality adds some complexity due to the co-dependency between assets. In general, the mutual interaction of two variables is measured by a **copula**, i.e., a bivariate cumulative probability defined as a function of the marginal cumulative probabilities of the two variables:

$$\phi(x_1, x_2) = C(F(x_1), F(x_2))$$

In this chapter, we will deal only with **multivariate Gaussian** distributions: it means that mutual dependencies among assets are measured, two at a time, by the coefficient of linear **correlation** or, more simply, the *correlation* ρ. This parameter is embedded in standard diffusion models such as Black–Scholes:

$$\begin{cases} \dfrac{\mathrm{d}S_i}{S_i} = \mu_i.\mathrm{d}t + \sigma_i.\mathrm{d}w_i \\ \\ \dfrac{\mathrm{d}S_j}{S_j} = \mu_j.\mathrm{d}t + \sigma_j.\mathrm{d}w_j \end{cases} \; \vdots \; \Rightarrow \rho_{i,j}\mathrm{d}t = \mathbf{E}(\mathrm{d}w_i.\mathrm{d}w_j)$$

5.1.2 The Gaussian case

Mutual dependencies in a group of n assets can be summarized then by a correlation matrix, derived from the **Covariance** matrix

$$\Sigma = \begin{pmatrix} \sigma_1^2 & \rho_{1,2}\sigma_1\sigma_2 & \cdots & \rho_{1,n}\sigma_1\sigma_n \\ \rho_{2,1}\sigma_1\sigma_2 & \sigma_2^2 & \cdots & \rho_{2,n}\sigma_2\sigma_n \\ \vdots & \vdots & \ddots & \vdots \\ \rho_{n,1}\sigma_1\sigma_n & \rho_{n,2}\sigma_2\sigma_n & \cdots & \sigma_n^2 \end{pmatrix}$$

The multivariate Gaussian density function of a set of correlated variates $x_i \equiv \mathcal{N}(\mu_i, \sigma_i)$ is written:

$$f(x_1, ..., x_n) = \frac{1}{\sqrt{2\pi^n |\Sigma|}} Exp(-1/2(x-\mu)^\dagger \Sigma^{-1}(x-\mu))$$

where $|\Sigma|$ stands for the determinant of Σ and

$$x - \mu = \begin{pmatrix} x_1 - \mu_1 \\ \vdots \\ x_n - \mu_n \end{pmatrix}$$

Since Monte-Carlo trials require the variates to be first generated independently, we shall build recursively a base of orthogonal or uncorrelated normalized random variables w_i^*, i.e., satisfying

$$\mathbf{E}(dw_i^* . dw_j^*) = \mathbf{E}(dw_i^*) . \mathbf{E}(dw_j^*) = 0$$

$$\mathbf{E}((dw_i^*)^2) = 1 * dt = dt$$

The vector (w_i^*) is mapped to (w_i) through a linear transformation:

$$w = [A].w^* \qquad ([A] = (a_{i,j}))$$

Originally, we state

$$w_1 = w_1^* \Rightarrow a_{1,1} = 1$$

The second row satisfies

$$w_2 = a_{2,1} w_1^* + a_{2,2} w_2^*$$

which yields

$$a_{2,1} = \rho_{1,2} = \rho_{2,1} \Rightarrow a_{2,2} = \sqrt{1 - \rho_{1,2}^2}$$

More generally,

$$\rho_{i,j} = \sum_{k=1}^{i} a_{i,k} a_{j,k}$$

$$\sum_{k=1}^{i} a_{i,k}^2 = 1$$

or, equivalently,

$$[A].[A]^\dagger = [\rho]$$

where $[A]$ is a lower triangular matrix provided that $[\rho]$ is a positive-definite matrix. Put differently, $[A]$ is a **pseudo-square root** of $[\rho]$ achieved by using a **Cholesky decomposition** algorithm.

Therefore, every Monte-Carlo simulation of an asset following a Black–Scholes-style diffusion model proceeds as follows:

- retrieve the correlation matrix $[\rho]$ and operate a Cholesky decomposition to get a lower triangular matrix $[A]$, such that $[A].[A]^{\dagger} = [\rho]$,
- simulate n i.i.d. (**i**ndependent **i**dentically **d**istributed) Gaussian variables w_i^* such that

$$w_i^* \equiv N(0, \sqrt{t}) \qquad i = 1, ..., n$$

$$\begin{pmatrix} w_1 \\ \vdots \\ w_n \end{pmatrix} = [A]. \begin{pmatrix} w_1^* \\ \vdots \\ w_n^* \end{pmatrix}$$

- derive the asset price from the trial solution

$$S_{i,t} = S_{i,0} Exp((r - \sigma_i^2/2)t + \sigma_i z_i \sqrt{t})$$

$$z_i = \sum_{k=1}^{i} a_{i,k} w_k^*$$

As an illustration, we give below the code of a plain-vanilla European call on a basket of five equally weighted assets with no intermediate coupon. The holder of the option is assumed to get 100% of the positive performance of this basket: let us denote

$$\frac{\Delta S_i}{S_i} = \frac{S_{i,t} - S_{i,0}}{S_{i,0}}$$

the payoff is then

$$Max\left(\frac{1}{n} \sum_{i=1}^{n} \frac{\Delta S_i}{S_i}, 0\right)$$

The code below is broken down into three steps:

- Step 1: retrieve market data from a spreadsheet and compute the lower triangular matrix *A*.
- Step 2: generate *n* iid Gaussian variates and calculate the resulting payoff solution. Reiterate this *N* times.
- Step 3: compute the mean payoff obtained from the *N* iterations.

```
Sub basketCall()

Dim i&
Dim n%: n = 5
Dim t!: t = 1
po = 0

Dim r!: r = 0.04
ReDim spot!(n), vol!(n), rho!(n, n)
ReDim rand!(n), Z!(n)
```

Step 1

```
For j = 1 To n
```

```
        spot(j) = 100
        vol(j) = 0.3
        For k = 1 To n
            rho(j, k) = Cells(j, k)
        Next k
    Next j

Dim trigo!(): trigo = Cholesky(rho)
```

Step 2

```
For i = 1 To 50000
    perf = 0
    For j = 1 To 5
        rand(j) = gauss(): Z(j) = 0
        For k = 1 To j
            Z(j) = Z(j) + trigo(j, k) * rand(k)
        Next k
    Next j
    For j = 1 To 5
        perf = perf + Exp((r - vol(j) ^ 2 / 2) * t + vol(j) * Z(j)
* Sqr(t)) / n
    Next j
    If perf - 1 > 0 Then po = po + (perf - 1)
Next i
```

Step 3

```
Debug.Print Exp(-r * t) * po / 50000

End Sub
```

Approximation As the size of the basket grows, this basket may be treated as one single asset $\hat{S}$ in order to price plain-vanilla options, provided that the approximation error is acceptable.

The calculation of the equivalent volatility $\hat{\sigma}$ is straightforward:

$$(n\hat{\sigma})^2 = \begin{pmatrix} \sigma_1 & \cdots & \sigma_n \end{pmatrix} . \begin{pmatrix} 1 & \rho_{1,2} & \cdots & \rho_{1,2} \\ \rho_{2,1} & 1 & \cdots & \rho_{2,n} \\ \vdots & \vdots & \ddots & \vdots \\ \rho_{n,1} & \rho_{n,2} & \cdots & 1 \end{pmatrix} . \begin{pmatrix} \sigma_1 \\ \vdots \\ \sigma_n \end{pmatrix}$$

or

$$\hat{\sigma} = \frac{1}{n} \sqrt{[\sigma]^\dagger . [\rho] . [\sigma]}$$

The appropriate VBA code to fix this is obvious:

```
Dim Ex#, Variance#

For i = 1 To n
    Ex = Ex + mu(i)
    For j = 1 To n
        Variance = Variance + vol(i) * vol(j) * correl(i, j)
    Next j
Next i
Ex = Ex / n: Variance = Variance / n^2
```

This approximation complies with tolerable accuracy for a basket of 10 components or more. Out of curiosity, we test prices obtained through the approximation method and the "real" price (see the code above), with a basket of five assets, on a 2-yr call, for different strikes: ATM, ATM $+ 25\%$, ATM $+ 50\%$.

The final payoff of the basket call is

$$Max\left(\frac{1}{n}\sum_{i=1}^{n}\frac{\Delta S_i}{S_i} - K, 0\right)$$

and the approximate payoff

$$Max\left(\frac{\Delta \hat{S}}{\hat{S}} - K, 0\right)$$

$$K = 0(\text{ATM}), K = 25\% \text{ and } K = 50\%$$

Notice that $\hat{S}$ is a fictitious asset with an initial price of 1 (100%). Three samples are chosen for the volatilities:

- Case 1: unique volatilities $\sigma = (30\%, ..., 30\%)$
- Case 2: $\sigma = (20\%, 25\%, 30\%, 35\%, 40\%)$
- Case 3: $\sigma = (40\%, 35\%, 30\%, 25\%, 20\%)$.

We assume the following correlation matrix:

$$\begin{pmatrix} 1 & 0.905 & 0.819 & 0.741 & 0.670 \\ 0.905 & 1 & 0.905 & 0.819 & 0.741 \\ 0.819 & 0.905 & 1 & 0.905 & 0.819 \\ 0.741 & 0.819 & 0.905 & 1 & 0.905 \\ 0.670 & 0.741 & 0.819 & 0.905 & 1 \end{pmatrix} \qquad (\rho(i,j) = e^{-0.1(|j-i|)})$$

Thus:

$$\text{Case 1: } \hat{\sigma}_1 = 27.80$$

$$\text{Case 2: } \hat{\sigma}_2 = 27.87$$

$$\text{Case 3: } \hat{\sigma}_3 = 27.87$$

Results from both methods are displayed in the table below:

Strike	case 1	MC	case 2	MC	case 3	MC
ATM	19.13	**19.15**	19.17	**19.1**	19.17	**19.11**
ATM+25%	10.17	**10.16**	10.21	**10.29**	10.21	**10.24**
ATM+50%	5.23	**5.23**	5.27	**5.36**	5.27	**5.38**

5.1.3 Exotics

Exotics are, most of the time, path-dependent. The final payoff is determined not only by the underlying asset price at maturity but several prices fixed throughout the instrument's lifetime, at anniversary dates. Therefore, one simulation trial consists, for each component of the basket, in drawing as many random variates as fixings.

Let us denote by n the number of components in the basket, p, the number of anniversary dates, $S_{i,j}$ the j-th fixing of the i-th component. Given $\Delta t_j = t_j - t_{j-1}$,

$$S_{i,j} = S_{i,j-1} \; Exp((r - \sigma_i^2/2)\Delta t_j + \sigma_i \sqrt{\Delta t_j} z(i,j))$$

Hence, one scenario needs $n \times p$ drawings of $z(i,j) \equiv N(0,1)$.

Among the wide range of existing path-dependent payoffs, we can mention:

- **Min/Max** options, struck on the minimum (resp. maximum) of one asset over the option lifetime;
- **Asian**-style options, struck on the continuous (daily fixed) or discrete time mean average of an asset;
- **Cliquet**-style options. Summarily, the performance of such options is measured with respect to different inception prices, fixed at successive reset dates. The most common version of this class of instruments yields

$$\frac{1}{n} \sum_{i=1}^{n} Max \left(\frac{S_i - S_{i-1}}{S_{i-1}}, 0 \right)$$

Most of Cliquet-style payoffs are capital guaranteed and often include additional tailor-made clauses.

The asset that is to be priced as an illustration is a Cliquet-style capital guaranteed instrument that yields the best performances of one component (equity, index...) among a basket, *one at a time*.

Let us assume a basket made up of 20 non-coupon-bearing assets (in the case where a coupon is expected between two anniversary dates, one may capitalize the flow over the period from the coupon payment date up to the next anniversary date). On each fixing date, regarding the period just elapsed:

1. the best performance is stored;
2. the best performer is discarded from the group.

Thus, every component is to be, at one time, the best performer. If we choose quarterly fixing dates, the resulting maturity is $20 \div 4 = 5y$.

Practically, every performance is based on the change from the inception date. At this time, the price of every asset, i.e., $S(i, 0)$ is called the **reference price**.

On any reset date t_j, we denote by $\pi(j)$ the index of the best performer:

$$Best(j) = \frac{S(\pi(j), j) - S(\pi(j), 0)}{S(\pi(j), 0)}$$

The final payoff is

$$Max \left(\frac{1}{20} \sum_{j=1}^{20} Best(j), 0 \right)$$

For the pricing algorithm, we adopt the following recipe: once the best performer is found, we re-initialize it to an arbitrary very low level so that it will be automatically discarded over the rest of the instrument's lifetime.

For the sake of conciseness, we instantiate volatilities with values uniformly distributed between 15% to 55%. Furthermore, we link correlations according to the following relation:

$$\rho(i,j) = e^{-0.04|i-j|}$$

```
Sub Appaloosa()
Dim i&, l&
Dim n%: n = 20
Dim t!: t = 0.25
po = 0

Dim r!: r = 0.04
ReDim spot#(n, n), vol#(n), rho#(n, n)
ReDim rand#(n), z#(n)

ReDim v#(n)
ReDim Best#(n)
Dim perf#

For i = 1 To n
    spot(0, i) = 100
    vol(i) = 0.15 + 0.02 * i
    For j = i To 20
        rho(i, j) = Exp(-0.04 * (j - i))
    Next j
Next i

Dim trigo#(): trigo = Cholesky(rho)

For l = 1 To 10000
    perf = 0
    For i = 1 To n
        v(i) = 0
    Next i
    For i = 1 To n
        For j = 1 To n
        rand(j) = gauss(): z(j) = 0
            For k = 1 To j
                z(j) = z(j) + trigo(j, k) * rand(k)
            Next k
        Next j
        For j = 1 To n
            If v(j) <> -100000 Then
                spot(i, j) = spot(i - 1, j) * Exp((r - vol(j) ^ 2 / 2) * t
+ vol(j) * z(j) * Sqr(t))
                v(j) = (spot(i, j) - spot(0, j)) / spot(0, j)
            End If

        Next j
        m = maxVector(v)

        Best(i) = v(m): v(m) = -100000
```

```
       perf = perf + Best(i) / n
   Next i
   po = po + max(perf, 0)
Next l

Debug.Print po / 10000 * Exp(-r * n * t)
End Sub
```

5.2 DISCRETIZATION SCHEMES

Let us consider a diffusion model of the form

$$dX_t = \alpha(X_t, t)dt + \sigma(X_t, t)dw_t$$

that is assumed intractable. To price a payoff $f(X_T)$, we have in any case to fix the problem of sampling the Ito integral:

$$X_T = \int_0^T \alpha(X_s, s)ds + \int_0^T \sigma(X_s, s)dw_s$$

Two popular schemes are widely used to approach this problem of valuing a continuously changing asset, each of them involving a **discretization scheme**.

First we divide the period $[0, T]$ into n sub-intervals $[t_i, t_{i+1}]$ such that

$$X_T = \sum_{i=1}^{n-1} (X_{t_{i+1}} - X_{t_i})$$

- the basic **Euler scheme** merely turns derivatives into increments, i.e.,

$$X_{t_{i+1}} = X_{t_i} + \alpha(X_{t_i})\Delta t_i + \sigma(X_{t_i})\Delta w_{t_i}$$

The Euler scheme arises from the first order expansion of ΔX_t without considering the impact of Δw_t^2, i.e., as if ΔX_t was simply deterministic.
- the **Milstein scheme** — this scheme is designed to take into consideration the convexity bias induced by Δw_t^2 in the first order Taylor expansion of ΔX_t:

$$X_{t_{i+1}} = X_{t_i} + \alpha(X_{t_i})\Delta t_i + \sigma(X_{t_i})\Delta w_{t_i} + 1/2\sigma(X_{t_i})\sigma'_x(X_{t_i})((\Delta w_{t_i})^2 - \Delta t)$$

σ'_x stands for the first derivative of $\sigma(X)$.

Pros and cons of these two methods are thoroughly investigated by Webber (2011). It emerges that Milstein is not always an improvement, despite the fact that the theoretical systematic error of the Milstein method is considerably lower than Euler's. Different criteria must be taken into account before making a choice (rate of convergence, bias, etc.).

5.3 VARIANCE REDUCTION TECHNIQUES

One major drawback of Monte-Carlo techniques is that their accuracy depends heavily on the efficiency of random number generators. The variability of the simulation results points to some potential error in the pricing. The mean error can be measured ex post by the observed standard deviation in the results. **Variance reduction** techniques are specifically designed to reduce this empirically observed standard deviation, without changing the RNG.

In this section, we will review three of them:

1. Antithetic variates
2. Importance sampling
3. Control variates.

5.3.1 Antithetic variates

Consider two equiprobable events measured by the variates X^+ and X^-. Denote by (X_i^+) and (X_i^-) the samples obtained from simultaneous simulation tests associated with these variables. Then, from

$$\hat{X} = \frac{1}{2}(X^+ + X^-)$$

we draw that

$$\mathbb{E}(\hat{X}) = \mathbb{E}(X^+) = \mathbb{E}(X^-)$$

and, assuming that X^+ and X^- are negatively correlated,

$$Var(\hat{X}) = \frac{1}{4}(Var(X^+) + Var(X^-) + 2\rho(X^+, X^-)Var(X^+)) \leq Var(X^+)) \tag{5.1}$$

Moreover, if we suppose that X_i^+ is one sample of a Wiener path, then

$$X_i^+ = g(\Delta w_1, .., \Delta w_n).$$

If we generate X^- such that

$$X_i^- = g(-\Delta w_1, -\Delta w_2, ..., -\Delta w_n)$$

then X^- verifies equation (5.1). As a result, by replicating scenarios $(\Delta w_1, \Delta w_2, ..., \Delta w_n)$ with their mirrored ones $(-\Delta w_1, -\Delta w_2, ..., -\Delta w_n)$, we generate samples of the same variables, although with reduced errors.

Put even more simply, if, for every trial (Δw_i) randomly generated, we generate deterministic $(-\Delta w_i)$, the distribution of the sum of outcomes will be trivially symmetrical.

Since the replication of the mirrored scenario does not demand the generation of random samples, the extra time induced is less than the time needed for an additional standard Monte-Carlo scenario. In most situations, provided that $\rho < 0$, this technique is profitable.

Moreover, recalling that Gaussian variates are built from uniform variates, we can add another degree of variance reduction in our implementation of this technique, by replicating also $u_i^+ \equiv \mathcal{U}[0, 1]$ with $u_i^- = 1 - u_i^+$. However, the extra cost in terms of computation time makes its benefit questionable.

5.3.2 Importance sampling

Although rare, some events can have a significant impact on the mean payoff. The idea behind Importance Sampling is to increase the frequency of these events. This happens for instance when we intend to price deep out-of-the-money options or, to some extent, barrier options. To put it shortly, let us denote by $h(s)$ a payoff structure on an asset S distributed normally. The Monte-Carlo estimate of $\mathbf{E}(h(s))$ is

$$\frac{1}{N}\sum_{i=1}^{N} h(S_i) \simeq \int_{\mathcal{F}} h(s)f(s)\mathrm{d}s$$

where $S_i \equiv N(\mu, \sigma^2 t)$.

When the option is out-of-the-money, a lot of samples result in $h(S_i) = 0$, which boils down at least to truncating randomly the domain of integration:

$$\frac{1}{N}\sum_{i=1}^{N} h(S_i) \simeq \int_{D \subset \mathcal{F}} h(s)f(s)\mathrm{d}s < \int_{\mathcal{F}} h(s)f(s)\mathrm{d}s$$

Moreover, if some knock-in/out provision is included, the impact will be substantially more severe.

In order to reduce the number of trials S_i for which $h(S_i) = 0$, we can modify the drift through a **change of probability**:

$$w_t \rightarrow w_t \pm \lambda t$$

and twist the payoff formula to preserve the fair value of the option. Incidentally, this method can be applied whatever the distribution of the underlying asset:

$$\int_{\mathcal{F}} h(s)f(s)\mathrm{d}s = \int_{\mathcal{F}} \frac{h(s)f(s)}{g(s)} g(s)\mathrm{d}s$$

$$g(s)\text{: new density}$$

$$\frac{h(s)f(s)}{g(s)}\text{: distorted payoff}$$

$\frac{f(s)}{g(s)}$ can also be viewed as the *density* $\frac{\mathrm{d}P^f}{\mathrm{d}P^g}$. Since the dynamics of S_t is fully determined by μ and σ, we can write

$$h(S_t) = h(S_0, \mu, \sigma, t)$$

Thus, according to Girsanov,

$$\mathbb{E}^{P_\mu}(h(S_0, \mu, \sigma, t)) = \mathbb{E}^{P_{\mu-\lambda}}(e^{(-\lambda w_t - \lambda^2 t/2)} h(S_0, \mu + \lambda\sigma, \sigma, t))$$

When dealing with call options, the more positive λ, the higher $P(h(S_0, \mu + \lambda\sigma, \sigma, t) > 0)$. Conversely, to increase the probability of exercise of an out-of-the-money put, choose a negative λ.

However, if λ is too high, the errors in the RNG may be magnified by the extreme values taken by the term $e^{(-\lambda w_t - \lambda^2 t/2)}$. The drift must be chosen to optimize the sampling efficiency, and thus to minimize the variance of the Monte-Carlo estimate.

Let us call P the risk-neutral probability and P^λ this measure drifted with λ. The variance of simulation estimates is, under P

$$\mathbb{E}^P(h^2(s)) - h_0^2 = V_\lambda$$

Under P^λ

$$\mathbb{E}^{P^\lambda}\left[h^2(s)\left(\frac{dP}{dP^\lambda}\right)^2\right] - h_0^2 = \mathbb{E}^P\left[h^2(s)\frac{dP}{dP^\lambda}\right] - h_0^2$$

Therefore, the sampling is optimal when

$$\mathbb{E}^P\left[h^2(s)\frac{dP}{dP^\lambda}\right]$$

is minimal. We can differentiate this expression under P, writing

$$\frac{\partial \mathbb{E}^P}{\partial \lambda}\left[h^2(s)\frac{dP}{dP^\lambda}\right] = \mathbb{E}^P\left[h^2(s)\frac{\partial}{\partial \lambda}\left(\frac{dP}{dP^\lambda}\right)\right]$$

since $h(s)$ is not λ-dependent. Let us assume the following change of drift $b_t = w_t - \lambda t$:

$$\frac{\partial}{\partial \lambda}\left(\frac{dP}{dP^\lambda}\right) = \frac{\partial}{\partial \lambda}Exp\left(-\lambda w_t + \frac{1}{2}\lambda^2 t\right) = -b_t Exp\left(-\lambda b_t - \frac{1}{2}\lambda^2 t\right)$$

$$Min_\lambda \mathbb{E}^P\left[h^2(s)(-b_t)Exp\left(-\lambda b_t - \frac{1}{2}\lambda^2 t\right)\right] = Min_\lambda \mathbb{E}^{P^\lambda}\left[h^2(s)(-b_t)Exp(-2\lambda b_t - \lambda^2 t)\right]$$

The convexity of V_λ allows us to reach its minimum through a gradient-style method, approaching the minimum by the recursive method

$$\lambda_{n+1} = \lambda_n - a_n g_n$$

where $g_n = \mathbb{E}^{P^\lambda}\left[h^2(s_n)(-b)exp(-2\lambda_n b - \lambda_n^2 t)\right]$ is an <u>unbiased</u> estimate of $\partial V_\lambda / \partial \lambda_n$

The function, displayed below, calculates the optimal drift for a call 1-yr, 70% out-of-the money.

```
Function ImpSamp(x!, vol!, t!, r!) As Single

Dim lambda!: lambda = (Log(x) / t - r) / vol

y = 0
    For i = 1 To 10000
        b = gauss() * Sqr(t)
        s = 100 * Exp((r + lambda * vol - vol ^ 2 / 2) * t + vol * b)
        y = y + (max(s - 100 * x, 0)) ^ 2 * (-b) * Exp(-2 * lambda * b
- lambda ^ 2 * t)
    Next i
    g = y / 10000
    a = Abs(1 / g)
```

```
For j = 1 To 100
    y = 0
    For i = 1 To 10000
        b = gauss() * Sqr(t)
        s = 100 * Exp((r + lambda * vol - vol ^ 2 / 2) * t + vol * b)
        y = y + (max(s - 100 * x, 0)) ^ 2 * (-b) * Exp(-2 * lambda * b
- lambda ^ 2 * t)
    Next i
    g = y / 10000
    lambda = lambda - a / Sqr(j) * g
Next j
ImpSamp = lambda

End Function
```

With a volatility of 30% and r=3%, we get $\lambda \simeq 2.44$ and a variance divided by 10!

Asian-style options In this paragraph, we will focus on discrete average options. Therefore, the payoff at maturity is

$$h(s_{t_1}, ..., s_{t_n}) = Max\left(\frac{1}{n} \sum_{i=1}^{n} s_{t_i} - K, 0 \right) \text{ for a call}$$

$$h(s_{t_1}, ..., s_{t_n}) = Max\left(K - \frac{1}{n} \sum_{i=1}^{n} s_{t_i}, 0 \right) \text{ for a put}$$

Let us assume that the fixing dates are equally spaced and denote by $\tau = t_i - t_{i-1}$. Then

$$S_{t_i} = S_i = S_{i-1} e^{((r-\sigma^2/2)\tau + \sigma w_i)}$$

Applying a change of numeraire to each period gives

$$\frac{dP}{dP^{\lambda_i}} = exp\left(-\lambda_i w_i + \frac{1}{2}\lambda_i^2 \tau \right) \qquad w_i \equiv N(0, \sqrt{\tau})$$

The density of the new measure is, therefore,

$$\frac{dP}{dP^{\lambda_1}} \frac{dP}{dP^{\lambda_2}} ... \frac{dP}{dP^{\lambda_n}} = \prod_{i=1}^{n} exp\left(-\lambda_i w_i + \frac{1}{2}\lambda_i^2 \tau \right) = \prod_{\lambda}$$

We seek the minimum of

$$\mathbb{E}^P\left[h^2(s) \prod_{\lambda} \right]$$

through the computation of n gradients

$$\frac{\partial}{\partial \lambda_i}\left(\prod_{\lambda} \right) = -b_i exp\left(-\lambda_i b_i - \frac{1}{2}\lambda_i^2 \tau \right) \prod_{j \neq i}^{n} exp\left(-\lambda_j w_j + \frac{1}{2}\lambda_j^2 \tau \right)$$

Since

$$w_i - b_i = \lambda_i \tau$$

and

$$\prod_{j \neq i}^{n} exp\left(-\lambda_j w_j + \frac{1}{2}\lambda_j^2 \tau\right)) = \prod_{\lambda} /exp\left(-\lambda_i w_i + \frac{1}{2}\lambda_i^2 \tau\right)$$

under $\mathbf{P}^{\lambda}$

$$\frac{\partial}{\partial \lambda_i}\left(\prod_{\lambda}\right) = -b_i exp\left(-\lambda_i b_i + \frac{1}{2}\lambda_i^2 \tau\right) \prod_{\lambda}$$

$$S_i = S_{i-1} exp\left((r + \lambda_i \sigma - \sigma^2/2)\tau + \sigma w_i\right)$$

Just as before, we build the sequence λ_i^n by recursion:

$$\lambda_i^{n+1} = \lambda_i^n - a_i^n g_i^n$$

$$g_i^n = \mathbb{E}^{P^{\lambda_i}}\left[-b_i exp\left(-\lambda_i^n b_i + \frac{1}{2}(\lambda_i^n)^2 \tau\right)\prod_{\lambda}\right]$$

If the option is not deep out-of-the-money, this algorithm may unfortunately diverge. In fact, it is quite unstable. First, whatever the periodicity of the fixings, you should take care that τ does not exceed three months. Secondly, the choice of the initial values a_i^0 is crucial. When the delta of the option increases, start with very low values such as a fraction of the rate r, or r itself. To initialize λ_i, you can, in any case, set

$$\lambda_i^0 = \frac{Ln(x)/t - r}{\sigma}$$

where x stands for the ratio $K/Spot$ and t is the duration of the instrument.

The function ImpSampAsia below calculates the optimal drifts for a 3-yr Asian call, 100% out-of-the-money ($x=2$), fixed quarterly.

```
Function ImpSampAsia(x!, vol!, t!, r!) As Single()

Dim n%: n = 12

ReDim lambda!(n), g!(n), a!(n)
ReDim s!(n), b!(n)
For j = 1 To n
    lambda(j) = (Log(3) / t - r) / vol
    a(j) = r
Next j

For l = 1 To 200
    For j = 1 To 12
        g(j) = 0
    Next j
    For i = 1 To 10000
```

```
        s(0) = 100: x = 0: prod = 1
        For j = 1 To n
            b(j) = gauss() * Sqr(t / n)
            s(j) = s(j - 1) * Exp((r + lambda(j) * vol - vol ^ 2 / 2) * t / n
+ vol * b(j))
            x = x + s(j)
            prod = prod * Exp(-lambda(j) * b(j) - lambda(j) ^ 2 * (t / n) / 2)
        Next j
        For j = 1 To n
            g(j) = g(j) + (max(x / n - 200, 0)) ^ 2 * (-b(j)) * Exp(-lambda(j)
* b(j) - lambda(j) ^ 2 * (t / n) / 2) * prod
        Next j
    Next i
    For j = 1 To 12
        g(j) = g(j) / 10000
        lambda(j) = lambda(j) - a(j) / Sqr(l) * g(j)
    Next j
Next l

For j = 1 To n
    Debug.Print lambda(j)
Next j

ImpSampAsia = lambda

End Function
```

Twenty simulations have been performed, with $\sigma = 0.3$ and $r = 4\%$. The drifts are displayed in Figure 5.1 and the estimates from both the standard and the importance sampling methods in Figure 5.2.

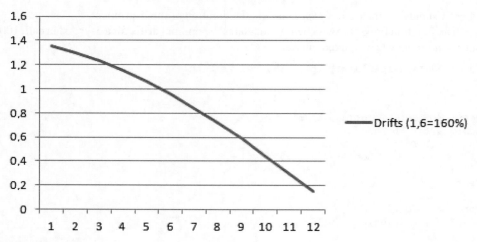

FIGURE 5.1 Solutions of the optimal sampling function ImpSampAsia

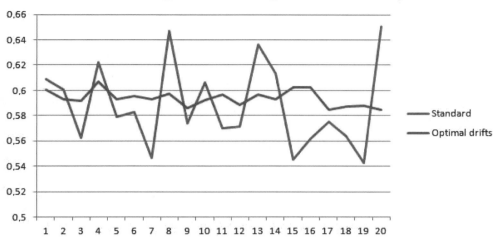

FIGURE 5.2   Simulation results

5.3.3 Control variates

This technique is used when we have two securities X and Y, similar in terms of risk exposure, and when a closed-form solution is available for one of them. By similarity, we mean that the impacts of stochastic perturbations on both instruments are well correlated. Combining a long position in one security and a short one in the other with adequate weights should lead to a low risk profile. Let us consider n replications of Monte-Carlo trials and the n pairs (X_i, Y_i) obtained. $\mathbb{E}(X)$ is to be estimated, while $\mathbb{E}(Y)$ is known. Let us call θ the ratio between the errors in the estimates of $\mathbb{E}(X)$ and $\mathbb{E}(Y)$:

$$\frac{1}{n}\sum_{i=1}^{n} X_i - \mathbb{E}(X) = \theta\left(\frac{1}{n}\sum_{i=1}^{n} Y_i - \mathbb{E}(Y)\right)$$

or

$$\mathbb{E}(X) = \frac{1}{n}\sum_{i=1}^{n} X_i - \theta\left(\frac{1}{n}\sum_{i=1}^{n} Y_i - \mathbb{E}(Y)\right)$$

At each trial, θ obviously changes, but we can seek its value which, on average, minimizes

$$Var(X_i - \theta(Y_i - \mathbb{E}(Y)))$$

Then,

$$\frac{1}{n}\sum_{i=1}^{n} X_i - \theta\left(\frac{1}{n}\sum_{i=1}^{n} Y_i - \mathbb{E}(Y)\right)$$

will provide a better estimator of $\mathbb{E}(X)$ than $\frac{1}{n} \sum_{i=1}^{n} X_i$

$$\frac{\partial}{\partial \theta} \left[Var(X) + \theta^2 \underbrace{Var(Y - \mathbb{E}(Y))}_{Var(Y)} - 2\theta \underbrace{Cov(X, Y - \mathbb{E}(Y))}_{Cov(X,Y)} \right] = 0$$

$$\theta = \frac{Cov(X, Y)}{Var(Y)}$$

A Monte-Carlo sampling using the control variate always operates as follows:

1. Calculate $\mathbb{E}(Y)$ analytically
2. Generate n pairs (X_i, Y_i)
3. Compute $Cov(X, Y) = \mathbb{E}((X_i - \overline{X})(Y_i - \overline{Y}))$
4. Compute an estimate of $\mathbb{E}(X) = \overline{X} - \frac{Cov(X, Y)}{Var(Y)}(\overline{Y} - \mathbb{E}(Y))$.

    In practice, only a few structures meet all the requirements to serve as control variates of assets needing Monte-Carlo simulations to be priced. As a matter of fact, either they have an analytical solution, but $Cov(X, Y)$ is weak, or they react in a similar way to the Brownian outcomes, but fail to provide a closed-form solution.

    Below, we give an example of implementation with a standard (but rare in real life) example. The structure to be priced is an arithmetic average of the performances of a basket of assets. As a control variate, we will use an option on the geometric average of the same basket.

    The payoff of the structure to price is given by

$$Max\left(\frac{1}{n} \sum_{i=1}^{n} \frac{S_i(T)}{S_i(0)} - K, 0\right)$$

In other words, this option is a call on the mean performance of an equi-weighted basket of assets, struck at K. In parallel, a call on the geometric average of the same basket states the following payoff:

$$Max\left[\left(\prod_{i=1}^{n} \frac{S_i(T)}{S_i(0)}\right)^{\frac{1}{n}} - K, 0\right]$$

From

$$S_i(T) = S_i(0)Exp\left(\mu_i T + \sigma_i w_i\right)$$

we draw

$$\prod_{i=1}^{n} \frac{S_i(T)}{S_i(0)} = Exp\left(\sum_{i=1}^{n} (\mu_i T + \sigma_i w_i)\right)$$

The argument of the exponential is a sum of correlated Gaussian variates. Its expectation is the sum of each variate's expectation and the variance is the sum of the covariance matrix, i.e.,

$$\mathbb{E}\left(\sum_{i=1}^{n} (\mu_i T + \sigma_i w_i) \right) = \sum_{i=1}^{n} \mu_i T$$

$$Var\left(\sum_{i=1}^{n} (\mu_i T + \sigma_i w_i) \right) = \sum_{i,j} \sigma_i \sigma_j \rho_{i,j} T$$

Thus,

$$\left(\prod_{i=1}^{n} \frac{S_i(T)}{S_i(0)} \right)^{\frac{1}{n}} = e^X$$

$$X \equiv N\left(\sum_{i=1}^{n} \mu_i T/n, \sum_{i,j} \sigma_i \sigma_j \rho_{i,j} T/n^2 \right) = N(\epsilon, V)$$

The fair price of the call is then written:

$$e^{-rt} \int_{Ln\,(K)}^{+\infty} (e^u - K) Exp\left(-\frac{1}{2} \frac{(u-\epsilon)^2}{V} \right) / \sqrt{2\pi V} \, du$$

which yields

$$e^{-rt} \left[e^{\epsilon + V/2} \left(1 - N\left(\frac{(Ln\,(K) - (\epsilon + V)}{\sqrt{V}} \right) \right) - K \left(1 - N\left(\frac{Ln\,(K) - \epsilon}{\sqrt{V}} \right) \right) \right]$$

Let us illustrate this with a 3-yr ATM call option on the average performance of a basket of five underlyings. Volatilities and correlations are retrieved from a worksheet named **Correls**. The payoff is written:

$$Max\left(\frac{1}{5} \sum_{i=1}^{5} \frac{S_i(T)}{S_i(0)} - 1, 0 \right)$$

This is the corresponding code:

```
Sub GeoAvg()

Dim K#: st = 1
Dim r#: r = 0.04
Dim t#: t = 3

Dim n&: n = 10000
Dim m%: m = 5

ReDim pay_off#(1 To n), cont_variate#(1 To n)

Dim correl#(): ReDim correl(m, m)
Dim Chol#()
```

```vba
Dim z#(): ReDim z(m)
Dim brown#(): ReDim brown(m)

Worksheets("Correls").Activate
For i = 1 To 5
    For j = 1 To 5
        correl(i, j) = Cells(i, j)
    Next j
Next i


Chol = Cholesky (correl)

Dim vol#(): ReDim vol(5)
Dim mu#(): ReDim mu(5)

For i = 1 To 5
    vol(i) = Cells(i, 7)
    mu(i) = r - vol(i) ^ 2 / 2
Next i


Dim Ex#, Variance#
Dim perf_avg#, perf_geo#

For i = 1 To 5
    Ex = Ex + mu(i) * t
    For j = 1 To 5
        Variance = Variance + vol(i) * vol(j) * correl(i, j) * t
    Next j
Next i
Ex = Ex / 5: Variance = Variance / 25

Price = Exp(Ex + Variance / 2) * (1 - norm((Log(st) - Variance - Ex) /
Sqr(Variance))) _
                    - st * (1 - norm((Log(st) - Ex) / Sqr(Variance)))

po = 0: cc = 0
Randomize
For j = 1 To 10000
perf_avg = 0: perf_geo = 1
For i = 1 To 5
    z(i) = gauss()

    brown(i) = 0
    For K = 1 To i
        brown(i) = brown(i) + Chol(i, K) * z(K)
    Next K
    perf = Exp(mu(i) * t + vol(i) * brown(i) * Sqr(t))
    perf_avg = perf_avg + perf
    perf_geo = perf_geo * perf

Next i

pay_off(j) = max(perf_avg / m - st, 0)
cont_variate(j) = max(perf_geo ^ (1 / m) - st, 0)
```

```
Next j

beta = WorksheetFunction.Covar(pay_off, cont_variate) /
WorksheetFunction.Var(pay_off)

Debug.Print Exp(-r * t) * (WorksheetFunction.Average(pay_off) + _
beta * (Price - WorksheetFunction.Average(cont_variate)))
Debug.Print Exp(-r * t) * WorksheetFunction.Average(pay_off)

End Sub
```

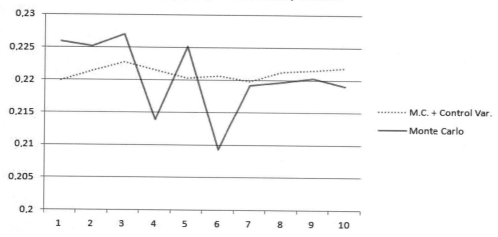

Sum of control variates Consider two payoffs V, W, and a control variate Z for which an analytical solution is available:

$$V = f(X) \qquad W = g(X) \qquad Z = V + W$$

Some current derivatives satisfy this feature, such as, for instance, continuous barrier options. In fact,

$$\text{Call d/i} + \text{Call d/o} = \text{European call}$$

Consider another two payoffs V, W, and a control variate Z for which an analytical solution is available.

Then, if $\beta = Cov(V_i, W_i)/Var(W_i)$,

$$V = \overline{V_i} + \beta(W - \overline{W_i}) = \overline{V_i} + \beta(Z - V - \overline{W_i})$$

$$V = \frac{\overline{V_i} + \beta(Z - \overline{W_i})}{1 + \beta}$$

This recipe can extend to more than two payoffs. We will illustrate this with a Cliquet call option with a cap restriction. Given the following payoff

$$V_{cap} = \frac{1}{n} \sum_{i=0}^{n-1} \left[\frac{S_{i+1}}{S_i} - 1 \right] \mathbb{1}_{110\% S_i > S_{i+1} > S_i}$$

the price of this call spread is the difference between the at-the-money V and 110% call V_{110}:

$$V_{cap} + V_{110} = V$$

where moreover

$$\text{Cliquet call} + \text{Cliquet put} = \mathbb{E} \left(\frac{S_{i+1}}{S_i} - 1 \right)$$

$$V + W = Z$$

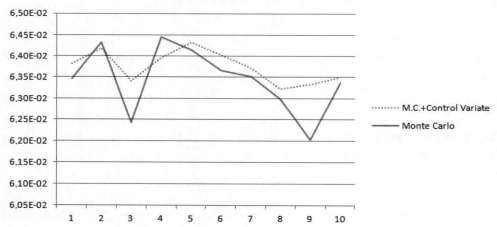

2-yr Cliquet call option/quarterly fixings

The general case   As payoffs grow in complexity, well-correlated control variates are hardly detectable: in that case, we may invoke the asset itself as control variate. Indeed, it is realistic to think that, at least once a week, on the week-end, time is not a major concern for the accurate valuing of a book of derivatives. More precisely, the same Monte-Carlo sampling can be used to price the derivative under new conditions and archived ones: given $f_t(..., x_i, ...)$, the price at t for which there exists an exact solution,

$$f_{t+\Delta t}(..., x_i + \Delta x_i, ...) = \bar{f}_{t+\Delta t}(..., x_i + \Delta x_i, ...) + \beta(f_t(..., x_i, ...) - \bar{f}_t(..., x_i, ...))$$

As an illustration, let us consider a basket of four assets and a 2-yr call option written on it. On each semi-annual monitoring date, the asset having performed best from inception is discarded from the basket but its performance is stored. Concretely, let us denote by $S_i, i = 1, ..., 4$, the prices of the underlyings, and by $t_i, i = 1, ..., 4$, the fixing dates:

- at t_1, if the best performance is $= (S_2(t_1) - S_2(0))/S_2(0) = Perf(2)$, asset #2 is discarded and $Perf(2)$ is archived.
- at t_2, the basket now contains three assets: we repeat the same process and discard, for instance, S_3, assuming #3 is the best performer among the three remaining assets – and again, up to t_4 The final payoff is

$$Max\left(\frac{1}{4}\sum_{i=1}^{4} Perf(i), 0\right)$$

The market data are stored in the *Data* sheet of the Excel file.

	A	B	C	D	E	F	G	H
1	Spots (t)	Vols (t)	Spots (t+Δt)	Vols (t+Δt)		Correlations		
2								
3	100	20%	110	19%	1	0.65	0.7	0.57
4	60	25%	65	23%	0.65	1	0.59	0.62
5	50	30%	48	30%	0.7	0.59	1	0.59
6	70	35%	76	32%	0.57	0.62	0.59	1

For the purposes of simplicity, and without questioning the validity of the method, we assume that the time to maturity is 2 years under both sets of market conditions. The control variate price, obtained with 500 000 paths, is 10.78%. This is the resulting code:

```
Sub Basket_Dim()

Dim K#: st = 1
Dim r#: r = 0.04
Dim t#: t = 2

Dim n&: n = 5000
ReDim v#(1 To n), w#(1 To n)

ReDim vol_init#(4), vol_fin#(4)
ReDim spot_init#(4), spot_fin#(4)
ReDim mu_init#(4), mu_fin#(4)

Dim correl#(): ReDim correl(4, 4)
Dim Chol#()
Dim z#(): ReDim z(4)
Dim brown#(): ReDim brown(4)

Worksheets("Data").Activate

For i = 1 To 4
    For j = 1 To 4
        correl(i, j) = Cells(2 + i, 4 + j)
    Next j
    spot_init(i) = Cells(i + 2, 1): spot_fin(i) = Cells(i + 2, 3)
    vol_init(i) = Cells(i + 2, 2): vol_fin(i) = Cells(i + 2, 4)
    mu_init(i) = r - vol_init(i) ^ 2 / 2
    mu_fin(i) = r - vol_fin(i) ^ 2 / 2
Next i
```

```vba
Chol = Cholesky (correl)
Randomize

Price = 0.1078

ReDim spot1#(4), perf1#(4)
ReDim spot2#(4), perf2#(4)

For l = 1 To 5000
    For j = 1 To 4
        spot1(j) = spot_init(j)
        spot2(j) = spot_fin(j)
    Next j
    perf_basket1 = 0: perf_basket2 = 0
    For i = 1 To 4
        For j = 1 To 4
            z(j) = gauss()
            brown(j) = 0
            For K = 1 To j
                brown(j) = brown(j) + Chol(j, K) * z(K)
            Next K
            If perf1(j) <> -10000 Then
                spot1(j) = spot1(j) * Exp(mu_init(j) * t / 4 + vol_init(j) *
Sqr(t / 4) * brown(j))
                perf1(j) = (spot1(j) - spot_init(j)) / spot_init(j)
            End If
            If perf2(j) <> -10000 Then
                spot2(j) = spot2(j) * Exp(mu_fin(j) * t / 4 + vol_fin(j) *
Sqr(t / 4) * brown(j))
                perf2(j) = (spot2(j) - spot_fin(j)) / spot_fin(j)
            End If
        Next j
        perf_basket1 = perf_basket1 + maxList(perf1)(1)
        perf_basket2 = perf_basket2 + maxList(perf2)(1)
        perf1(maxList(perf1)(2)) = -10000
        perf2(maxList(perf2)(2)) = -10000
    Next i
    w(l) = max(perf_basket1 / 4, 0)
    v(l) = max(perf_basket2 / 4, 0)
Next l

beta = WorksheetFunction.Covar(v, w) / WorksheetFunction.Var(w)

Debug.Print Exp(-r * t) * (WorksheetFunction.Average(v) + _
          beta * (0.1078 - WorksheetFunction.Average(w)))
Debug.Print Exp(-r * t) * WorksheetFunction.Average(v)
End Sub
```

In order to select the best performance on each fixing date and discard the asset responsible for it, we add a utility function:

```vba
Function maxList(v#()) As Double()

ReDim res#(2)
res(1) = v(1)
For i = 1 To UBound(v)
    If v(i) > res(1) Then res(1) = v(i): res(2) = i
```

```
Next i
maxList = res

End Function
```

The graph below comparing solutions, obtained with or without control variate, speaks for itself.

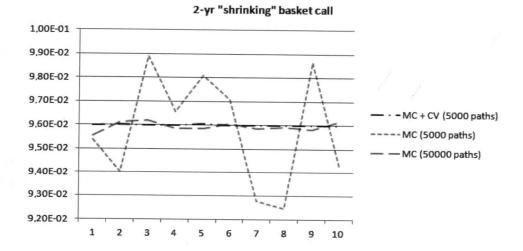

2-yr "shrinking" basket call

- ·-MC + CV (5000 paths)
- -----MC (5000 paths)
- — —MC (50000 paths)

CHAPTER 6

Yield Curve Models

6.1 SHORT RATE MODELS

6.1.1 Introduction

Basically, short rate dynamics yield the following expression:

$$\mathrm{d}r = \alpha(r, t)\mathrm{d}r + \sigma(r, t)\mathrm{d}w_t \tag{6.1}$$

or, more generally:

$$\mathrm{d}r = \alpha(r, t)\mathrm{d}r + \sigma(f(r), t)\mathrm{d}w_t$$

Depending on whether w_t is a single Brownian or a vector, the model is said to be **one-factor** or **multi-factor**. Also, the diffusion process can involve several correlated variables (e.g., the Gaussian additive model).

In the literature, it is common to read that models are classified into to two main categories:

- Equilibrium models, derived from general assumptions based on economic considerations that aim to model the short rate and draw the longer term rates from it;
- Arbitrage-free models, which are only concerned about fitting the parameters of the models with liquid market data.

In this section, we will address successively one-factor, two-factor, and forward curve models, without reference to any other criterion. Obviously, one chapter cannot cover the matter exhaustively, but the models presented give a global overview of the main features of interest rate modeling theory: further on, these models will be used for pricing some interest rate exotics.

The role of the forward measure By definition, under the forward measure Q^t, any asset denominated in zero-bonds has the following martingale property:

$$\frac{X_s}{B(s,t)} = \mathbb{E}^{Q_t}\left(\frac{X_t}{B(t,t)}/\mathcal{F}_s\right) = \mathbb{E}^{Q_t}(X_t/\mathcal{F}_s)$$

On the other hand, under the risk-neutral measure Q,

$$X_s = \mathbb{E}^Q\left(e^{-\int_s^t r(u)du} X_t/\mathcal{F}_s\right)$$

which yields

$$dQ^t/dQ = \frac{e^{-\int_s^t r(u)du}}{B(s,t)}$$

Provided that r_t is Gaussian,

$$\mathbb{E}(e^{r_t}) = e^{E(r_t)+Var(r_t)/2}$$

which simplifies significantly the computation of standard payoffs such as

$$\pi_s = B(s,t)\mathbb{E}^{Q_t}([X_t - K]^+(resp\,[K - X_t]^+)/\mathcal{F}_s)$$

Since both short rate models investigated here are gaussian, this measure will be called upon systematically in the process of cap/floor and swaption valuations.

6.1.2 Hull and White one-factor model

Short rate dynamics Hull and White introduce their model as an extension of Vasicek's, since the drift includes a deterministic function $\theta(t)$ that aims to fit the initial term structure, i.e.,

$$dr_t = (\theta(t) - ar_t)dt + \sigma dw_t$$

A change of variable $v_t = r_t.e^{at}$ leads to

$$dv_t = e^{at}\theta(t)dt + e^{at}\sigma dw_t \implies v_t - v_0 = \int_0^t (e^{as}\theta(s)ds + e^{as}\sigma dw_s)$$

Finally,

$$r_t = r_0e^{-at} + \int_0^t e^{-a(t-s)}\theta(s)ds + \int_0^t e^{-a(t-s)}\sigma dw_s$$

From some future date s,

$$r_t = r_se^{-a(t-s)} + \int_s^t e^{-a(t-u)}\theta(u)du + \int_s^t e^{-a(t-u)}\sigma dw_u \tag{6.2}$$

Since $e^{-at}\sigma$ is deterministic, r_t is Gaussian, and so is $\int_0^t r_s ds$, which will help us to calculate

$$B(0,t) = \mathbb{E}\left(e^{-\int_0^t r_s ds}\right)$$

In fact, given a Gaussian process X,

$$\mathbb{E}(e^X) = e^{E(X)+Var(X)/2}$$

We will use this feature to connect $\theta(t)$ with the zero-bond curve. From equation (6.2), we draw

$$-\int_0^t r_s ds = -r_0\frac{1-e^{-at}}{a} - \int_0^t \int_0^s e^{-a(s-u)}\theta(u)du\,ds + \int_0^t \int_0^s e^{-a(s-u)}\sigma dw_u ds$$

$$\mathbb{E}\left(-\int_0^t r_s ds\right) = -r_0\frac{1-e^{-at}}{a} - \int_0^t \int_0^s e^{-a(s-u)}\theta(u)du\,ds = -r_0\frac{1-e^{-at}}{a} - \phi(t) \quad (6.3)$$

$$\mathbb{V}\left(-\int_0^t r_s ds\right) = \mathbb{V}\left(\int_0^t \int_0^s e^{-a(s-u)}\sigma dw_u ds\right) = \mathbb{V}\left(\sigma \int_0^t \left[\int_0^s e^{au}dw_u\right]e^{-as}ds\right)$$

$$= \mathbb{V}\left(\sigma \int_0^t e^{as}\left[\int_s^t e^{-au}du\right]dw_s\right) = \mathbb{V}\left(\sigma \int_0^t -\frac{1}{a}e^{as}(e^{-at}-e^{-as})dw_s\right)$$

$$= \mathbb{V}\left(\sigma \int_0^t \frac{1-e^{a(t-s)}}{a}dw_s\right) = \frac{\sigma^2}{a^2}\mathbb{E}\left(\left[\int_0^t (1-e^{-a(t-s)})dw_s\right]^2\right) = \frac{\sigma^2}{a^2}\int_0^t (1-e^{-a(t-s)})^2 ds$$

from the Ito integral's property of isometry.

Finally,

$$\mathbb{V}\left(-\int_0^t r_s ds\right) = \frac{\sigma^2}{a^2}\left(t + \frac{2}{a}e^{-at} - \frac{1}{2a}e^{-2at} - \frac{1}{2a}\right)$$

Introducing $V_t = \mathbb{V}\left(-\int_0^t r_s ds\right)$,

$$B(0,t) = Exp\left(-r_0\frac{1-e^{-at}}{a} - \phi(t) + V(t)/2\right)$$

To fit the zero curve, $\phi(t)$ must therefore satisfy

$$e^{-\phi(t)} = B_{market}(0, t)Exp\left(r_0\frac{1 - e^{-at}}{a} - V(t)/2\right) \tag{6.4}$$

We draw from equation (6.4) a new expression of $B(s, t)$, mapped to the zero curve:

$$B(s, t) = Exp\left(-r_0\frac{1 - e^{-at}}{a}\right)\frac{B_{market}(0, t)}{B_{market}(0, s)}Exp(-(V(0, t) - V(0, s) - V(s, t))/2)$$

Options on ZC bonds   Under the risk-neutral measure Q, the theoretical price of a European call expiring at T on a zero-bond over $(T, T + \tau]$, is written:

$$\mathbb{E}^Q\left(e^{-\int_t^T r(s)ds}[B(T, T + \tau) - K]^+/\mathcal{F}_t\right)$$

We now carry on the calculation under the forward measure:

$$X_t = B(t, T)\mathbb{E}^{Q_T}\left(\frac{X_T}{B(T, T)}/\mathcal{F}_t\right) = \mathbb{E}^{Q_T}(X_T/\mathcal{F}_t)$$

Thus,

$$\frac{dQ^T}{dQ} = \frac{e^{-\int_t^T r(s)ds}}{B(t, T)} = \frac{Exp\left(-r_t\frac{(1-e^{-a(T-t)})}{a} - (\phi(T) - \phi(t)) - \int_t^T\int_t^s e^{-a(s-u)}\sigma dw_u ds\right)}{Exp\left(-r_t\frac{(1-e^{-a(t-s)})}{a} - (\phi(T) - \phi(t)) + V(t, T)/2\right)}$$

$$= Exp\left(-\int_t^T\int_t^s e^{-a(s-u)}\sigma dw_u ds - \frac{1}{2}V(t, T)\right)$$

$$= Exp\left(-\sigma\int_t^T\frac{1 - e^{a(T-s)}}{a}dw_s - \frac{1}{2}V(t, T)\right)$$

With the objective of calibrating a and σ with market prices of liquid assets (plain-vanilla options), we carry on our calculations at $t = 0$. Above, we established that the density dQ^T/dQ is of the form

$$\frac{dQ^T}{dQ} = Exp\left(-\int_0^T \epsilon_u dw_u - \int_0^T \frac{1}{2}\epsilon_u^2 du\right)$$

with

$$\epsilon_u = \sigma\frac{1 - e^{a(T-u)}}{a}$$

Therefore, under Q^T, the dynamics of r_t are

$$r_t = r_0 e^{-at} + \int_0^t e^{-a(t-s)}\theta(s)\mathrm{d}s + \int_0^t e^{-a(t-s)}\sigma \left[\mathrm{d}w_s^T - \frac{\sigma}{a}(1 - e^{a(t-s)})\mathrm{d}s \right]$$

where w^T is a standard Brownian under this measure.

$$r_t = r_0 e^{-at} + \int_0^t e^{-a(t-s)}\theta(s)\mathrm{d}s - \left[\frac{\sigma^2}{a^2}(1 - e^{-at}) - \frac{\sigma^2}{2a^2}(1 - e^{-2at}) \right] - \int_0^t e^{-a(t-s)}\sigma \mathrm{d}w_s^T$$

Now, we can conclude

$$ZBC(0) = \frac{1}{B(0,T)}\mathbb{E}^{Q_T}([B(T,T+\tau) - K]^+)$$

$Ln[B(T,T+\tau)]$ is an **affine** function of r_T, i.e.,

$$Ln[B(T,T+\tau)] = -\alpha(T,T+\tau)r_T + \beta(T,T+\tau)$$

with

$$\alpha(T,T+\tau) = -\frac{1 - e^{-a\tau}}{a}$$

$$\beta(T,T+\tau) = Ln\left(\frac{B_M(0,T+\tau)}{B_M(0,T)} - \frac{1}{2}(V(0,T+\tau) - V(0,T) - V(T,T+\tau)) \right)$$

Then,

$$ZBC(0) = \frac{1}{B(0,T)}\mathbb{E}^{Q_T}([Exp(-\alpha(T,T+\tau)r_T + \beta(T,T+\tau) - Exp(Ln(K))]^+) \qquad (6.5)$$

$$\mathbb{E}^{Q_T}(r_T) = r_0 e^{-aT} + \int_0^T e^{-a(T-s)}\theta(s)\mathrm{d}s - \left[\frac{\sigma^2}{a^2}\left(1 - e^{-aT}\right) - \frac{\sigma^2}{2a^2}(1 - e^{-2aT}) \right]$$

From equation (6.3):

$$\int_0^T e^{-a(T-s)}\theta(s)\mathrm{d}s = \frac{\partial\phi}{\partial T} = r_0 e^{-aT} + \frac{1}{2}\frac{\partial V(T)}{\partial T}$$

$$= r_0 e^{-aT} + \frac{\sigma^2}{2a^2}(1 - e^{-aT})^2$$

Denoting by $F(0, T)$ the market value at $t = 0$ of the instantaneous forward rate:

$$\mathbb{E}^{Q_T}(r_T) = F(0, t) + \frac{\sigma^2}{2a^2}(1 - e^{-aT})^2$$

$$V(r_T) = \frac{\sigma^2}{2a}(1 - e^{-2aT})$$

From equation (6.5) and $\frac{r_T - \mathbb{E}^{Q_T}(r_T)}{V(r_T)} \equiv \mathcal{N}(0, 1)$

$$ZBC(0, T, T + \tau, K) = B(0, T + \tau) * N(Z) - B(0, T)K * N(Z - \sigma_{ZB})$$

$$\sigma_{ZB} = \sqrt{V(r_T)}\frac{1 - e^{-a\tau}}{a}$$

$$Z = \frac{Ln\left(\frac{B(0, T+\tau)}{KB(0, T)}\right) + \frac{1}{2}\sigma_{ZB}^2}{\sigma_{ZB}}$$

Also:

$$ZBP(0, T, T + \tau, K) = B(0, T) * KN(-Z + \sigma_{ZB}) - B(0, T + \tau) * N(-Z)$$

Let us go on with shorter notations and set $F_{T,T+\tau} = F(T, T + \tau)$. The caplet payoff follows from ZBP since

$$Max\left(\frac{F_{T,T+\tau} - K}{1 + F_{T,T+\tau}.\tau}.\tau, 0\right) = Max\left(\frac{1 + \tau F_{T,T+\tau} - 1 - \tau K}{1 + F_{T,T+\tau}.\tau}, 0\right)$$

$$= Max\left(1 - \frac{1 + \tau K}{1 + F_{1,T+\tau}.\tau}, 0\right)$$

This coincides with the payoff of a put option on a zero-bond maturing at $T + \tau$ for a nominal of $1 + K.\tau$, struck at $1/(1 + K(\tau))$. The caplet price is thus

$$Caplet(t, T, T + \tau, K) = B(0, T) * N(-Z + \sigma_{ZB}) - B(0, T + \tau) * (1 + K(\tau))N(-Z)$$

$$Z = \frac{Ln\left(\frac{B(0, T + \tau)(1 + K\tau)}{B(0, T)}\right) + \frac{1}{2}\sigma_{ZB}^2}{\sigma_{ZB}}$$

Calibration with caplets' market prices In order to calibrate a and σ with the prices available in the cap market, we seek to minimize the estimator:

$$\sum_{i=1}^{n-1}(Caplet_{Black}(Fwd_i) - Caplet_{HW}(Fwd_i))^2$$

Since caplet volatilities are not quoted, only those of caps, we proceed as follows:

Step 1 Let us consider a forward rate term structure:

$$Fwd(i) = Fwd(0, i\Delta t, (i+1)\Delta t)$$

Denoting by $Cap_i(K)$ the market price of a cap, struck at K, that terminates at $t_i = i\Delta t$, we draw

$$Caplet(i) = Cap_{i+1}(Fwd(i)) - Cap_i(Fwd(i))$$

Step 2 Given the caplet price under the Black model (Black volatility= σ_B)

$$caplet(K, T, T + \tau, \sigma_B) = [Fwd(T, T + \tau)\tau. * N(d_1) - K * N(d_2)\tau]B(0, T + \tau)$$

$$d_1 = \frac{Ln\left(\frac{Fwd(T, T+\tau)}{K}\right) + \sigma_B^2 T/2}{\sigma_B \sqrt{T}} \qquad d_2 = d_1 - \frac{\sigma_B \sqrt{T}}{2}$$

we draw σ_B using the Newton-Raphson method. The code below calculates the implied volatility of a 3-mth caplet struck at K, with a market quote denoted by **target**. **dt** denotes the caplet duration (0.25 years), **t** is the maturity.

```
Function ImpliedCapletVol(t!, K!, target!, fwd!, vol!) As Single

Dim price!: price = 0
Dim vega!: vega = 0
Dim dt!: dt = 0.25

Const PI = 3.14159
Dim d1!, d2!

d1 = (Log(fwd / K) + vol ^ 2 / 2 * t) / vol / Sqr(t): d2 = d1 - vol * Sqr(t)
price = (fwd * norm(d1) - K * norm(d2)) * dt
vega = fwd * Sqr(t / (2 * PI)) * Exp(-d1 ^ 2 / 2) * dt

While Abs(price - target) > 0.000005

    vol = (target - price) / vega + vol

    d1 = (Log(fwd / K) + vol ^ 2 / 2 * t) / vol / Sqr(t): d2 = d1 - vol
    * Sqr(t)

    price = (fwd * norm(d1) - K * norm(d2)) * dt
    vega = fwd * Sqr(t / (2 * PI)) * Exp(-d1 ^ 2 / 2) * dt

Wend
ImpliedCapletVol = vol

End Function
```

We are now ready to proceed with the calibration itself. The choice of method is open. Our natural inclination to be lazy would prompt us to use the Excel solver facility. In fact, this ready-to-use tool is rather powerful (and fast!). Furthermore, the analytical formulae are quite concise, making a spreadsheet easy to build. However, whatever the Excel algorithm (three options in Office 2010) the solution depends very much on the initial values of the parameters to be fitted. The reason for this is, probably, that some distortion in the volatility term structure can significantly shift the estimator's minima.

As an alternative, you can use a more robust algorithm, such as Nelder-Mead, and compare with Excel solutions.

Here, we do not recommend the simulated annealing algorithm.

Excel solver　The spreadsheet looks like this:

Maturity	Forward	ValCap Mkt	VolCaplet	B(0,T)	σZB	z	ValCap HW	Δ^2
				0.99378882				
0.25	2.387%	0.000141095	12.00%	0.987893401	0.000749606	0.000374803	0.000297209	1.106449203
0.5	2.619%	0.00024459	13.50%	0.981468369	0.001059825	0.000529913	0.000417716	0.707822172
0.75	2.902%	0.000353918	14.50%	0.974399017	0.001297675	0.000648838	0.000508132	0.435732198
1	3.049%	0.000418669	14.25%	0.967028238	0.001498033	0.000749017	0.000582326	0.390898362
1.25	3.178%	0.000475538	14.00%	0.959405072	0.001674413	0.000837206	0.000645993	0.358446661
1.5	3.326%	0.000532749	13.80%	0.95149455	0.001833746	0.000916873	0.000701889	0.317483796
1.75	3.496%	0.000590827	13.60%	0.943251694	0.001980153	0.000990077	0.000751652	0.27220392
2	3.671%	0.000647625	13.40%	0.934672569	0.002116318	0.001058159	0.000796359	0.229661276
2.25	3.836%	0.000700214	13.20%	0.925793563	0.002244106	0.001122053	0.000836777	0.19503035
2.5	3.980%	0.000746602	13.00%	0.916672832	0.002364875	0.001182438	0.000873414	0.169852783
2.75	4.102%	0.000786539	12.80%	0.907367137	0.002479652	0.001239826	0.000906799	0.152897103
3	4.206%	0.000820421	12.60%	0.897925286	0.002589234	0.001294617	0.000937264	0.142417144
3.25	4.317%	0.000860007	12.50%	0.888338827	0.002694254	0.001347127	0.000965162	0.122272628
3.5	4.439%	0.000907591	12.50%	0.878588381	0.002795228	0.001397614	0.000990599	0.091459851
3.75	4.550%	0.000951969	12.50%	0.868706342	0.002892578	0.001446289	0.001013843	0.064996218
4	4.714%	0.001006476	12.50%	0.858588612	0.00298666	0.00149333	0.001035061	0.028401018
4.25	4.844%	0.001053152	12.50%	0.848316093	0.003077773	0.001538886	0.001054223	0.001016857
4.5	4.955%	0.001094837	12.50%	0.837936177	0.003166173	0.001583087	0.001071543	0.021276001
4.75	5.082%	0.001139091	12.50%	0.827423033	0.003252083	0.001626042	0.001087125	0.045620083
5	5.125%	0.001163501	12.50%	0.816954796	0.003335694	0.001667847	0.001101079	0.053649928
5.25	5.200%	0.001193859	12.50%	0.806470582	0.003417175	0.001708588	0.001113736	0.067112527
5.5	5.278%	0.001223954	12.50%	0.795967509	0.003496676	0.001748338	0.001125016	0.08083455
5.75	5.358%	0.001253375	12.50%	0.785446673	0.003574328	0.001787164	0.001135011	0.094436016
6	5.444%	0.001283167	12.50%	0.774900832	0.00365025	0.001825125	0.001143815	0.108599703
6.25	5.522%	0.001310245	12.50%	0.764348293	0.003724547	0.001862273	0.00115139	0.121241039
6.5	5.594%	0.001334565	12.50%	0.753806905	0.003797315	0.001898657	0.00115792	0.132361435
6.75	5.600%	0.001342618	12.50%	0.743398461	0.00386864	0.00193432	0.001163405	0.133480141
7	5.710%	0.001374093	12.50%	0.73293627	0.003938601	0.001969301	0.0011681	0.149911942
7.25	5.764%	0.001391406	12.50%	0.722524835	0.00400727	0.002003635	0.001171735	0.15787697
7.5	5.817%	0.001407556	12.50%	0.7121679	0.004074711	0.002037355	0.001174513	0.165565572
							Estimator:	6.119007448

As constraints, we put that σ(L4) and a(L5) must be positive (named vv and aa in the spreadsheet). The value of the estimator is displayed in J34.

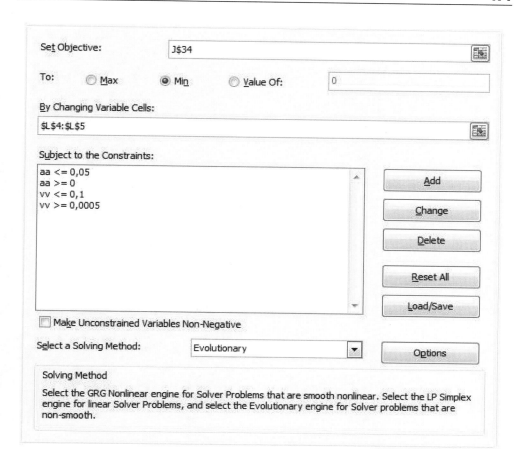

Nelder-Mead algorithm In the core engine of the algorithm, the simplex is a set of three vector-type elements (2 parameters to fit + 1). **HWpricingCaplet** plays the role of baseFunc (see §2.4.1) and the estimator is computed by **LeastSquare**.

```
Function HWpricingCaplet(x As Vector) As Double
HWpricingCaplet = LeastSquare(x.v(1), x.v(2))
End Function
```

```
Function LeastSquare(a#, v#) As Double
Dim i%
LeastSquare = 0
For i = 1 To 30
    LeastSquare = LeastSquare + (PrixHW(a, v, i) - Cap(i)) ^ 2
Next i
End Function
```

```
Function PrixHW(a#, v#, n%) As Single

Dim dt!: dt = 0.25
Dim vol!: vol = Sqr((1 - Exp(-2 * a * n * dt)) / (2 * a)) * v / a
* (1 - Exp(-a * dt))
Dim h!: h = Log(bd(n) / bd(n - 1) * (1 + Fd(n) * dt)) / vol + vol / 2

PrixHW = bd(n - 1) * norm(-h + vol) - (1 + Fd(n) * dt) * bd(n) * norm(-h)
End Function

Sub calibHW()

ReDim simp(3) As New Vector
ReDim w(3) As New Vector
Dim i%

Dim sr As Vector
Dim se As Vector
Dim soc As Vector
Dim sic As Vector
```

Below, we give arbitrary initial values to start the algorithm

```
For i = 1 To 3
    simp(i).nbEl = 2
    simp(i).v(1) = 0.001 + 0.002 * i
    simp(i).v(2) = 0.005 + 0.002 * i
Next i
```

Here, we retrieve market data from **IRdata**:

```
Worksheets("IRdata").Activate

ReDim bd(30), Fd(30), Vd(30), Cap(30)

bd(0) = Cells(3, 7)
For i = 1 To 30
    bd(i) = Cells(3 + i, 7)
    Fd(i) = Cells(3 + i, 4)
    Vd(i) = Cells(3 + i, 6)
    Cap(i) = Cells(3 + i, 5)
Next i

For m = 1 To 50

    simp = sort_vec_gen (simp,"HWpricingCaplet")

    Set sr = sum_vec(scalar(2, moy_vec(del(simp))), simp(3), -1)

    Select Case HWpricingCaplet(sr)

        Case HWpricingCaplet(simp(1)) To HWpricingCaplet(simp(2))
            simp = comp(del(simp), sr)
```

```
            Case Is < HWpricingCaplet(simp(1))
                Set se = sum_vec(scalar(2, sr), moy_vec(del(simp)), -1)

                If HWpricingCaplet(se) < HWpricingCaplet(sr) Then
                    simp = comp(del(simp), se)
                Else
                    simp = shrink(simp)
                End If

            Case HWpricingCaplet(simp(2)) To HWpricingCaplet(simp(3))
                Set soc = sum_vec(scalar(0.5, sr),
                scalar(0.5, moy_vec(del(simp))), 1)
                If HWpricingCaplet(soc) < HWpricingCaplet(sr) Then
                    simp = comp(del(simp), soc)
                Else
                    simp = shrink(simp)
                End If

            Case Is >= HWpricingCaplet(simp(3))
                Set sic = sum_vec(scalar(0.5, simp(3)),
                scalar(0.5, moy_vec(del(simp))), 1)
                If HWpricingCaplet(sic) < HWpricingCaplet(simp(3)) Then
                    simp = comp(del(simp), sic)
                Else
                    simp = shrink(simp)
                End If

        End Select

Next m

Debug.Print simp(2).v(1) & "   " & simp(2).v(2)
Debug.Print HWpricingCaplet(simp(1))

End Sub
```

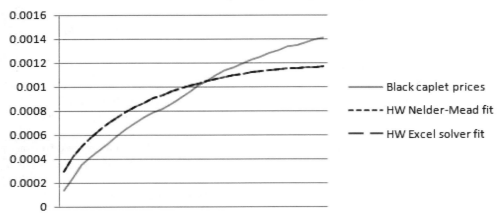

3–mth ATM caplet prices up to 7.5y

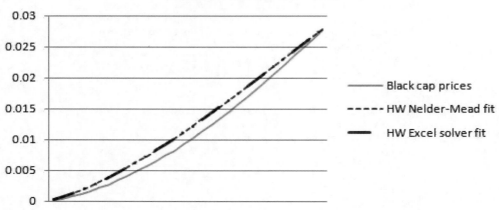

In some cases, the calibration may give rather poor results: the convergence between the solver and our algorithm is the only consolation. Actually, two parameters are not enough to fit the caplets curve. We could resort to time-dependent parameters, but it makes the trinomial tree-building rather intricate. We should bear in mind that this model is quite popular as a fast risk valuation model: consequently, adding parameters is, in that sense, counterproductive.

Trinomial tree   One common numerical solution to deal with exotics is the interest rate tree. For the building process, we split r_t into two processes $r_t = \hat{r}_t$ (stochastic) $+ \eta_t$ (deterministic) such that

$$d\hat{r}_t = -a\hat{r}_t t + \sigma w_t$$

and

$$d\eta_t = (\theta(t) - a\eta_t)dt$$

Indeed

$$dr_t = d\eta_t + d\hat{r}_t = \underbrace{(\theta(t) - a\eta_t)dt - a\hat{r}_t t} + \sigma w_t = (\theta(t) - ar_t)dt + \sigma dw_t$$

The building procedure will therefore be **two-step**:

- First we set up a recombining tree for the evolution of $\hat{r}_t$, starting from $\hat{r}_0 = 0$;
- Then, we twist the tree to incorporate the deterministic part (fitting the zero curve) η_t.

Step 1   We opt for a **trinomial** tree that brings a third degree of freedom for the diffusion of $\hat{r}$. Also, the tree will be symmetrical around $\hat{r} = 0$ so that $\Delta\hat{r}$ is constant, set to equal (see Hull (1997)):

$$\Delta\hat{r} = \sigma\sqrt{3\Delta t} = \Delta r \ (\eta \text{ plays no role in the volatility})$$

As an illustration, the first two timesteps look like this:

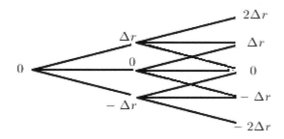

More generally, at the $i - th$ step, the values at each node are within the range

$$- i\Delta r, \quad - (i - 1)\Delta r,..., (i - 1)\Delta r, \quad i\Delta r$$

The mathematical expectation and variance of $(\widehat{r}_{t+\Delta t} - \widehat{r}_t)$ are approximated (first order expansion) by

$$\mathbb{E}(\widehat{r}_{t+\Delta t} - \widehat{r}_t) = - a\widehat{r}_t\Delta t$$

$$Var(\widehat{r}_{t+\Delta t} - \widehat{r}_t) = \sigma^2\Delta t$$

While the spacing Δr between two adjacent nodes is constant, the probabilities of transition between $i\Delta t$ and $(i + 1)\Delta t$ are contingent upon rate levels, i.e., $(i - j)\Delta r$. To avoid negative probabilities on one hand and take account of the mean-reversion on the other hand, we adjust the branching method when the rate goes too high or too low. Branching modes (a), (b), and (c), apply to (a) normal variations, (b) "low level" situations, (c) "high level" situations.

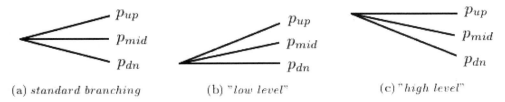

(a) *standard branching*   (b) *"low level"*   (c) *"high level"*

Practically, Hull & White have shown that probabilities are always positive when $(i - j)_{max}$ does not exceed the smallest integer greater than $0.184/(a\Delta t)$. In any case, however, if we denote by p_u, p_d, and p_m the probabilities that the rate moves up, down, or remains unchanged,

$$p_{up} + p_{mid} + p_{dn} = 1$$

$$p_{up}\Delta r_u + p_{mid}\Delta r_m + p_{dn}\Delta r_d = - aj\Delta r\Delta t$$

$$p_{up}\Delta r_u^2 + p_{mid}\Delta r_m^2 + p_{dn}\Delta r_d^2 = \sigma^2\Delta t + a^2j^2\Delta r^2\Delta t^2$$

Branching mode	(a)	(b)	(c)
$(\Delta r_u, \Delta r_m, \Delta r_d)$	$(\Delta r, 0, - \Delta r)$	$(2\Delta r, \Delta r, 0)$	$(0, - \Delta r, - 2\Delta r)$
$(p_{up}, p_{mid}, p_{dn})$	(p_u, p_m, p_d)	(l_u, l_m, l_d)	(h_u, h_m, h_d)

$$p_u = \frac{1}{6} + \frac{a^2 j^2 \Delta t^2 - aj\Delta t}{2}$$

$$p_m = \frac{2}{3} - a^2 j^2 \Delta t^2$$

$$p_d = \frac{1}{6} + \frac{a^2 j^2 \Delta t^2 + aj\Delta t}{2}$$

$$l_u = \frac{1}{6} + \frac{a^2 j^2 \Delta t^2 + aj\Delta t}{2}$$

$$l_m = -\frac{1}{3} - a^2 j^2 \Delta t^2 - 2aj\Delta t$$

$$l_d = \frac{7}{6} + \frac{a^2 j^2 \Delta t^2 + 3aj\Delta t}{2}$$

$$h_u = \frac{7}{6} + \frac{a^2 j^2 \Delta t^2 - 3aj\Delta t}{2}$$

$$h_m = -\frac{1}{3} - a^2 j^2 \Delta t^2 + 2aj\Delta t$$

$$h_d = \frac{1}{6} + \frac{a^2 j^2 \Delta t^2 - aj\Delta t}{2}$$

Step 2 η_t is the deterministic part of r_t, that is to say

$$\eta_t = r_0 e^{-at} + \int_0^t e^{-a(t-s)} \theta(s) ds$$

or

$$\eta_t = F(0, t) + \frac{\sigma^2}{2a^2}(1 - e^{-at})^2$$

$\eta_t = r_t - \hat{r}_t$ is an **instantaneous** rate that needs to be compounded over each timestep Δt so that, at each node

$$r(i\Delta t) = \hat{r}(i\Delta t) + \frac{1}{\Delta t} \int_{i\Delta t}^{(i+1)\Delta t} \eta_s ds$$

At first order

$$1 + \int_{i\Delta t}^{(i+1)\Delta t} F(0, s) ds \simeq \frac{B(0, i\Delta t)}{B(0, (i+1)\Delta t)}$$

Finally

$$\frac{1}{\Delta t} \int_{i\Delta t}^{(i+1)\Delta t} \eta_s ds \simeq \frac{1}{\Delta t} \left(\frac{B(0, i\Delta t)}{B(0, (i+1)\Delta t)} - 1 \right)$$

$$+ \frac{\sigma^2}{2a^2 \Delta t} \left[\Delta t + \frac{2}{a} \left(e^{-a(i+1)\Delta t} - e^{-ai\Delta t} \right) - \frac{1}{2a} \left(e^{-2a(i+1)\Delta t} - e^{-2ai\Delta t} \right) \right]$$

Since a picture often speaks a thousand words, the diagram below shows how the tree is implemented, "upstream and downstream" of **jmax**

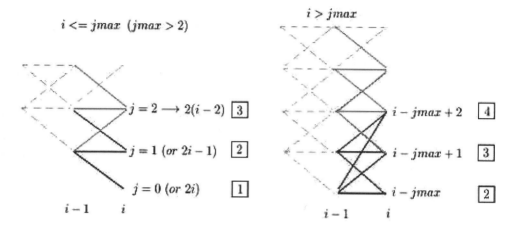

Code Once a and σ have been fitted with caplet prices, we are now ready to start building the trinomial tree. Below, we display the program to populate every node (i, j) with the appropriate forward rate $r_{i,j}$, and compute caplet prices, as a way of checking whether our tree is OK.

a and σ are declared at the top of the module for they will be invoked in the core tree-building program as well as in the computation of the probabilities p_u, p_d and p_m: those functions take only one argument, since prob(r(i,j)) depends solely on j.

```
Function pu(j#, dt#, a#) As Double
    pu = 1 / 6 + ((a ^ 2) * (j ^ 2) * (dt ^ 2) - a * j * dt) / 2
End Function
Function pm(j#, dt#, a#) As Double
    pm = 2 / 3 - a ^ 2 * j ^ 2 * dt ^ 2
End Function
Function pd(j#, dt#, a#) As Double
    pd = 1 / 6 + (a ^ 2 * j ^ 2 * dt ^ 2 + a * j * dt) / 2
End Function
Function lu(j#, dt#, a#) As Double
    lu = 1 / 6 + (a ^ 2 * j ^ 2 * dt ^ 2 + a * j * dt) / 2
End Function
Function lm(j#, dt#, a#) As Double
    lm = -1 / 3 - a ^ 2 * j ^ 2 * dt ^ 2 - 2 * a * j * dt
End Function
Function ld(j#, dt#, a#) As Double
    ld = 7 / 6 + (a ^ 2 * j ^ 2 * dt ^ 2 + 3 * a * j * dt) / 2
End Function
Function hu(j#, dt#, a#) As Double
    hu = 7 / 6 + (a ^ 2 * j ^ 2 * dt ^ 2 - 3 * a * j * dt) / 2
End Function
Function hm(j#, dt#, a#) As Double
    hm = -1 / 3 - a ^ 2 * j ^ 2 * dt ^ 2 + 2 * a * j * dt
End Function
Function hd(j#, dt#, a#) As Double
    hd = 1 / 6 + (a ^ 2 * j ^ 2 * dt ^ 2 - a * j * dt) / 2
End Function
```

```
***********************************************************************
```
testHW retrieves a forward rate curve from IRdata and calls HW1F to
build the tree and compute the price of ATM 3-mth caplets up to
5 years from now.
```
***********************************************************************
```

```vba
Sub testHW()

Worksheets("IRdata").Activate
ReDim f!(40)
For i = 1 To 40
    f(i) = Cells(i + 3, 4)
Next i
Call HW1F(f)
End Sub

Sub HW1F(Fwd!())

Dim a#: a = 0.05
vol = 0.005

Dim dt#: dt = 0.25

ReDim eta!(UBound(Fwd))

For i = 1 To UBound(Fwd)
    eta(i) = dt + 2 / a * (Exp(-a * (i + 1) * dt) - Exp(-a * i * dt)) _
           - 1 / (2 * a) * (Exp(-2 * a * (i + 1) * dt)
           - Exp(-2 * a * i * dt))
    eta(i) = vol ^ 2 / (2 * a ^ 2 * dt) * eta(i) + Fwd(i)
Next i

Dim dr!: dr = vol * Sqr(3 * dt)
Dim jmax#: jmax = Fix(0.184 / a / dt) + 1
```

```
***********************************************************************
```
The time horizon is 10 years (40 timesteps).
```
***********************************************************************
```

```vba
Dim r!(40, 80), p!(40, 80)

r(1, 0) = -dr + eta(1): r(1, 1) = eta(1): r(1, 2) = dr + eta(1)
p(1, 0) = 1 / 6: p(1, 1) = 2 / 3: p(1, 2) = 1 / 6
```

From $j = j_{max}$, the tree is twisted

```vba
For i = 2 To jmax
    For j = 0 To 2 * i
        r(i, j) = (-i + j) * dr + eta(i)
    Next j

    p(i, 0) = p(i - 1, 0) * pd(-(i - 1), dt, a)
    p(i, 1) = p(i - 1, 0) * pm(-(i - 1), dt, a) + _
              p(i - 1, 1) * pd(-(i - 1) + 1, dt, a)

    For j = 2 To 2 * i - 2
        p(i, j) = p(i - 1, j - 2) * pu(-(i - 1) + j - 2, dt, a) + _
```

```
                    p(i - 1, j - 1) * pm(-(i - 1) + j - 1, dt, a) + _
                    p(i - 1, j) * pd(-(i - 1) + j, dt, a)
        Next j

        p(i, 2 * i - 1) = p(i - 1, 2 * (i - 1) - 1) * pu(i - 2, dt, a) + _
                    p(i - 1, 2 * (i - 1)) * pm(i - 1, dt, a)
        p(i, 2 * i) = p(i - 1, 2 * (i - 1)) * pu(i - 1, dt, a)

Next i

For i = jmax + 1 To 40

    For j = i - jmax To i + jmax
        r(i, j) = (-i + j) * dr + eta(i)
    Next j

    p(i, i - jmax) = p(i - 1, i - 1 - jmax) * ld(-jmax, dt, a) + _
                p(i - 1, i - jmax) * pd(-jmax + 1, dt, a)
    p(i, i - jmax + 1) = p(i - 1, i - 1 - jmax) * lm(-jmax, dt, a) + _
                    p(i - 1, i - jmax) * pm(-jmax + 1, dt, a) + _
                    p(i - 1, i - jmax + 1) * pd(-jmax + 2, dt, a)
    p(i, i - jmax + 2) = p(i - 1, i - 1 - jmax) * lu(-jmax, dt, a) + _
                    p(i - 1, i - jmax) * pu(-jmax + 1, dt, a) + _
                    p(i - 1, i - jmax + 1) * pm(-jmax + 2, dt, a) + _
                    p(i - 1, i - jmax + 2) * pd(-jmax + 3, dt, a)

    For j = i - jmax + 3 To i + jmax - 3
        p(i, j) = p(i - 1, j - 2) * pu(j - 1 - i, dt, a) + _
                p(i - 1, j - 1) * pm(j - i, dt, a) + _
                p(i - 1, j) * pd(j + 1 - i, dt, a)
    Next j

    p(i, i + jmax - 2) = p(i - 1, i - 1 + jmax) * hd(jmax, dt, a) + _
                    p(i - 1, i - 2 + jmax) * pd(jmax - 1, dt, a) + _
                    p(i - 1, i - 3 + jmax) * pm(jmax - 2, dt, a) + _
                    p(i - 1, i - 4 + jmax) * pu(jmax - 3, dt, a)
    p(i, i - 1 + jmax) = p(i - 1, i + jmax - 1) * hm(jmax, dt, a) + _
                    p(i - 1, i + jmax - 2) * pm(jmax - 1, dt, a) + _
                    p(i - 1, i + jmax - 3) * pu(jmax - 2, dt, a)
    p(i, i + jmax) = p(i - 1, i + jmax - 1) * hu(jmax, dt, a) + _
                p(i - 1, i + jmax - 2) * pu(jmax - 1, dt, a)

Next i

caplet = 0
DF = 1 / (1 + 0.0225 * dt)
For i = 1 To 20
    s = 0
    For j = 0 To 2 * i
        s = s + p(i, j) * max(r(i, j) - Fwd(i), 0) * dt
    Next j
    DF = DF / (1 + Fwd(i) * dt)

Debug.Print s * DF
Next i

End Sub
```

6.1.3 Gaussian two-factor model

Short rate dynamics The process is the sum of two Gaussian processes $x_t + y_t$ and a deterministic function $\phi(t)$:

$$r_t = x_t + y_t + \phi(t) \quad t > 0$$

$$x_0 = y_0 = 0 \quad \phi(0) = r_0$$

x_t and y_t satisfy

$$dx_t = -a.x_t dt + \sigma_x.dw_x$$

$$dy_t = -b.y_t dt + \sigma_y.dw_y$$

$$< dw_x, dw_y) > (\mathbb{E}(dw_x, dw_y)) = \rho dt$$

$\phi(t)$ is determined so that r_t fits the yield curve, i.e.,

$$B(0, T) = \mathbb{E}^Q \left(Exp \left[-\int_0^T r_t dt \right] \right) = e^{-\int_0^T \phi(t)dt} \mathbb{E}^Q \left(Exp \left[-\int_0^T (x_t + y_t)dt \right] \right)$$

under the risk-neutral measure. More generally:

$$B(t, T) = e^{-\int_t^T \phi(s)ds} \mathbb{E}^Q \left(exp \left[-\int_t^T (x_s + y_s)ds \right] / \mathcal{F}_t \right)$$

Zero-coupon bonds Let us recall that a normal variable Z satisfies

$$\mathbb{E}(e^Z) = e^{E(Z) + \frac{1}{2}V(Z)}$$

where $V(Z)$ is the variance of Z. Applied to B(t,T), that yields

$$B(t, T) = Exp \left[-\int_t^T \phi(s)ds \right] Exp \left(\underbrace{\mathbb{E} \left[-\int_t^T (x_s + y_s)ds \right]}_{mean=E(t,T)} + \frac{1}{2} \underbrace{V \left[-\int_t^T (x_s + y_s)ds \right]}_{Variance=V(t,T)} \right)$$

$$E(t, T) = \frac{1 - e^{-a(T-t)}}{a} x_t + \frac{1 - e^{-b(T-t)}}{b} y_t$$

$$V(t, T) = \frac{\sigma_x^2}{a^2} \left[T - t + \frac{2}{a} e^{-a(T-t)} - \frac{1}{2a} e^{-2a(T-t)} - \frac{3}{2a} \right]$$

$$+ \frac{\sigma_y^2}{b^2} \left[T - t + \frac{2}{b} e^{-b(T-t)} - \frac{1}{2b} e^{-2b(T-t)} - \frac{3}{2b} \right]$$

$$+ 2\rho \frac{\sigma_x \sigma_y}{ab} \left[T - t - \frac{1 - e^{-a(T-t)}}{a} - \frac{1 - e^{-b(T-t)}}{b} - \frac{e^{-(a+b)(T-t)} - 1}{a + b} \right] \tag{6.6}$$

As a consequence, the function ϕ that fits the zero-coupon yield curve verifies, for some t and T:

$$Exp\left[-\int_t^T \phi(s)ds\right] = \frac{B_{market}(0,T)}{B_{market}(0,t)}.Exp\left(-\frac{1}{2}[V(0,T)-V(0,t)]\right)$$

Options on zero-coupon bonds The theoretical price of a European call on a zero-coupon bond is given under the risk-neutral measure Q:

$$\mathbb{E}^Q\left(e^{-\int_t^T r(s)ds}[B(T,T+\tau)-K]^+/\mathcal{F}_t\right)$$

Once again, for ease of calculation, we opt for the forward measure:

$$X_t = B(t,T)\mathbb{E}^{Q_T}(X_T/\mathcal{F}_t)$$

with

$$\frac{dQ_T}{dQ} = \frac{e^{-\int_t^T r(s)ds}}{B(t,T)} = e^{-\frac{1}{2}V(t,T)-\int_t^T (x_s+y_s)ds}$$

From the above, we know that

$$\int_t^T (x_s+y_s)ds$$

is normally distributed. Thus, dQ_T/dQ is of the form

$$Exp\left(-\int \theta(\sigma_x,\sigma_y,a,b,\rho,s,T)ds - \int \epsilon(\sigma_x,\sigma_y,a,b,\rho,s,T)dw_s\right)$$

$$= Exp\left(\int \left(\frac{\theta_s^2}{2}-\epsilon_s\right)ds\right) * Exp\left(-\int \frac{\theta_s^2}{2}ds - \int \theta_s dw_s\right)$$

By analogy with the Girsanov density, we obtain the dynamics of x_t and y_t under Q_T, thus $\mathbb{E}^{Q_T}[r_t]$ and $Var^{Q_T}[r_t](=Var^Q[r_t])$.

Finally, since the change of measure only modifies the drift,

$$Corr^{Q_T}[dx_t,dy_t] = <dx_t,dy_t> = \rho dt$$

For a comprehensive explanation of the options' pricing, see Brigo and Mercurio (2006). Finally the price at t of a European call expiring at T on a zero-bond maturing at $T+\tau$ is

$$Call(t,T,T+\tau,K) = B(t,T+\tau) * N\left(\frac{Ln(B(t,T+\tau)/(K.B(t,T)))}{\Sigma(t,T,T+\tau)} + \frac{1}{2}\Sigma(t,T,T+\tau)\right)$$

$$- B(t,T)K * N\left(\frac{Ln(B(t,T+\tau)/(K.B(t,T)))}{\Sigma(t,T,T+\tau)} - \frac{1}{2}\Sigma(t,T,T+\tau)\right) \qquad (6.7)$$

$$\Sigma(t, T, T + \tau)^2 = \frac{\sigma_x^2}{2a^3}[1 - e^{-a\tau}]^2[1 - e^{-2a(T-t)}]$$

$$+ \frac{\sigma_y^2}{2b^3}[1 - e^{-b\tau}]^2[1 - e^{-2b(T-t)}]$$

$$+ 2\rho\frac{\sigma_x\sigma_y}{ab(a + b)}[1 - e^{-a\tau}][1 - e^{-b\tau}][1 - e^{-(a+b)(T-t)}] \qquad (6.8)$$

$$Put(t, T, T + \tau, K) = -B(t, T + \tau).N\left(\frac{Ln(K.B(t, T)/(B(t, T + \tau))}{\Sigma(t, T, T + \tau)} - \frac{1}{2}\Sigma(t, T, T + \tau)\right)$$

$$+ B(t, T)K.N\left(\frac{Ln(K.B(t, T)/B(t, T + \tau))}{\Sigma(t, T, T + \tau)} + \frac{1}{2}\Sigma(t, T, T + \tau)\right) \qquad (6.9)$$

Caplets and floorlets   The caplet payoff is written

$$Max\left(\frac{F(T, T + \tau) - K}{1 + F(T, T + \tau).\tau}.\tau, 0)\right)$$

To simplify, let us denote $F(T, T + \tau) = F_{T,\tau}$

$$Max\left(\frac{F_{T,\tau} - K}{1 + F_{T,\tau}.\tau}.\tau, 0)\right) = Max\left(\frac{1 + \tau F_{T,\tau} - 1 - \tau K}{1 + F_{T,\tau}.\tau}, 0)\right)$$

$$= Max\left(1 - \frac{1 + \tau K}{1 + F_{T,\tau}.\tau}, 0)\right)$$

Invoking the same rationale as for the HW one-factor model, and using Σ as an abbreviation of $\Sigma(t, T, T + \tau)$, we can infer the caplet price:

$$caplet(K, T, T + \tau) = (1 + \tau K) \, Put(t, \underbrace{T, T + \tau}_{ZBdates}, \underbrace{1/(1 + \tau K)}_{strike})$$

which results in

$$caplet(K, T, T + \tau) = -(1 + \tau K)B(t, T + \tau) * N\left(\frac{1}{\Sigma}.Ln\left(\frac{B(t, T)}{(1 + \tau K).B(t, T + \tau)}\right) - \frac{1}{2}\Sigma\right)$$

$$+ B(t, T) * N\left(\frac{1}{\Sigma}.Ln\left(\frac{B(t, T)}{(1 + \tau K).B(t, T + \tau)}\right) + \frac{1}{2}\Sigma\right)$$

Calibration with market caplets   Here again, we will invoke the Excel solver facility and another custom method to calibrate a, b, σ_x, σ_y, ρ.

As regards the custom method, we go for the simulated annealing technique that allows us to find minima even remote from the initial parameters. However, some restrictions must be brought to σ_x, σ_y, and ρ, namely

$$\sigma_x > 0 \qquad \sigma_x > 0 \qquad -1 \le \rho \le +1$$

We will put that into practice to calibrate 3-mth caplets up to 5-year maturities (19 caplets). The market prices are assumed to derive from the Black model.

Arbitrarily, we choose to minimize the following estimator:

$$\frac{1}{n} \sum_{i=1}^{n(=19)} \frac{|BlackPrice(i) - CapletG2Price(i)|}{BlackPrice(i)} < 2\%$$

The iterations will stop when the estimator level falls below 2%.

Excel solver   The screen snapshot below displays only significant data: intermediate results are stored in masked cells. It is merely a suggestion for organizing your own spreadsheet. Remember that the **Evolutionary** is the most robust algorithmic method to reach a minimum.

Se<u>t</u> Objective:	$B$12			
To:	⦿ Max	⦿ Mi<u>n</u>	⦿ <u>V</u>alue Of:	0

<u>B</u>y Changing Variable Cells:

$B$3:$B$7

S<u>u</u>bject to the Constraints:

```
rho <= 1
rho >= -1
vx >= 0
vy >= 0
```

	A	B	E	F	K	L	M	P	Q
1			T	Vol caplet(i)	Discount Factor	strike(i)	val caplet(i)	ZBC	gap
2					0.990099013				
3	vx	0.0212448	0.25	0.135	0.980198503	0.040402	0.0002666	0.0002778	4.21%
4	vy	0.0245844	0.5	0.14	0.970299482	0.0408081	0.0003908	0.0003901	0.18%
5	a	0.5194518	0.75	0.145	0.960402966	0.0412182	0.0004955	0.0004744	4.24%
6	b	0.058568	1	0.1425	0.950509965	0.0416324	0.0005619	0.000544	3.19%
7	rho	-0.980727	1.25	0.14	0.940621495	0.0420508	0.0006168	0.0006039	2.09%
8			1.5	0.138	0.930738568	0.0424735	0.0006656	0.0006569	1.31%
9	tau	0.25	1.75	0.136	0.920862257	0.0429003	0.0007079	0.0007044	0.49%
10			2	0.134	0.910993576	0.0433315	0.000745	0.0007476	0.35%
11			2.25	0.132	0.901133597	0.043767	0.0007776	0.000787	1.21%
12	Target	0.3336759	2.5	0.13	0.891283393	0.0442068	0.0008063	0.0008233	2.11%
13	Error	0.0175619	2.75	0.128	0.881444037	0.0446511	0.0008316	0.0008568	3.03%
14			3	0.128	0.871616602	0.0450999	0.0008674	0.0008878	2.35%
15			3.25	0.128	0.861802161	0.0455531	0.0009015	0.0009166	1.68%
16			3.5	0.128	0.852001786	0.046011	0.000934	0.0009434	1.00%
17			3.75	0.128	0.842216611	0.0464734	0.0009651	0.0009683	0.32%
18			4	0.128	0.832447767	0.0469404	0.000995	0.0009914	0.36%
19			4.25	0.128	0.822696328	0.0474122	0.0010236	0.0010128	1.05%
20			4.5	0.128	0.812963367	0.0478887	0.0010511	0.0010328	1.74%
21			4.75	0.128	0.803250074	0.04837	0.0010775	0.0010512	2.44%

Simulated annealing   We may run different trials until we obtain a solution combining restrictive conditions, and an acceptable mean gap between market and Gaussian prices (here 2%). Five solutions are tabulated below:

a	b	σ_x	σ_x	ρ	Gap $(.10^{-2})$
0.1224	−0.000442	.01024	.01023	−0.83	1.714
0.00575	−0.008167	.00757	.01038	−0.846	1.852
−0.0566	0.142	.00842	.0107	−0.807	1.41
0.0497	−0.009	.0084	.01072	−0.86	1.75
0.2017	−0.02045	.01036	.00915	−0.811	1.69

Modifying some increments and launching five other trials, we find:

a	b	σ_x	σ_y	ρ	Gap $(.10^{-2})$
0.102	−0.00159	.0052	.00907	−0.841	1.9
0.103	−0.00657	.01	.0101	−0.827	1.72
0.112	0.00048	.00673	.00913	−0.798	1.9
0.118	0.000678	.001	.00652	−0.88	1.94
0.0872	−0.02025	.00922	.00922	−0.8	1.65

Code   The main procedure **calibG2cap()**:

- calls **capG2init** in order to retrieve basic market data (forward rates, caplets' Black volatilities...) and computes caplets' prices under the Black model. In addition, a first computation of the estimator is achieved to start the calibration process;

- instantiates a, b, σ_x, σ_y, and ρ;
- runs the calibration algorithm that invokes three functions:
  - **calibCap**, that computes the estimator sum to mimimize
  - **capletG**, that computes the Gaussian price of the ith caplet
  - **accept**, the core process of the simulated annealing algorithm.

The arrays of market data are merely declared as Single (obviously at the top of the module), since the calculations do not require double precision.

```
Dim bd!(), Fwd!(), volCaplet!(), valCapB!(), valCapG!()

Sub calibG2cap()

Dim z0!, z1!, z2!, z3!, z4!, dg!
Dim zz0!, zz1!, zz2!, zz3!, zz4!

Dim i%
capG2init

Dim T!: T = 50 / 2: m = 2
    z0 = 0.136: z1 = -0.02: z2 = 0.00033: z3 = 0.00587: z4 = -0.835
f0 = calibCap(z0, z1, z2, z3, z4)
    T = 50: m = 2
    While T > 1

        For j = 1 To 10
            zz0 = z0 + (0.5 - Rnd()) / 100
            zz1 = z1 + (0.5 - Rnd()) / 100
            zz2 = z2 + (0.5 - Rnd()) / 100
            zz3 = z3 + (0.5 - Rnd()) / 100
            zz4 = z4 + (0.5 - Rnd()) / 100
            f1 = calibCap(zz0, zz1, zz2, zz3, zz4)
            dg = f1 - f0
            If accept(dg, T) Then z0 = zz0: z1 = zz1: _
            z2 = zz2: z3 = zz3: z4 = zz4: f0 = f1
        Next j
        m = m + 1
        T = 50 / m
    Wend

Randomize
Debug.Print z0 & "  " & z1
Debug.Print z2 & "  " & z3 & "  " & z4
Debug.Print calibCap(z0, z1, z2, z3, z4) / (n - 1)
End Sub


*************************************************************
valCapB is the array of ATM caplets' prices under the Black model.
*************************************************************


Function calibCap(a!, b!, vx!, vy!, rh!) As Single
som = 0
Dim i%
For i = 1 To 19
```

```
        som = som + Sqr((valCapB(i) - capletG(a, b, vx, vy, rh, i)) ^ 2 /
valCapB(i) ^ 2)
Next i
calibCap = som
End Function

Function capletG(a!, b!, vx!, vy!, rh!, i%)

    ep = vx ^ 2 / (2 * a ^ 3) * (1 - Exp(-a * 0.25)) ^ 2
            * (1 -   Exp(-2 * a * i * 0.25)) _
            + vy ^ 2 / (2 * b ^ 3) * (1 - Exp(-b * 0.25)) ^ 2
            * (1 - Exp(-2 * b * i * 0.25)) _
            + 2 * rh * vx * vy / (a * b * (a + b)) * (1 - Exp(-a * 0.25)) _
            * (1 - Exp(-b * 0.25)) * (1 - Exp(-(a + b) * i * 0.25))
    ep = Sqr(Abs(ep))
    capletG = bd(i - 1) * norm(Log(bd(i - 1) / ((1 + 0.25 * Fwd(i)) _
    * bd(i))) / ep + 0.5 * ep) - (1 + 0.25 * Fwd(i)) * bd(i)
    * norm(Log(bd(i - 1) _
    / ((1 + 0.25 * Fwd(i)) * bd(i))) / ep - 0.5 * ep)

End Function

Sub capG2init()

Dim d1!, d2!
Dim n%: n = 20

a = 0.136: b = -0.02: sx = 0.00033: sy = 0.00587: rho = -0.835

ReDim bd(n)
ReDim Fwd(n)
ReDim volCaplet(n)
ReDim valCapB(n)
ReDim valCapG(n)

Dim eps!(): ReDim eps(n)

Dim i%

valCapB(0) = 0

Worksheets(7).Activate

For i = 0 To n-1
    bd(i) = Cells(2 + i, 11)
Next i

For i = 1 To n - 1
    Fwd(i) = Cells(2 + i, 12)
    volCaplet(i) = Cells(2 + i, 6)
    d1 = 0.5 * volCaplet(i) * Sqr(i * 0.25)
    d2 = d1 - volCaplet(i) * Sqr(i * 0.25)
    valCapB(i) = 0.25 * Fwd(i) * (norm(d1) - norm(d2)) * bd(i)
Next

For i = 1 To n - 1
```

```
eps(i) = sx ^ 2 / (2 * a ^ 3) * (1 - Exp(-a * 0.25)) ^ 2
      * (1 - Exp(-2 * a * i * 0.25)) _
      + sy ^ 2 / (2 * b ^ 3) * (1 - Exp(-b * 0.25)) ^ 2
      * (1 -     Exp(-2 * b * i * 0.25)) _
      + 2 * rho * sx * sy / (a * b * (a + b)) * (1 - Exp(-a * 0.25)) * _
      (1 - Exp(-b * 0.25)) * (1 - Exp(-(a + b) * i * 0.25))
eps(i) = Sqr(eps(i))
valCapG(i) = bd(i - 1) * norm(Log(bd(i - 1) / ((1 + 0.25 * Fwd(i))
* bd(i))) / eps(i) _
+ 0.5 * eps(i)) - (1 + 0.25 * Fwd(i)) * bd(i) * norm(Log(bd(i - 1) _
          / ((1 + 0.25 * Fwd(i)) * bd(i))) / eps(i) - 0.5 * eps(i))
Next i

End Sub

Public Function accept(a!, b!) As Boolean
Dim z!
If a < 0 Then
    accept = True
Else
    z = Exp(-a / b)
    If Rnd() < z Then
        accept = True
    Else
        accept = False
    End If
End If
End Function
```

Swaptions Let us assume a European-style swaption expiring at T, i.e., a right to enter into a fixed-rate paying swap ($w = 1$) or a fixed-rate receiving swap ($w = -1$), with payment times T_i, $i = 1,...,n$. Struck at K, the expression of the swaption payoff is

$$Max\left(w\left[\underbrace{1 - B(T,T_n)}_{floating\ leg} - \underbrace{\sum_{i=1}^{n} X\tau B(T,T_i)}_{fixed\ leg}\right],0\right)$$

Assuming that $T_{i+1} - T_i = \tau$ $\forall i$, and introducing the coupons c_i such that

$$c_i = X\tau \text{ for } i < n$$
$$c_n = 1 + X\tau$$

the swaption payoff may also be expressed as follows:

$$Max\left(w\left(1 - \sum_{i=1}^{n} c_i B(T,T_i)\right),0\right)$$

We have established previously that the price of any zero-bond $B(t, T)$ could be written

$$B(t, T) = I(\Phi) * exp(-\lambda(a)x_t - \lambda(b)y_t + V(a, b, \sigma_x, \sigma_y, \rho))$$

where $I(\Phi)$ is **deterministic**. The computation of the swaption price requires an integration of the sum $\sum B(T, T_i)$ depending on x_t and y_t, then weighted by the density $f(x_t, y_t)$, hence a (very) arduous issue. We settle straight away for the final expression, letting the reader explore the major steps of the proof in Brigo and Mercurio (2006). The swaption price writes

$$wB(0, T) \int_{-\infty}^{+\infty} \frac{exp\left(-1/2\left(\dfrac{x - \mu_x}{\eta_x}\right)^2\right)}{\eta_x\sqrt{2\pi}} \left[N(-wh_1(x)) - \sum_{i=1}^{n} \lambda_i(x)e^{\kappa_i(x)}N(-wh_2(x))\right] dx$$

$$w = \pm 1 \ (+1 \text{ for payer} - 1 \text{ for receiver}) \tag{6.10}$$

$$h_1(x) = \frac{\bar{y} - \mu_y}{\eta_y\sqrt{1 - \eta_{xy}^2}} - \frac{\eta_{xy}(x - \mu_x)}{\eta_x\sqrt{1 - \eta_{xy}^2}}$$

$$h_2(x) = h_1(x) + B(b, T, T_i)\eta_y\sqrt{1 - \eta_{xy}^2}$$

with

$$B(z, T, T_i) = \frac{1 - e^{-z(T_i - T)}}{z}$$

and $\bar{y}$ being the solution of

$$\sum_{i=1}^{n} c_i A(T, T_i)e^{-B(a,T,T_i)x}e^{-B(b,T,T_i)\bar{y}} = 1$$

$\mu_x, \mu_y, \eta_x, \eta_y$, and η_{xy} are given by

$$\mu_x = -\left(\frac{\sigma_x^2}{a^2} + \rho\frac{\sigma_x\sigma_y}{ab}\right)(1 - e^{-aT}) + \frac{\sigma_x^2}{2a^2}(1 - e^{-2aT}) + \frac{\rho\sigma_x\sigma_y}{b(a + b)}(1 - e^{-(a+b)T})$$

$$\mu_y = -\left(\frac{\sigma_y^2}{b^2} + \rho\frac{\sigma_x\sigma_y}{ab}\right)(1 - e^{-bT}) + \frac{\sigma_y^2}{2b^2}(1 - e^{-2bT}) + \frac{\rho\sigma_x\sigma_y}{a(a + b)}(1 - e^{-(a+b)T})$$

$$\eta_x = \sigma_x\sqrt{\frac{1 - e^{-2aT}}{2a}} \qquad \eta_y = \sigma_y\sqrt{\frac{1 - e^{-2bT}}{2b}}$$

$$\eta_{xy} = \frac{\rho\sigma_x\sigma_y}{(a + b)\eta_x\eta_y}(1 - e^{-(a+b)T})$$

Also:

$$\lambda_i(x) = c_i A(T, T_i)e^{-B(a,T,T_i)x}$$

with $A(T, T_i) = \dfrac{B_{market}(0, T_i)}{B_{market}(0, T)} . exp\left(\dfrac{1}{2}[V(T, T_i) - V(0, T_i) + V(0, T)]\right)$

$\kappa_i(x) = -B(b, T, T_i)\left(\mu_x - \dfrac{1}{2}(1 - \eta_{xy}^2)\eta_y^2 B(b, T, T_i) + \eta_{xy}\eta_y \dfrac{x - \mu_x}{\eta_x}\right)$

Numerical solution The swaptions' pricing comes up against two computational difficulties:

- the solving of the implicit equation

$$\sum_{i=1}^{n} c_i A(T, T_i) e^{-B(a, T, T_i)x} e^{-B(b, T, T_i)\bar{y}} = 1 \tag{6.11}$$

Fortunately, the first derivative of the left-hand side function is straightforward to calculate: this can be solved easily using *Newton-Raphson*.

- the calculation of the improper integral itself. The form of the integral

$$\int_{-\infty}^{+\infty} e^{-1/2\left(\frac{x-\mu_x}{\eta_x}\right)^2} g(x)dx$$

suggests that we use the *Hermite polynomials* approximation after a change of variable

$$u = \frac{x - \mu_x}{\sqrt{2}\eta_x}$$

The payer swaption is then written:

$$B(0, T)\int_{-\infty}^{+\infty} \frac{e^{-u^2}}{\sqrt{\pi}}\left[N(-h_1(u)) - \sum_{i=1}^{n} \lambda_i(u)e^{\kappa_i(u)}N(-h_2(u))\right]du$$

$$h_1(u) = \frac{\bar{y} - \mu_y}{\eta_y\sqrt{1 - \eta_{xy}^2}} - \frac{\sqrt{2}\eta_{xy}u}{\sqrt{1 - \eta_{xy}^2}}$$

$$h_2(u) = h_1(u) + B(b, T, T_i)\eta_y\sqrt{1 - \eta_{xy}^2}$$

$$\lambda_i(u) = c_i A(T, T_i)e^{-B(a, T, T_i)(\eta_x\sqrt{2}u + \mu_x)}$$

$$\kappa_i(u) = -B(b, T, T_i)\left(\mu_x - \frac{1}{2}(1 - \eta_{xy}^2)\eta_y^2 B(b, T, T_i) + \eta_{xy}\eta_y\sqrt{2}u\right)$$

$$\sum_{i=1}^{n} c_i A(T, T_i)e^{-B(a, T, T_i)(\sqrt{2}\eta_x u + \mu_x)} . e^{-B(b, T, T_i)\bar{y}} = 1$$

TABLE 6.1 Black prices (in %)

Exp I swap tenor	1y	2y	3y	4y	5y	6y	7y	8y	9y
1y	0.229	0.470	0.717	0.961	1.188	1.401	1.599	1.790	1.973
2y		0.341	0.690	1.035	1.356	1.656	1.936	2.205	2.465
3y			0.427	0.849	1.242	1.610	1.952	2.282	2.599
4y				0.487	0.940	1.365	1.760	2.140	2.507
5y					0.506	0.981	1.421	1.847	2.256
6y						0.519	1.002	1.467	1.916
7y							0.512	0.976	1.391
8y								0.504	0.960
9y									0.548

TABLE 6.2 G2 prices (in %)

Exp I swap tenor	1y	2y	3y	4y	5y	6y	7y	8y	9y
1y	0.282	0.558	0.816	1.049	1.256	1.439	1.600	1.741	1.863
2y		0.388	0.759	1.098	1.403	1.673	1.911	2.120	2.302
3y			0.453	0.876	1.260	1.603	1.907	2.174	2.407
4y				0.489	0.941	1.349	1.713	2.033	2.313
5y					0.507	0.972	1.391	1.762	2.088
6y						0.514	0.982	1.402	1.773
7y							0.512	0.976	1.391
8y								0.504	0.960
9y									0.492

A good approximation can be obtained with twenty 20 Gauss-Hermite abscissas.

$$\frac{B(0, T)}{\sqrt{\pi}} \sum_{k=1}^{20} H_k \cdot g(x_k)$$

$$g(x_k) = N(-h_1(x_k)) - \sum_{i=1}^{n} \lambda_i(x_k) e^{\kappa_i(x_k)} N(-h_2(x_k))$$

The calibration will be carried out on the following run of swaptions:

$$1y/1y, \ 1y/2y, \ ,..., \ 1y/9y$$

$$2y/1y, \ 2y/2y,..., \ 2y/8y$$

$$\vdots$$

$$9y/1y$$

The fitting of five parameters with $9 \times 8/2 = 36$ swaptions proves to be a tricky issue. We resort to the simulated annealing method, seemingly the most appropriate one, though it takes a pretty long time to give an acceptable solution for a majority of swaptions. Tables 6.1 and 6.2 provide prices issued from Black and G2 models while Table 6.3 highlights the pricing gap (in %) between the two models.

TABLE 6.3 (Black-G2)/G2 (in %)

Exp\swap tenor	1y	2y	3y	4y	5y	6y	7y	8y	9y
1y	**−23.13**	**−18.69**	**−13.78**	**−9.07**	−5.66	−2.68	−0.006	2.74	5.60
2y		**−13.86**	**−9.98**	−6.11	−3.46	−0.99	1.27	3.87	6.63
3y			−6.02	−3.12	−1.45	0.42	2.29	4.73	7.42
4y				−0.43	−0.09	1.15	2.66	5.01	7.72
5y					−0.22	0.83	2.15	4.59	7.47
6y						1.08	1.96	4.46	7.47
7y							1.78	4.59	7.71
8y								6.06	**8.89**
9y									**10.25**

```
Dim xH!(), wH!()
Dim a!, b!, sx!, sy!, rho!
Dim mu_x!, mu_y!, eta_x!, eta_y!, eta_xy!

Dim V!(), At!()

Dim str!(), sfwd!()
Dim volSwap!(), valSwap!() swaptions market volatilities and prices
Dim bd!()

Sub swapG2init()

Dim d1!, d2!

a = 0.575: b = 0.035: sx = 0.005: sy = 0.007: rho = -0.6

ReDim bd(10)
Dim swG!(): ReDim swG(10, 10)
Dim swB!(): ReDim swB(10, 10)

ReDim sfwd(10, 10)

ReDim V(10, 10)
ReDim At(10, 10)

For i = 0 To 9
    For j = i + 1 To 10
    dt = (j - i)
        V(i, j) = sx ^ 2 / a ^ 2 * (dt + 2 / a * Exp(-a * dt) - 1 _
        / (2 * a) * Exp(-2 * a * dt) - 3 / (2 * a)) _
            + sy ^ 2 / b ^ 2 * (dt + 2 / b * Exp(-b * dt) - 1 _
            / (2 * b) * Exp(-2 * b * dt) - 3 / (2 * b)) _
            + 2 * rho * sx * sy / (a * b) * (dt + (Exp(-a * dt) - 1) _
            / a + (Exp(-b * dt) - 1) / b - (Exp(-(a + b) * dt) - 1) /
            (a + b))
    Next j
Next i

ReDim swaps(10), sumbd(10)
```

```
ReDim volSwap(10, 10)
ReDim valSwap(10, 10)

Dim DF!(): ReDim DF(10)
Worksheets(10).Activate

sumbd(0) = 0: bd(0) = 1
For i = 1 To 10
    swaps(i) = Cells(2 + i, 4)
    bd(i) = (1 - sumbd(i - 1) * swaps(i)) / (1 + swaps(i))
    sumbd(i) = sumbd(i - 1) + bd(i)
Next i
For i = 1 To 9
    For j = i + 1 To 10
        sfwd(i, j) = (bd(i) - bd(j)) / (sumbd(j) - sumbd(i))
        Cells(2 + i, 6 + j) = sfwd(i, j)
    Next j
Next i
For i = 1 To 9
    For j = i + 1 To 10
        dt = (j - i)
        At(i, j) = bd(j) / bd(i) * Exp(0.5 * (V(i, j) - V(0, j) + V(0, i)))
    Next j
Next i

For i = 1 To 9
    For j = i + 1 To 10
        volSwap(i, j) = Cells(i + 32, j + 6)
        volSwap(i, j) = 0.13
    Next j
Next i

For i = 1 To 9
    For j = i + 1 To 10
        d1 = 0.5 * volSwap(i, j) * Sqr(i)
        d2 = d1 - volSwap(i, j) * Sqr(i)
        valSwap(i, j) = sfwd(i, j) * (norm(d1) - norm(d2))
        * (sumbd(j) - sumbd(i))
        Cells(12 + i, 6 + j) = valSwap(i, j)
    Next j

Next

ReDim wH!(32), xH!(32)

Worksheets("Hermite").Activate

For i = 1 To 20
    xH(i) = Cells(i, 8): wH(i) = Cells(i, 10)
Next i

End Sub

Function swapG(a!, b!, sx!, sy!, rho!, n%, p%) As Single

Dim yy!, h1!, h2!, k%, d1!, d2!
```

```
mu_x = -(sx ^ 2 / a ^ 2 + rho * sx * sy / a / b) * (1 - Exp(-a * n)) _
+ sx ^ 2 / (2 * a ^ 2) * (1 - Exp(-2 * a * n)) _
    + rho * sx * sy / (b * (a + b)) * (1 - Exp(-(a + b) * n))
mu_y = -(sy ^ 2 / b ^ 2 + rho * sx * sy / a / b) * (1 - Exp(-b * n)) _
+ sy ^ 2 / (2 * b ^ 2) * (1 - Exp(-2 * b * n)) _
    + rho * sx * sy / (a * (a + b)) * (1 - Exp(-(a + b) * n))
eta_x = sx * Sqr((1 - Exp(-2 * a * n)) / (2 * a))
eta_y = sy * Sqr((1 - Exp(-2 * b * n)) / (2 * b))
eta_xy = rho * sx * sy / (a + b) / (eta_x * eta_y) * (1 - Exp(-(a + b) * n))

For i = 0 To 9
    For j = i + 1 To 10
    dt = (j - i)
        V(i, j) = sx ^ 2 / a ^ 2 * (dt + 2 / a * Exp(-a * dt) - 1 _
        / (2 * a) * Exp(-2 * a * dt) - 3 / (2 * a)) _
            + sy ^ 2 / b ^ 2 * (dt + 2 / b * Exp(-b * dt) - 1 _
            / (2 * b) * Exp(-2 * b * dt) - 3 / (2 * b)) _
            + 2 * rho * sx * sy / (a * b) * (dt + (Exp(-a * dt) - 1) _
            / a + (Exp(-b * dt) - 1) / b - (Exp(-(a + b) * dt) - 1)
            / a( + b))
    Next j
Next i

For i = 1 To 9
    For j = i + 1 To 10
        dt = (j - i)
        At(i, j) = bd(j) / bd(i) * Exp(0.5 * (V(i, j) - V(0, j) + V(0, i)))
    Next j
Next i

Dim x!


*****************************************************************
x: every Hermite node for which the implicit equation is solved.
*****************************************************************


For m = 1 To 20
x = xH(m)

    yy = 0.1
    f = impY(sfwd(n, p), n, p, x, yy)
    divf = DimpY(sfwd(n, p), n, p, x, yy)
    While Abs(f - 1) > 0.00001
        yy = yy + (1 - f) / divf
        f = impY(sfwd(n, p), n, p, x, yy)
        divf = DimpY(sfwd(n, p), n, p, x, yy)
    Wend
d2 = 0
    h1 = (yy - mu_y) / eta_y / Sqr(1 - eta_xy ^ 2) - eta_xy * Sqr(2)
        * x / Sqr(1 - eta_xy ^ 2)
    d1 = norm(-h1)
    For k = n + 1 To p
        h2 = h1 + Bt(b, n, k) * eta_y * Sqr(1 - eta_xy ^ 2)
```

```
            d2 = d2 + sfwd(n, p) * At(n, k) * Exp(-Bt(a, n, k)
                * (eta_x * Sqr(2) * x + mu_x)) * _
                Exp(-Bt(b, n, k) * (mu_y - 0.5 * (1 - eta_xy ^ 2) * eta_y ^ 2
                    * Bt(b, n, k) _
                + eta_xy * eta_y * Sqr(2) * x)) * norm(-h2)
        Next k
        d2 = d2 + At(n, p) * Exp(-Bt(a, n, p) * (eta_x * Sqr(2) * x + mu_x)) * _
            Exp(-Bt(b, n, p) * (mu_y - 0.5 * (1 - eta_xy ^ 2) * eta_y ^ 2
                * Bt(b, n, p) _
            + eta_xy * eta_y * Sqr(2) * x)) * norm(-h2)
        som = som + wH(m) * (d1 - d2) * Exp(-x ^ 2)

Next m

swapG = som / Sqr(PI) * Sqr(2) * bd(n)

End Function
```

```
Function Bt(z!, i%, j%) As Single
Bt = (1 - Exp(-z * (j - i))) / z
End Function
```

```
*********************************************************************
```
Functions impY and DimpY play the roles of *f* and *f′* in the Newton-Raphson algorithm.
```
*********************************************************************
```

```
Function impY(s!, i%, j%, u!, y!) As Single
Dim k%
impY = At(i, j) * Exp(-Bt(a, i, j) * (eta_x * Sqr(2) * u + mu_x)
      - Bt(b, i, j) * y)
For k = i + 1 To j
    impY = impY + s * At(i, k) * Exp(-Bt(a, i, k) * (eta_x * Sqr(2)
        * u + mu_x) - Bt(b, i, k) * y)
Next k
End Function
```

```
Function DimpY(s!, i%, j%, u!, y!) As Single
Dim k%
DimpY = -Bt(b, i, j) * At(i, j) * Exp(-Bt(a, i, j) * (eta_x * Sqr(2)
        * u + mu_x) - Bt(b, i, j) * y)
For k = i + 1 To j
    DimpY = DimpY - Bt(b, i, k) * s * At(i, k) * Exp(-Bt(a, i, k)
            * (eta_x * Sqr(2) * u + mu_x) _
    - Bt(b, i, k) * y)
Next k
End Function
```

```
Sub algoHW()

Dim z0!, z1!, z2!, z3!, z4!, dg!
Dim zz0!, zz1!, zz2!, zz3!, zz4!

z0 = 0.773: z1 = 0.082: z2 = 0.0023: z3 = 0.01: z4 = -0.7

swapG2init
```

```
Dim T!: T = 50 / 2: m = 2
z0 = 0.773: z1 = 0.082: z2 = 0.0033: z3 = 0.01: z4 = -0.7

f0 = calib(z0, z1, z2, z3, z4)
While T > 5

    For j = 1 To 10
        zz0 = z0 + (0.5 - Rnd()) / 100
        zz1 = z1 + (0.5 - Rnd()) / 500
        zz2 = z2 + (0.5 - Rnd()) / 500
        zz3 = z3 + (0.5 - Rnd()) / 500
        zz4 = z4 + (0.5 - Rnd()) / 100
        f1 = calib(zz0, zz1, zz2, zz3, zz4)
        dg = f1 - f0
        If accept(dg, T) Then z0 = zz0: z1 = zz1: z2 = zz2: z3 = zz3:
        z4 = zz4: f0 = f1
    Next j
    m = m + 1
    T = 50 / m
Wend
Randomize
Debug.Print z0 & "   " & z1
Debug.Print z2 & "   " & z3 & "   " & z4
Debug.Print calib(z0, z1, z2, z3, z4) / 45 & "   " & compteur

Worksheets(10).Activate
Dim n%, p%
For n = 1 To 9
    For p = n + 1 To 10
        Cells(22 + n, 6 + p) = swapG(z0, z1, z2, z3, z4, n, p)
    Next p
Next n

End Sub
```

```
Function calib(a!, b!, vx!, vy!, rh!) As Single
calib = 0
Dim i%, j%
For i = 1 To 9
    For j = i + 1 To 10
        calib = calib + Sqr((valSwap(i, j)
                 - swapG(a, b, vx, vy, rh, i, j)) ^ 2) / valSwap(i, j)
    Next j
Next i

End Function
```

Binomial approximation   One of the most common numerical solutions to price exotic interest rate derivatives remains the binomial tree. When dealing with a two-factor process, we fix the problem by combining two binomial trees in order to build a *quadrinomial tree*.

Let us denote by p and q the probabilities that x and y move up. The form of r_t diffusion process as the sum of two Gaussian variables x_t and y_t forces the increments Δx_t and Δy_t to be constant. If we want the trees to be recombining,

$$\text{down movement} + \text{up movement} = 0$$

As a consequence, given x and y at t

$$\mathbb{E}(x(t + \Delta t)) = p(x + \Delta x) + (1 - p)(x - \Delta x) \simeq x(1 - a\Delta t)$$

$$\mathbb{E}(y(t + \Delta t)) = q(y + \Delta y) + (1 - q)(y - \Delta y) \simeq y(1 - b\Delta t)$$

$$Var(x(t + \Delta t)) = p(x + \Delta x)^2 + (1 - p)(x - \Delta x)^2 - x^2(1 - a\Delta t)^2 = \sigma_x^2 \Delta t$$

$$Var(y(t + \Delta t)) = p(y + \Delta y)^2 + (1 - p)(y - \Delta y)^2 - y^2(1 - b\Delta t)^2 = \sigma_y^2 \Delta t$$

A first-order approximation leads to

$$\Delta x = \sigma_x \sqrt{\Delta t} \quad p = \frac{1}{2} - \frac{x.a}{2\sigma_x}\sqrt{\Delta t}$$

$$\Delta y = \sigma_y \sqrt{\Delta t} \quad q = \frac{1}{2} - \frac{y.b}{2\sigma_y}\sqrt{\Delta t}$$

Let us consider $p(i, j)$ the probability of an upward/downward movement of (x, y) from every node as represented in the chart below:

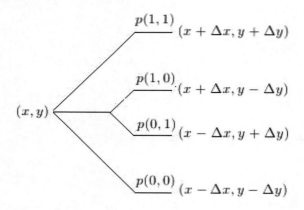

As the increments Δx and Δy are constant over the tree's lifetime, the values of $x + y$ at each node are easily computable. In fact, at $t = i\Delta t$,

$$x(i, j) = (2j - i)\Delta x \qquad y(i, k) = (2k - i)\Delta y$$

The computation of probabilities is a bit more tricky. Let us consider the tree as an "inverted pyramid". In the graph below two adjacent steps i and $i + 1$ are superposed (actually in our example, $i = 2$). Three situations are possible (noted (1), (2), and (3) on the graph zone):

1. **(1)** : corner to corner: 1 path) (e.g., $(2, 0, 0) \rightarrow (3, 0, 0)$)
2. edge to edge: 2 paths (e.g., $(2, 0, 2)$ or $(2, 1, 2) \rightarrow (3, 1, 3)$)
3. inside the square: 4 paths (e.g., $(2, 1, 0)$ or $(2, 2, 0)$ or $(2, 1, 1)$ or $(2, 2, 1) \rightarrow (3, 2, 1)$)

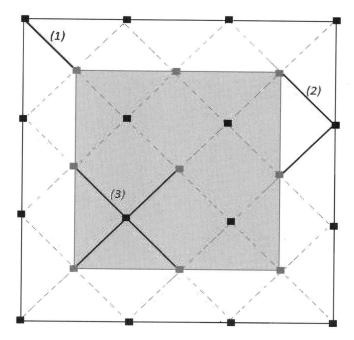

In the code below, a 5-yr maturity tree has been implemented to price 3-mth duration caplets up to 5 years. Therefore, a 3-mth timestep seems to be a logical choice. In other words, each node provides an occurrence of the underlying LIBOR fixing.

```
Sub treeG2()
```

```
Dim fwHW!(), fwd!()
ReDim fwHW!(20, 20, 20)
ReDim fwd(19)
Dim DF!()
ReDim DF(19)

Dim nb%()
ReDim nb(19, 19, 19)
Dim p!()
ReDim p(19, 19, 19)
Dim x!(), y!()
ReDim x(19, 19), y(19, 19)

'    retrieval forward market

For i = 0 To 19
    fwd(i) = 0.04 * Exp(0.01 * i)
Next i
DF(0) = 1 / (1 + fwd(0) * 0.25)
For i = 1 To 19
    DF(i) = DF(i - 1) / (1 + fwd(i) * 0.25)
Next i

Dim vx!, vy!, a!, b!, rho!
```

```
vx = 0.00376: vy = 0.00979
a = 0.541: b = 0.0542
rho = -0.99

Dim dt!: dt = 0.25
Dim dx!: dx = vx * Sqr(dt)
Dim dy!: dy = vy * Sqr(dt)

For i = 1 To 19
    For j = 0 To i
        x(i, j) = (2 * j - i) * dx
        y(i, j) = (2 * j - i) * dy
    Next j
Next i

Dim zu!: zu = (1 + rho) / 4
Dim zd!: zd = (1 - rho) / 4
Dim z2!: z2 = Sqr(dt) / (4 * vx * vy)

Dim puu!(), pud!(), pdu!(), pdd!()
ReDim puu!(19, 19, 19), pud!(19, 19, 19), pdu!(19, 19, 19), pdd!(19, 19, 19)

Dim phi!()
ReDim phi(19)
phi(0) = fwd(0)

For i = 1 To 19
phi(i) = fwd(i) + vx ^ 2 / 2 / a ^ 2 * (1 - Exp(-a * i * 0.25)) ^ 2
    phi(i) = phi(i) + vy ^ 2 / 2 / a ^ 2 * (1 - Exp(-b * i * 0.25)) ^ 2
                    + rho * vx * vy / a / b * (1 - Exp(-a * i * 0.25))
                    * (1 - Exp(-b * i * 0.25))
Next i

nb(1, 0, 0) = 1: nb(1, 1, 0) = 1: nb(1, 0, 1) = 1: nb(1, 1, 1) = 1

fwHW(0, 0, 0) = phi(0)
p(1, 1, 1) = (1 + rho) / 4
p(1, 1, 0) = (1 - rho) / 4
p(1, 0, 1) = (1 - rho) / 4
p(1, 0, 0) = (1 + rho) / 4

fwHW(1, 1, 1) = phi(1) + dx + dy
fwHW(1, 1, 0) = phi(1) + dx - dy
fwHW(1, 0, 1) = phi(1) - dx + dy
fwHW(1, 0, 0) = phi(1) - dx - dy

For i = 2 To 19
    For j = 1 To i
        For k = 1 To i

p(i, j, k) = p(i - 1, j - 1, k - 1) * (zu - (b * vx * y(i - 1, k - 1) _
    + a * vy * x(i - 1, j - 1)) * z2) _
            + p(i - 1, j, k - 1) * (zd - (b * vx * y(i - 1, k - 1) _
            - a * vy * x(i - 1, j)) * z2) _
            + p(i - 1, j - 1, k) * (zd + (b * vx * y(i - 1, k) _
            - a * vy * x(i - 1, j - 1)) * z2) _
```

```
                + p(i - 1, j, k) * (zu + (b * vx * y(i - 1, k) _
                + a * vy * x(i - 1, j)) * z2)

fwHW(i, j, k) = fwHW(i - 1, j - 1, k - 1) + dx + dy + (phi(i) - phi(i - 1))

        Next k
    Next j

    fwHW(i, 0, 0) = fwHW(i - 1, 0, 0) - dx - dy + _
    (phi(i) - phi(i - 1))
    p(i, 0, 0) = p(i - 1, 0, 0) * (zu + (b * vx * y(i - 1, 0) + a
    * vy * x(i - 1, 0)) * z2)
    fwHW(i, i, 0) = fwHW(i - 1, i - 1, 0) + dx - dy + (phi(i) - phi(i - 1))
    p(i, i, 0) = p(i - 1, i - 1, 0) * (zd + (b * vx * y(i - 1, 0) - a * vy
    * x(i - 1, i - 1)) * z2)
    fwHW(i, 0, i) = fwHW(i - 1, 0, i - 1) - dx + dy + (phi(i) - phi(i - 1))
    p(i, 0, i) = p(i - 1, 0, i - 1) * (zd - (b * vx * y(i - 1, i - 1) - a
    * vy * x(i - 1, 0)) * z2)
    fwHW(i, i, i) = fwHW(i - 1, i - 1, i - 1) + dx + dy
    + (phi(i) - phi(i - 1))
    p(i, i, i) = p(i - 1, i - 1, i - 1) * (zu - (b * vx * y(i - 1, i - 1) + a
    * vy * x(i - 1, i - 1)) * z2)

    For l = 1 To i - 1

    fwHW(i, 0, l) = fwHW(i - 1, 0, l - 1) - dx + dy + (phi(i) - phi(i - 1))
    p(i, 0, l) = p(i - 1, 0, l - 1) * (zd - (b * vx * y(i - 1, l - 1) - a
    * vy * x(i - 1, 0)) * z2) _
                + p(i - 1, 0, l) * (zu + (b * vx * y(i - 1, l) + a * vy
                * x(i - 1, 0)) * z2)

    fwHW(i, i, l) = fwHW(i - 1, i - 1, l - 1) + dx + dy
    + (phi(i) - phi(i - 1))
    p(i, i, l) = p(i - 1, i - 1, l - 1) * (zu - (b * vx * y(i - 1, l - 1) + a
    * vy * x(i - 1, i - 1)) * z2) _
                + p(i - 1, i - 1, l) * (zd + (b * vx * y(i - 1, l) - a * vy
                * x(i - 1, i - 1)) * z2)

    fwHW(i, l, 0) = fwHW(i - 1, l - 1, 0) + dx - dy + (phi(i) - phi(i - 1))
    p(i, l, 0) = p(i - 1, l - 1, 0) * (zd + (b * vx * y(i - 1, 0) - a
    * vy * x(i - 1, l - 1)) * z2) _
                + p(i - 1, l, 0) * (zu + (b * vx * y(i - 1, 0) + a * vy
                * x(i - 1, l)) * z2)

    fwHW(i, l, i) = fwHW(i - 1, i - 1, l - 1) + dx + dy + (phi(i)
                    - phi(i - 1))
    p(i, l, i) = _
            p(i - 1, l - 1, i - 1) * _
            (zu - (b * vx * y(i - 1, i - 1) + a * vy
            * x(i - 1, l - 1)) * z2) _
        + p(i - 1, l, i - 1) * _
            (zd - (b * vx * y(i - 1, i - 1) - a * vy * x(i - 1, l)) * z2)

    Next l
Next i
Dim cc!(19)
For i = 1 To 19
```

```
w = 0
    For j = 0 To i
        For k = 0 To i
            cc(i) = cc(i) + p(i, j, k) * max(fwHW(i, j, k) - fwd(i), 0) * 0.25
            w = w + p(i, j, k)
        Next k
    Next j
    Debug.Print cc(i) * DF(i)
    ' checking that the sum of p(i,j) at each step is 1
    Debug.Print w
Next i
End Sub
```

Monte-Carlo scenarios   We choose to discretize the process, using the basic *Euler scheme*, i.e., the dynamics are then written:

$$\Delta x_i = x_{i+1} - x_i = -a.x_i\Delta t + \sigma_x\sqrt{\Delta t}z_x$$

$$\Delta y_i = y_{i+1} - y_i = -b.y_i\Delta t + \sigma_y\sqrt{\Delta t}z_y$$

$$\phi_i = F_{i,i+1} + \frac{v_x^2}{2a^2}(1 - e^{a.i\Delta t})^2 + \frac{v_y^2}{2b^2}(1 - e^{b.i\Delta t})^2$$

$$+ \rho\frac{v_xv_y}{ab}(1 - e^{a.i\Delta t})(1 - e^{b.i\Delta t})$$

z_1 and z_2 being independent standard normal RVs:

$$z_x = z_1 \qquad z_y = \rho z_1 + \sqrt{1 - \rho^2}z_2$$

The code below prices 3-mth duration caplets up to 5 years (from $3m/3m$ to $4.75y/3m$), i.e., the same caplets than for the quadrinomial tree method, using the same parameters.

```
Sub hwMC()

Dim x!, y!
Dim phi!(): ReDim phi(19)

Dim dt!: dt = 0.25
```

```
Dim Fwd!(), DF!(): ReDim Fwd(19), DF(19)
phi(0) = Fwd(0)

Dim caplet!(19)

For i = 0 To 19
    Fwd(i) = 0.04 * Exp(0.01 * i)
Next i
DF(0) = 1 / (1 + Fwd(0) * 0.25)
For i = 1 To 19
    DF(i) = DF(i - 1) / (1 + Fwd(i) * 0.25)
Next i

Dim vx!, vy!, a!, b!, rho!
vx = 0.0054123: vy = 0.0087792
a = 0.1305263: b = 0.0127878
rho = -0.78784

For i = 1 To 19
    phi(i) = Fwd(i) + vx ^ 2 / 2 / a ^ 2 * (1 - Exp(-a * i * 0.25)) ^ 2 _
                    + vy ^ 2 / 2 / b ^ 2 * (1 - Exp(-b * i * 0.25)) ^ 2 _
                    + rho * vx * vy / a / b * (1 - Exp(-a * i * 0.25)) _
                    * (1 - Exp(-b * i * 0.25))
Next i

For m = 1 To 20000
    x = 0: y = 0
    For i = 1 To 19
        z1 = gauss()
        z2 = rho * z1 + gauss() * Sqr(1 - rho ^ 2)

        x = x - a * x * dt + vx * z1 * Sqr(dt)
        y = y - b * y * dt + vy * z2 * Sqr(dt)

        caplet(i) = caplet(i) + max(x + y + phi(i) - Fwd(i), 0) * 0.25
    Next i
Next m

For i = 1 To 19
    Debug.Print caplet(i) / 20000 * DF(i)
Next i

End Sub
```

The results obtained from the tree and Monte-Carlo seem tolerably close except for short maturity caplets where the values obtained from the tree look quite unstable. This is essentially attributable to the relative importance of the elementary timestep compared to the caplet duration. The table below is a recap of the prices issued from both numerical algorithms vs prices issued from close formulae (Black and G2 models):

Maturity	Black price ($\times 10^{-3}$)	Analytical G2($\times 10^{-3}$)	Quad. tree($\times 10^{-3}$)	M.C.($\times 10^{-3}$)
3m	0.267	0.278	0.277	0.276
6m	0.391	0.391	0.293	0.389
9m	0.496	0.475	0.403	0.47
12m	0.562	0.544	0.447	0.542
15m	0.617	0.604	0.547	0.6
18m	0.666	0.657	0.598	0.652
21m	0.708	0.704	0.676	0.7
24m	0.745	0.747	0.715	0.744
27m	0.778	0.786	0.773	0.788
30m	0.806	0.822	0.805	0.823
33m	0.832	0.855	0.85	0.859
36m	0.867	0.886	0.878	0.892
39m	0.902	0.914	0.915	0.92
42m	0.934	0.941	0.94	0.949
45m	0.965	0.966	0.973	0.974
48m	0.995	0.989	0.995	0.994
51m	1.02	1.01	1.02	1.02
54m	1.05	1.03	1.04	1.04
57m	1.08	1.05	1.07	1.06

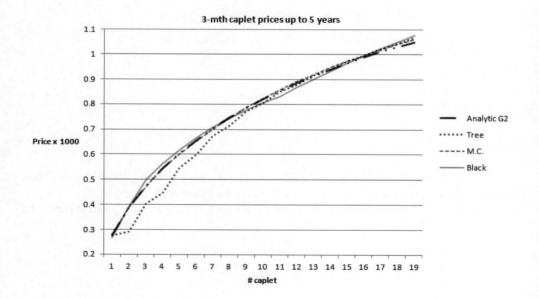

6.1.4 Hull and White two-factor model

Short rate dynamics The one-factor H & W model is enhanced by the addition of a factor π_t correlated with r_t:

$$dr_t = (\theta(t) + \pi_t - ar_t)dt + \sigma dw_t$$

$$d\pi_t = -b\pi_t dt + \sigma_\pi dz_t$$

$$\rho = \rho(dw_t, dz_t)$$

Brigo (Brigo and Mercurio, 2006) shows the analogy between the HW two-factor and G2 models through the following correspondence:

HW 2F	G2
a	a
b	b
σ	$\sqrt{\sigma_x^2 + \sigma_y^2 + 2\rho\sigma_x\sigma_y}$
σ_π	$\sigma_y(a - b)$
ρ	$\dfrac{\sigma_x\rho + \sigma_y}{\sqrt{\sigma_x^2 + \sigma_y^2 + 2\rho\sigma_x\sigma_y}}$
$\theta(t)$	$\dfrac{d\phi(t)}{dt} + a\phi(t)$

Monte-Carlo implementation Retrieving the previous parameters, we can apply the MC method and verify that both models coincide.

Model	σ_x	σ_x	a	b	ρ
G2	0.0054123	0.0087792	0.1305263	0.0127878	−0.78784
HW	0.0056123	0.00103	0.1305263	0.0127878	0.805

Some changes are to be made to the G2 algorithm:

```
Dim theta!(): ReDim theta(19)
...
For i = 1 To 19
    phi(i) = ...
    theta(i) = (phi(i) - phi(i - 1)) / 0.25 + a * phi(i - 1)
Next i
```

$$(\phi \rightarrow \theta = \tfrac{d\phi}{dt} + a\phi)$$

```
For m = 1 To 50000
    x = 0: r = Fwd(0)
    For i = 1 To 19
        z1 = gauss()
        z2 = rho * z1 + gauss() * Sqr(1 - rho ^ 2)
```

```
      x = x - b * x * dt + vy * z2 * Sqr(dt)
      r = r + (theta(i) + x - a * r) * dt + vx * z1 * Sqr(dt)

      caplet(i) = caplet(i) + max(r - Fwd(i), 0) * 0.25
   Next i
Next m

For i = 1 To 19
   Debug.Print caplet(i) / 50000 * DF(i)
Next i
```

G2($\times 10^{-3}$)	HW($\times 10^{-3}$)	Δ(in bps)
0.276	0.286	0.11
0.0.665	0.687	0.22
1.135	1.175	0.4
1.677	1.736	0.59
2.277	2.357	0.8
2.929	3.035	1.05
3.63	3.762	1.32
4.374	4.532	1.58
5.162	5.341	1.79
5.985	6.187	2.02
6.844	7.069	2.25
7.736	7.98	2.44
8.657	8.919	2.62
9.606	9.883	2.77
10.58	10.873	2.94
11.574	11.885	3.12
12.591	12.92	3.29
13.635	13.977	3.42
14.697	15.055	3.58

The maximum discrepancy observed between ATM cap prices (up to 5 years) is 4 bps: this could be reduced, using a shorter timestep.

6.2 FORWARD RATE MODELS

The two models presented in this section are the **Heath-Jarrow-Morton** framework (Heath, Jarrow, and Morton, 1992) applicable to *instantaneous* forward rates and the **Brace Gatarek Musiela** model (Brace, Gatarek, and Musiela, 1997), applicable to LIBOR rates. The BGM model is also designated as **LIBOR Market Model**: for now, we will use LMM instead of BGM, to avoid confusion with the Benhamou Gobet Miri method (see Chapter 7). If we denote by f the continuous rate, and fwd the LIBOR, the generic form of these models is

$$df(t, T) = \alpha(t, T)dt + \sigma(t, T)dw_t \tag{6.12}$$

and

$$\frac{dfwd(t, T_i)}{fwd(t, T_i)} = \mu(t, T_i).dt + \sigma(t, T_i).dw_i \tag{6.13}$$

The similarity between the dynamics above and the Black diffusion model makes the calibration of caplets and floorlets straightforward. Furthermore, Black volatilities and the LMM caplet (resp. floorlet) "mean" volatilities coincide.

Some difficulty arises when dealing with path-dependent assets which are priced through Monte-Carlo sampling of the whole forward curve. This does not really matter as long as we price caplets **separately**: indeed, under the appropriate forward martingale measure (Q^T or Q^{T_i}), the dynamics of each forward rate are, either of the form

$$df(t, T) = \sigma(t, T)dw_t$$

or

$$\frac{dfwd(t, T_i)}{fwd(t, T_i)} = \sigma(t, T_i).dw_i$$

By contrast, the sampling of the **entire forward term structure** in one go needs to use one single measure. In general, namely under any forward martingale measure, the presence of a drift term yields

$$\mathbb{E}^Q(f(t, t)) \neq f(0, t)$$

$$\mathbb{E}^Q(fwd(T_i, T_i)) \neq fwd(0, T_i)$$

Therefore, it appears at first glance that ATM cap prices cannot match ATM floors. In practice, they still coincide, since discount factors are not calculated from the market forwards' term structure on the calculation date (say $t = 0$), but inferred from scenarios where correlations between forward rates are taken into consideration.

6.2.1 Generic Heath-Jarrow-Morton

Up to now, we have linked bond prices and short rate dynamics under the "natural" probability measure thanks to the relation

$$B(t, T) = \mathbb{E}\left[Exp\left(-\int_t^T r_s ds\right)\right]$$

We can also link $B(t, T)$ to the continuum of forward rates $f(t, s)$, observed at t and settled at s:

$$B(t, T) = Exp\left(-\int_t^T f(t, s)ds\right) \tag{6.14}$$

There are different implementations of the HJM model according to the dimension of the Brownian motion: for instance, the **d-factor** HJM model assumes that w_t is a d-dimensional Brownian motion. We should then write equation (6.12) more explicitly:

$$df(t, T) = \alpha(t, T)dt + \sigma(t, T)^\dagger.dw_t$$

In practice, w_t is a linear combination of stationary independent Brownian motions so that the dynamics of $f(t, T)$ can be developed:

$$df(t, T) = \alpha(t, T)dt + \sum_{i=1}^{d} \sigma_i(t, T)dw_{i,t}$$

Given two correlated forward rates $f(t, T_j)$ and $f(t, T_k)$,

$$< df(t, T_j), df(t, T_k) > \; = \rho_{j,k}\sigma(t, T_j)\sigma(t, T_k)$$

From equation (6.9), we draw that

$$f(t, T) = - \frac{\partial Ln(B(t, T))}{\partial T} = f(0, T) + \int_0^t \alpha(s, T)ds + \int_0^t \sigma(s, T)^\dagger.dw_s$$

Let us calculate $Ln(B(t, T))$:

$$- \int_t^T f(t, s)ds = - \int_t^T f(0, s)ds - \int_t^T \left(\int_0^t \alpha(s, u)ds \right)du - \int_t^T \left(\int_0^t \sigma(s, u)^\dagger.dw_s \right)du$$

Reversing the order of integration to underline the stochastic term (Fubini's rule) leads to

$$- \int_t^T f(t, s)ds = - \int_t^T f(0, s)ds - \int_0^t \left(\int_t^T \alpha(s, u)du \right)ds - \int_0^t \left[\int_t^T \sigma(s, u)du \right]^\dagger.dw_s \quad (6.15)$$

$$- \int_t^T f(0, s)ds = - \int_t^0 f(0, s)ds - \int_0^T f(0, s)ds$$

$$= \int_0^t f(0, s)ds + Ln(B(0, T))$$

We now introduce the instantaneous spot rate $r_t = f(t, t)$:

$$\int_0^t f(0, s)ds = \int_0^t r_s ds - \int_0^t \left(\int_0^s \alpha(u, s)du \right)ds - \int_0^t \left(\int_0^s \sigma(u, s)^\dagger.dw_u \right)ds$$

Incorporating r_t and reorganizing (6.11) (see Musela and Rutkowski (1998)) leads to

$$Ln(B(t, T)) = Ln(B(0, T)) + \int_0^t r ds - \int_0^t \left(\int_s^T \alpha(s, u)du \right)ds - \int_0^t \left[\int_s^T \sigma(s, u)du \right]^\dagger.dw_s$$

To link the dynamics of $B(t, T)$ and $Ln(B(t, T))$, we state that dB is of the form

$$dB = \alpha_B dt + \sigma_B^\dagger . dw_t$$

$$dLn(B) = \left(r_t - \int_t^T \alpha(t, u) du\right) dt - \left(\int_t^T \sigma(t, u) du\right)^\dagger . dw_t$$

From the Ito formula, we also have

$$dLn(B) = dB/B - \frac{1}{2B^2} d < B, B >$$

$$= \left(\frac{\alpha_B}{B} - \frac{1}{2B^2} Var\left[\int_t^T \sigma(t, u) du\right]\right) dt + \frac{1}{B}\sigma_B^\dagger . dw_t$$

Finally,

$$dB(t, T) = B(t, T)(a(t, T)dt + b(t, T).dw_t)$$

with

$$a(t, T) = r_t - \int_t^T \alpha(t, u) du + \frac{1}{2} Var\left(\int_t^T \sigma(t, u) du\right)$$

$$b(t, T) = -\left(\int_t^T \sigma(t, u) du\right)^\dagger$$

We proceed now with a change of probability Q such that the dynamics of $B(t, T)$ under Q are written:

$$\frac{dB(t, T)}{B(t, T)} = \mathbf{r_t} dt + b_t . dw_t$$

Under this (risk-neutral) measure, $\mathbb{E}^Q\left(e^{-\int_0^t r_s ds} B(t, T)\right) = B(0, T)$

We can now derive the dynamics of

$$f(t, T) = -\frac{\partial Ln(B(t, T))}{\partial T} \quad \text{under } Q$$

$$df(t, T) = \frac{-\partial}{\partial T}\left[r_t - \frac{1}{2}b(t, T).b(t, T)^\dagger\right] dt - \frac{\partial b(t, T)}{\partial T} . dw_t$$

Recalling that $b(t, T) = -\left(\int_t^T \sigma(t, u) du\right)^\dagger$, we infer the core arbitrage-free HJM diffusion process:

$$df(t, T) = \left(\sigma(t, T)^\dagger . \int_t^T \sigma(t, u) du\right) dt + \sigma(t, T)^\dagger . dw_t$$

Implementation model   Since no closed solutions are available in the HJM generic frame, we choose to discretize time and the forward rates: moreover, some assumptions are required. It is common to reduce the number of factors to one, two, or three, given the important correlations between forward rates.

By the way, a single-factor dynamics assuming some deterministic form $\sigma(t, T)$ for the volatility can be easily solved.

In the case of two-factor models, some discretization is needed and volatility is commonly chosen to verify

$$\sigma(t, T_i) = \sigma(T_i - t)$$

In this section, we are concerned with calibration: it implies that our implementation allows an optimal flexibility, meaning that we use a lot of parameters, yet without burdening the calculation.

Our choice fell on an n-**factor model** with **constant volatilities** and **correlations**:

$$\|\sigma(t, T_i)\| = \|\sigma_i\|$$

This choice may seem outrageous, since remote forward rates are driven by the long-term end of the swap curve, thus technical factors, while closer ones react to money-market ups and downs. However, this implementation allows a satisfactory fit to the cap market prices.

Calibration with caplets   Let us set, without any loss of generality, $t_{i+1} - t_i = \tau$ where t_i, $i = 1,...,n$ stands for the fixing dates. The calibration will address forward rates $f(t, t_i)$ such that

$$f(t, t_i)\tau = \left[\frac{B(t, t_i)}{B(t, t_{i+1})}\right] - 1$$

As we adopt an n-factor model, let us denote by $A = (a_{ij})$ the Cholesky lower triangular matrix such that

$$A.A^{\dagger} = [\rho_{i,j}]$$

where

$$\rho_{i,j} = \frac{< df(t, t_i), df(t, t_j) >}{\|\sigma(t, t_i)\|.\|\sigma(t, t_j)\|} = \frac{< df(t, t_i), df(t, t_j) >}{\sigma_i \sigma_j}$$

At t, the ATM caplet price for the corresponding forward is written

$$B(t, t_{i+1})\mathbb{E}^{Q}([f(t_i, t_i) - f(t, t_i)]^{+}\tau)$$

where Q stands for the forward martingale measure. We approximate

$$\sigma(t_j, t_i)^{\dagger}.\int_{t_j}^{t_i} \sigma(t_j, u)\mathrm{d}u$$

with

$$(\sigma_i)^{\dagger}.\sum_{k=j}^{i-1} \tau(\sigma_k)$$

For better readability, we set $\sigma_i = \|\sigma_i\|$: then

$$\sigma(t_j, t_i)^\dagger . \int_{t_j}^{t_i} \sigma(t_j, u) du \simeq \sigma_i \sum_{k=j}^{i-1} \sigma_k \tau \sum_{l=1}^{k} a_{i,l} a_{j,l}$$

$$= \sigma_i \left(\tau \sum_{k=j}^{i-1} \rho_{k,i} \sigma_k \right)$$

$$f(t_{j+1}, t_i) - f(t_j, t_i) = \mu(i,j)\tau + (\sigma_i)^\dagger . \Delta w$$

where

$$\mu(i,j) = \sigma_i \left(\sum_{k=j}^{i-1} \rho_{k,i} \sigma_k \right)$$

Then, from $t = 0$,

$$f(t_i, t_i) = f(0, t_i) + \tau \sigma_i \left(\sum_{j=1}^{i-1} \mu(i,j) \right) + \sigma(i)^\dagger . (w_i - w_0)$$

To return to the ATM caplet price: given

$$\Delta w_i = \Delta z \sqrt{t_i} (\Delta z \equiv N(0,1))$$

and

$$\tilde{\mu}_i t_i = \tau \sigma_i \left(\sum_{j=1}^{i-1} \mu(i,j) \right)$$

$$B(0, t_{i+1}) \mathbb{E}^Q ([f(t_i, t_i) - f(0, t_i)]^+ \tau) = B(0, t_i) \mathbb{E}^Q ([\tilde{\mu}_i t_i + \sigma(i) \Delta w_i]^+ \tau)$$

The affine form of the payoff formula allows us to conclude:

$$\mathbb{E}^Q ([\tilde{\mu}_i t_i + \sigma(i) \Delta w_i]^+) = \sigma(i) \sqrt{t_i} \mathbb{E}^Q \left(\left[\frac{\tilde{\mu}_i \sqrt{t_i}}{\sigma_i} + \Delta Z \right]^+ \right)$$

$$= \sigma(i) \sqrt{t_i} \int_{-\lambda_i}^{+\infty} \frac{e^{-u^2/2}}{\sqrt{2\pi}} (u + \lambda_i) du \qquad , \lambda_i = \frac{\tilde{\mu}_i \sqrt{t_i}}{\sigma(i)}$$

Finally,

$$Caplet(i) = B(0, t_i) \left(\sigma(i) \sqrt{t_i} \left[\lambda_i N(\lambda_i) + \frac{e^{-\lambda_i^2/2}}{2\pi} \right] . \tau \right)$$

The HJM model is, in theory, not compatible with log-normal dynamics, so that caplet prices depend, to some extent, on correlations. In practice, the observed impact of $\rho_{i,j}$ coefficients is marginal. In the graph below, we have compared Black and HJM at-the-money volatilities using three different correlation matrices:

1. Correl 1 $\rho_{i,j} = e^{-0.1\tau(j-i)}, \quad j > i$
2. Correl 2 $\rho_{i,j} = e^{-0.35(j\tau)^{0.5}-0.35(i\tau)^{0.5}}, \quad j > i$
3. Uncorrelated $(\rho_{i,j}) = Id$.

Note that Correl 1 and Correl 2 are typical standard assumptions for the estimation of

$$\frac{< df(t, t_i)/f(t, t_i), df(t, t_j)/f(t, t_j) >}{\|\sigma(t, t_i)\|.\|\sigma(t, t_j)\|}$$

when needed (see the LMM model in the next section). As a matter of fact, in the range of usually observed volatilities,

$$\rho\left(\frac{df_i}{f_i}, \frac{df_j}{f_j}\right) \simeq \rho(df_i, df_j)$$

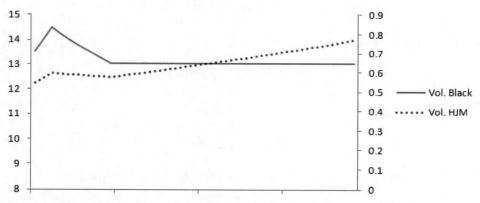

The matrices below (Tables 6.4 and 6.5) display correlations for $\tau = 1$: these do not actually correspond to the quarterly fixed caps we have chosen to calibrate our implementation, but help visualize how correlations between remote forward rates are valued.

TABLE 6.4   Correlation matrix # 1 $(\rho_{i,j} = \rho_{i+k,j+k})$

1	0.975	0.951	0.928	0.905	0.882	0.861	0.839	0.819	0.799
	1	0.975	0.951	0.928	0.905	0.882	0.861	0.839	0.819
		1	0.975	0.951	0.928	0.905	0.882	0.861	0.839
			1	0.975	0.951	0.928	0.905	0.882	0.861
				1	0.975	0.951	0.928	0.905	0.882
					1	0.975	0.951	0.928	0.905
						1	0.975	0.951	0.928
							1	0.975	0.951
								1	0.975
									1

TABLE 6.5 Correlation matrix # 2

1	0.975	0.951	0.928	0.905	0.882	0.861	0.839	0.819	0.799	
	1	0.946	0.903	0.866	0.834	0.806	0.781	0.758	0.736	
		1	0.954	0.916	0.882	0.852	0.825	0.801	0.779	
			1	0.96	0.924	0.893	0.865	0.839	0.816	
				1	0.963	0.931	0.902	0.875	0.85	
					1	0.966	0.936	0.908	0.883	
						1	0.969	0.94	0.914	
							1	0.97	0.943	
								1	0.972	
									1	

Cholesky triangular matrix #1										
1	0	0	0	0	0	0	0	0	0	0
0.975	0.221	0	0	0	0	0	0	0	0	0
0.951	0.215	0.221	0	0	0	0	0	0	0	0
0.928	0.210	0.215	0.221	0	0	0	0	0	0	0
0.905	0.205	0.210	0.215	0.221	0	0	0	0	0	0
0.882	0.200	0.205	0.210	0.215	0.221	0	0	0	0	0
0.861	0.195	0.200	0.205	0.210	0.215	0.221	0	0	0	0
0.839	0.190	0.195	0.200	0.205	0.210	0.215	0.221	0	0	0
0.819	0.185	0.190	0.195	0.200	0.205	0.210	0.215	0.221	0	0
0.799	0.181	0.185	0.190	0.195	0.200	0.205	0.210	0.215	0.221	0
0.779	0.176	0.181	0.185	0.190	0.195	0.200	0.205	0.210	0.215	0.221

Code First, we start with the coding of **CapletHJM** and **divCapHJM**, i.e., the core engine of our
calibration.

```
Public Function CapletHJM(v#, s#, t#, n As Long) As Double
Dim x#: x = s * Sqr(t * n)
CapletHJM = v * Sqr(t * n) * (x * norm(x) + Exp(-0.5 * x ^ 2) / Sqr(2 * PI))
* df(n) * t
End Function
```

```
Public Function divCapHJM(v#, s#, t#, n As Long) As Double
divCapHJM = (CapletHJM(v + 0.0001, s, t, n) - CapletHJM(v - 0.0001, s, t, n))
   / 0.0002
End Function
```

The functions **drift** and **VarToDoubleArray** displayed below are needed to adjust the correlation matrix as time passes: in fact, **trigDrift** is a lower triangular matrix (from Cholesky decomposition) of type Variant, that needs to be converted into Double().

For a better understanding of the algorithm, it is important to catch the main steps:

- p denotes the duration of the cap against 3-mth LIBOR ($= p * 0.25$ years).
- $f(1)$ denotes the <u>spot</u> theoretical rate at each monitoring date, and $Fwd(i)$ is the <u>forward</u> market rate (as of $t = 0$).

Over the i-th step:

- (p-i) forward rates are sampled
- the payoff of the maturing i-th ATM caplet (resp floorlet), i.e.,

$$\text{Max}(f(1)\text{-Fwd}(i), 0)(\text{resp. Max}(\text{Fwd}(i) - f(1), 0)$$

is calculated
- this payoff is added to the accumulated previous payoffs: the sum is then capitalized, using **capi**:

$$\text{capi} = (1 + f(1) * \Delta t)$$

which gives

$$\text{cap}(i) = \text{cap}(i - 1) * \text{capi} + \text{Max}(f(1) - \text{Fwd}(i), 0) * \Delta t$$

$$\text{flr}(i) = \text{flr}(i - 1) * \text{capi} + \text{Max}(\text{Fwd}(i) - f(1), 0) * \Delta t$$

The factors capi are compounded so as to populate the vector **capit**:

$$\text{capit}(i) = \text{capit}(i - 1) * \text{capi}$$

- the total cap (resp. floor) payoff is then incorporated to sumcap(i) (resp sumflr(i)), then discounted using

$$\frac{1}{capit(i)}$$

and, finally, averaged.

```
Public Function drift(t#(), n&) As Double()

ReDim result#(UBound(t) - n, UBound(t) - n)
For i = n + 1 To UBound(t)
    For j = n + 1 To UBound(t)
        result(i - n, j - n) = t(i, j)
    Next j
Next i
drift = result

End Function

Public Function VarToDoubleArray(v As Variant) As Double()

VarToDoubleArray = v
End Function
```

The correlation matrix must be shifted at each iteration since as time to maturity diminishes:

$$\text{CorrelDrift}(0) = \begin{pmatrix} 1 & \rho_{1,2} & \rho_{1,3} & \cdots & \cdots & \rho_{1,n} \\ \rho_{2,1} & 1 & \rho_{2,3} & \cdots & \cdots & \rho_{2,n} \\ \rho_{3,1} & \rho_{3,2} & 1 & \cdots & \cdots & \rho_{3,n} \\ \rho_{4,1} & \rho_{4,2} & \rho_{4,3} & \cdots & \cdots & \rho_{4,n} \\ \vdots & \vdots & \vdots & \cdots & \cdots & \vdots \end{pmatrix}$$

$$\text{CorrelDrift}(1) = \begin{pmatrix} 1 & \rho_{1,2} & \rho_{1,3} & \cdots & \cdots & \rho_{1,n} \\ \rho_{2,1} & 1 & \rho_{2,3} & \cdots & \cdots & \rho_{2,n} \\ \rho_{3,1} & \rho_{3,2} & 1 & \cdots & \cdots & \rho_{3,n} \\ \rho_{4,1} & \rho_{4,2} & \rho_{4,3} & \cdots & \cdots & \rho_{4,n} \\ \vdots & \vdots & \vdots & \cdots & \cdots & \vdots \end{pmatrix}$$

$$\text{CorrelDrift}(2) = \begin{pmatrix} 1 & \rho_{1,2} & \rho_{1,3} & \cdots & \cdots & \rho_{1,n} \\ \rho_{2,1} & 1 & \rho_{2,3} & \cdots & \cdots & \rho_{2,n} \\ \rho_{3,1} & \rho_{3,2} & 1 & \cdots & \cdots & \rho_{3,n} \\ \rho_{4,1} & \rho_{4,2} & \rho_{4,3} & \cdots & \cdots & \rho_{4,n} \\ \vdots & \vdots & \vdots & \cdots & \cdots & \vdots \end{pmatrix}, \text{ etc.}$$

df is declared outside **calibHJM** since it must visible from **CapletHJM**.

```
Public df#(),cap#()
Sub calibHJM()

Dim i&, p%
p = 40
Dim t#: t = 0.25

ReDim f#(p - 1), f0#(p - 1), cap#(p - 1)
ReDim sig#(p - 1), sum_sig#(p - 1)
Dim mu#(): ReDim mu(p - 1, p - 1)

ReDim volCaplet#(p - 1), valCaplet#(p - 1)
ReDim sumcap#(p - 1), sumflr#(p - 1), cap#(p - 1), flr#(p - 1), capit#(p - 1)
ReDim Fwd#(p - 1), discFwd#(p - 1)

ReDim df(p - 1)

ReDim volCaplet#(p - 1)
volCaplet(1) = 0.135
volCaplet(2) = 0.14
volCaplet(3) = 0.145
volCaplet(4) = 0.1425
For i = 5 To 10
    volCaplet(i) = 0.14 - (i - 5) * 0.002
Next i
```

```vba
For i = 11 To p - 1
    volCaplet(i) = 0.13
Next i

ReDim Fwd#(p - 1), discFwd#(p - 1)
Fwd(0) = 0.04: discFwd(0) = 1 / (1 + Fwd(0) * 0.25)
For i = 1 To p - 1
    Fwd(i) = Fwd(0) * Exp(i * 0.01)
    discFwd(i) = discFwd(i - 1) / (1 + Fwd(i) * 0.25)
Next i

ReDim valCaplet#(p - 1)
For i = 1 To p - 1
    valCaplet(i) = Fwd(i) / 4 * discFwd(i) * _
    (norm(0.5 * volCaplet(i) * Sqr(i * 0.25)) - norm(-0.5 * vol-
Caplet(i) * Sqr(i * 0.25)))
    sv = sv + valCaplet(i)
    Debug.Print sv
Next i

Dim Correl#(): ReDim Correl(p - 1, p - 1)
Dim n As Long

For i = 1 To p - 1
    Correl(i, i) = 1
    For j = i To p - 1
        Correl(i, j) = Exp(-0.35 * ((j / 4) ^ 0.5 - (i / 4) ^ 0.5))
        Correl(j, i) = Correl(i, j)
    Next
Next

ReDim correlDrift(p - 1) As Variant
ReDim trigDrift(p - 1) As Variant

For i = 1 To p - 1
    correlDrift(i) = drift(Correl, i - 1)
    trigDrift(i) = Cholesky(VarToDoubleArray(correlDrift(i)), p - (i - 1))
Next i

ReDim brown#(p - 1), z#(p - 1)

Dim x#, s#, y#, dy#

For i = 1 To p - 1
    x = volCaplet(i) * Fwd(i)
    sum_sig(i) = 0
    For j = i - 1 To 1 Step -1
        For K = j To 1
            sum_sig(i) = sum_sig(i) + sig(K) * Correl(K, i)
        Next K
    Next j
    s = sum_sig(i) * t
    y = CapletHJM(x, s, t, i, discFwd(i)): dy = divCapHJM(x, s, t, i, dis-
cFwd(i))

    While Abs(valCaplet(i) - y) > 0.00002
```

```
                x = x + (valCaplet(i) - y) / dy
                s = sum_sig(i) * t
                y = CapletHJM(x, s, t, i, discFwd(i)): dy = div-
CapHJM(x, s, t, i, discFwd(i))
        Wend

        sig(i) = x
Next i

For i = 1 To p - 1
    For j = 1 To i
        mu(i, j) = 0
        For K = j To i - 1
            mu(i, j) = mu(i, j) + sig(i) * sig(K) * Correl(i, K) * t
        Next K
    Next j
Next i

ReDim f#(p - 1), f0#(p - 1), cap#(p - 1)
Randomize

For i = 1 To 20000
    For K = 1 To p - 1
        f0(K) = Fwd(K)
    Next K

    For l = 1 To p - 1

        For j = 1 To p - 1
            brown(j) = gauss()
        Next j

        For j = 1 To p - 1
            z(j) = 0
            For K = 1 To j
                z(j) = z(j) + trigDrift(l)(j, K) * brown(K)
            Next K
            f(j) = f0(j) + mu(l - 1 + j, 1) * t + sig(l - 1 + j) * z(j)
            * Sqr(t)

        Next j
        If l > 1 Then
            cap(l) = cap(l - 1) * capi + WorksheetFunction.max(f(1)
            - Fwd(1), 0) * t
            flr(l) = flr(l - 1) * capi + WorksheetFunction.max(Fwd(1)
            - f(1), 0) * t
        Else
            cap(l) = WorksheetFunction.max(f(1) - Fwd(1), 0) * t
            flr(l) = WorksheetFunction.max(Fwd(1) - f(1), 0) * t
            capit(0) = 1 / discFwd(0)
        End If
        capi = (1 + f(1) * t)
        capit(l) = capit(l - 1) * capi

        For K = 1 To p - 1 - l
            f0(K) = f(K + 1)
```

```
        Next K
    Next l
    For l = 1 To p - 1
        sumcap(l) = sumcap(l) + cap(l) / capit(l)
        sumflr(l) = sumflr(l) + flr(l) / capit(l)
    Next l
Next i

For K = 1 To p - 1
Debug.Print sumcap(K) / 20000 & "   " & sumflr(K) / 20000
Next K

End Sub
```

Numerical results The graph below demonstrates the efficiency of the calibration process: in fact, despite the deficiencies of the random number generator, HJM and Black prices overlap almost perfectly.

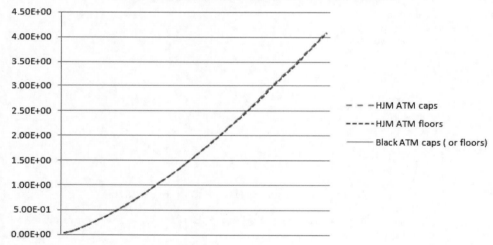

HJM vs Black ATM 3-mth cap(floor) prices up to 10y (%)

6.2.2 LMM (LIBOR market model)

The LMM model is a discretized geometric Brownian model on a market (e.g., LIBOR) rate. Let us denote by fwd_i the forward rate applied to the period spanning from t_i and t_{i+1}. The discussion process is given by:

$$\frac{\mathrm{d}fwd_i}{fwd_i} = \mu_i.\mathrm{d}t + \sigma_i.\mathrm{d}w_i \qquad (6.16)$$

Let us call $B(t; t_i)$, the price at t of an asset paying one unit at t_i, and Q_i, the probability under which the price of any asset, normalized by $B(t, t_i)$, is martingale.

$$\frac{X_t}{B(t, t_i)} = \mathbb{E}^{Q_i}(X_{t_i}/\mathcal{F}_t)$$

Recalling that $B(t, t_i)$ is the discount factor for the period $[t, t_i]$,

$$\frac{1}{B(0, t_1)}.(1 + Fwd_1.\tau) = \frac{1}{B(0, t_2)}$$

$$\implies Fwd_1 = (B(0, t_1) - B(0, t_2))/B(0, t_2)\tau$$

is martingale under Q_2 and then has a null drift:

$$\frac{dFwd_1}{Fwd_1} = \sigma_1 dw_1$$

Likewise $1/(1 + Fwd_2.\tau)$ is Q_2-martingale since

$$\frac{1}{B(0, t_2)}.(1 + Fwd_2.\tau) = \frac{1}{B(0, t_3)}$$

$$\implies \frac{1}{1 + Fwd_2.\tau} = \frac{B(0, t_3)}{B(0, t_2)}$$

Under this measure, its drift is nul. According to Ito,

$$d\left(\frac{1}{1 + Fwd_2\tau}\right) = \frac{-dFwd_2\tau}{(1 + Fwd_2\tau)^2} + \frac{1}{2}.\left[\frac{2}{(1 + Fwd_2\tau)^3}\right].[\sigma_2^2 Fwd_2^2 dt]$$

This condition is satisfied if

$$\frac{-\mu_2\tau Fwd_2 dt}{(1 + Fwd_2\tau)^2} + \frac{\sigma_2^2 Fwd_2^2 dt}{(1 + Fwd_2\tau)^3} = 0 \implies \mu_2 = \frac{\sigma_2^2 Fwd_2}{1 + Fwd_2\tau}$$

For the purposes of conciseness, let us denote Fwd_i by F_i and $B(0, t_i)$ by B_i.

$$\frac{1}{1 + F_2\tau} * \frac{1}{1 + F_3\tau} = \frac{B_4}{B_2}$$

is Q_2-martingale. Applying the **Integration by parts** rule,

$$d\left(\frac{1}{1 + F_2\tau} * \frac{1}{1 + F_3\tau}\right) =$$

$$d\left(\frac{1}{1 + F_2\tau}\right) * \frac{1}{1 + F_3\tau} + \frac{1}{1 + F_2\tau} * d\left(\frac{1}{1 + F_3\tau}\right)$$

$$+ d < \frac{1}{1 + F_2\tau}, \frac{1}{1 + F_3\tau} > \qquad (6.17)$$

We know from the above that the drift of $d\left(\frac{1}{1+F_2\tau}\right) * \frac{1}{1+F_3\tau}$ is null.

Also,

$$d < \frac{1}{1+F_2\tau}, \frac{1}{1+F_3\tau} > = \frac{\tau F_2\sigma_2}{(1+F_2\tau)^2} \cdot \frac{\tau F_3\sigma_3}{(1+F_3\tau)^2} \cdot \rho_{23}dt$$

where ρ_{23} is the instantaneous correlation between F_2 and F_3.

Finally,

$$\mu_3 = \sigma_3 \cdot \frac{\tau\rho_{23}\sigma_2 F_2}{1+F_2\tau} + \sigma_3 \cdot \frac{\tau\sigma_3 F_3}{1+F_3\tau}$$

Under Q_n, $1 + F_{n-1}.\tau$ is martingale, and so are

$$(1 + F_{n-1}.\tau)(1 + F_{n-2}.\tau),...$$

$$(1 + F_{n-1}.\tau)(1 + F_{n-2}.\tau)...(1 + F_{n-k}.\tau).$$

Recursively, we can give the general formula of F_k dynamics with respect to B_i numeraire:

- if k>i, $dF_k = \sigma_k F_k \sum\limits_{j=i+1}^{k} \frac{\tau\rho_{kj}\sigma_j F_j}{1+F_j\tau}dt + \sigma_k F_k.dw_k$

- if k<i, $dF_k = -\sigma_k F_k. \sum\limits_{j=k+1}^{i} \frac{\tau\rho_{kj}\sigma_j F_j}{1+F_j\tau}dt + \sigma_k F_k.dw_k$

- if i=k, $dF_k = \sigma_k F_k.dw_k$

Cap/floor pricing The LMM dynamics, through the expression of the drift, indicate some correlations between forward rates, which is not taken into account in the framework of the Black model. However, both models are consistent when dealing with caplets' pricing since every single caplet may be valued regardless of the others, the only factor to consider being the volatility. In the framework of LMM, we are entitled to choose the most adequate numeraire for each caplet, i.e., the martingale measure. All we have to do is to ensure that Black-style volatilities are consistent with the instantaneous σ_i given in equation (6.15).

Theoretically, we should assume some function for $\sigma_i(t) = f_i(t)$ with parameters to be fitted to verify

$$\sigma^2_{i,market} = \frac{1}{t_i} \int\limits_{0}^{t_i} \sigma^2_i(u)du = \overline{\sigma}^2_i$$

For instance, Rebonato (1999) suggested

$$\sigma_i(t) = k_i[(a + b(t_i - t))e^{-c(t_i-t)} + d].\mathbb{1}_{t\leq t_i}$$

For the sake of simplification, our timestep for the discretization will be the caplet's duration. For instance, a cap against 3-mth LIBOR will be discretized quarterly: practically, this means approximating σ_i with the **Black's caplet volatility**.

The correlation issue Though correlation is not an issue to worry about when pricing a single caplet, it is to be accounted for when sampling the whole forward curve. This is what we intend to do in order to check that our implementation of the model actually gives valuations close enough to the market cap prices.

For that purpose, we must adopt an arbitrary, but realistic, correlations function.

Common sense dictates that correlations are to be positive. Also, correlations between adjacent forward rates $(\rho_{i,i+1})$ are logically close to 1 and the smaller $|j - i|$ the larger $\rho_{i,j}$. For instance, Jäckel suggests the generic function

$$\rho_{i,j}(t) = e^{-\beta|(t_i - t)^\gamma - (t_j - t)^\gamma|} . \mathbb{1}_{t \leq \min(t_i, t_j)} \tag{6.18}$$

with $\beta = 0.35$ and $\gamma = 0.5$. Jäckel shows that simplifying () with $\beta = 0.1$ and $\gamma = 1$ brings no significant change in the pricing of Bermudan swaptions. This approximation can therefore apply to assets with similar risk profiles, such as cancelable swaps or CMS swaps that will be investigated in Chapter 8.

As with $\sigma_i(t)$, $\rho_{i,j}(t)$ must be understood as the **instantaneous correlation** factor between $F_i(t)$ and $F_j(t)$: thus, in the framework of our discretized implementation, the coefficients $\rho_{i,j}$ should be averaged, and in any case one question remains: what change is to be made in $\overline{\rho_{i,j}}$ when moving one step ahead?

Notice that this problem, which also pertains to forward rates and volatilities, is easily fixed for these parameters: at the i-th step

- F_{i-1} takes the place of F_i
- σ_i remains constant, to fit the market prices (Black-style).

How about correlations? In fact, assuming $\gamma = 1$, the problem solves itself:

1. $\rho_{i,j}$ is no longer time-dependent, indeed: $\overline{\rho_{i,j}} = \rho_{i,j}$.
2. $\rho_{i,j} = \rho_{i+m,j+m}$: thus, any shift in the correlation matrix, as we saw in the course of our HJM implementation (see §6.2.1), has no impact on the value of $\rho_{i,j}$, which can be considered as constant over time.

Discretization Over the time increment Δt, we adopt the Euler scheme:

$$F_k(t + \Delta t) = F_k(t).Exp((\mu_k - \overline{\sigma}_k^2/2)\Delta t + \overline{\sigma}_k.\Delta w_k)$$

Before starting to code, we have to choose one suitable measure Q_k. Heuristically speaking, or more simply for reasons of symmetry, Q_1 or Q_n both seem relevant choices. In this section, we arbitrarily choose Q_k so that μ_k depends on $(F_2, F_3, ..., F_k)$.

Another problem arises along with the stochasticity of the drift, contingent on the evolution of the forward rates curve. When dealing with deterministic drifts, one can fix the issue by averaging the instantaneous drift over the desired period. Regarding the present model, it should be accounted that all the $F_k = F_{t_k}(t)$ become $F_{t_k + \Delta t}$ (in the algorithm, F_k becomes F_{k-1}) over each timestep. Therefore, the relevant drift to apply between t and $t + \Delta t$ is somewhere between μ_k and μ_{k-1}. One straightforward, but in practice efficient, way to cope with it is to opt for

$$\frac{1}{2}(\mu_k + \mu_{k-1})$$

This adjustment method, called **predictor-corrector**, is implemented as follows:

1. First, sampling $F_k(t + \Delta t) = F_k(t).exp((\mu_k(F_k, F_{k-1}, ...) - \overline{\sigma}_k^2/2)\Delta t + \overline{\sigma}_k.\Delta w_k)$

2. Then recomputing $\hat{\mu}_k(\widehat{F}_k, F_{k-1}, ...))$ with $\widehat{F}_k = F_k(t + \Delta t)$ calculated previously. The calculation of $\widehat{F}_{k-1}...$ is not required since F_k plays the prominent role in the dynamics of dF_k.

3. Finally we obtain $F_k(t + \Delta t) = F_k(t).exp\left(\left(\frac{(\mu_k + \hat{\mu}_k)}{2} - \overline{\sigma}_k^2/2\right)\Delta t + \overline{\sigma}_k.\Delta w_k\right)$

Code The code below aims to check that our implementation of the model complies with the market cap prices. The main steps of the algorithm are similar to the HJM implementation (see above):

- p denotes the duration of the cap against 3-mth LIBOR ($= p * 0.25$ years);
- $Fwd(1)$ denotes the spot theoretical rate at each monitoring date, and $Fwd0(i)$ is the forward market rate (as of $t = 0$).

Over the i-th step

- (p-i) forward rates are sampled;
- the payoff of the maturing i-th ATM caplet (resp. floorlet), i.e.,

$$\text{Max(Fwd(1)-Fwd0(i),0) (resp. Max(Fwd0(i)-Fwd(1), 0)}$$

is calculated
- this payoff is added to the accumulated previous payoffs: the sum is then capitalized, using **capi**:

$$\text{capi} = (1 + \text{Fwd}(1) * \Delta t)$$

which gives

$$\text{cap(i)} = \text{cap(i - 1)} * \text{capi} + Max(\text{Fwd}(1) - \text{Fwd0(i)},0) * \Delta t$$

$$\text{floor(i)} = \text{floor(i - 1)} * \text{capi} + \text{Max(Fwd0(i) - Fwd(1),0)} * \Delta t$$

The *capi* factors are compounded so as to populate the vector **capit**:

$$\text{capit(i)} = \text{capit(i - 1)} * \text{capi}$$

- the total cap (resp. floor) payoff is then incorporated to sumcap(i) (resp. sumfloor(i)), then discounted using

$$\frac{1}{capit(i)}$$

and, finally, averaged.

```
Public Sub LMMCap(p%)

ReDim alea!(p) 'gaussian variates
ReDim mu!(p), muB!(p)  'drift and corrected drift
ReDim FwdB!(p), Fwd0!(p)  'corrected forward and market forward
Dim t!:t=0.25 'timestep
```

```
************************************************************************
```
To make this code ready-to-use, we retrieve the market data in the body of the procedure. See
Figures 6.1 and 6.2.
```
************************************************************************
```

```
Redim Fwd!(p),discFwd!(p),caplet!(p),volCaplet!(p)
Redim sumcap!(p),cap!(p),sumfloor!(p),floor!(p),capit!(p)

ReDim correl#(p - 1, p - 1)
Dim i As Long
For i = 1 To p - 1
    For j = i To p - 1
        correl(i, j) = Exp(-0.1 * (j - i) *t)
        correl(j, i) = correl(i, j)
    Next
Next

Fwd(0) = 0.04: discFwd(0) = 1 / (1 + Fwd(0) * t)

For i = 1 To p - 1
    Fwd(i) = 0.04 * Exp(0.01 * i)
    discFwd(i) = discFwd(i - 1) / (1 + Fwd(i) * 0.25)
Next

volCaplet(1) = 0.135
volCaplet(2) = 0.14
volCaplet(3) = 0.145
volCaplet(4) = 0.1425
For i = 5 To 10
    volCaplet(i) = 0.14 - (i - 5) * 0.002
Next i
For i = 11 To p - 1
    volCaplet(i) = 0.128
Next i

Dim d1#, d2#
For i = 1 To p - 1
    d1 = volCaplet(i) * Sqr(i * t) / 2
    d2 = d1 - volCaplet(i) * Sqr(i * t)
    caplet(i) = (norm(d1) - norm(d2)) * t * discFwd(i)
Next
```

```
************************************************************************
```
corr is an array of variant type: each element is a correlation matrix
Each trig(i) is the Cholesky decomposition of corr(i)
Since there are (p-1) steps in one scenario, we need p-1 correlation matrices.
Remember that, at each step, the correlation matrix is shifted, so are volCaplet(i) and Fwd(i)
```
************************************************************************
```

```
ReDim corr(p - 1) As Variant
ReDim trig(p - 1) As Variant

For i = 1 To p - 1
    corr(i) = DoubleToVarArray(drift(Correl, i - 1))
    trig(i) = Cholesky(VarToDoubleArray(corr(i)))
```

$$\begin{pmatrix} \sigma_1 \\ \sigma_2 \\ \vdots \\ \sigma_n \end{pmatrix} \begin{pmatrix} 1 & \rho_{1,2} & \rho_{1,3} & \cdots & \rho_{1,n} \\ \rho_{2,1} & 1 & \rho_{2,3} & \cdots & \rho_{2,n} \\ \rho_{3,1} & \rho_{3,2} & 1 & \cdots & \rho_{3,n} \\ \vdots & \vdots & \vdots & \cdots & \vdots \end{pmatrix}$$

FIGURE 6.1   Step 1: Caplets' volatilities and correlations

$$\begin{pmatrix} \sigma_1 \\ \sigma_2 \\ \vdots \\ \sigma_n \end{pmatrix} \begin{pmatrix} 1 & \rho_{1,2} & \rho_{1,3} & \cdots & \rho_{1,n} \\ \rho_{2,1} & 1 & \rho_{2,3} & \cdots & \rho_{2,n} \\ \rho_{3,1} & \rho_{3,2} & 1 & \cdots & \rho_{3,n} \\ \vdots & \vdots & \vdots & \cdots & \vdots \end{pmatrix}$$

FIGURE 6.2   Step 2: Same parameters one step ahead

```
Next i

For i = 0 To p - 1
    Fwd0(i) = Fwd(i)
Next

For l = 1 To 10000

    For i = 1 To p - 1
        Fwd(i) = Fwd0(i)
    Next

Randomize

For i = 1 To p - 1
    m = i - 1
    For K = 1 To p - i
        alea(K) = gauss()
    Next K

    Fwd(1) = Fwd(1) * _
    Exp(-0.5 * volCaplet(1 + m) ^ 2 * t + volCaplet(1 + m) * alea(1) *
Sqr(t))


    For j = 2 To p - i
        mu(j) = 0: muB(j) = 0

        For K = 2 To j
            mu(j) = _
            mu(j) + volCaplet(j + m) * Fwd(K) * t * vol-
Caplet(K + m) * corr(i)(K, j) / (1 + Fwd(K) * t)
        Next K

        brown = 0
        For K = 1 To j
```

```
            brown = brown + trig(i)(j, K) * alea(K)
        Next K


        '    predictor corrector
        FwdB(j) = Fwd(j) * _
        Exp(mu(j) * t - 0.5 * volCaplet(j + m) ^ 2 * t + vol-
Caplet(j + m) * brown * Sqr(t))


        For K = 1 To j - 1
            muB(j) = muB(j) _
            + volCaplet(j + m) * FwdB(K) * t * vol-
Caplet(K + m) * corr(i)(K, j) / (1 + FwdB(K) * t)
        Next K


        Fwd(j) = Fwd(j) * _
        Exp(0.5 * (mu(j) + muB(j)) * t _
                - 0.5 * volCaplet(j + m) ^ 2 * t + vol-
Caplet(j + m) * brown * Sqr(t))


    Next j
    If i > 1 Then
        cap(i) = cap(i - 1) * capi + WorksheetFunc-
tion.Max(Fwd(1) - Fwd0(i), 0) * t
        floor(i) = floor(i - 1) * capi + WorksheetFunc-
tion.Max(Fwd0(i) - Fwd(1), 0) * t
    Else
        cap(i) = WorksheetFunction.Max(Fwd(1) - Fwd0(i), 0) * t
        floor(i) = WorksheetFunction.Max(Fwd0(i) - Fwd(1), 0) * t
        capit(0) = 1 / discFwd(0)
    End If
        capi = (1 + Fwd(1) * t)
        capit(i) = capit(i - 1) * capi
    For K = 1 To p - i - 1
        Fwd(K) = Fwd(K + 1)
    Next K
Next i
    For i = 1 To p - 1
        sumcap(i) = sumcap(i) + cap(i) / capit(i)
        sumfloor(i) = sumfloor(i) + floor(i) / capit(i)
    Next i
Next l

For i = 1 To p - 1
Debug.Print sumcap(i) / 10000 & "  " & sumfloor(i) / 10000 & "  " & caplet(i)
Next i

End Sub
```

Numerical results Using 10 000 paths and a basic RNG, we matched LMM and market cap prices up to 10-yr maturities. Our implementation of LMM proves to be satisfactory since the gap between market prices (Black model) and the cap/floor valuations using Monte-Carlo is within the range $[-2bps, +2bps]$.

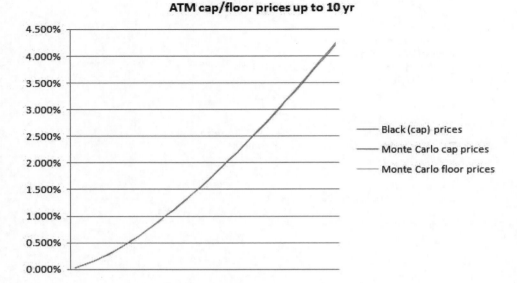

Calibration with swaptions   As usual, in order to facilitate the calibration, we first assume that fixed and floating payments occur at the same dates in the underlying swaps. In our implementation, the timestep is the payment frequency and the Euler scheme will be amended by a drift correction (see above).

Therefore, given an n-year term divided into $n.x$ periods (e.g., $x = 2$ when payments are semi-annual), the number of correlations to be adjusted is

$$1 + 2 + \dots + (n.x - 1) = \frac{n.x(n.x - 1)}{2}$$

(omitting Fwd_0 that plays no part in the scenario). On the other hand, we count the same number of forward swaps (the underlying assets of swaptions) with maturities of less than n years.

Swap numeraire   In a first attempt, we try to derive some swap dynamics using a relevant numeraire, as for the forward rates curve. Let us denote by $SW_n(t, T)$ the market rate at t of an n-year swap starting at T, and by $B(t, T_i)$, the price at t of a zero-bond paying 1 unit at $T + \tau i$: the payment frequency is assumed to be τ. The theoretical swap rate is given by

$$SW_n(t, T).\tau.(B(t, T_1) + B(t, T_2) + \dots + B(t, T_n)) = 1 - B(t, T_n)$$

$$\implies SW_n(t, T) = \frac{1 - B(t, T_n)}{\sum\limits_{i=1}^{n} B(t, T_i)}$$

Under the numeraire of $(B(t, T_1) + B(t, T_2) + \dots + B(t, T_n))$, the forward swap rate is martingale: in fact, this numeraire is called the **swap numeraire**.

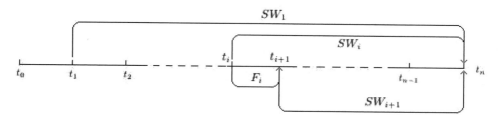

However, finding a closed relation between the dynamics of two adjacent swaps, i.e., $SW_i(t, T)$ and $SW_{i+1}(t, T)$, turns out not to be practicable since the forward rates are not geometric normal, as a result of their stochastic drift. Moreover, whereas forward rate instantaneous volatilities are *deterministic*, the expression of swap instantaneous volatilities unveils some degree of stochasticity due to the drift, contingent on the forward term structure at any time.

An approximate formula for swaption volatilities Let us denote by $SW(i, m)$ the **co-terminal swap rates**, i.e., expiring i years from today maturing m years from today. By definition

$$\sum_{k=i}^{m-1} [SW_t(i, m) - f(k)] \tau_k B_t(k + 1) = 0$$

Assuming that $\tau_k = \tau$, and denoting by $w_t(k, m)$ the quantity

$$w_t(k, m) = B_t(k + 1) / \sum_{j=i}^{m-1} B_t(j + 1)$$

$SW(i, m)$ can be reformulated as follows:

$$SW(i, m) = \sum_{k=i}^{m-1} w_t(k) f(k)$$

Otherwise

$$\frac{dSW(i, m)}{SW(i, m)} = \sum_{k=i}^{m-1} \frac{\partial SW(i, m)}{\partial f(k)} \frac{df(k)}{SW(i, m)}$$

For the purposes of conciseness, we denote $SW_i = SW(i, m)$ and $f_i = f(i)$

$$\frac{dSW_i}{SW_i} = \sum_{k=i}^{m-1} \frac{\partial SW_i}{\partial f_k} \frac{df_k}{f_k} \frac{f_k}{SW_i}$$

From $Cov(df_k/f_k, df_l/f_l) = (\rho_{k,l}\sigma_k\sigma_l)\tau$, we draw

$$Cov(dSW_i/SW_i, dSW_j/SW_j) = \left(\sum_{k=i}^{m-1} \sum_{l=j}^{m-1} \frac{\partial SW_i}{\partial f_k} \frac{\partial SW_j}{\partial f_l} \frac{f_k}{SW_i} \frac{f_l}{SW_j} \rho_{k,l}\sigma_k\sigma_l \right) \tau \qquad (6.19)$$

From equation (6.19), we draw the theoretical SW_i instantaneous volatility

$$\sigma^2(SW_i) = \frac{\sum\limits_{k=i}^{m-1} \sum\limits_{l=i}^{m-1} \partial SW_i/\partial f_k . \partial SW_i/\partial f_l . f_k f_l \rho_{k,l} \sigma_k \sigma_l}{\left(\sum\limits_{k=i}^{m-1} w_t(k) f_k \right)^2}$$

Rebonato (2002) has brought to light the fact that $\sigma(SW_{i,m})$ (or $\sigma(SW_i)$) calculated at $t = 0$ yields a good approximation in order to match the Black volatility as implied from the swaptions' market prices. Introducing a new "weight" w' defined by

$$w'_i = w_i + \sum_k f_k \frac{\partial w_k}{\partial f_i}$$

and stating

$$\eta'_{k,l}(t) = \frac{w'_k(t) f_k(t) w'_l(t) f_l(t)}{\left(\sum\limits_{j=i}^{m-1} w_t(j) f_j \right)^2}$$

then

$$\sigma^2(SW_i) \simeq \sum\limits_{k=i}^{m-1} \sum\limits_{l=i}^{m-1} \eta'_{k,l}(t = 0) \rho_{k,l} \sigma_k \sigma_l$$

Denoting by $[C^{SW}]$ and $[C^F]$ respectively the co-terminal swap rates and forward rates covariance matrix, this can be put matricially:

$$[C^{SW}] = [Z^{F \to SW}].[C^F].[Z^{F \to SW}]^{\dagger}$$

On one hand, the computation of $Z^{F \to SW}_{k,l}$ is rather tedious (see Jäckel 2002): on the other hand, the fitting of correlations to match swaptions' market prices requires no complex calibration algorithms, but only to compute $Z^{F \to SW}_{k,l}(t)$ at $t = 0$. The calibration will consist in adjusting the correlation matrix $(\rho_{k,l})$ so as to verify

$$\sigma^2_{market}(SW_i)(t) = \sum\limits_{k=i}^{m-1} \sum\limits_{l=i}^{m-1} Z^{F \to SW}_{i,k}(0) \underbrace{\left[\frac{1}{i\Delta t - t} \int\limits_t^{i\Delta t} \rho_{k,l}(t) \sigma_k \sigma_l dt \right]} Z^{F \to SW}_{i,l}(0)$$

In general, the term between square brackets must be "piecewise" integrated, since the time to expiration is discretized. Fortunately, our model for $\rho_{j,l}(t) = \rho_{j,l}(0)$ leads to a tremendous simplification:

$$\int\limits_t^T \sigma_i(t) \sigma_j(j) \rho_{i,j} du/(T - t) = \sigma_i(t) \sigma_j(j) \rho_{i,j}$$

Therefore

$$[C^{SW}] = [Z^{F \to SW}].[C^F].[Z^{F \to SW}]^\dagger$$

$$= [Z^{F \to SW}].[(\rho_{i,j}\sigma_i\sigma_j)(T - t)].[Z^{F \to SW}]^\dagger$$

The forward-forward **correlation** adjusted matrix is obtained by rescaling $[(\rho_{i,j}\sigma_i\sigma_j)(T - t)]$.

$$[Correl^F] = [\rho_{i,j}\sigma_i\sigma_j]$$

The calibration goes roughly like this:

- compute $Z_{i,j}^{F \to SW}$ and draw the coordinates of the swap correlation $[Correl^{SW}]$ matrix from them
- compute the pseudo-square root $[B]$ of this matrix through a Cholesky decomposition:

$$[B][B]^\dagger = [Correl^{SW}]$$

- build a diagonal matrix $[\epsilon]$ with

$$\epsilon_{i,j} = \sigma_{i,j}^{market}\delta_{i,j}$$

   This matrix will "rescale" the swap correlations obtained from the forwards' correlation matrix
- finally, compute

$$[A] = Z^{-1}[\epsilon][B]$$

   and the market-adjusted covariance matrix $[C] = [A][A]^\dagger$

Code   Below, we adopt a linearly increasing swaption volatility, from 10.5% up to 12.8% while caplets' volatilities remain unchanged from the last calibration program (see above). As before, the data are retrieved inside the **CalibSwaption** procedure. The forward correlation matrix is quite standard, i.e.,

$$\rho_{i,j} = e^{-0.1(j-i)0.25}\mathbb{1}_{j>i}$$

```
Public Sub CalibSwaption(p%)

ReDim alea!(p)
ReDim mu!(p), muB!(p)
ReDim FwdB!(p), Fwd0!(p)
Dim t!:t=0.25 'timestep

ReDim correl(p - 1, p - 1)
Dim i As Long
For i = 1 To p - 1
    For j = i To p - 1
        correl(i, j) = Exp(-0.1 * (j - i) / 4)
        correl(j, i) = correl(i, j)
    Next
Next
```

```
ReDim corr(p - 1) As Variant
ReDim trig(p - 1) As Variant

Fwd(0) = 0.04: discFwd(0) = 1 / (1 + Fwd(0) * t)

For i = 1 To p - 1
    Fwd(i) = 0.04 * Exp(0.01 * i)
    discFwd(i) = discFwd(i - 1) / (1 + Fwd(i) * t)
Next

volCaplet(1) = 0.135
volCaplet(2) = 0.14
volCaplet(3) = 0.145
volCaplet(4) = 0.1425
For i = 5 To 10
    volCaplet(i) = 0.14 - (i - 5) * 0.002
Next i
For i = 11 To p - 1
    volCaplet(i) = 0.128
Next i

For i = 1 To p - 1
    volSwap(i) = 0.105 + CSng(i) / CSng(p - 1) * (0.128 - 0.105)
Next
```

At this stage, we compute swaption Black prices and display them in a sheet called "Swap".

```
Sheets("Swap").Activate
Dim d1#, d2#

For i = 1 To p - 1
    sumdisc = 0
    For j = i To p - 1
        sumdisc = sumdisc + discFwd(j)
    Next
    swapFwd(i) = (discFwd(i - 1) - discFwd(p - 1)) / sumdisc / t
    strikeSwap(i) = swapFwd(i)
    d1 = (Log(swapFwd(i) / strikeSwap(i)) + 0.5 * vol-
Swap(i) ^ 2 * (i * t)) / volSwap(i) _
    / Sqr(i * t)
    d2 = d1 - volSwap(i) * Sqr(i * t)
    valSwap(i) = (swapFwd(i) * norm(d1) - strikeSwap(i)
    * norm(d2)) * sumdisc * t
    Cells(i + 2, 2) = valSwap(i)
Next
```

The calibration starts here: the matrices that play a part in the fit of the correlations are now declared. The computation of Zswap(i,j)=z(i,j) is in Jäckel (2002) pp 166–167.

```
ReDim swaption(p - 1)
ReDim covFwd(p - 1, p - 1), Zswap(p - 1, p - 1), invZswap(p - 1, p - 1), _
```

```
    Temp(p - 1, p - 1), AAFwd(p - 1, p - 1), covar(p - 1, p - 1), _
    Epsilon(p - 1, p - 1), covSwap(p - 1, p - 1)

    ReDim Aswap(p - 1), Bswap(p - 1)

    For i = 1 To p - 1
        For j = 1 To p - 1
            covFwd(i, j) = volCaplet(i) * volCaplet(j) * correl(i, j)
        Next
    Next

    For i = 1 To p - 1
        For j = i To p - 1
            Aswap(i) = Aswap(i) + discFwd(j) * Fwd(j) * t
            Bswap(i) = Bswap(i) + discFwd(j) * t
        Next
    Next

    For i = 1 To p - 1
        For j = i To p - 1
            Zswap(i, j) = discFwd(j) * Fwd(j) * t / Aswap(i) + _
            (Aswap(i) * Bswap(j) - Aswap(j) * Bswap(i)) * Fwd(j) * t / _
            (Aswap(i) * Bswap(i)) / (1 + t * Fwd(j))
        Next
    Next

    '***********************************************************
    sig is the array of instantaneous swap volatilites,
    computed from the initial correlation matrix.
    '***********************************************************
    ReDim x!(p - 1), sig!(p - 1)

    For i = 1 To p - 1
        For K = i To p - 1
            y = 0
            For l = i To p - 1
                y = y + covFwd(K, l) * Zswap(i, l)
            Next l
            x(i) = x(i) + Zswap(i, K) * y
        Next K

        sig(i) = Sqr(x(i))
    Next i

    For i = 1 To p - 1
        sumdisc = 0
        For j = i To p - 1
            sumdisc = sumdisc + discFwd(j)
        Next
        d1 = (Log(swapFwd(i) / strikeSwap(i)) + 0.5 * sig(i) ^ 2 * (i * t)) / _
            sig(i) / Sqr(i * t)
        d2 = d1 - sig(i) * Sqr(i * t)
        Cells(i + 2, 3) = (swapFwd(i) * norm(d1) - strikeSwap(i) * _ norm(d2))
            * sumdisc * t
    Next
```

```vba
invZswap = InverseMatrice(Zswap)

covSwap = MatMult(Zswap, MatMult(covFwd, matTranspose(Zswap)))

ReDim vol!(p - 1)
For i = 1 To p - 1
    vol(i) = Sqr(covSwap(i, i))
Next i
For i = 1 To p - 1
    For j = 1 To p - 1
        covSwap(i, j) = covSwap(i, j) / vol(i) / vol(j)
    Next
Next

Temp = Cholesky(covSwap, p)

For i = 1 To p - 1
    For j = 1 To p - 1
        If i = j Then
        Epsilon(i, j) = volSwap(i)
        Else: Epsilon(i, j) = 0
        End If
    Next j
Next i

AAFwd = MatMult(invZswap, MatMult(Epsilon, Temp))

covar = MatMult(AAFwd, matTranspose(AAFwd))

For i = 1 To p - 1
    For j = 1 To p - 1
        correl(i, j) = covar(i, j) / Sqr(covar(i, i) * covar(j, j))
    Next j
Next i

For i = 1 To p - 1
    corr(i) = DoubleToVarArray(drift(Correl, i - 1))
    trig(i) = Cholesky(VarToDoubleArray(corr(i)))
Next i

For i = 1 To p - 1
    swaption(i) = 0
    sumDF(i) = 0
    Fwd0(i) = Fwd(i)
Next
Randomize

For l = 1 To 4000

    For i = 1 To p - 1
        Fwd(i) = Fwd0(i)
        FwdB(i) = Fwd0(i)
        sumDF(i) = 0
    Next

    For i = 1 To p - 1
        m = i - 1
```

```
        For K = 1 To p - i
            alea(K) = Acklam(Rnd()): c = c + 1
        Next K

        Fwd(1) = Fwd(1) * Exp(-0.5 * volCaplet(1 + m) ^ 2 * t _
        + volCaplet(1 + m) * alea(1) * Sqr(t))
        DF(1) = 1 / (1 + Fwd(1) * t)
        sumDF(1) = DF(1)

        For j = 2 To p - i
            mu(j) = 0: muB(j) = 0

            For K = 2 To j
                mu(j) = mu(j) + volCaplet(j + m) * Fwd(K) * t * vol-
Caplet(K + m) * corr(i)(K, j) _
                / (1 + Fwd(K) * t)
            Next K

            brown = 0
            For K = 1 To j
                brown = brown + trig(i)(j, K) * alea(K)
            Next K

'    predictor corrector
            FwdB(j) = Fwd(j) * _
            Exp(mu(j) * t - 0.5 * volCaplet(j + m) ^ 2 * t + vol-
Caplet(j + m) * brown * Sqr(t))

            For K = 2 To j
                muB(j) = muB(j) + _
                volCaplet(j + m) * FwdB(K) * t * vol-
Caplet(K + m) * corr(i)(K, j) / (1 + FwdB(K) * t)
            Next

            Fwd(j) = Fwd(j) * Exp(0.5 * (mu(j) + muB(j)) * t - _
                            0.5 * volCaplet(j + m) ^ 2 * t + vol-
Caplet(j + m) * brown * Sqr(t))

            DF(j) = DF(j - 1) / (1 + Fwd(j) * t)
            sumDF(j) = sumDF(j - 1) + DF(j)

        Next j

        swaption(i) = swaption(i) + Max(1 - DF(p - i) - strikeSwap(i) * t *
        sumDF(p - i), 0)

        For K = 1 To p - i - 1
            Fwd(K) = Fwd(K + 1)
        Next K
    Next i

Next l

For i = 1 To p - 1
Cells(i + 2, 15) = swaption(i) / 4000 * discFwd(i - 1)
Next i

End Sub
```

Numerical results The graph below displays the swaption prices obtained from the calibration program above. Let us remark that, despite the very poor RNG used, the variance observed on the swaptions was surprisingly low.

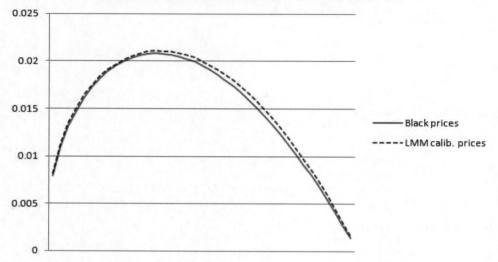

Co-terminal (option+swap=10y) ATM swaption prices

CHAPTER 7

Stochastic Volatilities

Until now, all the dynamics we use to price assets have been characterized by a Brownian term in the form of

$$\sigma^{\dagger}.dW_t$$

The volatility array was assumed to be **deterministic**, referring to one particular asset, such as one stock, or one forward rate, and one maturity.

Unfortunately, this Brownian noise does not reflect the way assets prices actually react to broad upward or downward moves. For the needs of a more reliable risk assessment, this basic model had to be enhanced or, at least, amended.

At the inception of the options industry, a smile effect was added to the volatility term structure in the form of positive or negative spreads according to the type of securities. For instance, regarding put equity options, out-of-the-money implied volatilities were higher than at-the-money ones. As a matter of fact, volatility curves became *volatility surfaces*. The convexity of these surfaces determined the **smile effect**.

Some authors have established that market prices of European-style options determined one unique diffusion process. **Dupire** (1994) stated the following relationship mapping instantaneous volatilities to option prices:

$$\frac{\partial \hat{C}(S, t, K)}{\partial t} = \frac{1}{2}\sigma(S, t, K)^2 K^2 \frac{\partial^2 \hat{C}(S, t, K)}{\partial K^2} - rK\frac{\partial \hat{C}(S, t, K)}{\partial K}$$

A further step is taken when considering the volatility as randomly distributed. As a result, some additional dynamics related to the instantaneous volatility are needed to complete the model, such as in the **Heston model** (Heston, 1993):

$$dS_t = \mu S_t dt + \sqrt{v_t}S_t dW_t \qquad (7.1a)$$

$$dv_t = \kappa(\theta - v_t)dt + \eta\sqrt{v_t}dB_t \qquad (7.1b)$$

$$\sigma_t = \sqrt{v_t} \qquad (7.1c)$$

$$< dW_t, dB_t > = \rho dt \qquad (7.1d)$$

This **stochastic volatility** model will be presented in the next section with applications in equity-based derivatives. In a further section, we will introduce a **Constant Elasticity Volatility** (CEV) model for LIBOR forward rates, the SABR model.

7.1 THE HESTON MODEL

From equation (7.1), Heston derived the European call price in the following form:

$$C(S_t, K, v_t, \tau) = S_t P_1(S_t, K, v_t, \tau) - Ke^{-r\tau} P_2(S_t, K, v_t, \tau)$$

where τ denotes the time to maturity.

In the equation above, P_1 and P_2 figure probabilities, just as N_1 and N_2 figure probabilities in the Black–Scholes (BS) vanilla European option's price.

For $j = 1, 2$,

$$P_j = \frac{1}{2} + \frac{1}{\pi} \int_0^{+\infty} Re \left[\frac{e^{-i\phi Ln\,(K)} f_j}{i\phi} \right] d\phi$$

with

$$f_j = exp\,[C_j + D_j v_t + i\phi Ln\,(S_t)]$$

$$C_j = ri\phi\tau + \frac{\kappa\theta}{\sigma^2} \left[(b_j - \rho\sigma i\phi + d_j)\tau - 2Ln \left(\frac{1 - g_j e^{d_j\tau}}{1 - g_j} \right) \right]$$

$$D_j = \frac{(b_j - i\phi\rho\sigma + d_j)}{\sigma^2} \left[\frac{1 - e^{d_j\tau}}{1 - g_j e^{d_j\tau}} \right]$$

$$g_j = \frac{(b_j - i\phi\rho\sigma + d_j)}{(b_j - i\phi\rho\sigma - d_j)}$$

$$d_j = \sqrt{(\rho\sigma i\phi - b_j)^2 - \sigma^2(2u_j i\phi - \phi^2)}$$

$$u_1 = 1/2, \quad u_2 = -1/2$$

$$b_1 = \kappa - \rho\sigma, \quad b_2 = \kappa$$

7.1.1 Code

Given the integration domain, i.e., $[0, +\infty)$, we will use the **Gauss-Laguerre** approximation quadrature method. Let us denote by $w_L(k)$ and $x_L(k)$ the weights and nodes of the quadrature:

$$P_j \simeq \frac{1}{2} + \frac{1}{\pi} \sum_{k=1}^{n} w_L(k) Re \left[\frac{e^{-ix_L(k)Ln\,(K)} f_j(x_L(k)}{ix_L(k)} \right]$$

The calculation of the right-hand side of the formula requires the carrying out of operations on complex numbers such as addition or division, and, moreover, exponentiation and square root extraction. As a reminder:

$$a + ib = (a^2 + b^2) \left(\frac{a}{a^2 + b^2} + i\frac{b}{a^2 + b^2} \right)$$

$$= (a^2 + b^2)(cos(\alpha) + isin(\alpha))$$

giving

$$\alpha = arctan(b/a)$$

From

$$\sqrt{cos(\alpha) + isin(\alpha)} = e^{i\alpha/2}(\text{De Moivre})$$

we conclude

$$\sqrt{cos(\alpha) + isin(\alpha)} = \sqrt{a^2 + b^2}(cos(b/2a) + isin(b/2a))$$

Basic arithmetical operations are achieved through user-developed functions on a custom-type variable **Complex** implemented in a class module.

```
Complex
Public re As Double
Public im As Double

'Instantiation of complex number
Public Function Compx(a As Double, b As Double) As Complex

Dim c As New Complex
c.re = a
c.im = b
Set Compx = c
End Function

'Addition
Public Function AddCompx(a As Complex, b As Complex) As Complex

Dim c As New Complex
c.re = a.re + b.re
c.im = a.im + b.im
Set AddCompx = c
End Function

'Sum for complex numbers
Public Function SumCompx(a() As Complex) As Complex

Dim c As New Complex
For i = 1 To UBound(c)
    Set c = AddCompx(c, a(i))
Next i
Set SumCompx = c
End Function
```

```vba
'Subtraction
Public Function SubCompx(a As Complex, b As Complex) As Complex

Dim c As New Complex
c.re = a.re - b.re
c.im = a.im - b.im
Set SubCompx = c
End Function

'Multiplication
Public Function MultCompx(a As Complex, b As Complex) As Complex

Dim c As New Complex
c.re = a.re * b.re - a.im * b.im
c.im = a.re * b.im + a.im * b.re
Set MultCompx = c
End Function

'Division
Public Function DivCompx(a As Complex, b As Complex) As Complex

Dim c As New Complex
c.re = (a.re * b.re + a.im * b.im) / (b.re ^ 2 + b.im ^ 2)
c.im = (a.im * b.re - a.re * b.im) / (b.re ^ 2 + b.im ^ 2)
Set DivCompx = c
End Function

'Square
Public Function SqCompx(a As Complex) As Complex

Dim c As New Complex
c.re = a.re ^ 2 - a.im ^ 2
c.im = 2 * a.re * a.im
Set SqCompx = c
End Function

'Square root extraction
Public Function SqrtCompx(a As Complex) As Complex

Dim c As New Complex
w = Sqr(a.re ^ 2 + a.im ^ 2)
u = Atn(a.im / a.re)
c.re = Sqr(w) * Cos(u / 2)
c.im = Sqr(w) * Sin(u / 2)
Set SqrtCompx = c
End Function

'Exponential
Public Function ExpCompx(a As Complex) As Complex

Dim c As New Complex
c.re = Exp(a.re) * Cos(a.im)
c.im = Exp(a.re) * Sin(a.im)
Set ExpCompx = c
End Function
```

```
'Neperian log
Public Function LnCompx(a As Complex) As Complex

Dim c As New Complex
w = (a.re ^ 2 + a.im ^ 2) ^ 0.5
c.re = Log(w)
c.im = Atn(a.im / a.re)
Set LnCompx = c
End Function


Function HestonP1(rho#, eta#, phi#, kappa#, theta#, tau#, K#, S#, r#, v#)
As Double

Dim z#, b1#
Dim g1 As Complex, d1 As Complex, C As Complex, D As Complex
Dim f1 As Complex, a As Complex, b As Complex
u1 = 0.5
z = rho * eta * phi
b1 = kappa - rho * eta
Set d1 = SqrtCompx(SubCompx(SqCompx(SubCompx(Compx(0, z),
Compx(b1, 0))), MultCompx(Compx(eta ^ 2, 0), _
        SubCompx(Compx(0, 2 * u1 * phi), Compx(phi ^ 2, 0)))))
Set g1 = DivCompx(SubCompx(AddCompx(Compx(b1, 0), d1), Compx(0, z)), _
        SubCompx(SubCompx(Compx(b1, 0), d1), Compx(0, z)))

Set C = AddCompx(Compx(0, r * phi * tau), MultCompx
(Compx((kappa * theta) / eta ^ 2, 0), _
        SubCompx(MultCompx(SubCompx(AddCompx(Compx(b1, 0), d1),
Compx(0, z)), Compx(tau, 0)), _
        MultCompx(Compx(2, 0), _
        LnCompx(DivCompx(SubCompx(Compx(1, 0), MultCompx(g1, _
        ExpCompx(MultCompx(d1, Compx(tau, 0))))),
SubCompx(Compx(1, 0), g1)))))))

Set D = MultCompx(DivCompx(SubCompx(Compx(1, 0), ExpCompx
(MultCompx(d1, Compx(tau, 0)))), _
        SubCompx(Compx(1, 0), MultCompx(g1, ExpCompx
(MultCompx(d1, Compx(tau, 0)))))), _
        DivCompx(SubCompx(AddCompx(Compx(b1, 0), d1),
Compx(0, z)), Compx(eta ^ 2, 0)))

Set f1 = ExpCompx(AddCompx(AddCompx(C, MultCompx(D, Compx(v, 0))),
Compx(0, phi * Log(S))))
Set a = ExpCompx(Compx(0, -phi * Log(K)))
Set b = DivCompx(MultCompx(a, f1), Compx(0, phi))

HestonP1 = b.re
End Function


Function HestonP2(rho#, eta#, phi#, kappa#, theta#, tau#, K#, S#, r#, v#)
As Double

Dim z#, b2#
Dim g2 As Complex, d2 As Complex, C As Complex, D As Complex
Dim f2 As Complex, a As Complex, b As Complex
u2 = -0.5
z = rho * eta * phi
```

```vba
b2 = kappa
Set d2 = SqrtCompx(SubCompx(SqCompx(SubCompx(Compx(0, z),
Compx(b2, 0))), MultCompx(Compx(eta ^ 2, 0), _
        SubCompx(Compx(0, 2 * u2 * phi), Compx(phi ^ 2, 0)))))
Set g2 = DivCompx(SubCompx(AddCompx(Compx(b2, 0), d2), Compx(0, z)), _
        SubCompx(SubCompx(Compx(b2, 0), d2), Compx(0, z)))

Set C = AddCompx(Compx(0, r * phi * tau), MultCompx(Compx
((kappa * theta) / eta ^ 2, 0), _
        SubCompx(MultCompx(SubCompx(AddCompx(Compx(b2, 0), d2),
Compx(0, z)), Compx(tau, 0)), _
        MultCompx(Compx(2, 0), _
        LnCompx(DivCompx(SubCompx(Compx(1, 0), MultCompx(g2, _
        ExpCompx(MultCompx(d2, Compx(tau, 0)))))),
SubCompx(Compx(1, 0), g2)))))))

Set D = MultCompx(DivCompx(SubCompx(Compx(1, 0),
ExpCompx(MultCompx(d2, Compx(tau, 0)))), _
        SubCompx(Compx(1, 0), MultCompx(g2,
ExpCompx(MultCompx(d2, Compx(tau, 0)))))), _
        DivCompx(SubCompx(AddCompx(Compx(b2, 0), d2),
Compx(0, z)), Compx(eta ^ 2, 0)))

Set f2 = ExpCompx(AddCompx(AddCompx(C, MultCompx(D, Compx(v, 0))),
Compx(0, phi * Log(S))))
Set a = ExpCompx(Compx(0, -phi * Log(K)))
Set b = DivCompx(MultCompx(a, f2), Compx(0, phi))

HestonP2 = b.re
End Function

Function HestonCall(rho#, eta#, kappa#, theta#, tau#, K#, S#, r#, v#) As Double

Worksheets("Laguerre").Activate

ReDim xL(20), wL(20)
p1 = 0: p2 = 0

For i = 1 To 20
    xL(i) = Cells(i, 5): wL(i) = Cells(i, 7)
Next i

For i = 1 To 20
    p1 = p1 + wL(i) * HestonP1(rho, eta, xL(i), kappa, theta, tau,
K, S, r, v)
    p2 = p2 + wL(i) * HestonP2(rho, eta, xL(i), kappa, theta, tau,
K, S, r, v)
Next i

p1 = 0.5 + (1 / PI) * p1
p2 = 0.5 + (1 / PI) * p2

If p1 < 0 Then p1 = 0
If p1 > 1 Then p1 = 1
If p2 < 0 Then p2 = 0
If p2 > 1 Then p2 = 1
HestonCall = S * p1 - K * Exp(-tau * r) * p2
```

```
If HestonCall < 0 Then HestonCall = 0

End Function
```

7.1.2 A faster algorithm

In this section, we will examine the Benhamou, Gobet, and Miri (2009) approximation method, applied to a piecewise constant parametrization of the Heston model. In a first paragraph, we will just scratch the surface of the BGM approach (not to be confused with Brace Gatarek Musiela) and establish their formula for a single European put. Then, we extend these formulae to a string of dates.

European put approximation Setting F as the forward price, we define $X_t = Ln\,(F_t)$, yielding

$$dX_t = -\frac{1}{2}v_t dt + \sqrt{v_t}dW_t$$

Recalling the dynamics of v_t in the Heston model,

$$dv_t = \kappa(\theta - v_t)dt + \eta\sqrt{v_t}dB_t$$

under the filtration $\mathcal{F}(B_t)$ generated by B_t, the European put option price on a non-bearing coupon asset is written:

$$e^{-rt}\mathbb{E}(\mathbb{E}([K - e^{X_t}]^+/\mathcal{F}(B_t)))$$

Thus, for every scenario $B_{0<t<T}$, the mean variance

$$\frac{1}{T}\int_0^T v_t dt$$

is well determined. Since X_t SDE is a Black-Scholes diffusion process, given $K = e^{X_0}$ (ATM put) we can rewrite the put price as follows:

$$\text{Put(Heston)} = \mathbb{E}\left(Put_{BS}(\underbrace{X_0 + \int_0^T \rho\sqrt{v_t}dB_t - \int_0^T \frac{\rho^2}{2}v_t dt}_{Strike}, \underbrace{\int_0^T (1 - \rho^2)2v_t dt}_{variance})\right)$$

Benhamou considers v_t^ϵ, the perturbed version of v_t satisfying

$$dv_t^\epsilon = \kappa(\theta - v_t^\epsilon)dt + \eta\epsilon\sqrt{v_t^\epsilon}dB_t$$

The idea is to use the methodology of the small volatility of volatility expansion in order to attain a rather accurate approximation of the put, using the derivatives of $\partial^i v_t^\epsilon/\partial\epsilon^i|_{\epsilon=0}$. From

$$dv_t^\epsilon = \kappa(\theta - v_t^\epsilon)dt \tag{7.2}$$

we draw

$$v_t^0 = (v_0^0 - \theta)e^{-\kappa t} + \theta$$

Therefore

$$V_0 = \int_0^T v_t^0 dt = \frac{\theta - v_0^0}{\kappa}(e^{-\kappa T} - 1) + \theta T$$

Let us denote $y = V_0$: when $\epsilon = 0$, the solution is a proxy BS put price:

$$Put_{BS}(x, y) = Ke^{-rT}N\left(\frac{1}{\sqrt{y}}Ln\left[\frac{K}{e^{x+rT}}\right] + \frac{1}{2}\sqrt{y}\right) - e^x N\left(\frac{1}{\sqrt{y}}Ln\left[\frac{K}{e^{x+rT}}\right] - \frac{1}{2}\sqrt{y}\right)$$

Benhamou finds a solution for $\epsilon = 1$, through an expansion around the proxy BS price:

$$P_{Heston}(x, y) \simeq P_{BS}(x, y)$$

$$+ a_{1,t}\frac{\partial^2}{\partial xy}P_{BS}(x, y) + a_{2,t}\frac{\partial^3}{\partial x^2 y}P_{BS}(x, y)$$

$$+ b_{0,t}\frac{\partial^2}{\partial y^2}P_{BS}(x, y) + b_{2,t}\frac{\partial^4}{\partial x^2 y^2}P_{BS}(x, y)$$

with

$$a_{1,T} = \int_0^T \int_{t_1}^T e^{\kappa t_1}\rho_{t_1}\eta_{t_1}v_{t_1}^0 e^{-\kappa t_2}dt_1 dt_2$$

$$a_{2,T} = \int_0^T \int_{t_1}^T \int_{t_2}^T e^{\kappa t_1}\rho_{t_1}\eta_{t_1}v_{t_1}^0\rho_{t_2}\eta_{t_2}e^{-\kappa t_3}dt_1 dt_2 dt_3$$

$$b_{0,T} = \int_0^T \int_{t_1}^T \int_{t_2}^T e^{2\kappa t_2}\eta_{t_1}^2 v_{t_1}^0 e^{-\kappa t_2}e^{-\kappa t_3}dt_1 dt_2 dt_3$$

$$b_{2,T} = \frac{a_{1,T}^2}{2}$$

$$a_1 = \rho\eta(p_0 v_0^0 + p_1\theta) \quad a_2 = (\rho\eta)^2(q_0 v_0^0 + q_1\theta)$$

$$b_0 = \eta^2(r_0 v_0^0 + r_1\theta) \quad b_2 = \frac{a_1^2}{2}$$

$$p_0 = \frac{e^{-\kappa T}(-\kappa T + e^{\kappa T} - 1)}{\kappa^2}$$

$$p_1 = \frac{e^{-\kappa T}(\kappa T + e^{\kappa T}(\kappa T - 2) + 2)}{\kappa^2}$$

$$q_0 = \frac{e^{-\kappa T}(-\kappa T(\kappa T + 2) + 2e^{\kappa T} - 2)}{2\kappa^3}$$

$$q_1 = \frac{e^{-\kappa T}(2e^{\kappa T}(\kappa T - 3) + \kappa T(\kappa T + 4) + 6)}{2\kappa^3}$$

$$r_0 = \frac{e^{-2\kappa T}(-4e^{\kappa T}\kappa T + 2e^{2\kappa T} - 2)}{4\kappa^3}$$

$$r_1 = \frac{e^{-2\kappa T}(4e^{\kappa T}(\kappa T + 1) + e^{2\kappa T}(2\kappa T - 5) + 1)}{4\kappa^3}$$

Code For the sake of readibility, we use **finite differences** to estimate the partial derivatives:

$$\frac{\partial^{i+j}}{\partial x^i y^j} P_{BS}(x, y)$$

For instance, $\frac{\partial^2}{\partial y^2} P_{BS}$ is numerically calulated using

```
HputYY = (HputY(x, k, y + 0.01, t, r) - _
    HputY(x, k, y - 0.01, t, r)) / 0.02

Public Function Hput(x#, k#, y#, t#, r#) As Double

Hput = k * Exp(-r * t) * norm(Log(k / Exp(x + r * t)) / Sqr(y)
+ 0.5 * Sqr(y)) - _
Exp(x) * norm(Log(k / Exp(x + r * t)) / Sqr(y) - 0.5 * Sqr(y))
End Function

Public Function HputX(x#, k#, y#, t#, r#) As Double

HputX = (Hput(x + 0.05, k, y, t, r) - Hput(x - 0.05, k, y, t, r)) / 0.1
End Function

Public Function HputY(x#, k#, y#, t#, r#) As Double

HputY = (Hput(x, k, y + 0.01, t, r) - Hput(x, k, y - 0.01, t, r)) / 0.02
End Function

Public Function HputYY(x#, k#, y#, t#, r#) As Double

HputYY = (HputY(x, k, y + 0.01, t, r) - HputY(x, k, y - 0.01, t, r)) / 0.02
End Function

Public Function HputXY(x#, k#, y#, t#, r#) As Double

HputXY = (HputX(x, k, y + 0.01, t, r) - HputX(x, k, y - 0.01, t, r)) / 0.02
End Function

Public Function HputXXY(x#, k#, y#, t#, r#) As Double

HputXXY = (HputXY(x + 0.05, k, y, t, r) - HputXY(x - 0.05, k, y, t, r)) / 0.1
End Function

Public Function HputXXYY(x#, k#, y#, t#, r#) As Double

HputXXYY = (HputXXY(x, k, y + 0.01, t, r) - HputXXY(x, k, y - 0.01, t, r))
/ 0.1
End Function
```

****

The put pricing is carried out by the following function **BGM**.

****

```vba
Function BGM(theta#, v#, kappa#, rho#, eta#, S#, K#, t#, r#) As Double

Dim y#: y = (v - theta) / kappa * (1 - Exp(-kappa * t)) + theta * t

Dim p0#: p0 = Exp(-kappa * t) * _
(-kappa * t + Exp(kappa * t) - 1) / kappa ^ 2

Dim p1#: p1 = Exp(-kappa * t) * _
(kappa * t + Exp(kappa * t) * (kappa * t - 2) + 2) / kappa ^ 2

Dim q0#: q0 = Exp(-kappa * t) * _
(-kappa * t * (kappa * t + 2) + 2 * Exp(kappa * t) - 2) / (2 * kappa ^ 3)

Dim q1#: q1 = Exp(-kappa * t) * _
(2 * Exp(kappa * t) * (kappa * t - 3) + kappa * t *
(kappa * t + 4) + 6) / (2 * kappa ^ 3)

Dim r0#: r0 = Exp(-2 * kappa * t) * _
(-4 * kappa * t * Exp(kappa * t) + 2 * Exp(2 * kappa * t) - 2) /
(4 * kappa ^ 3)

Dim r1#: r1 = Exp(-2 * kappa * t) * _
(4 * (kappa * t + 1) * Exp(kappa * t) + Exp(2 * kappa * t)
* (2 * kappa * t - 5) + 1) _
/ (4 * kappa ^ 3)

Dim a1#, a2#, b0#, b2#
a1 = rho * eta * (p0 * v + p1 * theta)
a2 = (rho * eta) ^ 2 * (q0 * v + q1 * theta)
b0 = eta ^ 2 * (r0 * v + r1 * theta)
b2 = a1 ^ 2 / 2
Dim x#: x = Log(S)

BG = Hput(x, K, y, t, r) + a1 * HputXY(x, K, y, t, r) + _
                          a2 * HputXXY(x, K, y, t, r) + _
                          b0 * HputYY(x, K, y, t, r) + _
                          b2 * HputXXYY(x, K, y, t, r)

BGM = max(BGM, K * Exp(-r * t) - S + 0.02)
'0.02 aims at avoiding negative volatilities in the course of calibra-
tion since Gauss quadrature truncates deep in-the-money options' prices

End Function
```

This method works remarkably well: it is of great help at the calibration stage. The tables (Tables 7.1–7.3) below provide evidence of the method's accuracy.

We compare results obtained from the Heston closed formula with 20 Gauss-Laguerre nodes and from the approximation method, for different values of K (at and out-of-the-money), ρ and η.

TABLE 7.1 6-mth European put

K	$\rho = 0$ $\eta = 0.1$	$\rho = 0.5$ $\eta = 0.1$	$\rho = 0$ $\eta = 0.3$	$\rho = 0.5$ $\eta = 0.3$
70	0.215 *0.215*	0.168 *0.171*	0.241 *0.243*	0.113 *0.119*
85	1.905 *1.905*	1.817 *1.818*	1.895 *1.897*	1.624 *1.626*
100	7.225 *7.224*	7.229 *7.224*	7.148 *7.14*	7.158 *7.11*

TABLE 7.2 1-yr European put

K	$\rho = 0$ $\eta = 0.1$	$\rho = 0.5$ $\eta = 0.1$	$\rho = 0$ $\eta = 0.3$	$\rho = 0.5$ $\eta = 0.3$
70	1.078 *1.078*	0.965 *0.969*	1.105 *1.108*	0.774 *0.784*
85	4.114 *4.114*	4.01 *4.008*	4.064 *4.061*	3.74 *3.714*
100	10.12 *10.12*	10.131 *10.125*	10.004 *9.998*	10.028 *9.96*

TABLE 7.3 2-yr European Put

K	$\rho = 0$ $\eta = 0.1$	$\rho = 0.5$ $\eta = 0.1$	$\rho = 0$ $\eta = 0.3$	$\rho = 0.5$ $\eta = 0.3$
70	3.048 *3.048*	2.906 *2.907*	3.041 *3.04*	2.605 *2.596*
85	7.32 *7.319*	7.23 *7.226*	7.238 *7.234*	6.954 *6.9*
100	13.773 *13.773*	13.797 *13.788*	13.641 *13.635*	13.696 *13.611*

The other parameters are fixed ($r = 0.03$, $v_0^0 = 0.07$, $\kappa = 2$ and $\theta = 0.1$). Approximation values are in *italics*.

Piecewise constant parameters   Since market prices for plain-vanilla options cover different strikes and different maturities, we can hardly afford to fit our model using only five parameters. One solution would consist in calibrating the model for each maturity, in order to get a set $V(t_i)$, $\theta(t_i)$, $\eta(t_i)$, $\kappa(t_i)$, $\rho(t_i)$, for each term. One question arises: which parameters to use between t_i and t_{i+1}, when pricing, for instance, Asian-style calls?

Once again, we will resort to BGM and discretize the time space with piecewise constant (forward) parameters. The interval $[0, T)$ is divided into n sub-intervals $[T_i, T_{i+1})$, $i = 0,...,n$ and we adopt the following asumptions:

- $\rho = \rho_{i+1}$, $\theta = \theta_{i+1}$ and $\eta = \eta_{i+1}$ are piecewise constants
- κ is being fixed all over $[0, T)$
- for reasons of stability in the process of calibration, we will cheat with the model, also considering V as a parameter that will be adjusted for each period $[t_i, t_{i+1})$. This is justified by potential gaps between prices in the market volatility surface that sometimes put the calibration process in jeopardy. In practice, given equation (7.2),

$$dv_t^\epsilon = \kappa(\theta - v_t^\epsilon)dt$$

we are to adjust $V(i)$ using the recursive relationship:

$$V(i) = e^{-\kappa(t_{i+1}-t_i)}(V(i-1) - \theta(i)) + \theta(i)$$

Benhamou, Gobet, and Miri introduced the integral operators $w_{t,T}^{k,l}$ defined as follows:

$$w_{t,T}^{k,l} = \int_t^T e^{ku} l_u du$$

where $k \in \mathbb{R}$ and $l : [0, T] \mapsto \mathbb{R}$, an RCLL (**R**ight **C**ontinuous **L**imits **L**eft, i.e., allowing processes with jumps) function. By definition,

$$w_{t,T}^{(k_1,l_1),\dots,(k_n,l_n)} = w_{t,T}^{(k_1,l_1} w_{.,T}^{(k_2,l_2),\dots,(k_n,l_n)}$$

For instance,

$$w_{t,T}^{(k_1,l_1),(k_2,l_2)} = \int_t^T e^{k_1 t_1} l_{t_1} w_{t_1,T} dt_1 = \int_t^T e^{k_1 t_1} l_{t_1} \left(\int_{t_1}^T e^{k_2 t_2} l_{t_2} dt_2 \right) dt_1$$

Furthermore, let us define

$$\tilde{w}_{t,T}^{k_1,\dots,k_n} = w_{t,T}^{(k_1,1),\dots,(k_n,1)}$$

For convenience, let us write $v_0 = v_0^0$

Up to T_{i+1}, the coefficients a_1, a_2, b_0, and b_2 are written:

$$a_{1,T_{i+1}} = a_{1,T_i} + \tilde{w}_{T_i,T_{i+1}}^{-\kappa} \tilde{w}_{1,T_i} + \rho_{T_{i+1}} \eta_{T_{i+1}} f_{\kappa,v_{0,T_i}}^1 (\theta_{T_{i+1}}, T_i, T_{i+1})$$

$$a_{2,T_{i+1}} = a_{2,T_i} + \tilde{w}_{T_i,T_{i+1}}^{-\kappa} \alpha_{T_i} + \rho_{T_{i+1}} \eta_{T_{i+1}} \tilde{w}_{T_i,T_{i+1}}^{0,-\kappa} \tilde{w}_{1,T_i} + (\rho_{T_{i+1}} \eta_{T_{i+1}})^2 f_{\kappa,v_{0,T_i}}^2 (\theta_{T_{i+1}}, T_i, T_{i+1})$$

$$b_{0,T_{i+1}} = b_{0,T_i} + \tilde{w}_{T_i,T_{i+1}}^{-\kappa} \beta_{t_i} + \tilde{w}_{T_i,T_{i+1}}^{-\kappa,-\kappa} \tilde{w}_{2,T_i} + \eta_{T_{i+1}}^2 f_{\kappa,v_{0,T_i}}^0 (\theta_{T_{i+1}}, T_i, T_{i+1})$$

$$\alpha_{T_{i+1}} = \alpha_{T_i} + \rho_{T_{i+1}} \eta_{T_{i+1}} (T_{i+1} - T_i) \tilde{w}_{1,T_i} + (\rho_{T_{i+1}} \eta_{T_{i+1}})^2 g_{\kappa,v_{0,T_i}}^1 (\theta_{T_{i+1}}, T_i, T_{i+1})$$

$$\beta_{T_{i+1}} = \beta_{T_i} + \tilde{w}_{T_i,T_{i+1}}^{-\kappa} \tilde{w}_{2,T_i} + \eta_{T_{i+1}}^2 g_{\kappa,v_{0,T_i}}^2 (\theta_{T_{i+1}}, T_i, T_{i+1})$$

$$\tilde{w}_{1,T_{i+1}} = \tilde{w}_{1,T_i} + \rho_{T_{i+1}} \eta_{T_{i+1}} h_{\kappa,v_{0,T_i}}^1 (\theta_{T_{i+1}}, T_i, T_{i+1})$$

$$\tilde{w}_{2,T_{i+1}} = \tilde{w}_{2,T_i} + \eta_{T_{i+1}}^2 h_{\kappa,v_{0,T_i}}^2 (\theta_{T_{i+1}}, T_i, T_{i+1})$$

$$v_{0,T_{i+1}} = e^{-\kappa(T_{i+1}-T_i)}(v_{0,T_i} - \theta_{T_{i+1}}) + \theta_{T_{i+1}}$$

The following functions form part of $a_{1,T}, a_{2,T}$ and $b_{0,T}$:

$$f_{\kappa,v_0}^0 (\theta, t, T) = \frac{e^{-2\kappa T}(e^{2\kappa t}(\theta - 2v_0) + e^{2\kappa t}((-2\kappa t + 2\kappa T - 5)\theta + 2v_0) + 4e^{\kappa(t+T)}((-\kappa t + \kappa T + 1)\theta + \kappa(t - T)v_0))}{4\kappa^3}$$

$$f_{\kappa,v_0}^1 (\theta, t, T) = \frac{e^{-\kappa T}(e^{\kappa T}((-\kappa t + \kappa T - 2)\theta + v_0) - e^{\kappa t}((\kappa t - \kappa T - 2)\theta - \kappa t v_0 + \kappa T v_0 + v_0)}{\kappa^2}$$

$$f_{\kappa,v_0}^2 (\theta, t, T) = \frac{e^{-\kappa(t+3T)}(2e^{\kappa(t+3T)}((\kappa(T - t) - 3)\theta + v_0) + e^{2\kappa(t+T)}((\kappa(\kappa(t - T) - 4)(t - T) + 6)\theta - (\kappa(\kappa(t - T) - 2)(t - T) + 2)v_0))}{2\kappa^3}$$

$$g^1_{\kappa,v_0}(\theta,t,T) = \frac{2e^{\kappa T} + e^{\kappa t}(\kappa^2(t-T)^2)v_0 - (\kappa(\kappa(t-T)-2)(t-T)+2)\theta)}{2\kappa^2}$$

$$g^2_{\kappa,v_0}(\theta,t,T) = \frac{e^{-\kappa T}(2e^{\kappa T}\theta - e^{2\kappa t}(\theta - 2v_0) + 2e^{\kappa(t+T)}(\kappa(t-T)(\theta-v_0)-v_0))}{2\kappa^2}$$

$$h^1_{\kappa,v_0}(\theta,t,T) = \frac{e^{\kappa T}\theta + e^{\kappa t}((\kappa(t-T)-1)\theta + \kappa(T-t)v_0)}{\kappa}$$

$$h^2_{\kappa,v_0}(\theta,t,T) = \frac{(e^{\kappa t}-e^{\kappa T})(e^{\kappa t}(\theta-2v_0))-e^{\kappa T}\theta}{2\kappa}$$

Code

```
Public Function f0(n%) As Double

f0 = Exp(-2 * x3 * n * dt) * ( _
                    Exp(2 * x3 * (n - 1) * dt) * (x1 - 2 * v(n)) + _
                    Exp(2 * x3 * n * dt) * ((2 * x3 * dt - 5)
* x1 + 2 * v(n)) + _
                    4 * Exp(x3 * (2 * n - 1) * dt)
* ((x3 * dt + 1) * x1 - x3 * dt * v(n)))
f0 = f0 / (4 * x3 ^ 3)
End Function
```

```
Public Function f1(n%) As Double

Dim temp#: temp = (1 + x3 * dt)
f1 = Exp(-x3 * n * dt) * (Exp(x3 * n * dt) * ((x3 * dt - 2) * x1 + v(n)) - _
Exp(x3 * (n - 1) * dt) * ((-x3 * dt - 2) * x1 + v(n) * temp))

f1 = f1 / x3 ^ 2
End Function
```

```
Public Function f2(n%) As Double

Dim temp#: temp = Exp(2 * x3 * (2 * n - 1) * dt)
* ((-x3 * (-x3 * dt - 4) * dt + 6) * x1 - _
(-x3 * (-x3 * dt - 2) * dt + 2) * v(n))
f2 = Exp(-x3 * (4 * n - 1) * dt) * ( _
                    2 * Exp(x3 * (4 * n - 1) * dt)
* ((x3 * dt - 3) * x1 + v(n)) + temp)
f2 = f2 / (2 * x3 ^ 3)
End Function
```

```
Public Function g1(n%) As Double

g1 = 2 * Exp(x3 * n * dt) * x1 + Exp(x3 * (n - 1) * dt)
* ((x3 * dt) ^ 2 * v(n) - _
(x3 * (x3 * dt + 2) * dt + 2) * x1)
g1 = g1 / (2 * x3 ^ 2)
End Function
```

```
Public Function g2(n%) As Double

g2 = Exp(-x3 * n * dt) * (Exp(2 * x3 * n * dt)
* x1 - Exp(2 * x3 * (n - 1) * dt) * _
```

```vba
(x1 - 2 * v(n)) + 2 * Exp(x3 * (2 * n - 1) * dt)
* (-x3 * dt * (x1 - v(n)) - v(n)))
g2 = g2 / (2 * x3 ^ 2)
End Function

Public Function h1(n%) As Double

h1 = Exp(x3 * n * dt) * x1 + Exp(x3 * (n - 1) * dt)
* ((-x3 * dt - 1) * x1 + x3 * dt * v(n))
h1 = h1 / x3
End Function

Public Function h2(n%) As Double

h2 = (Exp(x3 * (n - 1) * dt) - Exp(x3 * n * dt))
* (Exp(x3 * (n - 1) * dt) * _
(x1 - 2 * v(n)) - Exp(x3 * n * dt) * x1)
h2 = h2 / (2 * x3)
End Function

Public Function v(n%) As Double

If n = 1 Then
    v = v0
Else
    v = Exp(-x3 * dt) * (v(n - 1) - x1) + x1
End If
End Function

Public Function w1(n%)

If n = 1 Then
    w1 = rho(1) * eta(1) * h1(1)
Else
    w1 = w1(n - 1) + rho(n) * eta(n) * h1(n)
End If
End Function

Public Function w2(n%) As Double

If n = 1 Then
    w2 = eta(1) ^ 2 * h2(1)
Else
    w2 = w2(n - 1) + eta(n) ^ 2 * h2(n)
End If
End Function

Public Function alpha(n%) As Double

If n = 1 Then
    alpha = rho(1) ^ 2 * eta(1) ^ 2 * g1(1)
Else
    alpha = alpha(n - 1) + rho(n) * eta(n) * dt * w1(n - 1)
+ rho(n) ^ 2 * eta(n) ^ 2 * g1(n)
End If
End Function
```

```
Public Function beta(n%) As Double

If n = 1 Then
    beta = eta(1) ^ 2 * g2(1)
Else
    beta = beta(n - 1) + ww1(n) * w2(n - 1) + eta(n) ^ 2 * g2(n)
End If
End Function

Public Function ww1(n%) As Double

    ww1 = (Exp(-x3 * (n - 1) * dt) - Exp(-x3 * n * dt)) / x3
End Function

Public Function ww0(n%) As Double

    ww0 = (Exp(-x3 * n * dt) * (-x3 * dt - 1) + Exp(-x3 * (n - 1) * dt))
/ x3 ^ 2
End Function

Public Function ww2(n%) As Double

    ww2 = (Exp(-x3 * (n - 1) * dt) - Exp(-x3 * n * dt)) ^ 2 / (2 * x3 ^ 2)
End Function

Public Function a1(n%) As Double

If n = 1 Then
    a1 = rho(1) * eta(1) * f1(1)
Else
    a1 = a1(n - 1) + ww1(n) * w1(n - 1) + rho(n) * eta(n) * f1(n)
End If
End Function

Public Function a2(n%) As Double

If n = 1 Then
    a2 = (rho(1) * eta(1)) ^ 2 * f2(1)
Else
    a2 = a2(n - 1) + ww1(n) * alpha(n - 1) + rho(n) * eta(n)
* ww0(n) * w1(n - 1) + _
    (rho(n) * eta(n)) ^ 2 * f2(n)
End If
End Function

Public Function b0(n%) As Double

If n = 1 Then
    b0 = eta(1) ^ 2 * f0(1)
Else
    b0 = b0(n - 1) + ww1(n) * beta(n - 1) + ww2(n) * w2(n - 1)
+ eta(n) ^ 2 * f0(n)
End If
End Function
```

7.1.3 Calibration

Here comes the critical step, as usual. Obviously, the BGM fast pricing formulae will be of great help, the choice of the algorithm still remaining a delicate issue since no standard optimization method performs miracles alone given the many local minima. Practitioners currently combine global optimization techniques with local ones. In this section, we suggest the use of the Nelder-Mead algorithm, in a first step, then refining our search, computing the estimator using a grid of parameters in the vicinity of the solutions.

Different estimators are available: we choose to minimize

$$\sum_{i,j} \frac{|\sigma^{i,j}_{Hest.implied} - \sigma^{i,j}_{BS}|}{\sigma^{i,j}_{BS}}$$

where

- $\sigma^{i,j}_{Hest.implied}$ are BS volatilities implied from Heston prices
- $\sigma^{i,j}_{BS}$ are volatilities given by the market
- i and j stand for the indices of maturites and strikes.

The code below performs a calibration on semi-annual forward periods, up to 5 years (Table 7.4 describes the market volatility surface to fit with). The algorithm is two-stage, i.e., the Nelder-Mead algorithm is followed by trivial valuations using a grid of parameters and selecting the minimum. To be honest, the second stage does not bring remarkable improvements. By contrast, **a good choice of the simplex** at the origin is definitely the **key** to the efficiency of your program.

Numerical results   The volatility surface chosen to test our implementation is quite standard.

TABLE 7.4   BS volatility surface 6m → 5y

T\K	70	80	90	100	110	120	130
6m	33	29.5	27	25	24	23.25	22.5
1y	30.5	27.5	25.5	24	23.25	22.75	22
18m	28.5	26	24.25	23	22.25	21.75	21
2y	27	25	23.5	22.5	22	21.5	20.75
30m	25.5	24.25	22.75	22	21.5	21	20.5
3y	24.5	23	22	21.5	21	20.5	20
42m	24.5	23	22	21.5	21	20.5	20
4y	24.5	23	22	21.5	21	20.5	20
54m	24.5	23	22	21.5	21	20.5	20
5y	24.5	23	22	21.5	21	20.5	20

The calibration results are given by $\kappa = 1.08$ and the following table:

exp.	θ	V	ρ	η
6m	0.0952	0.0665	−0.747	0.348
1y	0.0764	0.0563	−0.842	0.252
18m	0.0621	0.0568	−0.83	0.241
2y	0.0554	0.0587	−0.78	0.251
2.5y	0.0512	0.0592	−0.793	0.253
3y	0.046	0.0589	−0.799	0.252
3.5y	0.0462	0.06	−0.772	0.258
4y	0.0478	0.0603	−0.764	0.259
4.5y	0.0478	0.06	−0.773	0.257
5y	0.0478	0.06	−0.773	0.257

The charts below show Heston prices after calibration of the piecewise constant parameters, for three maturities: 6 months, 2 years, and 5 years (Tables 7.5–7.7). The weakness of the algorithm lies, unfortunately, in at-the-money options, where the difference between BS and Heston implied volatility reaches 1.3%, possibly caused by an inflection of the volatility smile on this point.

Code First, declare these variables to be visible in the whole module.

```
Dim y#()
Dim dt#
Dim r#
Dim volHeston#(7)
Public rho#(), eta#(), theta#()
Public v0#, kappa#

Sub testBGM(n%)

Dim simp() As New Vector
ReDim simp(6) As New Vector
Dim w(6) As New Vector
Dim i%, l%

dt = 0.5
r = 0.03

Dim sr As Vector
Dim se As Vector
Dim soc As Vector
Dim sic As Vector
```

TABLE 7.5   6-mth put options 70-130 strike

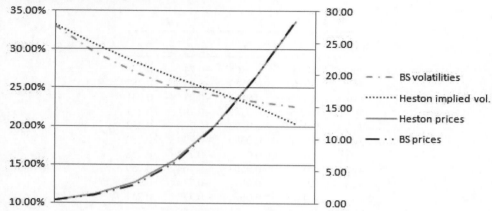

TABLE 7.6   2-yr put options 70-130 strike

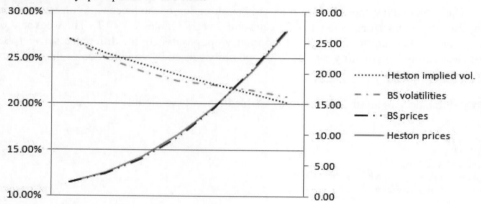

TABLE 7.7   5 yr put options 70-130 strike

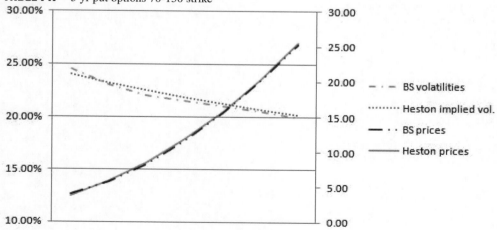

****

The market put prices are supposed to be have been retrieved from an Excel file and stored in **VolPutB(n,j)**, where n stands for the index of the maturity and j the index of the strike. Some initial arbitrary values are chosen for the Heston parameters simplex:

$$v(1) \rightarrow \theta$$
$$v(2) \rightarrow V$$
$$v(3) \rightarrow \kappa$$
$$v(4) \rightarrow \rho$$
$$v(5) \rightarrow \eta$$

****

```
putHestoninit

ReDim rho(n), eta(n), theta(n), y(n)

For l = 1 To n
    If l = 1 Then
        For i = 1 To 6
            simp(i).nbEl = 5
            simp(i).v(1) = 0.02 + 0.05 * i
            simp(i).v(2) = 0.05 + 0.006 * i
            simp(i).v(3) = 0.5 + 0.3 * i
            simp(i).v(4) = -1 + 0.1 * i
            simp(i).v(5) = 0.2 + i * 0.05
        Next i
    Else
        For i = 1 To 6
            simp(i).v(1) = theta(l - 1) - 0.05 + 0.02 * i
            simp(i).v(2) = 0.05 + 0.004 * i
            simp(i).v(3) = kappa
            simp(i).v(4) = -1 + 0.1 * i
            simp(i).v(5) = 0.2 + i * 0.02
        Next i
    End If

For m = 1 To 250

    simp = sort_vec(simp, 1)

    Set sr = sum_vec(scalar(2, moy_vec(del(simp))), simp(6), -1)
```

****

baseFunction is the core procedure of the Nelder-Mead algorithm: It calls the function **CalibHestonVol** that minimizes the estimator.

****

```
    Select Case baseFunction(sr, 1)
        Case baseFunction(simp(1), 1) To baseFunction(simp(5), 1)
            simp = comp(del(simp), sr)

        Case Is < baseFunction(simp(1), 1)
            Set se = sum_vec(scalar(2, sr), moy_vec(del(simp)), -1)

            If baseFunction(se, 1) < baseFunction(sr, 1) Then
                simp = comp(del(simp), se)
            Else
                simp = shrink(simp)
            End If
```

```
        Case baseFunction(simp(5), 1) To baseFunction(simp(6), 1)
            Set soc = sum_vec(scalar(0.5, sr),
scalar(0.5, moy_vec(del(simp))), 1)
            If baseFunction(soc, 1) < baseFunction(sr, 1) Then
                simp = comp(del(simp), soc)
            Else
                simp = shrink(simp)
            End If

        Case Is >= baseFunction(simp(6), 1)
            Set sic = sum_vec(scalar(0.5, simp(6)),
scalar(0.5, moy_vec(del(simp))), 1)
            If baseFunction(sic, 1) < baseFunction(simp(6), 1) Then
                simp = comp(del(simp), sic)
            Else
                simp = shrink(simp)
            End If

    End Select
```

****

Some additional conditions must be imposed here:

1. κ must <u>not</u> be modified
2. the **Feller condition** (to ensure that variances cannot be negative)

$$2\kappa\theta > \eta^2$$

3. $1 > \rho > -1$

****

```
    For i = 1 To 6
        If l > 1 Then simp(i).v(3) = kappa
        simp(i).v(1) = max(simp(i).v(1), 1.001 * simp(i).v(5) ^ 2 /
(2 * simp(i).v(3))) 'Feller
        If simp(i).v(4) < -1 Then simp(i).v(4) = -1
    Next i

Next m

theta(l) = simp(1).v(1)
rho(l)   = simp(1).v(4)
eta(l)   = simp(1).v(5)

If l = 1 Then
    kappa = simp(1).v(3)
End If
```

****

Here, we refine our search for the minimum with a pricing grid around the parameters previously found.

****

```
Dim ww As New Vector
Set ww = simp(1)

    wwmin = baseFunction(ww, 1)
    www1 = ww.v(1): www5 = ww.v(5): www2 = ww.v(2): www4 = ww.v(4)
    For i = 1 To 10
        ww.v(1) = (1 + 0.005 * (i - 5)) * www1
        For j = 1 To 10
            ww.v(5) = (1 + 0.005 * (j - 1)) * www5
            For m = 1 To 10
                ww.v(2) = (1 + 0.005 * m) * www2
                For p = 1 To 10
                    ww.v(4) = (1 + 0.008 * (p - 8)) * www4
                    www = baseFunction(ww, 1)
                    If www < wwmin Then wwmin = www
                Next p
            Next m
        Next j
    Next i

[Heston].Activate
For p = 1 To 7
    Cells(2 * l + 1, p) = _
    BGMpiecewise(ww.v(1), ww.v(2), ww.v(3), ww.v(4), ww.v(5),
100, 100 * (1 + (p - 4) * 0.1), 1, 0.03)
    Cells(2 * l + 1, p) = putB(l, p)
Next p

Next l
End Sub

Public Function baseFunction(x As Vector, n%) As Single

baseFunction = calibHestonVol(x.V(1), x.V(2), x.V(3), x.V(4), x.V(5), n)
End Function

Public Function calibHestonVol(z1#, z2#, z3#, z4#, z5#, n%) As Double

Dim d1#, d2#, target#, Price#, vega#
calibHestonVol = 0

    For j = 1 To 7
        volHeston(j) = VolPutB(n, j)

        target = BGMpiecewise(z1, z2, z3, z4, z5, 100, 100 *
(1 + (j - 4) * 0.1), n, r)

        d1 = (-Log(1 + (j - 4) * 0.1) + (r + volHeston(j) ^ 2 / 2)
* n * dt) _
            / (volHeston(j) * Sqr(n * dt))
        d2 = d1 - volHeston(j) * Sqr(n * dt)

        Price = _
        100 * (norm(d1) - 1) - 100 * (1 + (j - 4) * 0.1)
* Exp(-r * n * dt) * (norm(d2) - 1)
        vega = Exp(-d1 ^ 2 / 2) / Sqr(2 * PI) * 100 * Sqr(n * dt)
```

```
        While Abs(target - Price) > 0.015
            volHeston(j) = volHeston(j) + (target - Price) / vega
            d1 = (-Log(1 + (j - 4) * 0.1) +
(r + volHeston(j) ^ 2 / 2) * n * dt) _
            / (volHeston(j) * Sqr(n * dt))
            d2 = d1 - volHeston(j) * Sqr(n * dt)
            Price = 100 * (norm(d1) - 1) - _
            100 * (1 + (j - 4) * 0.1) * Exp(-r * n * dt) * (norm(d2) - 1)
            vega = Exp(-d1 ^ 2 / 2) / Sqr(2 * PI) * 100 * Sqr(n * dt)
        Wend

        calibHestonVol = calibHestonVol + Abs((volHeston(j)
- VolPutB(n, j))) / VolPutB(n, j)
    Next j

End Function

Public Function BGMpiecewise(z1#, z2#, z3#, z4#, z5#, S#, K#, n%, r#) As Double

dt = 0.5: v0 = z2
x1 = z1: x2 = z2: x3 = z3: x4 = z4: x5 = z5
Dim x#: x = Log(S)
Dim t#: t = n * dt
Dim i%
If n = 1 Then
    rho(1) = x4: eta(1) = x5: theta(1) = x1
End If

For i = 1 To n
    y(i) = y(i - 1) + (V(i) - x1) / x3 * (1 - Exp(-x3 * dt)) + x1 * dt
Next i

BGMpiecewise = Hput(x, K, y(n), t, r) + a1(n) * HputXY(x, K, y(n), t, r) _
                            + a2(n) * HputXXY(x, K, y(n), t, r) _
                            + b0(n) * HputYY(x, K, y(n), t, r) _
                            + a1(n) ^ 2 / 2 * HputXXYY
(x, K, y(n), t, r)
'End If
BGMpiecewise = max(BGMpiecewise, K * Exp(-r * n * dt) - S + 0.02)

End Function
```

7.2 BARRIER OPTIONS

Since volatility determines the probability of reaching a knock-in/out level, steep smile curvature can impact substantially the price of barrier options. Whatever the volatility model, either smiled, local, or stochastic, this issue must be considered, especially when the spot gets closer to the knocking level.

To put this into practice under the Heston dynamics, the most straightforward way is to discretize $[0, T]$ and sample a number of paths, given a subdivision $T = n\Delta t$. For instance, the payoff of a down-and-in call will be given by

$$(S_T - K)^+ 1_{min(S_{t_i})<bar}.$$

However, this straightforward approach meets practical difficulties:

- It is easy to show how such a discretization leads to **pricing biases**. In fact, the probability of hitting some barrier at t_i *or* t_{i+1} is less than *between* t_i and t_{i+1}. Increasing the monitoring frequency modestly reduces this bias, bringing on the other hand considerable extra computation cost.
- Without the help of advanced variance reduction techniques, solutions are unstable.

Some discretization schemes have been put forward in relation to variance reduction techniques, such as **Conditional Quasi-Monte-Carlo sampling** (see Achtsis, Cools, and Nuyens (2013) and Imai and Tan (2006)).

In this section, we introduce an original algorithm using the formula yielding the probability for an asset of attaining some level S_T without hitting a barrier over $[0; T]$ (see § 3.5.1).

The idea is to generate samples $S(t_{i+1})$ from $S(t_i)$, and, conditional on $S(t_i)$, to estimate the likelihood that S has hit the barrier over $[t_{i-1}, t_i]$. The formula obtained in § 3.5.1 is only valid under the BS model, but we may imagine that, if periods between monitoring dates were short enough, the **variance** parameter might be treated like a **constant**. As a matter of fact, this seems to be quite a strong assumption, especially as standard Brownian paths and Heston-style paths differ significantly: applying this method to a large lapse of time would surely lead to serious mispricings. Empirically, for $\Delta t_i \simeq 5 \times 10^{-4}$, this method is conclusive.

Let us break down the methodology into simple steps.

Step 1 Let us start by choosing a discretization scheme. Our implementation requires us to sample the variance parameter V_i first, then the asset price S_i or, instead, $Ln(S_i)$, which is more tractable. Also, we will choose, at no significant extra cost, the Milstein scheme: let us recall remind that, given the dynamics of V_t, i.e.,

$$dV_t = \kappa(\theta - V_t)dt + \eta\sqrt{V_t}dw_t = a(V_t)dt + b(V_t)dw_t$$

the Milstein discretization is written:

$$\Delta V_i \simeq a(V_i)\Delta t + b(V_i)\Delta w_i + \frac{1}{2}b(V_i)b'(V_i)((\Delta w_i)^2 - \Delta t)$$

$$= \kappa(\theta - V_i)\Delta t + \eta\sqrt{V_i}\Delta w_i + \frac{1}{2}\eta\sqrt{V_i}\eta\frac{1}{2\sqrt{V_i}}((\Delta w_i)^2 - \Delta t)$$

$$= \kappa(\theta - V_i)\Delta t + \eta\sqrt{V_i}\sqrt{\Delta t}z_i^1 + \frac{1}{4}\eta^2\Delta t((z_i^1)^2 - 1) \quad (z_i^1 \equiv N(0, 1))$$

Regarding $Ln(S_i)$:

$$Ln(S_{i+1}) = Ln(S_i) + \left(r - \frac{V_i}{2}\right)\Delta t + \sqrt{V_i}\sqrt{\Delta t}(\rho z_i^1 + \sqrt{1 - \rho^2}z_i^2) \tag{7.3}$$

Step 2 On each monitoring date, we draw a uniform variate $\mathbf{u} \equiv \mathcal{U}_{[0,1]}$, assumed to figure the probability of hitting a given level throughout the last period: for example, for a down-and-in option:

$$u = P(MinS_{t_i < t \leq t_{i+1}} < S_{min}|S_{i+1} \in ds) = F_{min}(S_{min})$$

and, for an up-and-in option:

$$u = P(MaxS_{t_i < t \leq t_{i+1}} > S_{max}|S_{i+1} \in ds) = F_{max}(S_{max})$$

Put differently:

$$S_{max} \ (\text{resp } S_{min}) = F_{max}^{-1}(u)(\text{resp} = F_{min}^{-1}(u))$$

Clearly, if $F_{max}^{-1}(u) > bar$, the barrier is deemed to have been hit as the law of the maximum $F_{max}(S_{max}) = u$. We base our valuation of F_{max}^{-1} on the formula established in § 3.5.1 for

$$\mathbb{E}^P(1_{Max(S_t)>Bar,S_T<K})$$

To find $P(Max(S_t) > Bar, S_T \in ds)$, we need to compute the first derivative:

$$\frac{\partial}{\partial K}_{|K=S}(P(Max(S_t) > Bar, S_T < K))$$

Using the notations of § 3.5.1, $(H = Bar, \ X = K)$,

$$P(Max(S_t) > Bar, S_T \in ds) = \frac{\partial}{\partial X}((H/S_0)^{2\lambda-2}N(-y+\sigma^*\sqrt{T}))$$

The conditional expectation is written:

$$P(Max(S_t) > Bar|S_T \in ds) = P(Max(S_t) > Bar, S_T \in ds)/P(S_T \in ds)$$

After calculation,

$$P(Max(S_t) > Bar|S_T \in ds) = \left(\frac{Bar}{S_0}\right)^{2Ln\,(s/Bar)/\sigma^2 T}$$

Calling $b = Ln\,(Bar/S_0)$ and $s = Ln\,(S/S_0)$,

$$b = F_{max}^{-1}(u) = \frac{s + \sqrt{s^2 - 2\sigma^2 TLn(u)}}{2} \tag{7.4}$$

Returning to the dynamics of V_i,

$$\Delta V_i = \kappa(\theta - V_i)\Delta t + \eta\sqrt{V_i}\sqrt{\Delta t}z_i^1 + \frac{1}{4}\eta^2\Delta t((z_i^1)^2 - 1) \tag{7.5}$$

Written differently,

$$\sqrt{V_i}\sqrt{\Delta t}z_i^1 = \frac{1}{\eta}(\Delta V_i - \kappa(\theta - V_i)\Delta t + \frac{1}{4}\eta^2\Delta t((z_i^1)^2 - 1))$$

The trick is to replace the Brownian term $\sqrt{V_i}\sqrt{\Delta t}z_i^1$ in equation (7.3) to get

$$Ln\,(S_{i+1}/S_i) = \left(r - \frac{V_i}{2}\right)\Delta t + \frac{\rho}{\eta}(\Delta V_i - \kappa(\theta - V_i)\Delta t$$

$$- \frac{1}{4}\eta^2\Delta t((z_i^1)^2 - 1)) + \sqrt{V_i}\sqrt{\Delta t}\sqrt{1 - \rho^2}z_i^2$$

Finally,

$$Ln\,(S_{i+1}/S_i) - \frac{\rho}{\eta}\Delta V_i = \left(r - \frac{V_i}{2}\right)\Delta t - \frac{\rho}{\eta}\left(\kappa(\theta - V_i)\Delta t + \frac{1}{4}\eta^2\Delta t((z_i^1)^2 - 1)\right)$$
$$+ \sqrt{V_i}\sqrt{\Delta t}\sqrt{1 - \rho^2}z_i^2$$
$$= \left(r - \frac{V_i}{2} - \frac{\rho}{\eta}(\kappa(\theta - V_i) + \frac{1}{4}\eta^2((z_i^1)^2 - 1))\right)\Delta t + \sqrt{V_i}\sqrt{\Delta t}\sqrt{1 - \rho^2}z_i^2$$

Feeling guilty to assume that ΔV_i is constant on $[t_i, t_{i+1}]$, we opt for the mean value of V_t to sample S_{i+1}.

$Ln\,(S_{i+1}/S_i)$ is affine, shifted by $-\frac{\rho}{\eta}\Delta V_i$: we thus apply equation (7.4), with the following changes:

$$\sigma^2 \rightarrow \left(1 - \rho^2\right) V_i$$
$$b \rightarrow b - \frac{\rho}{\eta}\Delta V_i$$
$$s = Ln\,(S_{i+1}/S_i) \rightarrow s = s - \frac{\rho}{\eta}\Delta V_i$$

7.2.1 Numerical results

The graphs on page 259 compare prices obtained for down-and-in calls, with respect to different strikes, and different models. The maturity of 3 months is arbitrarily chosen to be short but not too short. Indeed, short maturities induce more convexity, thus more risk, and the smile curvature is steeper, highlighting the gap between BS and Heston valuation outcomes. On the other hand, volatilities of 1 month or less are uncontrollable. To capture the dizzying smile slope, a jump process must be incorporated into the original dynamics: only robust random number generators can help then. We may console ourselves with the thought that, when considering the risk taken by a very short option with a close barrier, it is already too late!

7.2.2 Code

```
Sub HestonCall_DI()

Dim S#, K#: S = 100: K = 110
Dim bar#: bar = 87.5
Dim ok As Boolean

Dim x#: x = Log(S)
Dim y#: y = Log(bar)

Dim t#, r#: r = 0.03: t = 0.25

Dim kappa#, theta#, eta#, b#, rho#
kappa = 1.5: theta = 0.25: eta = 0.7: rho = -0.85
Dim va#: va = 0.068
```

```
Randomize

pay_off = 0: n = 500
For i = 1 To 2000
    x1 = Log(S) : va2 = va
    ok = False
    For j = 1 To n
     z1 = gauss(): z2 = Sqr(1 - rho ^ 2) * gauss()
```

****

Here comes the Milstein discretization:

****

```
        deltaV = kappa * (theta - va2) * t / n + eta * Sqr(va2)
* z1 * Sqr(t / n) _
        + 0.25 * eta ^ 2 * (t / n * z1 ^ 2 - t / n)
        va1 = va2 + deltaV / 2
        x2 = x1 + (r - va1 / 2 - rho * kappa / eta * (theta - va1))
* t / n + _
          Sqr(va1) * z2 * Sqr(t / n) + rho * deltaV / eta-_
        rho*0.25*eta*(z1^2-1)*t/n
        va2 = va2 + deltaV
        If x2 < y Then
           ok = True
        Else
```

****

$$b = F_{max}^{-1}(u) = \frac{s + \sqrt{s^2 - 2\sigma^2 T Ln(u)}}{2}$$

****

```
        log_b = Log(bar) - x1: log_s = x2 - x1 - rho * deltaV / eta
        u = Rnd() + 0.0000001
        If (log_s - Sqr(log_s ^ 2 - 2 * (1 - rho ^ 2)
* va2 * t / n * Log(u))) / 2 _
             < log_b - rho * deltaV / eta / 2 Then ok = True
      End If
      x1 = x2
    Next j

    If ok Then
        pay_off = pay_off + max(Exp(x2) - K, 0)
    End If
Next i
Debug.Print pay_off / 2000 * Exp(-r * t)

End Sub
```

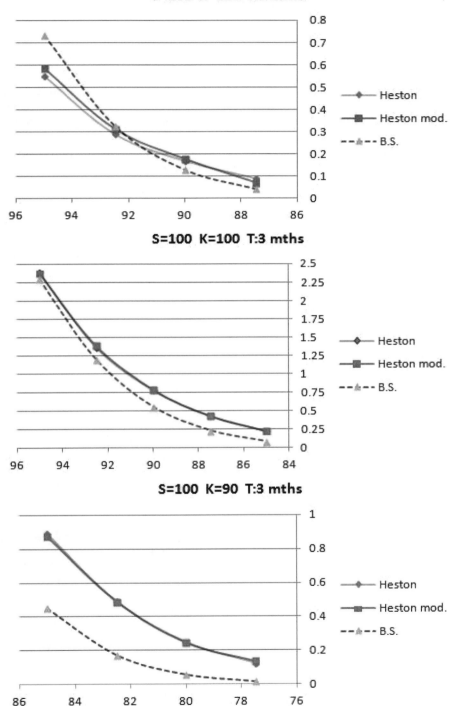

7.3 ASIAN-STYLE OPTIONS

"Asian-style" here designates any payoff of the form

$$f(S, T) = f(S(t_1), S(t_2), ..., S(t_n = T))$$

Path simulations under Heston with a plain Monte-Carlo method give disappointing results, as we noted above. In this section, we propose an alternative option that consists in sampling $S_i = S(t_i)$ under the Black–Scholes model, then shifting the outcomes in order to stick to Heston distribution.

Practically speaking, we will use an analogy between the BS formula for European options and the Heston closed-form solution. Given the BS call price formula, i.e.,

$$Put(S, K, \sigma, t, r) = SN(d1) - Ke^{-rt}SN(d2)$$

where

$$d2 = \frac{Ln\,(S/K) + (r - \sigma^2/2)t}{\sigma\sqrt{t}}$$

a well-known result states that

$$P(S_t > K) = N(d2) = N_2$$

In fact,

$$S_t = S_0 Exp\,((r - \sigma^2/2)t + \sigma\sqrt{t}z_t)$$

$$P(S_t > K) = P(Ln\,(S_t) > Ln\,(K))$$

$$= P\left(z_t < \frac{Ln\,(S_t/K) + (r - \sigma^2/2)t}{\sigma\sqrt{t}}\right)$$

$$= N(d2)$$

The same probability under the Heston model is (see (7.1)). $P_2(S, K, \upsilon_0, t)$.

Both N_2 and P_2 are functions of S/K, which will be of great help in our methodology. Let us denote by $\boldsymbol{P}_{BS}$ and $\boldsymbol{P}_{Heston}$ the following probabilities:

$$P_{BS}(x) = P_{BS}(S/K > x) = N_2(S, K)$$

$$P_{Heston}(x) = P_{Heston}(S/K > x) = P_2(S, K)$$

As a matter of fact, from $S(t = 0) = S_0$, we can sample S_i:

$$N_2(S_i) = P_{BS}(x_i) = P_{Heston}(x_i^*) \Rightarrow x_i^* = P_{Heston}^{-1}(P_{BS}(x_i))$$

$$\Rightarrow S_i^* = K.P_{Heston}^{-1}(P_{BS}(S_i/K))$$

Therefore, the simulation proceeds like this:

$$S_1 = S_0 Exp\ ((r - \sigma^2/2)t_1 + \sigma\sqrt{t_1}z_1) = S_0 x_1$$
$$\Rightarrow S_1^* = S_0 P_{Heston}^{-1}(P_{BS}(x_1))$$
$$S_2 = S_1^* Exp\ ((r - \sigma^2/2)(t_2 - t_1) + \sigma\sqrt{t_2 - t_1}z_2) = S_1^* x_2$$
$$\Rightarrow S_2^* = S_1^* P_{Heston}^{-1}(P_{BS}(x_2))$$

etc.

To calculate S_i^*, we choose a faster method: instead of computing $P_{Heston}^{-1}(P_{BS}(x_i))$ for each sample x_i we store the already calculated $P_{Heston}(x_i)$ and $P_{BS}(x_i)$ in a range $[x_{min}, x_{max}]$: the truncation of the x-space ($x_{max} < \infty$) and the number of abscissa x_i are contingent on the timestep and the accuracy requirements.

From experience, a quarterly timestep requires not more than 2500 abscissa from 0 to 2.5.

Code As an illustration, we price hereafter a 1-year at-the-money call on the arithmetic average of four quarterly fixings, i.e.,

$$\text{payoff} = Max\left(\frac{1}{4}\sum_{i=1}^{4} S_i - K, 0\right)$$

The values are stored in three columns of the "Heston" worksheet

$$Col\ 1 : P_{Heston}(i \times 1\text{‰})$$
$$Col\ 2 : i \times 1\text{‰}$$
$$Col\ 3 : P_{BS}(i \times 1\text{‰})$$

The computation and storage of the values displayed in these columns are achieved by two procedures:

- the subroutine **initDistrib** that passes Heston parameters and the option's timestep as arguments to **HestonDistrib**
- the function **HestonDistrib** that computes the 2500 values $P_{Heston}(x_i)$ using 30 Laguerre nodes.

Thus, the index of the line is directly given by $i = Int(S_i/0.2)$ and, subsequently, $u = N_2(0.2 \times i)$ is interpolated from the values displayed in column 1. We highly recommend not to approximate S^* from a polynomial interpolation that always turns out to be rather inaccurate. However, it is possible to use the solution provided by this polynomial in order to reduce the range of values needed for the interpolation (a much more drastic truncation).

```
Public Sub initDistrib()

Dim x#()
x = HestonDistrib(-0.8, 0.348, 1.08, 0.1, 0.25, 100, 80, 0.03, 0.07)
```

```
End Sub

Public Function HestonDistrib(rho#, eta#, kappa#, theta#, tau#,
K#, S#, r#, V#) As Double()

Worksheets("Laguerre").Activate
ReDim xL(30), wL(30)
For i = 1 To 30
    xL(i) = Cells(i, 1): wL(i) = Cells(i, 2)
Next i

Dim j#
ReDim pdist#(2500)

Worksheets("Heston").Activate
For j = 1 To 2500
    p2 = 0
    For i = 1 To 30
        p2 = p2 + wL(i) * HestonP2(rho, eta, xL(i), kappa, theta, tau,
1 / (0.001 * j), r, V)
    Next i
    p2 = 0.5 + (1 / PI) * p2
    If p2 < 0 Then p2 = 0
    If p2 > 1 Then p2 = 1
    pdist(j) = 1 - p2
    If j > 3 Then Cells(j, 1) = pdist(j)
Next j

HestonDistrib = pdist

End Function
```

The subroutine **BSHestonAsia** generates 10 000 x 4 samples of x_i and draws $P_{BS}(x_i)$ (next cell on the right). Then, this value **cumBS** is passed to **Hest** that finds the interpolated value. The interpolation is performed from $x > 0.207$: this is necessary because our approximative valuation of P_{Heston} using 30 Laguerre nodes states that, for $x <= 0.207$, this probability is 0.

Attention must be paid to the saving in terms of computation time that may be challenged by the interpolation process which is rather slow. As quoted before, the solution would be to restrict your search of interpolated value to a much smaller range than [A207:A2500]. The best way to proceed is first to compute the coefficients of the polynomial $Q(X)$ (using e.g. polyFit see ch. 2) fitting the relationship

$$x^* = P_{Heston}^{-1}(P_{BS}(x)) = Q(x)$$

and, then, truncate the interpolation to a smaller range $[x^* - \Delta x^*, x^* + \Delta x^*]$, Δx^* arbitrarily chosen "neither too large, nor too narrow."

```
Sub BSHestonAsia()

Dim S#, x#

Dim r#, vol#, t#
r = 0.03: vol = 0.3: t = 0.25

Dim cumBS#
```

```
Dim mu#: mu = (r - vol ^ 2 / 2) * t
Dim i#, n&
Dim po#


Worksheets("Heston").Activate
Randomize
For i = 1 To 10000
    moy = 0: S = 90
    For j = 1 To 4
        z = gauss()
        x = Exp(mu + vol * Sqr(t) * z)
        If x < 2.5 Then
            n = Round(1000 * x, 0)
            cumBS = Cells(n, 3)
            S = Hest(cumBS)(1) * S
        Else
            S = 2.5 * S
        End If
      moy = moy + S
    Next j
    po = po + max(moy/4 - 100, 0)
Next i
Debug.Print po / 10000 * Exp(-r * 4 * t)


End Sub


Function Hest(x#) As Double()

Dim res#(): ReDim res(2)
res = interpol(x, [A207:A2500], [B207:B2500])
res(2) = 206 + res(2)
Hest = res
End Function


Public Function interpol(x#, v1 As Range, v2 As Range) As Double()

Dim res#(): ReDim res(2)
For i = 1 To v1.Count
    If x < v1(i) Then Exit For
Next i
res(1) = (x - v1(i)) * (v2(i + 1) - v2(i)) / (v1(i + 1) - v1(i)) + v2(i)
res(2) = 206 + i
interpol = res
End Function
```

7.4 SABR MODEL

SABR is the acronym for **S**tochastic **A**lpha **B**eta **R**ho. In fact, the SABR dynamics of the forward rate F_k under its martingale measure Q_k are

$$dF_k(t) = V(t)F_k(t)^\beta dZ_k$$

$$dV(t) = \eta V(t)dW_k$$

$$V(0) = \alpha$$

$$Corr(dZ_k, dW_k) = \rho$$

This seminal expression shows that SABR is aimed at capturing caplets' volatility smiles. Yet, this model is also used for modeling the dynamics of a swap starting at T_i and ending at T_j under the swap numeraire $Q(i,j)$:

$$dS(t, T_i, T_j) = V(t)S(t, T_i, T_j)^\beta dZ(t, T_i, T_j)$$

$$dV(t) = \eta V(t)dW(t, T_i, T_j)$$

$$V(0) = \alpha$$

$$Corr(dZ(t, T_i, T_j), dW(t, T_i, T_j)) = \rho$$

7.4.1 Caplets

The price at $t = 0$ of a caplet struck at K, starting at T for a duration of τ is

$$\tau.B(0, T + \tau)(F(T, T + \tau).N(d_1) - K.N(d_2))$$

$$d_1 = \frac{Ln\,(F(T, T + \tau)/K + (\sigma_{SABR}^2/2)T}{\sigma_{SABR}\sqrt{T}} \qquad d_2 = d_1 - \sigma_{SABR}\sqrt{T}$$

The authors of the model obtained an approximate closed-form solution for the value of σ^{SABR}, in terms of an expansion of $Ln\,(K/F(0, T, T + \tau))$, i.e., roughly the distance in percentage between the actual strike K and the ATM strike (in fact $F(0, T, T + \tau)$). For ease of presentation, we note $F(0, T, T + \tau) = F(0)$

$$\sigma^{SABR}(K, F(0)) \simeq$$

$$\frac{\alpha}{F(0)^{1-\beta}} \left(1 - \frac{1}{2}(1 - \beta - \rho\lambda)Ln\,(K/F(0)) + \frac{1}{12}((1 - \beta)^2 + (2 - 3\rho^2)\lambda^2)Ln^2(K/F(0))\right)$$

$$\lambda = \eta F(0)^{1-\beta}/\alpha$$

7.4.2 Code

```
Dim smiles!(), capletB!(), volCapletB!()
Sub capSABRinit()

Dim d1!, d2!

ReDim bd(20)
ReDim Fwd(20)

Dim i%
Dim n%: n = 20

Worksheets(2).Activate
Dim nS%: nS = Range([B4], [B4].End(xlToRight)).Count
ReDim smiles(20, nS)
ReDim volCapletB(20, nS)
ReDim capletB(20, nS)

For i = 1 To 20
    For j = 1 To nS
        smiles(i, j) = Cells(i + 3, j + 1)
    Next j
Next i

Worksheets(1).Activate

For i = 0 To 19
    bd(i) = Cells(2 + i, 11)
Next i

For i = 1 To n - 1
    Fwd(i) = Cells(2 + i, 12)
    For j = 1 To nS
        volCapletB(i, j) = Cells(2 + i, 6) + smiles(i, j)
        d1 = (-Log(1 + (j - 4) * 0.05) + 0.5 * volCapletB(i, j) ^ 2
* i * 0.25) _
        / (volCapletB(i, j) * Sqr(i * 0.25))
        d2 = d1 - volCapletB(i, j) * Sqr(i * 0.25)
        capletB(i, j) = 0.25 * (Fwd(i) * norm(d1) - Fwd(i)
* (1 + (j - 4) * 0.05) * norm(d2)) _
            * bd(i)
    Next j
Next i

End Sub

Sub algoSABR()

Dim z1!, z2!, z3!, z4!, dg!
Dim zz1!, zz2!, zz3!, zz4!

z1 = 0.1: z2 = 0.5: z3 = 0.05: z4 = 0

capSABRinit

Dim T!: T = 50 / 2: m = 2
```

```
f0 = calibSABR(z1, z2, z3, z4, 5)

T = 50 / 2: m = 2

While T > 10 ^ (-1)
    Randomize
    For j = 1 To 100
        zz1 = z1 + (0.5 - Rnd()) / 500
        zz2 = z2 + (0.5 - Rnd()) / 50
        zz3 = z3 + (0.5 - Rnd()) / 500
        zz4 = z4 + (0.5 - Rnd()) / 100
        f1 = calibSABR(zz1, zz2, zz3, zz4, 5)
        dg = f1 - f0
        If accept(dg, T) Then z1 = zz1: z2 = zz2: z3 = zz3: z4 = zz4: f0 = f1
    Next j
    m = m + 1
    T = 50 / m
Wend

Worksheets(2).Activate
Dim p!

For p = 1 To 7

        Cells(2, 10 + p) = capletS(z1, z2, z3, z4, 5, p - 4)
        Cells(3, 10 + p) = capletB(5, p)

Next p

End Sub
```

```
Public Function capletS(z1!, z2!, z3!, z4!, i%, n!) As Single

Dim vS!
Dim lda!: lda = z3 * Fwd(i) ^ (1 - z2) / z1
Dim x!: x = Log(1 + n * 0.05)
Dim d1!, d2!

vS = z1 / Fwd(i) ^ (1 - z2) * (1 - 0.5 * (1 - z2 - lda * z4) * x + _
    1 / 12 * ((1 - z2) ^ 2 + (2 - 3 * z4 ^ 2) * lda ^ 2) * x ^ 2)

d1 = (-x + 0.5 * vS ^ 2 * i * 0.25) / (vS * Sqr(i * 0.25)):
d2 = d1 - vS * Sqr(i * 0.25)
capletS = 0.25 * bd(i) * (Fwd(i) * norm(d1) - Fwd(i) * Exp(x) * norm(d2))

End Function
```

```
Public Function calibSABR(z1!, z2!, z3!, z4!, i%) As Single

calibSABR = 0
Dim j!
For j = -3 To 3 Step 1
calibSABR = calibSABR + Sqr((capletB(i, j + 4)
- capletS(z1, z2, z3, z4, i, j)) ^ 2) / capletB(i, j + 4)
Next j

End Function
```

CHAPTER 8

Interest Rate Exotics

Interest rate exotics are a class of tailor-made interest rate-related assets that cover a wide range of payoffs. To investigate this area exhaustively would necessitate devoting a complete volume to the subject. In this section, we shall develop three popular payoffs, which over time have become "standard" instruments: CMS swaps, cancelable swaps, and one of the many versions of Target Redemption Notes. This will give us the opportunity to put theory into practice. To price the CMS and cancelable swaps, we will use two different models and share the results obtained from them. The TARN will be valued under the HJM model, with and without the help of factor reduction techniques (PCA).

8.1 CMS SWAPS

In the interbank market, reference rates are basically classified in three categories:

- overnight rates (e.g., EONIA), included in the calculation of short-term swaps;
- monetary rates, ranging from 1 month to 1 year in duration, such as the LIBOR benchmark;
- longer term rates, such as swap rates, generally named Constant Maturity Swap, with durations of more than 2 years.

The CMS reference generates a new class of derivatives:

- In a vanilla IRS, the benchmark floating rate payment frequency must comply with the period referenced: a 6-mth LIBOR is to be paid semi-annually.
- In a CMS swap, the floating reference, which is a **long-term** reference rate, is generally paid annually, which induces a **convexity** effect.

In fact, the only way to hedge a CMS swap is to trade forward swaps with **changing notionals**, contingent on the **shape of the yield curve**. Delta hedge adjustments are needed as long as the curve moves. According to whether your hedging swap is **payer or receiver**, you will be **gamma negative or positive**. In any case, the spread between the plain-vanilla forward rate and the CMS swap rate will increase: consequently, volatility plays a noticeable role in a CMS swap pricing.

What does <u>gamma</u> mean, actually?

While the delta (or **hedge ratio**) is the first derivative of an option value with respect to the underlying price, the gamma is its second derivative: it measures, then, the convexity. According to your position in options, i.e., short or long, this gamma can be positive or negative. Given the positive convexity of a plain-vanilla European option (the delta increases along with the probability to exercise the option), an option's buyer (resp. seller) will be gamma positive (resp. negative). This is one obvious reason why the option's price increases with the volatility of the underlying asset.

Ex: In this section, we choose to value:

- a 5-yr CMS swap maturing in 5 years (**4 fixings**, the 5-yr CMS spot is obviously not counted);
- using an implementation of HJM and LMM models successively.

The pricing will obviously be done through the Monte-Carlo simulation method, using discrete timesteps set to quarters of a year. Practically speaking, the time horizon is the maturity of the last CMS fixing date + 5 years, i.e., 5-1+5 years.

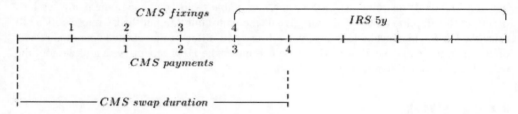

The algorithm is quite straightforward: at each anniversary date t_i ($t_1 = 1y$, $t_2 = 2y$, etc.) the sampled values of $fwd(1)$, $fwd(2)$,..., $fwd(20)$, will determine the discount factors $df(1)$, $df(2)$,.., $df(5)$ as of t_i. Note that, in t_i and $df(i)$, i stands for the index of the **year**, while in $fwd(j)$, j is a **quarterly** index. For instance, setting $\tau = 0.25$,

$$df(1) = \frac{1}{\displaystyle\prod_{j=1}^{4}(1 + fwd(j) * \tau)}$$

The resulting value of the CMS rate is then

$$CMS_{5y} = \frac{1 - df(5)}{\displaystyle\sum_{j=1}^{20} df(j)}$$

All these fixings will be accumulated in **Flow(i)**, then averaged and discounted with the initial values (as of today) of $df(\mathbf{2})$, $df(\mathbf{3})$, etc.

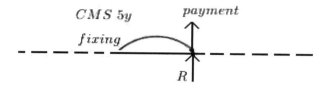

8.1.1 Code

Under the HJM model All you have to do is copy and paste the statements that are common with **CalibHJM** (Chapter 6 §6.2.1), especially the laborious calibration process, and add a few lines following the forward rates' sampling step.

```
Sub CMS_HJM()

Dim Flow #(4)
```

****
Paste here the initialization of the market parameters (caplet volatilities, discount rates, etc.) and the calibration statements. The next step is forwards $f(i)$ sampling.
****

```
    For i = 1 To 5000
     For K = 1 To p - 1
         f0(K)  = Fwd(K)
     Next K

     For l = 1 To p - 1

         For j = 1 To p - 1
             brown(j) = gauss()
         Next j

         For j = 1 To p - 1
             z(j) = 0
             For K = 1 To j
                 z(j) = z(j) + trigDrift(l)(j, K) * brown(K)
             Next K
             f(j) = f0(j) + mu(l - 1 + j, l) * t + sig(l - 1 + j) * z(j)
* Sqr(t)

         Next j

         For K = 1 To p - 1 - l
             f0(K)  = f(K + 1)
         Next K
     Next l
```

```
*********************************************************
```
Here we begin the calculation of CMS fixing = (1 - df(20))/sumCP.
```
*********************************************************
```

```
        If l Mod 4 = 0 And l < 17 Then
            sumCP = 0
            df(1) = 1 / (1 + f(1) * 0.25)
            For j = 2 To 20
                df(j) = df(j - 1) / (1 + f(j) * 0.25)
                If j Mod 4 = 0 Then
                    sumCP = sumCP + df(j)
                End If
            Next j
            Flow(l / 4) = Flow(l / 4) + (1 - df(20)) / sumCP

        End If

          For K = 1 To 35 - l
             f0(K) = f(K + 1)
        Next K

Next l

Next i

sumdisc=0
For i = 1 To 4
sumdisc = sumdisc + discFwd(4 * i + 4)
sumFlow = sumFlow + Flow(i) * discFwd(4 * i + 4)
Next i

Debug.Print sumFlow / 10000 / sumdisc

End Sub
```

Under the LMM model   The core of the program, in essence the calibration and forward rate samplings, is similar to the HJM one. We declare once again **Flow**, the array of the 5-yr CMS fixings, at the top of the procedure.

```
Public Sub CMS_LMM()
Dim Flow#(4)

For i = 1 To p - 1
    Fwd0(i) = Fwd(i)
Next i

For l = 1 To 5000

    For i = 1 To p - 1
        Fwd(i) = Fwd0(i)
        FwdB(i) = Fwd0(i)
    Next
    Flow = 0
    prodCP = 0

    For i = 1 To p - 1
        m = i - 1
```

```
         For K = 1 To p - i
             alea(K) = gauss()
         Next K

         Fwd(1) = Fwd(1) * Exp(-0.5 * volCaplet(1 + m) ^ 2 * 0.25 + _
         volCaplet(1 + m) * alea(1) * Sqr(0.25))

         df(1) = 1 / (1 + Fwd(1) * 0.25)

         For j = 2 To p - i
             mu(j) = 0: muB(j) = 0

             For K = 2 To j
                 mu(j) = mu(j) + _
                 volCaplet(j + m) * Fwd(K) * 0.25 * volCaplet(K + m) *
corr(i)(K, j) / (1 + Fwd(K) * 0.25)
             Next K

             brown = 0
             For K = 1 To j
                 brown = brown + trig(i)(j, K) * alea(K)
             Next K

         '   predictor corrector
             FwdB(j) = Fwd(j) * Exp(mu(j) * 0.25 - 0.5 * volCaplet(j + m)
^ 2 * 0.25 + _
             volCaplet(j + m) * brown * Sqr(0.25))

             For K = 2 To j
                 muB(j) = muB(j) + _
                 volCaplet(j + m) * FwdB(K) * 0.25 * volCaplet(K + m)
* corr(i)(K, j) / (1 + FwdB(K) * 0.25)
             Next
             Fwd(j) = Fwd(j) * Exp(0.5 * (mu(j) + muB(j)) * 0.25 - _
             0.5 * volCaplet(j + m) ^ 2 * 0.25 + vol-
Caplet(j + m) * brown * Sqr(0.25))
             df(j) = df(j - 1) / (1 + Fwd(j) * 0.25)

         Next j
```

```
*****************************************************
```
The CMS fixings are calculated here:
```
*****************************************************
```

```
         If i Mod 4 = 0 And i < 17 Then
             sumCP = 0
             df(1) = 1 / (1 + Fwd(1) * 0.25)
             For j = 2 To 20
                 df(j) = df(j - 1) / (1 + Fwd(j) * 0.25)
                 If j Mod 4 = 0 Then
                     sumCP = sumCP + df(j)
                 End If
             Next j
             Flow(i / 4) = (Flow(i / 4) + (1 - df(20)) / sumCP)
         End If
         For K = 1 To p - i - 1
             Fwd(K) = Fwd(K + 1)
         Next K
     Next i
```

```
Next 1
sumdisc = 0
For i = 1 To 4
    sumFlow = sumFlow + Flow(i) * discFwd(4 * i + 4)
    sumdisc = sumdisc + discFwd(4 * i + 4)
Next i
Debug.Print sumFlow / 5000

End Sub
```

8.2 CANCELABLE SWAPS

A cancelable swap is a vanilla swap where one counterparty has the right to terminate the swap on one or more fixed dates at no cost. In some sense, it looks like a swap with a Bermudan swaption embedded. The difference between them is:

- in a cancelable swap, the swap **expiry** is fixed;
- in a Bermudan swaption, the **duration** of the underlying swap is fixed.

For instance, a 7-yr receiver swaption, cancelable every year, encapsulates a series of 1y/6y (1y option and 6y swap), 2y/5y,..., 6y/1y swaptions, where the ny/(7-n)y option is contingent upon the other not being exercised on the preceding anniversary dates.

Obviously, when the rightholder pays (resp. receives) the fixed rate in the initial swap, this rate is higher (resp. lower) than the plain-vanilla swap rate for the same term. Under market conditions, the fair price of the Bermudan option must balance the negative value of the swap with no option:

$$\text{Bermudan swaption price} + \text{Swap value (without right attached)} = 0$$

For the pricing of this derivative, we will opt for (1) the LMM model, associating Monte-Carlo scenarios and **regressions** to tackle the early termination issue. This choice is almost instinctive, since one scenario consists in generating rates of swap expiring at the same date.

Nonetheless, it appears helpful to compare the LMM price with the solution obtained from other numerical methods. A natural choice would be the binomial approach, such as the Gaussian two-factor model. After all, this solution is the easiest to account for early exercise terms. If we demonstrate that both pricings give narrow solutions, the benefit is going to be twofold:

1. It can be regarded as a mutual self-validation of the models implemented.
2. The computation time is much quicker with a quadrinomial tree algorithm. Therefore, it is worth applying it for **risk management** purposes, provided the greeks are assumed to be close.

8.2.1 Code

The algorithm developed in the code below consists in setting arbitrarily a strike price for the Bermudan swaption, then computing the net present value:

$$\text{Bermudan swaption price} + \text{swap (without right attached)}$$

We, then, modify the strike, increasing or decreasing it with the annual amortization of the swaption flat price. Put mathematically, it gives

$$\text{amort}(i) = \text{annual amortization} = \text{Bermudan flat price}/\sum_{i=1}^{n} df(i)$$

the strike of the swaption becomes

$$\text{modified strike} = \text{strike} \pm \text{amort}(i)$$

This method converges rapidly (three or four swaptions calculations are enough). As usual, until the sampling iterations of the forward rates, the algorithm remains immutable. The only difference is the storage of all the swap prices generated by Monte-Carlo scenarios that necessitates the creation of long size arrays **fx** and **ef**: these arrays are to be populated before the regression process starts. The degree of the polynomial obtained from the regression is set arbitrarily to **3**.

We display here, for a better understanding, the complete code from the beginning of the forwards sampling. For the regression, we use a function named **regression** which is similar to polyFit (see Chapter 2 on mathematical algorithms).

```
Public Sub CanSwaption()

strikeSwap = 0.05
Dim p%: p = 20

n = 10000

ReDim fx#(n, p), ef%(n, p)
Dim a#, b#, c#: c = 1
```

r(n,p-1) is the vector of discount rates at each timestep of the regression.

```
Dim r#()

Dim x#(), y#(), reg#()
ReDim x#(n), y#(n)

ReDim swaption(n, p - 1)
ReDim r(n, p - 1)

For i = 1 To p - 1
    sumDF(i) = 0
    Fwd0(i) = Fwd(i)
Next
Randomize

For l = 1 To n

    For i = 1 To p - 1
        Fwd(i)  = Fwd0(i)
        FwdB(i) = Fwd0(i)
        sumDF(i) = 0
    Next
```

```
    For i = 1 To p - 1

        For K = 1 To p - i
            alea(K) = gauss(): c = c + 1
        Next K

        Fwd(1) = Fwd(1) * Exp(-0.5 * volCaplet(1) ^ 2 * 0.25 +
volCaplet(1) * alea(1) * Sqr(0.25))
        r(1, i) = Fwd(1)
        DF(1) = 1 / (1 + Fwd(1) * 0.25)
        sumDF(1) = DF(1)

        For j = 2 To p - i
            mu(j) = 0: muB(j) = 0

            For K = 2 To j
                mu(j) = mu(j) + volCaplet(j + m) * Fwd(K) * 0.25 *
volCaplet(K + m) * corr(i)(K, j) _
                    / (1 + Fwd(K) * 0.25)
            Next K

            brown = 0
            For K = 1 To j
                brown = brown + trig(i)(j, K) * alea(K)
            Next K

    '    predictor corrector
            FwdB(j) = Fwd(j) * Exp(mu(j) * 0.25 - 0.5 * volCaplet(j + m)
^ 2 * 0.25 + _
                volCaplet(j + m) * brown * Sqr(0.25))

            For K = 2 To j
                muB(j) = muB(j) + (volCaplet(j + m) * FwdB(K) * 0.25
* volCaplet(K + m) * corr(i)(K, j) _
                    / (1 + FwdB(K) * 0.25))
            Next k
            Fwd(j) = Fwd(j) * Exp(0.5 * (mu(j) + muB(j)) * 0.25 - 0.5
* volCaplet(j + m) ^ 2 * 0.25 + _
                volCaplet(j + m) * brown * Sqr(0.25))
            DF(j) = DF(j - 1) / (1 + Fwd(j) * 0.25)

        Next j

        swaption(1, i) = 1 - DF(p - i) - strikeSwap * 0.25 * sumDF(p - i)
        For K = 1 To p - i - 1
            Fwd(K) = Fwd(K + 1)
        Next K
    Next i

Next 1

    For i = 1 To n
        If swaption(i, p - 1) > 0 Then fx(i, p - 1) = swaption(i, p - 1):
ef(i, p - 1) = 1
    Next i
```

```
For l = p - 2 To 1 Step -1

    c = 1
    For i = 1 To n
        If swaption(i, l) > 0 Then x(c) = swaption(i, l)
        y(c) = fx(i, l + 1) / (1 + r(i, l) * 0.25): ef(i, l) = 1: c = c + 1
    Next i
    ReDim Preserve x(c - 1)
    ReDim Preserve y(c - 1)

    reg = regression(x, y, 2)

    a1 = reg(1): a2 = reg(2): a3 = reg(3)

    For i = 1 To n
        If ef(i, l) = 1 Then
            If a1 * swaption(i, l) ^ 2 + a2 * swaption(i, l) + a3
< swaption(i, l) Then
                fx(i, l) = swaption(i, l)
                For m = l + 1 To p
                ef(i, m) = 0
                Next m
            Else
                ef(i, l) = 0: fx(i, l) = fx(i, l + 1) / (1 + r(i, l) * 0.25)
            End If
        End If
    Next i

    ReDim x(n)
    ReDim y(n)

Next l

For i = 1 To n
    For j = 1 To p - 1
        po = po + ef(i, j) * swaption(i, j)
    Next j
Next i

Debug.Print po / n + (swap(p - 1) - strikeSwap) * 0.25 * discFwd(p - 1)

End Sub

Public Function regression(x#(), y#(), n%) As Double()

Dim m As Long: m = UBound(x)

ReDim res#(n + 1)

ReDim mat#(n + 1, n + 1)
ReDim cib#(n + 1)

Dim matInv#()

For i = 1 To n + 1
    cib(i) = 0
    For j = 1 To n + 1
```

```
        mat(i, j) = 0
        For K = 1 To m
            mat(i, j) = mat(i, j) + x(K) ^ (2 * n + 2 - i - j)
        Next K
    Next j
    cib(i) = 0
    For K = 1 To m
        cib(i) = cib(i) + y(K) * x(K) ^ (n + 1 - i)
    Next K
Next i
matInv = GaussJordan(mat)

If matNul(matInv) Then
    regression = res
Else
    res = MatMult(matInv, cib)
    regression = res
End If

End Function
```

8.2.2 Tree approximation

The quadrinomial tree constraint   The main obstacle to implementing the quadrinomial tree methodology is the number of paths that increases exponentially with the duration of the instrument. Let us point the node (i, j, k), and denote by

$$S(i, j, k, m)$$

the price of an m-step maturity swap starting from this node (for which the corresponding forward is $Fwd(i, j, k)$). The calculation of $S(i, j, k, m)$ needs to build the tree of zero-bonds. Given the general form of $Fwd(i, j, k)$

$$Fwd(i, j, k) = \phi(i) + x(i, j) + y(i, k)$$

the zero-bonds tree is regrettably *non-recombining*. Indeed

$$(1 + (\phi(i) + x(i, j) - \Delta x + y(i, k) - \Delta y)\tau).(1 + (\phi(i + 1) + x(i, j) + \Delta x + y(i, k) + \Delta y)\tau)$$

$$\neq$$

$$(1 + (\phi(i) + x(i, j) + \Delta x + y(i, k) + \Delta y)\tau).(1 + (\phi(i + 1) + x(i, j) - \Delta x + y(i, k) - \Delta y)\tau)$$

As a result, the number of paths for an N-step zero-bond tree is 4^N.

Algorithm   To overcome the obstacle, we are going to cheat a little bit: In place of calculating the discount factors from the tree, we will use the zero-bond prices in the continuous time framework, as given by []:

$$B(t, T) = \frac{B_{market}(0, T)}{B_{market}(0, t)}.$$

$$\exp\left(-\frac{1}{2}[V(0, T) - V(0, t) - V(t, T)] - \frac{1 - e^{-a(T-t)}}{a}x_t - \frac{1 - e^{-b(T-t)}}{b}y_t\right)$$

This will help us substantially for the computation of swap prices at each node (l, j, k) of the tree.

Practically, given

$$dt = 0.25, \quad \text{for quarterly timesteps}$$

$$N * dt, \quad \text{time horizon of the tree}$$

the discount factor $B(t, T)$ is calculated at each node, between $t = l * dt$, and $T = (l + m) * dt$, $m = 1, 2, ..., N - l$.

Finally, the intrinsic value of the option is

$$\text{strike} * B(l.dt, N.dt) * dt \quad - \quad \left(1 - \sum_{m=1}^{N-1} B(l.dt, (l + m).dt)\right)$$

This is to be compared with the option value obtained from backward induction: obviously, the option prices at step N are nil. In the piece of code below, the steps of this algorithm are detailed.

```
For l = N-1 To 1 Step -1
For j = 0 To 1
    For k = 0 To 1
        DFbond(l, j, k) = 0
        For m = 1 To N - 1
            discount = DF(l + m - 1) / DF(l - 1) * Exp(-(1 -
Exp(-a * m * dt)) / a * x(l, j) -  _
            (1 - Exp(-b * m * dt)) / b * y(l, k)) * _
                    Exp(Variance(a, b, vx, vy, rho, l * dt,
(l + m) * dt) / 2 - _
                    Variance(a, b, vx, vy, rho, 0,
(l + m) * dt) / 2 + _
                    Variance(a, b, vx, vy, rho, 0, l * dt) / 2)

            DFbond(l, j, k) = DFbond(l, j, k) + discount

        Next m
        opt(l, j, k) = max(strike * DFbond(l, j, k) * dt -
(1 - discount), opt(l, j, k))

Next k
Next j
```

- discount: $B(l.dt, N.dt)$
- DFbond: $\sum_{m=1}^{N-l} B(l.dt, (l + m).dt)$
- Variance: $V(t, T)$ (see 6.2.1 Gaussian Two-Factor model for the variance formula)
- opt: Bermudan swaption price.

Noting that the forward rate at one node is $fwHW(i, j, k)$, the recursive algorithm for the option pricing goes like this:

```
For j = 0 To l - 1
      For k = 0 To l - 1
            opt(l - 1, j, k) = (puu(l - 1, j, k) * opt(l, j + 1, k + 1) + _
                      pud(l - 1, j, k) * opt(l, j + 1, k) + _
                      pdu(l - 1, j, k) * opt(l, j, k + 1) + _
                      pdd(l - 1, j, k) * opt(l, j, k)) /
(1 + fwHW(l - 1, j, k) * dt)
      Next k
   Next j
```

To ensure that the $\phi(i)$ fits the initial forward curve $Fwd(i)$, we proceed as follows:

- compute fswap(i) = $\mathbb{E}_{j,k}(fwHW(i,j,k))$

- set $\phi(i)$ = Fwd(i)-fswap(i)

- adjust fwHW(i,j,k) = fwHW(i,j,k)+$\phi(i)$.

Code   In the program below, we price a Bermudan receiver swaption on a 7-yr swap 3-mth fixed vs 3-mth float.

```
Public Function CancelSwap(strike!, n%)

Dim fwHW!(), sw!()
ReDim fwHW!(n, n, n), bond!(n, n, n), DFbond!(n, n, n)
ReDim Fwd(n), DF(n), sw(n / 4)

Dim opt!(), swp!()
Dim i%, j%, k%, l%

Dim nb%()
ReDim nb(n, n, n)
Dim p#()
ReDim p(n, n, n)

ReDim x(n, n), y(n, n)

'    retrieval forward market
dt = 0.25
For i = 0 To n
    Fwd(i) = 0.04 * Exp(0.01 * i)
Next i
DF(0) = 1 / (1 + Fwd(0) * dt)
For i = 1 To n
    DF(i) = DF(i - 1) / (1 + Fwd(i) * dt)
Next i

vx = 0.02: vy = 0.007
a = 0.65: b = 0.0397
rho = -0.7

Dim dx!: dx = vx * Sqr(dt)
Dim dy!: dy = vy * Sqr(dt)

For i = 1 To n
```

```
    For j = 0 To i
        x(i, j) = (2 * j - i) * dx
        y(i, j) = (2 * j - i) * dy
    Next j
Next i

zu = (1 + rho) / 4
zd = (1 - rho) / 4
z2 = Sqr(dt) / (4 * vx * vy)

Dim phi#()
ReDim phi(n)

fwHW(0, 0, 0) = Fwd(0)
p(1, 1, 1) = (1 + rho) / 4: p(1, 1, 0) = (1 - rho) / 4
 p(1, 0, 1) = (1 - rho) / 4: p(1, 0, 0) = (1 + rho) / 4

fwHW(1, 1, 1) = phi(1) + dx + dy
fwHW(1, 1, 0) = phi(1) + dx - dy
fwHW(1, 0, 1) = phi(1) - dx + dy
fwHW(1, 0, 0) = phi(1) - dx - dy

For i = 2 To n
    For j = 1 To i
        For k = 1 To i

p(i, j, K) = _
    p(i - 1, j - 1, K - 1) * (zu - (b * vx * y(i - 1, K - 1) + a * vy
* x(i - 1, j - 1)) * z2) _
    + p(i - 1, j, K - 1) * (zd - (b * vx * y(i - 1, K - 1) - a * vy
* x(i - 1, j)) * z2) _
    + p(i - 1, j - 1, K) * (zd + (b * vx * y(i - 1, K) - a * vy
* x(i - 1, j - 1)) * z2) _
    + p(i - 1, j, K) * (zu + (b * vx * y(i - 1, K) + a * vy
* x(i - 1, j)) * z2)

fwHW(i, j, K) = fwHW(i - 1, j - 1, K - 1) + dx + dy + (phi(i) - phi(i - 1))

        Next K
    Next j

fwHW(i, 0, 0) = fwHW(i - 1, 0, 0) - dx - dy + (phi(i) - phi(i - 1))
p(i, 0, 0) = p(i - 1, 0, 0) * (zu + (b * vx * y(i - 1, 0) + a * vy
* x(i - 1, 0)) * z2)
fwHW(i, i, 0) = fwHW(i - 1, i - 1, 0) + dx - dy + (phi(i) - phi(i - 1))
p(i, i, 0) = p(i - 1, i - 1, 0) * (zd + (b * vx * y(i - 1, 0) - a * vy
* x(i - 1, i - 1)) * z2)
fwHW(i, 0, i) = fwHW(i - 1, 0, i - 1) - dx + dy + (phi(i) - phi(i - 1))
p(i, 0, i) = p(i - 1, 0, i - 1) * (zd - (b * vx * y(i - 1, i - 1) - a * vy
* x(i - 1, 0)) * z2)
fwHW(i, i, i) = fwHW(i - 1, i - 1, i - 1) + dx + dy + (phi(i) - phi(i - 1))

p(i, i, i) = p(i - 1, i - 1, i - 1) * _
    (zu - (b * vx * y(i - 1, i - 1) + a * vy * x(i - 1, i - 1)) * z2)

    For l = 1 To i - 1
```

```
fwHW(i, 0, 1) = fwHW(i - 1, 0, 1 - 1) - dx + dy + (phi(i) - phi(i - 1))
p(i, 0, 1) = p(i - 1, 0, 1 - 1) * _
    (zd - (b * vx * y(i - 1, 1 - 1) - a * vy * x(i - 1, 0)) * z2) _
    + p(i - 1, 0, 1) * (zu + (b * vx * y(i - 1, 1) + a * vy
* x(i - 1, 0)) * z2)

fwHW(i, i, 1) = fwHW(i - 1, i - 1, 1 - 1) + dx + dy + (phi(i) - phi(i - 1))
p(i, i, 1) = p(i - 1, i - 1, 1 - 1) * _
    (zu - (b * vx * y(i - 1, 1 - 1) + a * vy * x(i - 1, i - 1)) * z2) _
    + p(i - 1, i - 1, 1) * (zd + (b * vx * y(i - 1, 1) - a *
vy * x(i - 1, i - 1)) * z2)

fwHW(i, 1, 0) = fwHW(i - 1, 1 - 1, 0) + dx - dy + (phi(i) - phi(i - 1))
p(i, 1, 0) = p(i - 1, 1 - 1, 0) * _
    (zd + (b * vx * y(i - 1, 0) - a * vy * x(i - 1, 1 - 1)) * z2) _
    + p(i - 1, 1, 0) * (zu + (b * vx * y(i - 1, 0) + a * vy
* x(i - 1, 1)) * z2)

fwHW(i, 1, i) = fwHW(i - 1, i - 1, 1 - 1) + dx + dy + (phi(i) - phi(i - 1))
p(i, 1, i) = p(i - 1, 1 - 1, i - 1) * _
    (zu - (b * vx * y(i - 1, i - 1) + a * vy * x(i - 1, 1 - 1)) * z2) _
    + p(i - 1, 1, i - 1) * (zd - (b * vx * y(i - 1, i - 1) - a * vy
* x(i - 1, 1)) * z2)
    Next l
Next i

ReDim fswap!(n)
For i = 0 To n
    fswap(i) = 0
    For j = 0 To i
        For k = 0 To i
            fswap(i) = fswap(i) + p(i, j, k) * fwHW(i, j, k)
        Next k
    Next j
    phi(i) = Fwd(i) - fswap(i)

Next i

For i = 0 To n
    For j = 0 To i
        For k = 0 To i
            fwHW(i, j, k) = fwHW(i, j, k) + phi(i)
        Next k
    Next j
Next i

For j = 0 To n
    For k = 0 To n
        bond(n, j, k) = 100
    Next k
Next j

For i = n - 1 To 0 Step -1
    For j = 0 To i
        For k = 0 To i
```

```
                bond(i, j, k) = (bond(i + 1, j, k) * (zu + (b * vx * y(i, k)
+ a * vy * x(i, j)) * z2) _
                + bond(i + 1, j + 1, k + 1) * (zu - (b * vx * y(i, k) + a * vy
* x(i, j)) * z2) _
                + bond(i + 1, j + 1, k) * (zd + (b * vx * y(i, k) - a * vy
* x(i, j)) * z2) _
                + bond(i + 1, j, k + 1) * (zd - (b * vx * y(i, k) - a * vy
* x(i, j)) * z2)) _
                / (1 + fwHW(i, j, k) * dt)
        Next k
    Next j
Next i
sumDF1 = 0: sumDF2 = 0

ReDim opt(n, n, n), swp(n, n, n)
z = 0
For l = 27 To 1 Step -1
For j = 0 To l
    For k = 0 To l
        DFbond(l, j, k) = 0
        For m = 1 To 28 - l
            discount = DF(l + m - 1) / DF(l - 1)
* Exp(-(1 - Exp(-a * m * dt)) / a * x(l, j) - _
            (1 - Exp(-b * m * dt)) / b * y(l, k)) * _
            Exp(Variance(a, b, vx, vy, rho, l * dt, (l + m) * dt) / 2 - _
                Variance(a, b, vx, vy, rho, 0, (l + m) * dt) / 2 + _
                Variance(a, b, vx, vy, rho, 0, l * dt) / 2)

            DFbond(l, j, k) = DFbond(l, j, k) + discount

        Next m
        opt(l, j, k) = max(strike * DFbond(l, j, k) * dt - (1 - discount),
opt(l, j, k))

    Next k
Next j
For j = 0 To l - 1
        For k = 0 To l - 1
        opt(l - 1, j, k) = (puu(l - 1, j, k) * opt(l, j + 1, k + 1) + _
                            pud(l - 1, j, k) * opt(l, j + 1, k) + _
                            pdu(l - 1, j, k) * opt(l, j, k + 1) + _
                            pdd(l - 1, j, k) * opt(l, j, k)) /
(1 + fwHW(l - 1, j, k) * dt)
        Next k
    Next j

Next l

CancelSwap = opt(0, 0, 0)
End Function
```

8.3 TARGET REDEMPTION NOTE

Target **R**edemption **N**otes (TARNS) are coupon-paying capital guaranteed notes. The common feature of all TARN-style assets is that the overall amount received by the holder is determined at inception. While the anniversary dates are fixed, payments are uncertain. To make them attractive, these structures can offer high yields for the first year or two, the residual payment timing being subject to either the performance of an underlying asset or trigger conditions. When the trigger is activated, or the sum of coupons already paid exceeds the overall amount under contract, the note automatically terminates. Most of the time, investors make profits as the note expires early.

The imagination of structurers in innovating knows no limit. Here we will price an original structure within the class of assets termed **inverse floater snowball**. This structure combines different features:

1. As for an inverse floater, the coupon rate has an inverse relationship to a short-term benchmark rate (commonly LIBOR).
2. Each coupon depends on the previous one. More precisely,

$$coupon(i + 1) = coupon(i) + x\%$$

3. When the cap is attained, the capital is redeemed and the last coupon is scaled down so that the cap is hit exactly.

Consider the following structure

> Maturity: 7 years
>
> Coupon periodicity: annual
>
> $Coupon(i + 1) = Coupon(i) + 1\% - \alpha \quad LIBOR\ 6m$
>
> $Coupon(1) = 7\%$
>
> Redemption at par + last coupon
>
> Cap:25%

The pricing of this structure will be carried out according to HJM forward rates dynamics. We will use successively:

1. a standard algorithm using the whole correlation matrix and 7×4 factors;
2. a version of this program with a reduced number of factors, obtained from the pseudo-square root of the correlation matrix (function **pseudo**).

8.3.1 Code

Standard algorithm   As usual, the indispensable arrays of market data are created outside the the procedure.

```
Dim Fwd#(), discFwd#(), valCaplet#(), volCaplet#()

Sub TARN_HJM()

Dim i&
```

```
Dim p%: p = 28
ReDim coupon#(p / 4)
ReDim total_capi#(p / 4)

coupon(1) = 0.07
Dim sum_coupons#: sum_coupons = 0

Dim cap#: cap = 0.3
Dim alpha#: alpha = 0.4

Dim t#: t = 0.25
```

From this point, the calibration algorithm starts. We then go straight to the cash flows sampling

```
ReDim f#(p - 1), f0#(p - 1)

Price = 0: n_iter = 1000

For i = 1 To n_iter

    sum_coupons = 0: remaining = cap
    For K = 1 To p - 1
        f0(K) = Fwd(K)
    Next K
    For K = 1 To p / 4
        total_capi(K) = 0
    Next K

    For l = 1 To p - 1
        For j = 1 To 28 - l
            brown(j) = gauss()
        Next j
        capi(l, 0) = 1
        For j = 1 To 28 - l
            z(j) = 0
            For K = 1 To j
                z(j) = z(j) + trigDrift(l)(j, K) * brown(K)
            Next K
            f(j) = f0(j) + mu(l - 1 + j, l) * t + sig(l - 1 + j) *
z(j) * Sqr(t)
            capi(l, j) = capi(l, j - 1) * (1 + f(j) * t)
        Next j
```

$$capi(l,j) = \prod_{k=l}^{j}(1 + f(k) * t)$$

Since anniversary dates are yearly, the sum of coupons already received must be compounded with $capi(l, 4)$.

```
        If l = 4 Then sum_coupons = coupon(1): total_capi(l / 4 + 1)
= coupon(1) * capi(l, 4): _
            remaining = cap - sum_coupons

        If l Mod 4 = 0 And l >= 8 Then
            Libor = (capi(l, 2) - 1) / (2 * t): _
            coupon(l / 4) = max(coupon(l / 4 - 1) + 0.01 - alpha * Libor, 0)
```

```
                    sum_coupons = sum_coupons + coupon(l / 4)
                    If sum_coupons > cap Then
                        total_capi(l / 4) = total_capi(l / 4) * capi(l, 4)
+ remaining
                        Price = Price + (total_capi(l / 4) + 1) * discFwd(l):
l = 99
                    Else
                        total_capi(l / 4 + 1) = (total_capi(l / 4)
+ coupon(l / 4)) * capi(l, 4)
                        remaining = cap - sum_coupons
                        If l = 24 Then
                            total_capi(l / 4 + 1) = total_capi(l / 4 + 1)
+ remaining: l = p - 1
                        End If
                    End If
            End If

            For K = 1 To p - 1 - l
                f0(K) = f(K + 1)
            Next K

    Next l

    If l = 28 Then Price = Price + (total_capi(l / 4) + 1)
* discFwd(p - 1): early = early + 1

Next i

Debug.Print Price * 100 / n_iter & "   " & FormatNumber(100 * early /
n_iter, 2) & "%" _
& " early terminations"

End Sub
```

Reducing the number of factors   The calibration program is not modified. The main change lies in the generation of the pseudo-square root A of the correlation matrix, i.e.,

$$A.A^{\dagger} = C$$

Out of it, we keep only the m leftmost columns:

$$\begin{pmatrix} a_{1,1} & \cdots & a_{1,m} & a_{1,m+1} & \cdots & a_{1,n} \\ a_{2,1} & \cdots & a_{2,m} & a_{2,m+1} & \cdots & a_{2,n} \\ \vdots & \vdots & \vdots & \vdots & \vdots & \vdots \\ a_{n,1} & \cdots & a_{n,m} & a_{n,m+1} & \cdots & a_{n,n} \end{pmatrix}$$

Subsequently, only m independent Gaussian variates Δw_k^* have to be sampled at each step to simulate the forward rates $Fwd(i)$:

$$\Delta w_i = \sum_{k=1}^{m} a_{i,k} \Delta w_k^*$$

Given the correlations usually observed in the market, $m = 3$ factors are enough.

The problem that arises at this stage is that, denoting A_m the "reduced" matrix, namely

$$A_m = \begin{pmatrix} a_{1,1} & \cdots & a_{1,m} \\ a_{2,1} & \cdots & a_{2,m} \\ \vdots & \vdots & \vdots \\ a_{n,1} & \cdots & a_{n,m} \end{pmatrix}$$

$$A_m.A_m^\dagger - C = [\Delta C] \neq [0]$$

In particular, the elements of the diagonal are inferior to 1. In practice if we set $\Delta A = A - A_m$, and set $M = A(\Delta A^\dagger)$, it is easy to show that M must verify

$$M + M^\dagger \cong C - A_m.A_m^\dagger$$

This cannot be solved since the number of unknown variables is superior to the rank of M. Some approximative corrections can be made, such as, for instance, rescaling A_m with the quadratic sum of the diagonal of C, noticing that the differences are greater in the vicinity of this very diagonal.

In this section, we just adopt A_m with $m = 2$ or 3. The changes in the original code are as follows:

1. create a new matrix A_m called **correlPCA**: this matrix is the pseudo-inverse of **correlDrift**

```
ReDim correlDrift(p - 1) As Variant
ReDim correlPCA(p - 1) As Variant

For i = 1 To p - 1
    correlDrift(i) = drift(Correl, i - 1)
    correlPCA(i) = pseudo(VarToDoubleArray(correlDrift(i)))
Next i
```

2. When the time comes to sample the forward rates, replace j with m: that's it.

```
For j = 1 To m
        brown(j) = gauss()
    Next j

    capi(1, 0) = 1
    For j = 1 To 28 - 1
        z(j) = 0
        For K = 1 To m
            z(j) = z(j) + correlPCA(1)(j, K) * brown(K)
        Next K
```

One can bring some refinement to the algorithm, shifting from the model with reduced factors to the standard model when $m > 28 - l + 1$. What is remarkable in this example is that $m = 2$ is enough to obtain close prices for both the standard and the modified algorithms. On the other hand, the gain in terms of computation time saving ($\cong -40\%$) is noticeable, but not spectacular.

Bibliography

Achtsis, N., Cools, R., Nuyens D. (2013) Conditional Sampling for Barrier Option Pricing under the Heston Model, http://arxiv.org/pdf/1207.6566.pdf.

Acklam, P.J. (2003) An Algorithm for Computing the Inverse Normal Cumulative Distribution Function, http://home.online.no/~pjacklam/notes/invnorm/.

Antonov, I.A. and Saleev, V.M. (1979) An Economic Method of Computing lp-sequences, *USSR Computational Mathematics and Mathematical Physics,* 19(1), 252–256.

Benhamou, E., Gobet, E., and Miri, M. (2009) Expansion Formulas for European Options in a Local Volatility Model, *International Journal of Theoretical and Applied Finance,* 13(4), 603–634.

Bjerksund, P. and Stensland, G. (1993) American Exchange Options and a Put-call Transformation: A Note, *Journal of Business Finance and Accounting,* 20(5), 761–764.

Brace A., Gatarek D., and Musiela M. (1997) The Market Model of Interest Rate Dynamics, *Mathematical Finance,* 7(2) 127–155.

Brigo, D. and Mercurio, F. (2006) *Interest Rate Models – Theory and Practice*, 2nd edn, Springer Finance.

Dupire, Bruno (1994) Pricing with a Smile, *Risk,* 7(1), 18–20.

Geman, H., El Karoui, N., and Rochet, J.C. (1995) Changes of Numeraire, Changes of Probability Measures and Pricing of Options, *Journal of Applied Probability,* 32(2), 443–458.

Glasserman, Paul (2003) *Monte Carlo Methods in Financial Engineering: 53 (Stochastic Modelling and Applied Probability)*, Springer-Verlag, pp. 303–316.

Haug, Espen Gaarder (1999) Barrier Put-call Transformations, http://citeseerx.ist.psu.edu/viewdoc/summary?doi=10.1.1.40.7963.

Heath, D., Jarrow, R., and Morton, A. (1992) Bond Pricing and the Term Structure of Interest Rates: A New Methodology, *Econometrica,* 60, 77–105.

Heston Steven, L. (1993) A Closed-form Solution for Options with Stochastic Volatility, with Application to Bond and Currency Options, *Review of Financial Studies,* 6, 327–343.

Hoare, T. (1962) Quicksort, *Computer Journal,* 5(1), 10–16.

Hull, John C. (1997) *Options, Futures and Other Derivatives*, 3rd edn, Prentice-Hall, p. 439.

Hull, John C. and White, Alan (1990) Pricing Interest Rate Derivative Securities, *The Review of Financial Studies*, 3, 573–592.

Imai, J. and Tan, K.S. (2006) A General Dimension Reduction Technique for Derivative Pricing, *Journal of Computational Finance,* 10(2), 129–155.

Ito, Kiyoshi (1944) Stochastic Integral, *Proceedings of the Imperial Academy Tokyo*, Vol. 20, pp. 519–524.

Jackel, Peter (2002) *Monte-Carlo Methods in Finance,* John Wiley & Sons, Ltd (Wiley Finance).

Joe, S., and Kuo, F. (2010) Sobol Sequence Generator, http://web.maths.unsw.edu.au/~fkuo/sobol/.

Joe, S. and Kuo, F.Y. (2003) Remark on Algorithm 659: Implementing Sobol's quasirandom sequence generator, *ACM Transactions on Mathematical Software,* 29, 49–57.

Joe, S. and Kuo, F.Y. (2008) Constructing Sobol Sequences with Better Two-dimensional Projections, *SIAM Journal on Scientific Computing,* 30, 2635–2654.

Karatzas, I. and Shreve, S. (1991) Brownian Motion and Stochastic Calculus: 113 (Graduate Texts in Mathematics), Springer, pp. 149–153.

Knuth, Donald (1998) *The Art of Computer Programming*, Vol. 3, 2nd edn, Addison-Wesley.

L'Ecuyer, Pierre (1994) Uniform Random Number Generator, *Annals of Operations Research,* 53, December, 77-120.

Lamberton, Damien and Lapeyre, Bernard (1997) *Introduction au calcul stochastique appliqué à la finance*, 2nd edn, Editions Ellipses.

Lidl, Rudolf and Niederreiter, Harald (1996) *Finite Fields,* Cambridge University Press.

Marsaglia, George and Tsang, Wai Wan (1984, A Fast Easily Implemented Method for Sampling from Decreasing or Symmetric Unimodal Density Functions, *SIAM Journal of Scientific and Statistical Computing,* 5, 349–359.

Matsumoto, M. and Nishimura, T. (1998) Mersenne Twister: A 623-dimensionally equidistributed uniform pseudo-random number generator, *ACM Transactions on Modeling and Computer Simulation,* 8(1), 3–30.

Musiela, M. and Rutkowski, M. (1998) Martingale Methods in Financial Modelling (Stochastic Modelling and Applied Probability), Springer, p. 36.

Nelder, J.A. and Mead, R. (1965) A Simplex Method for Function Minimization, *Computer Journal,* 7(4), 308–313.

Oksendal, Bernt (2000) *Stochastic Differential Equations,* Springer.

Poole, David (2010) *Linear Algebra: A Modern Introduction*, 3rd edn, Brooks/Cole.

Rebonato, Riccardo (1999) *Volatility and Correlation,* John Wiley & Sons Ltd.

Rebonato, Riccardo (2002) *Modern Pricing of Interest-rate Derivatives,* Princeton University Press, pp. 304–305.

Sedgewick, Robert (1998) *Algorithms in C*, 3rd edn, Addison-Wesley, pp. 273–281.

Shell, Donald (1959) A High-speed Sorting Procedure, *Communications of the ACM,* 2(7), July, 30–32.

Vasicek, O.A. (1977) An Equilibrium Characterisation of the Term Structure, *Journal of Financial Economics,* 5, 177–188.

Webber, Nick (2011) *Implementing Models of Financial Derivatives: Object Oriented Applications with VBA,* John Wiley & Sons, Ltd (Wiley Finance).

Zaanen, Adriaan (1996) *Introduction to Operator Theory in Riesz Spaces,* Springer.